HADRIAN AND THE CITIES OF THE ROMAN EMPIRE

HADRIAN AND THE CITIES
OF THE ROMAN EMPIRE

Mary T. Boatwright

PRINCETON UNIVERSITY PRESS   PRINCETON AND OXFORD

Copyright © 2000 by Princeton University Press
Published by Princeton University Press, 41 William Street,
Princeton, New Jersey 08540
In the United Kingdom: Princeton University Press,
3 Market Place, Woodstock, Oxfordshire OX20 ISY
All Rights Reserved

Third printing, and first paperback printing, 2003
Paperback ISBN 0-691-09493-4

*The Library of Congress has cataloged the cloth edition
of this book as follows*

Boatwright, Mary Taliaferro.
Hadrian and the cities of the Roman empire / Mary T. Boatwright.
p. cm.
Includes bibliographical references and index.
ISBN 0-691-04889-4 (cloth : alk. paper)
1. Hadrian, Emperor of Rome, 76–138—Influence. 2. Emperors—
Rome—Biography. 3. Patron and client—Rome. 4. Cities and towns—
Rome—Administration. 5. Rome—History—Empire,
30 B.C.–284 A.D.
I. Title.
DG295.B62   2000
937.07′092—dc21
[B]   99-41096

British Library Cataloging-in-Publication Data is available

This book has been composed in Galliard

Printed on acid-free paper. ∞

www.pupress.princeton.edu

Printed in the United States of America

5   7   9   10   8   6   4

ISBN-13: 978-0-691-09493-9 (pbk.)

To My Parents

VICTOR TALIAFERRO BOATWRIGHT

AND

MARY HOWARD BOATWRIGHT

Contents

Illustrations and Tables

Acknowledgments

THE INSPIRATION for this book hit me in 1981, on a hot and windswept hill in southern Spain. There, at the site of Hadrian's home town, Italica, Pilar León excitedly showed me the excavations she had just begun. Enough evidence had already emerged to indicate that a huge structure once rose here at the summit of Italica. The few objects found so far suggested a date in the Hadrianic period; more intriguingly, the design of the whole seemed to correspond to that of the Library of Hadrian in distant Athens. Our minds raced as we discussed the implications of the similarity. The excitement stayed with me long after I returned home to Durham, and continued through my involvement in other research.

The generosity of the Howard Foundation, Duke University's Research Council, and the National Endowment for the Humanities enabled me to return to that initial puzzle and to complete this work. In 1986–87, the George A. and Eliza Gardner Howard Foundation granted me a fellowship, which I used to begin research into Hadrian's building donations throughout the Roman empire. As I delved ever deeper into the ancient material, however, I realized that it would not be enough to look at only his buildings and architectural achievements. Similar terminology, and equal enthusiasm, attended his other expressions of interest to communities: what I needed to investigate was Hadrian's overall pattern of beneficence to cities throughout the Roman world. A succession of annual grants from Duke's Research Council (1987–90, 1992–95) allowed me to attempt this more ambitious project by paying for research support by talented Duke undergraduate and graduate students. Their dedication and cheerfulness have been essential to my project. Duke's Research Council also funded my inspirational visit to Spain and Portugal in 1981, two weeks in Turkey in 1988, two weeks in southern France in 1993, and three weeks in Greece and Turkey in 1996. These trips, added to previous travel in Italy, Spain, France, Yugoslavia, Greece, Israel, Libya, and Tunisia, have immeasurably contributed to my understanding of the Roman world, although I cannot claim to have seen every city Hadrian benefited or visited. A fellowship from the National Endowment for the Humanities, in 1995–96, allowed me to complete the bulk of my manuscript.

Many individuals have assisted my work. Foremost are my husband, Paul Feldblum, and our two sons, Joseph and Sammy. In addition to editing and discussing much of this research, Paul has provided inestimable support in every other way. Both our boys have spent their entire lives with this book, and their novel questions have helped keep my perspective fresh. My sister, M. Dorsey Boatwright, greatly helped me with all things Spanish. Many thanks go to my student research assistants, consistently lively companions: Darryl Phillips, Jeannine Uzzi, Craig Gibson, Joe Romero, Laura Hostetler, Joel Allen, Aaron DeLong, Erik Sass, Kara Bryant, Sandy Cash, Mitch Watts, David Bird, and Erin Gregory. Also at Duke, only the grace of my entire department allowed me to take my NEH leave in 1995–96. Various colleagues have shared their specialized knowledge. Kent J. Rigsby has steadily supplied references, advice, editorial work, and erudition, particularly pertaining to the Greek East. Lawrence Richardson, jr, graciously opened his vast knowledge and his library. Diskin Clay read my section on heroes' tombs, offering information on the Tomb of Archilochus on Paros. For matters Egyptian, I have turned to John F. Oates, Peter van Minnen, and Joshua D. Sosin. John G. Younger and Paul Rehak explored Greek sites with me, as I "tagged along" with John's "Duke in Ancient Greece" summer program in 1996. Dale Martin was my intrepid fellow traveler in Turkey that year. In this group of friends and colleagues, to whom I am deeply appreciative, also belong Richard J. A. Talbert and Jerzy Linderski of the University of North Carolina at Chapel Hill: I have turned to them more than once for help on maps, politics, and inscriptions.

The generosity of colleagues further afield has also been fundamental. From the start Pilar León has been unstinting in her support. The splendid conference she and Antonio Caballos organized in Seville in 1994, on the 2200th anniversary of Italica's founding, introduced me to a most congenial group: Marianne Bergmann, Werner Eck, Hartmut Galsterer, Fernando Fernández, Simon Keay, Isabel Rodá, and José Manuel Rodríguez Hidalgo. The conference, the new friends made there, and Pilar and Antonio themselves have all been inspiring. Giorgio Ortolani, of Rome, shared his knowledge of Hadrianic architecture (and his photographs), Susan Walker her plans and experience. Now, at the end of the book, I also thank my editors at Princeton University Press, Joanna Hitchcock and Brigitta van Rheinberg, as well as Antony R. Birley and the other reader of my manuscript. Their suggestions have made this book more compelling.

I dedicate this book to my parents, Victor T. and Mary H. Boatwright. They have encouraged my work wholeheartedly, and my father lent his extraordinary editing skills to my earlier chapters. Although he gently deprecated his advice as "nit-picking," his discerning queries pushed me to think, and I hope to write, more clearly. More fundamentally, however, he and my mother influenced my fascination with Hadrian and the Roman world. Embracing many Roman ideals, my parents seem to replicate some of Hadrian's own qualities. They have always been devoted to both the life of their community and the life of the mind. My father gave untold hours to philanthropic societies, zoning boards, local drama, and other organizations. He edited the newsletter of the local historical society: like Hadrian, he championed history, doing all he could to keep its relevance dynamic. He read voraciously and critically: again like Hadrian, he wanted to know everything, and he could not endure carelessness. My mother's lifelong involvement in state and local politics impressed on me how vital such work is to society and government, and how essential politics are to identity. She shares Hadrian's conviction that life is not worth living without literature, poetry, art, beauty, and wit. May this book reflect, at least a little, my profound love and respect for both my parents. I wish only that it could have appeared before my father's untimely death.

January 31, 1999

Abbreviations

In citing periodicals, standard references, and ancient authors and works, I have generally followed the conventions of the *Oxford Classical Dictionary* and of the *American Journal of Archaeology*. For Greek inscriptions from newer corpora, such as the volumes of *Inschriften griechischer Städte aus Kleinasien* published in Bonn beginning in 1972, I have used G. H. R. Horsley and J. A. L. Lee, "A Preliminary Checklist of Abbreviations of Greek Epigraphic Volumes," *Epigraphica* 56 (1994): 129–69. Listed below are less familiar abbreviations appearing in my notes and text.

AE	*L'Année épigraphique: Revue des publications épigraphiques relatives à l'antiquité romaine.* Paris, 1888–
AltPerg	*Altertümer von Pergamum*
ANRW	Temporini, H., and W. Haase, eds. *Aufstieg und Niedergang der römischen Welt.* Berlin, 1972–
AntAfr	*Antiquités africaines*
ArchEspArq	*Archivo Español de Arqueología*
ASAA	*Annuario della Scuola archeologica di Atene*
Aur. Vict. *Caes.*	Sextus Aurelius Victor. *De Caesaribus,* ed. F. Pichlmayr and R. Gruendel. 2nd ed. Leipzig, 1970
BGU	*Aegyptische Urkunden aus d. Kgl. Museen zu Berlin. Griechische Urkunden.* Berlin, 1895–1926
BMC, Emp.	Mattingly, H. *Coins of the Roman Empire in the British Museum.* Vol. I– . London, 1923–
BMC, Lycaonia	Hill, G. F. *British Museum Catalogue of the Greek Coins of Lycaonia.* London, 1900
Bonner HAC	*Bonner Historia Augusta Colloquium*
Bruns[7]	Bruns, C. G., ed. *Fontes iuris romani antiqui.* 2 vols. 7th ed. by O. Gradenwitz. Tübingen, 1909
Buecheler, *Carm. Epig.*	Buecheler, F. *Carmina latina epigraphica.* 2 vols. With supplement by E. Lommatzsch. Leipzig, 1895–1926

Bull.Ep.	Robert, J., and L. Robert. *Bulletin épigraphique.* Appearing in the annual issues of *REG,* items are cited by the year and the number of the entry within the survey.
Cass. Dio	Dio Cassius. *Roman History,* ed. E. W. Cary. London, 1914–27
Chron. Pasch.	*Chronicon Paschale.* Ed. L. Dindorf. *CSHB* 1832
CIG	Boeckh, A., ed. *Corpus inscriptionum Graecarum.* 4 vols. Berlin, 1828–77
CIL	*Corpus inscriptionum Latinarum.* 16 vols. Berlin, 1863–
CILA	J. González Fernández, ed. *Corpus de Inscripciones Latinas de Andalucía. Volumen II: Sevilla. 2. La Vega (Italica).* Seville, 1991
CodJ	Krueger, P., ed. *Codex Iustinianus. Corpus iuris civilis, Vol. II.* Berlin, 1929
CollEFR	Collection de l'École Française de Rome
CollLat	Collection Latomus
CSHB	*Corpus scriptorum historiae Byzantinae.* 50 vols. Bonn, 1828–97
CTh	Mommsen, T., ed. *Theodosiani libri XVI cum Constitutionibus Sirmondianis.* Berlin, 1905
Dig.	Mommsen, T., ed. *Digesta. Corpus iuris civilis, Vol. I.* Berlin, 1893
DizEpig	De Ruggiero, E., ed. *Dizionario epigraphico di antichità romane.* Vol. I– . Rome, 1895–
EE	*Ephemeris Epigraphica, Corporis inscriptionum Latinarum Supplementum.* Berlin, 1873–1913
EpigAnat	*Epigraphica Anatolica*
Epit. de Caes.	*Epitome de Caesaribus.* Ed. F. Pichlmayr and R. Gruendel. 2nd ed. Leipzig, 1970
FIRA	*Fontes iuris romani antejustiniani.* Ed. S. Roccobono et al. 2nd ed. Florence, 1968–69
GCS	*Die griechischen christlichen Schriftsteller.* Leipzig, 1897–
HA	*Scriptores Historiae Augustae.* Ed. E. Hohl. 2 vols. Second Teubner edition corrected by C. Samberger and W. Seyfarth. Leipzig, 1971
HS	sestertius (pl., sesterces), standard Roman monetary unit. In Hadrian's day 4 sesterces = 1 denarius = 1 drachma, and the annual

	pay for a Roman legionary soldier was 1,200 HS.
IBulg	Mihailov, G., ed. *Inscriptiones Graecae in Bulgaria repertae.* Sofia, 1956–66
ICret	Guarducci, M. *Inscriptiones Creticae.* Rome, 1935–50
IEJ	*Israel Exploration Journal*
IG	*Inscriptiones Graecae.* Berlin, 1873–
IGR	Cagnat, R., et al., eds. *Inscriptiones Graecae ad res Romanas pertinentes.* 3 vols. (I, III, IV). Paris, 1901–27
IGUR	Moretti, L. *Inscriptiones Graecae urbis Romae.* Rome, 1968–79
IK	*Inschriften griechischer Städte aus Kleinasien.* Bonn, 1972–
ILAf.	Cagnat, R., and A. Merlin, eds. *Inscriptions latines d'Afrique (Tripolitaine, Tunisie, Maroc).* Paris, 1923
ILAlg.	Gsell, S., et al., eds. *Inscriptions latines d'Algérie.* 2 vols. Paris, 1922, 1957
ILLRP	A. Degrassi, *Inscriptiones Latinae liberae rei publicae.* Florence, 1957–63
ILS	Dessau, H., ed. *Inscriptiones Latinae selectae.* Berlin, 1892–1916
ILT	Merlin, A. *Inscriptions latines de la Tunisie.* Paris, 1944
IMS	Mirkovič, M., S. Dusanic, et al. *Inscriptions de la Mésie Supérieure.* Belgrade, 1976–82
Insc. Ital.	*Inscriptiones Italiae.* Rome, 1931–
IRT	Reynolds, J. M., and J. B. Ward Perkins. *The Inscriptions of Roman Tripolitania.* Rome, 1952
IstMitt	*Mitteilungen des Deutschen Archäologischen Instituts, Istanbuler Abteilung*
Jerome, *Chron.* Helm	Helm, R., ed. *Eusebius Werke. Siebenter Band. Die Chronik des Hieronymus. Hieronymi Chronicon. GCS* 47. Berlin, 1956
JJP	*Journal of Juristic Papyrology*
JÖAI	*Jahreshefte des Österreichischen archäologischen Instituts in Wien*
MAMA	Calder, W. M., et al., eds. *Monumenta Asiae minoris antiqua.* 9 vols. Manchester, 1928–
MDAI (A)	*Mitteilungen des Deutschen Archäologischen Instituts, Athenische Abteilung*

n.d.	no date
NSc	*Notizie degli scavi di antichità*
OGIS	*Orientis Graeci inscriptiones selectae*
Oliver, #	Oliver, J. H. *Greek Constitutions of the Early Roman Emperors from Inscriptions and Papyri.* Memoirs of the American Philosophical Society, 178. Philadelphia, 1989. # refers to document number in this edition.
PG	Migne, J. P. *Patrologiae cursus completus. Series Graeca.* 161 vols. Paris, 1857–66
PIR²	Groag, E., A. Stein, et al. *Prosopographia imperii Romani saec. I. II. III.* 2nd ed. Berlin and Leipzig, 1933–
PL	Migne, J. P. *Patrologiae cursus completus. Series Latina.* 221 vols. Paris, 1844–1900
RAN	*Revue archéologique de Narbonnaise*
RE	Pauly, A. F. von, G. Wissowa, et al., eds. *Real-Encyclopädie der classischen Altertums-wissenschaft.* Stuttgart, 1893–1972
RE Suppl.	Wissowa, G., et al., eds. *Paulys Real-Encyclopädie der classischen Altertumswissenschaft. Supplementbände.* 15 vols. Stuttgart, 1903–78
RIC	Mattingly, H., and E. A. Sydenham. *The Roman Imperial Coinage.* London, 1923–
Robert, *Hellenica*	Robert, L. *Hellenica.* Vol. I– . Limoges and Paris, 1940–
RömMitt	*Mitteilungen des Deutschen Archäologischen Instituts, Römische Abteilung*
SEG	*Supplementum epigraphicum Graecum.* Leiden, 1923–
Smallwood, #	Smallwood, E. M. *Documents Illustrating the Principates of Nerva, Trajan and Hadrian.* Cambridge, Eng., 1966. # refers to the document number in this edition.
Syll.³	Dittenberger, W. *Sylloge inscriptionum Graecarum.* 3rd ed. 4 vols. Leipzig, 1915–24
TAM	Kalinka, E., et al., eds. *Tituli Asiae Minoris.* Vienna, 1901–
ZRG	*Zeitschrift der Savigny-Stiftung für Rechtsgeschichte*

HADRIAN AND THE CITIES OF THE ROMAN EMPIRE

CHAPTER 1

Roman Cities and Roman Power:
The Roman Empire and Hadrian

THE ROMAN EMPIRE was far-flung and disparate during the reign of the emperor Hadrian (A.D. 117–38). With the Mediterranean basin as its heart, it stretched north, south, and east to cover almost three thousand miles, from modern England, the Atlantic, and Germany, up the Nile, and to Syria and Armenia. Although climate, an agricultural economy, and a generalized Greco-Roman culture united most of the Mediterranean littoral, these commonalities did not extend far inland. Difficulties of land transport and communications isolated regions from one another.[1] Each of the forty-some Roman provinces of the time had its own political, ethnic, religious, and cultural histories, in which figured prominently the date and means of its falling under Roman control.[2] Possibly as many as sixty million persons inhabited the Roman empire of Hadrian's day, with only some 20 percent estimated as living above subsistence level. These fortunate few dwelled in the cities scattered along coastlines, rivers, and at land passes, probably more than two thousand in all and most dense in North Africa, Italy, and coastal Asia Minor.[3] Beyond the borders were client-king-

---

[1] C. Starr, *The Roman Empire* (New York, 1982), 3–4. Isolation was the norm even within areas now considered a unit (e.g., Patterson 1987, esp. 138, 144).

[2] The provinces were: Britannia; the two Germaniae (Inferior; Superior); the four Gallic provinces (Belgica, Lugdunensis, Aquitania, Narbonensis); the three Iberian provinces (Tarraconensis, Baetica, Lusitania); the two Mauretaniae (Tingitana, Caesariensis); Africa; Cyrenaica (including Crete); Aegyptus; Arabia; Judaea (called Syria Palaestina by the very end of Hadrian's reign); Cyprus; Syria; Cilicia; Cappadocia; Galatia; Lycia-Pamphylia; Asia; Bithynia-Pontus; Thracia; the two Moesiae (Inferior, Superior); Dacia; Macedonia; Achaea; Dalmatia; Epirus; the two Pannoniae (Inferior, Superior); Noricum; Raetia; the Alpine provinces (Cottiae, Maritimae, and by now perhaps the Alpes Atrectianae et Graiae or Poeninae); Sardinia and Corsica (perhaps separate provinces by this time); and Sicilia.

[3] Most do not distinguish chronologically their estimates of population and number of cities; e.g., G. Charles-Picard, *La Civilisation de l'Afrique romaine* (Paris, 1959), 48, posits more than 200 cities in Africa Proconsularis, with 10 in a ten-km radius of Dougga; Mackie 1983, i, "over 500" in Roman Spain, apparently including non-Roman communities; H. Nissen, *Italische Landeskunde*, Vol. II.1, *Die Städte* (Berlin, 1902), 3, ca. 500 in Roman Italy. Josephus, *BJ* 2.16.4, and Apollonius of Tyana, *Ep.* 58, specify "500 cities" for Asia, and C. Habicht, "New Evidence on the Province of Asia," *JRS* 65 (1975): 67, holds for at least 300; S. Mitchell 1993, I:243, counts 130 for Bithynia-Pontus, Paphlagonia, Galatia and Lycaonia, Phrygia, Mysia, and Lydia. Hopkins 1978, 70, estimates 900 for Africa, Iberia, and Italy, and

doms, tribes allied with Rome, and more hostile tribes and nomads. Yet only some 350 elite officials in Rome, Italy, and the provinces oversaw the imperial government, and perhaps merely 350,000 to 400,000 armed men sufficed to protect the empire from internal and external dangers.[4]

A fundamental question of the Roman empire concerns its cohesion. Rome's immense domain had been acquired, gradually but seemingly inexorably, through constant warfare during the Roman republic. The first emperor, Augustus, and his successors apparently realized that Rome could no longer sustain its sovereignty simply by continued physical violence. Instead, norms of law, religion, politics, economy, community interest, and cultural values consolidated the Roman empire, at least until the second third of the third century.[5] Compliance with these patterns was not uniform or absolute during this lengthy period of the *pax Augusta* (the Augustan peace), in which Hadrian's reign is a kind of midpoint, but armed uprisings were exceptional after a region's initial incorporation into the empire.[6] Rome never neglected its military, and the state retaliated against defiant resistance swiftly and mercilessly. The Third Jewish Revolt of A.D. 132–35, to be discussed in chapter 8, illustrated to all, including Hadrian, the devastating consequences of rejecting Roman norms and taking up arms against the state. Compliance was more practical than coercion, both for Rome and for the provinces. But compliance requires that the subordinate acknowledge, more or less willingly, the norms of the dominant power. The history of the Roman empire is marked by the interplay of persuasion and force in the relationships between Rome, on the one hand, and its cities and provinces, on the other.

The reign of Hadrian offers a particularly good opportunity to assess this interaction, particularly as it was played out at the level of Rome's cities.

---

in his *Conquerors and Slaves* (Cambridge, Eng., 1978), 68–69, estimates that 32 percent of the six million inhabitants of Italy were urban residents, ca. one million in Rome. For the relatively small population of most Roman cities (2,000–10,000), see chapter 6 of Duncan-Jones 1982. G. Sjoberg, *The Preindustrial City* (Glencoe, IL, 1960), 83, holds that in preindustrial societies about 90 percent of the total population must work on the land.

[4] Levick 1985, 1; cf. Garnsey and Saller 1987, 21–26. There may have been as few as 150 Roman elite officials, one for every 350,000–400,000 subjects (Hopkins 1980, 121). By "elite officials" I mean senatorial governors, legionary legates, equestrian procurators, and the like, but not the Roman senate in session in Rome or the more than five hundred equestrian officers serving in the provincial armies and the Roman garrison. Birley 1981, 39–43, holds for more than 400,000 men in Rome's armed forces at this time, about 100,000 more than generally assumed.

[5] Whittaker 1997, 144, points to Augustus's complete refashionings of the army and the city as the "instruments of power to realize . . . imperial ideology."

[6] S. L. Dyson, "Native Revolt Patterns in the Roman Empire," *ANRW* II.3 (1975): 138–75; Whittaker 1997, 155–56.

The ancient writers celebrate Hadrian for his liberality to cities, but as a rule they speak imprecisely. Cassius Dio, Hadrian's biographer, Pausanias, Fronto, and others give pride of place to Hadrian's building projects, in part because these were the most lasting and tangible form of imperial benefaction. They also note engineering projects such as the dredging of harbors, financial measures such as the temporary or permanent remission of taxes, and social changes such as the establishment of games in a city.[7] Inscriptions,[8] and to a lesser extent coins,[9] furnish more detail and more instances of Hadrian's interactions with cities, and supplementary information comes from documentary papyri and recondite treatises such as those of the Roman land surveyors. The available evidence shows that more than 130 cities were affected by the personal attention of Hadrian, a number that helps quantify the ancient acclaim for his civic munificence.

Despite ancient and modern agreement that Hadrian fostered cities throughout the empire to an extent rarely matched in Roman history, so far there has been no analysis of the grounds and meaning of this commonplace. Scholars have examined various facets of his civic work; for example, F. Grelle, J. Gascou, and M. Zahrnt have focused on Hadrian's changes of municipal status, and H. Jouffroy and S. Mitchell cover his public building in North Africa and Italy, and in the eastern provinces, respectively.[10] I have investigated Hadrian's activity that influenced life in the

---

[7] E.g., Cass. Dio 69.5.2–3: Hadrian aided allied and subject cities most munificently, and he saw more cities than any other, assisting almost all of them variously with water supply, harbors, food, public works, money and various honors; *HA, Hadr.* 19.2, 20.5: Hadrian built something and gave games in almost every city, and he donated aqueducts "without end" in his own name; *HA, Hadr.* 9.6: Hadrian went to Campania and aided all the towns there by his benefactions and distributions (*beneficia, largitiones*); Pausanias 1.5.5: Hadrian built, restored, and embellished temples, and gave gifts to both Greek and foreign (barbarian) cities; Fronto, *Princ. Hist.* 11, p. 209 VDH (see chapter 2, n. 41): one can see monuments of Hadrian's journeys in many cities in Asia and Europe; *Epit. de Caes.* 14.4–5: Hadrian restored entire cities as he journeyed with a corps of builders and artisans; *Orac. Sibyll.* 12.166–68: Hadrian gave temples everywhere. These passages reappear in my text.

[8] In Oliver, about a fourth of the ca. 160 imperial addresses to magistrates or citizens of particular cities, from the reign of Augustus to A.D. 265, originate with Hadrian during his twenty-one-year reign. This is proportionally more than for any other emperor, even accounting for the "epigraphic habit" that contributed to an overall rise of inscriptions from the late Republic to the early third century (cf. MacMullen 1982).

[9] Coins struck in Rome commemorate Hadrian generally as the "restitutor" of entire provinces and regions: e.g., Toynbee 1934, 5, and passim.

[10] For changes of civic status, see chapter 3; for Hadrian's public building, chapters 6 and 7, and Blake, Bishop, and Bishop 1973. D'Orgeval 1950, 222–30, provides lists of cities whose juridical standing, name, title, or the like Hadrian changed, but these are not accurate enough to be useful. The topic of Hadrian's civic work occurs frequently in scholarship on quite different subjects: e.g., Isaac 1992, 352–59, investigates Hadrian's "urbanization" in his discussion of imperial attention to the military, though taking a minimalist view of Hadrian's municipal activity.

capital city of Rome.[11] But no one has attempted to compile and interpret all of Hadrian's different interactions with cities throughout the Roman empire. This I now aim to do, because I see Hadrian's personal involvement in Roman cities as intrinsic to the continuance of the Roman empire itself. Even though our evidence tends to report only successful pleas, the collected data let us see that Hadrian's municipal activity was predominantly positive. His benefactions, and their fame, decidedly helped to persuade Rome's provincials to cooperate with the ruling power.

As F. Millar and others have eloquently argued, the roles played by the Roman emperor were essential to the empire. Regardless of the particular merits or faults characterizing any one occupant of the throne, the emperor was the *pater patriae* (the father of the fatherland), ultimately deemed personally responsible for the welfare of each inhabitant.[12] This "beneficial ideology," in the words of V. Nutton,[13] was demonstrated daily, in many different guises, throughout the Roman world. Coins carried the imperial image encircled by legends broadcasting the imperial virtues.[14] Statues, reliefs, and paintings of the emperor and his family embellished temples and other public buildings and spaces, as well as private houses.[15] General oaths were sworn on the ruling emperor's "genius" (procreative spirit) as well as by earlier deified emperors, and at an emperor's accession, citizens of cities swore to protect his safety forever (e.g., *ILS* 190, *OGIS* 532).[16] Public processions, sacrifices, and games involving the imperial cult periodically enlivened municipal life.[17] But these and other symbolic representations of beneficent imperial power could remain forceful only with some factual basis. Something more than symbols was required to induce, generation after generation, those swearing to uphold the Roman emperor and empire actually to contribute energy and property to this cause.

---

[11] Boatwright 1987.

[12] Millar 1977, 363–463, with postscript of 1992 reprint (636–52). Cotton 1984, 265–66, dates to the principate of Trajan an important shift in the concept of the emperor. She holds that under Trajan the concept of the emperor as a *parens,* a parent whose indulgence could be begged for but was not automatically merited, supplanted the "image of the *princeps civilis,* the *princeps* as a fellow-citizen, a fellow-senator, an equal, a friend-amicus."

[13] Nutton 1978, 209.

[14] See Wallace-Hadrill 1986 on the nature of the persuasive language of imperial coinage; cf. T. Hölscher, *Staatsdenkmal und Publicum. Vom Untergang der Republik bis zur Festigung des Kaisertums in Rome. Xenia* (Constance, 1984).

[15] For one example of the vastly varying imagery and ideology of such images, see R. R. R. Smith, "The Imperial Reliefs from the Sebasteion at Aphrodisias," *JRS* 77 (1987): 88–138. Fronto remarks on the ubiquity of images of Marcus Aurelius when he was still only a "caesar" in Antoninus Pius's house (*Ad M. Caes.* 4.12 [VDH p. 67]). The passage, *HA, Marc.* 18.5–6, notes that an image of Marcus Aurelius was expected in every house that could afford it, located even with the household gods. See Hannestad 1986, 222.

[16] See also the sources collected in Levick 1985, 116–36.

[17] Fishwick 1987–92, II.1:475–590; Price 1984b, 101–32; and chapter 5 of this volume.

Positive reinforcement came through personal appearances of the emperor and, more lastingly, through manifest imperial favor.[18] At times this largesse graced an individual, as can be seen in the numerous inscriptions marking personal commendation by the emperor: for instance, M. Fabius Paulinus, honored by a dedication from his fellow townsmen in Ilerda (modern Lérida in northeast Spain), was "raised to equestrian status by Hadrian" (*CIL* II 4269). Such individualized attention was instrumental to the system of personal patronage underlying the social structure of the Roman empire.[19] It was one way Hadrian and other emperors encouraged the provincial elite to assume liturgies (public duties involving expense and usually personal service) and to contribute to their cities and Rome.[20]

Again the sources primarily document favorable attention: Hadrian is even said to have dropped earlier animosities upon assuming the throne, content simply to ignore his erstwhile enemies (*HA, Hadr.* 17.1). But we also hear, for example, that "in the case of some who clashed with him Hadrian thought it sufficient to write to their native cities the bare statement that they did not please him" (Cass. Dio 69.23.2). In a similar but more personalized instance, the sophist Favorinus gave in to Hadrian in a dispute about grammar, despite being in the right, because, as he said to friends, he was unwilling not to yield to the commander of thirty legions (*HA, Hadr.* 15.13, cf. Philostr. *VS* 489). The ostensibly nonchalant remark expresses well the tension between persuasion and force that was inherent in all exchanges with the emperor.

Rather than focusing on Hadrian's dealings with select individuals, however, I investigate benefactions affecting whole cities, for these interactions should be understood as systemic. Their existence and repetition reveal that imperial patronage was intrinsic to the endurance of the empire.[21] Although Hadrian's benefaction to a city was typically mediated or "bro-

[18] For Hadrian's trips, see Halfmann 1986; Syme 1988; T. D. Barnes, *JRA* 2 (1989): 247–61; and J.-L. Mourgues, *JRS* 80 (1990): 219–22. Aelius Aristides claims that in order to secure loyalty, the emperor has no need to tour the empire or visit individual peoples; he can simply use correspondence from Rome (*On Rome* 33). Birley 1997, 303n. 10, 357, reads Aristides' words as criticism of Hadrian, contra Oliver 1953, 919. We see below and in chapter 2 the significance of displayed imperial missives, and Swain 1996, 278, notes the importance to Aristides of "the emperor's epistolary support" in his long struggle for immunity and status.

[19] See Saller 1982; Veyne 1990; Millar 1983, esp. 77–78.

[20] The emperor's effects on the municipal elite, and the lives and ambitions of these provincial notables, have begun to be explored in fascinating detail for various cities of this era, such as Sparta (see Cartledge and Spawforth 1989), Ephesus (Rogers 1991), and Oenanda (Wörrle 1988). See also A. R. Birley, "Hadrian and Greek Senators," *ZPE* 116 (1997): 209–45.

[21] I do not, however, subscribe to the view expressed most notably by A. H. M. Jones in his numerous works on Greek cities, that cities simply served their Roman overlords. Wallace-Hadrill 1989, 4–6, remarks on the importance of assessing patronage in the ancient world as part of the "state" rather than as merely individual relationships.

kered" by a member or members of the municipal elite, as documented in various cases treated in this book, the city benefited as a whole, celebrated the benefaction as a whole, and was reaffirmed as a whole. Roman cities were much more than built-up and densely populated areas. They were always considered individual peoples, a fact reflected in their proper nomenclature as ethnic plurals rather than as place names. They combined an urban agglomeration of buildings and services, including administrative and governmental ones, with the land (*territorium* or *chora*) furnishing the basic livelihood for inhabitants of "city" and "countryside" alike.[22]

The obligations cities undertook for the Roman emperor and state were heavy ones, especially the collection of taxes and census registration. Tasks less onerous, because imposed more sporadically, included recruitment of armed men, supply of animals for transport, provision of hospitality and transportation for travelers on official business, and shelter, equipment, and supplies for journeying soldiers and the army. Such duties to the central Roman government were offset by a high degree of local autonomy. Individual cities were left to themselves, as a general rule, to oversee their own public buildings and cults, the maintenance of their water supply and baths, local law and order, and embassies to Roman officials, including the emperor.[23] They were also free to negotiate other relationships, with different cities in the area or farther afield (as we see especially in chapter 5), and with powerful individuals who were not serving officially at the time (as indicated in chapters 3 and 4). Despite isolating barriers of travel, transportation, and communications, albeit less severe during the second cen-

---

[22] Reynolds 1988, 15: e.g., *Carthaginienses* rather than *Carthago* refers to the city we know of as Carthage. Note the order of elements that constitute a city for Pausanias (10.4.1): "if one can give the name of a city (*polis*) to those [the city of Panopeus, in Phocis] who possess no government offices, no gymnasium, no theatre, no market-place, no water descending to a fountain, but live in bare shelters just like mountain cabins, right on a ravine. Nevertheless, they have boundaries with their neighbours, and even send delegates to the Phocian assembly" (trans. W. H. S. Jones, *Pausanias: Description of Greece*, Loeb edition, vol. IV [London, 1965], p. 383). For the economy of Roman cities, which were not simply "consumers," see Hopkins 1978 and, e.g., J. Nollé, "Pamphylische Studien 6–10," *Chiron* 17 (1987): 254–64 (focusing on third-century Pamphylian Side and Perge). In the early third century Ulpian characterized living in a Roman city as enjoying its functions as a place of economic and judicial transactions, and its offerings of public baths, attendance at shows, and participation in religious festivals (*Dig.* 50.1.27.1). Hadrian's benefactions encompassed all these urban amenities.

[23] Garnsey and Saller 1987, 32–34; with more detail from inscriptions, Reynolds 1988, 28–39. For tax collection and census registration, Brunt 1981, 163–66; transport, S. Mitchell, "Requisitioned Transport in the Roman Empire: A New Inscription from Pisidia," *JRS* 66 (1976): 106–31; recruitment, Brunt 1974b, C. P. Jones, "The Levy at Thespiae under Marcus Aurelius," *GRBS* 12 (1971): 45–48, and B. Isaac, "Military Diplomata and Extraordinary Levies for Campaigns," in *Heer und Integrationspolitik: Die römischen Militärdiplome als historische Quelle,* ed. W. Eck and H. Wolff, Passauer historische Forschungen 2 (Cologne, 1986), 258–64.

tury of the empire than at other times in ancient history, Roman cities had intricate networks of relationships. In each case the relationship was reciprocal. But rarely, if ever, were the strengths of the involved parties equal, and constant negotiation was needed to manage these relationships advantageously for both sides.

Such negotiation was undertaken for cities by their leading citizens. In addition to making political decisions, a town's magistrates and council were responsible for the fulfillment of that town's duties: they would personally have to make good shortfalls of taxes, for example. Spotty evidence indicates that from the end of the first century A.D., some cities experienced the reluctance, or incapacity, of individuals to take on municipal posts. From this, P. Garnsey, S. Mitchell, and others have argued for a progressive and marked decline of the "urban aristocracy," holding that as early as the beginning of the second century there was a diminution of the voluntary participatory character of the Roman empire as it had evolved since Augustus took power.[24]

The necessary corollary of this averred trend would be ever greater imperial control and interference as Rome extracted from cities what it needed to provision the armies, to maintain the court, to sustain games, distributions, and construction at Rome and elsewhere, and to ensure other functions deemed essential. Drawing in part on the correspondence between Trajan and Pliny the Younger, whom Hadrian's predecessor appointed as *legatus Augusti* (delegate of the emperor) to oversee the disorderly province of Bithynia-Pontus around 111,[25] some scholars have argued that the central government began to encroach on cities' autonomy by the beginning of the second century A.D.[26] Yet the domineering and rapacious Roman governors, soldiers, and officials, so unforgettably depicted in late inscriptions, legal codes, and literature, are rhetorically exaggerated even for the third and fourth centuries, and cannot be sustained generally for the second.[27]

Although recent research has shown that in Achaea, for example, there were fewer cities in the Roman imperial period than in preceding centuries,[28] on the

---

[24] Garnsey 1974, 232–38; S. Mitchell 1984, 124–25 (based esp. on Dio of Prusa). Jacques 1984, ix–xvii, discusses earlier expressions of this theory. See also chapter 3, n. 43 in my volume.

[25] His exact title was *legatus Augusti pro praetore consulari potestate* (delegate of the emperor with the rank of propraetor, but with consular powers). For title and date, see lines 2 and 3 of Smallwood, #230 (= *ILS* 2927), and W. Eck, "Jahres- und Provinzialfasten der senatorischen Statthalter von 69/70 bis 138/139," *Chiron* 12 (1982): 349.

[26] See, e.g., Pliny *Ep.* 10.23–24: cities needed permission from Rome to erect new buildings; *Ep.* 10.47–48: emperors could and did override a city's right to handle its own affairs. Reynolds 1988, 41–46, discusses these and similar passages; cf. Garnsey and Saller 1987, 34–40.

[27] Jacques 1984, xii–xiv. I argue in chapter 4 that Hadrian's *curatores rei publicae* (city overseers) were usually local men, not strangers imposed on the city from outside.

[28] Alcock 1993.

whole their leading citizens apparently evinced little or no reluctance to assume municipal responsibilities through most of the second century. In the second-century empire some famous men, such as Favorinus, Aelius Aristides, and Dio of Prusa, squirmed to get out of their public service[29]—who among us pays our taxes gladly?—but through that century enough others were honored to serve their cities that Rome and its provinces continued to flourish. Despite both the positivistic nature of most extant evidence and the painful awareness of Rome's abusive potential that Favorinus and some others express,[30] indications of functionally negative relations between Rome and the provincial cities begin to accumulate only toward the end of the second century.[31]

Indeed, R. Duncan-Jones has recently used building inscriptions to argue that the reigns of Hadrian and his successor, Antoninus Pius, generally witnessed a surge of construction in cities of the Roman empire.[32] He attributes this rise to the effects of Hadrian's policies, which demonstrate "concern for the fiscal and economic well-being of the empire, as well as exceptional involvement by the emperor in local affairs."[33] Noting some of Hadrian's activity I discuss in chapters 5 and 6, Duncan-Jones highlights Hadrian's general remission of unpaid taxes, worth 900 million sesterces, early in his reign.[34] Not only was this the largest tax remission up to

[29] See esp. Millar 1983 for an illuminating collection of petitions for immunities.

[30] For example, Plutarch counsels a young man entering local politics to remember always "the boots of the Roman governor poised above his head" (*Mor.* 813). See also Apul. *Met.* 4.9, Aristides *Or.* 50; cf. P. Desideri, "La vita politica cittadina nell'Impero: Lettura dei *praecepta gerendae rei publicae* e dell'*an seni res publica gerenda sit,*" *Athenaeum* 64 (1986): 371–81; F. Millar, "The World of the Golden Ass," *JRS* 71 (1981): 63–75; more generally, Swain 1996.

[31] See chapter 3, n. 43. Reynolds 1988, 51, holds for the vitality of Roman cities to at least A.D. 200. Duncan-Jones 1990, 159–73, esp. 170, argues that "the lack of direct indications of strain in the municipal system" in first-century legal rulings, inscriptions, and papyri should not be overemphasized, since these sources have much greater frequency and detail beginning in the second century. Polemo, for example, was not at all reluctant to take on "the expensive honors that came with his social position" (Gleason 1995, 23–24).

[32] Although he examines only Syria, Italy, Spain, Lepcis, Sabratha, and Thugga (Duncan-Jones 1990, 59–67). Working from the figures of Jouffroy (1986) for Africa, F. Jacques, "L'Urbanisme en Italie et en Afrique romaines," *JRA* 2 (1989): 242–44, sees a steady rise of public building after Trajan, with its apogee from A.D. 160 to 218.

[33] Duncan-Jones 1990, 66. Yet nothing points to a conscious policy on Hadrian's part materially to improve whole cities or provinces. Pausanias's remark that the Megarians were so cursed for an ancient misdeed that they were the only Greeks not even Hadrian could make more prosperous (1.36.3; Loeb translation) suggests to me the casual nature of the emperor's benevolence. See also Halfmann 1986, 191, and Alcock 1993, 160.

[34] Duncan-Jones 1990, 66–67: the rulings affecting money-changing at Pergamum, sale of olive oil in Athens, and land drainage at Coronea. He also mentions the *lex Hadriana de ruderibus agris,* which encouraged cultivation of unused or virgin land and the growing of vines and olives (*FIRA* 1.102, *AE* 1958, 9), Hadrian's reduction of the payment demanded from mine operators starting new concessions in government-owned mines (Smallwood, #439), and Hadrian's building, visits, and holding of local magistracies.

Hadrian's time, but the general amnesty was to last for fifteen years (*ILS* 309 = *CIL* VI 967, cf. Cass. Dio 69.8.1[2] and 71.32.2, and *BMC, Emp.* III, p. 417, #1207).[35] Local spending apparently rose as a result of actual money freed up and a concomitant change in economic outlook.[36] The increased expenditure on buildings by individuals and by towns (collectively) marks both the general prosperity of the era and its emphasis on urban amenities.

How much of these phenomena can we attribute to Hadrian himself and how much to larger political and social tendencies, such as competition between families, individuals, and even cities?[37] Hadrian was famous for his complex and self-contradictory personality (e.g., *HA, Hadr.* 14.11, *Epit. de Caes.* 14.6). His biography and Cassius Dio, the two most substantial literary sources, stress his competitiveness, his restlessness, and his brilliance (*HA, Hadr.* 20.7, 23.1; Cass. Dio 69.3.2–3). He had wide interests and insatiable curiosity (Tert. *Apol.* 5.7; *HA, Hadr.* 14.8–10, 15.10–16.11; Cass. Dio 69.3.1, 69.5.1, 69.11.3). Unpleasant when coupled with his pedantic insistence on being the only one hailed as correct (as when he had to best Favorinus, other sophists, or the scholars of Alexandria's Museum),[38] such intellectual qualities impelled him to climb Syrian Mt. Casius to see the sun rise, to travel up the Nile, and to devour local lore while traveling outside Italy for more than half of his twenty-one-year reign (*HA, Hadr.* 14.3, 17.8; Cass. Dio 69.9.1–2). Hadrian was indulgent with friends and acquaintances and met new people easily, although his intense competitiveness made him solitary (*HA, Hadr.* 15.1–2, 22.4; Cass. Dio 69.5.1–2, 69.6.2–3, 69.7.1–4, 69.17.3–18.1). Letters and speeches remaining from Hadrian's prolific output (see chapter 2) substantiate the literary sources' depiction of a man doggedly thorough in law and governance, meticulous in detail and thought, sensitive to difference, and as attuned to the common man as to the upper classes (*HA, Hadr.* 17.5–7, 21.1–3, 22.1; Cass Dio 69.6.2–3, 69.16.3).

The ideology of the Roman empire held that good emperors manifest magnanimity by public building in Rome, Italy, and the provinces, and no Roman emperor was oblivious of the importance of cities for the empire (cf. Dio Chrys. *Or.* 47.13). Moreover, each new emperor had to outdo his

---

[35] Duncan-Jones 1990, 66, where he also notes Hadrian's drastic reduction of taxes on crown land in Egypt and his postponement of money taxes near the end of his reign (Smallwood, ##460, 462), and his ruling that tax-farmers should not be forced to renew contracts against their will (*Dig.* 49.14.6, cf. Cass. Dio 69.16.2).

[36] Both the cited inscription, from 118, and the pertinent passage of the biography (*HA, Hadr.* 7.6) note increased "security" as an effect of the remission.

[37] Duncan-Jones 1990, 59–60, 170–71, cautiously addresses this key question, citing these three factors. I discuss competition between cities in the conclusion to chapter 5.

[38] *HA, Hadr.* 14.8–9, 15.10–13, 16.1–11, 20.2; Cass. Dio 69.3.1–4, 69.3.6; Syme 1965, 243–49, and n. 48 below.

predecessors in some way.[39] Although the pattern was thus set for Hadrian's benefactions with cities, he seems to have gone further than required. Hadrian's immediate predecessor, Trajan, had contributed lavishly to building in Rome and more modestly to public works elsewhere. In both spheres Hadrian surpassed him in quantity, and the predominantly religious, rather than utilitarian, aspect of Hadrian's imperial work further contrasted with Trajan's.[40] Antoninus Pius's building activity consisted largely of roadwork, some restoration, and completion of works begun or promised by Hadrian (for example, the aqueduct at Athens, discussed in chapter 7):[41] in sum, much less than what is recorded for Hadrian and evincing much less initiative and imagination.

Indeed, no Roman emperor devoted as much personal attention to cities throughout the empire as did Hadrian, except perhaps Augustus himself.[42] Yet the situations in which these two emperors undertook their activity differed greatly. Augustus had to restore urban structures and encourage order after cataclysmic warfare in extensive areas, including Italy and much of the Greek East.[43] Elsewhere, as in North Africa, Spain, and parts of Gaul, he had to establish civic organs with which Rome could cooperate.[44] In contrast, Hadrian came to the throne of an empire already urbanized, many of whose cities now possessed more or less uniform administrations. Thanks to better communications made possible by the *pax Augusta* (the imperial peace), the empire of Hadrian's day was relatively familiar with the mores, laws, language, and material culture of Rome itself. Hadrian's avoidance of war and his decisive withdrawal from the untenable borders established by Trajan allowed him to direct Rome's resources toward munificence.[45] The evidence for Hadrian's personality, as biased as some of it may be, indicates that the number and variety of Hadrian's benefactions were due to Hadrian himself, their geographical spread was intentional, and their nuances were deliberate.

[39] See Millar 1977, 420–34, and Kloft 1970; for the concept of surpassing one's predecessors, e.g., J. Elsner, "Constructing Decadence: The Representation of Nero as Imperial Builder," in *Reflections of Nero: Culture, History, and Representation,* ed. J. Elsner and J. Masters (Chapel Hill, NC, 1994), 112–27.

[40] E.g., Garzetti 1974, 329–39, noting especially Trajan's attention to roads and harbors; J. Bennett, *Trajan, Optimus Princeps* (Bloomington, IN, 1997), 138–60. Syme 1965, 244, points to Hadrian's particular sensitivity to his contrast to Trajan.

[41] Garzetti 1974, 451–53.

[42] S. Mitchell 1987, 333–36, discusses the history and significance of a ruler's public or sacred buildings for the benefit of his community, beginning in the Hellenistic period and citing the main literary references for Roman emperors.

[43] Keppie 1983, 114–22; cf. E. Gabba, "Urbanizzazione e rinnovamenti urbanistici nell'Italia centro-meridionale del I sec. a.C.," *StudClassOr* 21 (1972): 73–112; F. C. Bourne, *The Public Works of the Julio-Claudians and Flavians* (Princeton, NJ, 1946), 16–20.

[44] Gros and Torelli 1992, 237–42.

[45] See, e.g., *HA, Hadr.* 5.1–2, Cass. Dio 69.5; Garzetti 1974, 381–82.

As we see throughout this book, the actual interaction between Hadrian and many cities was associated with a renewal, preservation, or promotion of the unique history of that place. Again, it cannot be determined conclusively how much of this effect was due to Hadrian and how much to larger trends. Hadrian was famed for almost perversely archaistic predilections (e.g., *HA, Hadr.* 16.5–6; see chapter 6 on tombs). Yet many cities at this same time were also fascinated with their most remote past, displaying their heroic founders and venerable traditions in sculpture and architecture throughout the Greek East.[46] The privileging of the past, evinced by Hadrian and by cities from the end of the first through the second centuries A.D., is also conspicuous in the contemporaneous literary and cultural movement known as the Second Sophistic.[47] Many of the most famous exponents of the Second Sophistic, such as Favorinus, Polemo of Smyrna, Aelius Aristides, and Herodes Atticus, are connected with Hadrian in some way, and appear in my text. But we cannot attribute solely or even chiefly to Hadrian the cultural influence they and other such stars exerted. Indeed, given the rocky relations that Cassius Dio and others depict between emperor and sophists, we might expect the reverse.[48]

But here we are decidedly turning to the wrong set of questions; more important, and more appreciable in the data I have assembled, is the tenor of the past that Hadrian's municipal benefactions evoked. This "past" was inseparable from Hadrian and contemporary Roman might. S. Walker and A. J. Spawforth have brilliantly demonstrated, for instance, how closely tied to Hadrian himself was the Panhellenion, his re-creation of Athens's preeminence in the Greek world.[49] In Athens and many other cities, Hadrian's appreciation of local history and his interest in the recondite may have helped define the form his imperial largesse took as the restoration of a monument, the support of a festival, or something else that recalled the city's past. Regardless of its configuration, by his benefaction Hadrian effectively appropiated that past into the ongoing history of the Roman empire.[50]

My evidence for this process allows us to assess in a more nuanced way the topic of Romanization. The term *Romanization* traditionally has been used to describe assimilation by provincials, especially provincial elites, of Roman culture in all its variety, from materials and art forms to personal

---

[46] See Curty 1995, 254–63, and Scheer 1993 on legendary founders; and, for an example of this trend's architectural and sculptural expression, M. T. Boatwright, "The City Gate of Plancia Magna in Perge," in *Roman Art in Context: An Anthology,* ed. E. D'Ambra (Englewood Cliffs, NJ, 1993), 189–207.

[47] E.g., Anderson 1993, Andrei 1984, and earlier fundamental works, such as Bowersock 1969, and Bowie 1982.

[48] See Bowersock 1969, 50–53; Gleason 1995, 146–47.

[49] Spawforth and Walker 1985 and 1986. I discuss the Panhellenion in chapter 7.

[50] Cf. M. Bloch, "The Past and the Present in the Present," *Man* 12 (1977): 278–92, and A. Appadurai, "The Past as a Scarce Resource," *Man* 16 (1981): 201–19.

nomenclature and Roman law. Recent work has emphasized, however, that acculturation during the Empire was not simply a transferral of Roman culture to the "uncultured" non-Romans the empire encompassed. Rather, the interaction of Romans and provincials provided a stimulus for continual modification of dominant and subordinate cultures alike.[51] This give-and-take is manifested most clearly in Rome's interactions with the provinces in which Greek was the primary language, many of which were around the Aegean Sea, and long before Hadrian's era Rome's elite and not-so-elite had embraced Greek learning and cultural achievements.[52] Hadrian himself was derided as a "Graeculus," a little Greekling (*HA, Hadr.* 1.5, *Epit. de Caes.* 14.2), because of his deep and abiding interest in Greek literature, history, and learning. But in the Latin West as well as the Greek East Hadrian's work manifested his attentiveness to cities' particular traditions, as when he assumed a city's highest magistracy in absentia, or restored or completed temples begun long before the Romans' arrival.

Through his constant municipal activity, and particularly through his boons affecting religion, Hadrian ensured that the beneficent image of the Roman emperor was inextricably woven into the patterns of daily life in cities of the Roman world. Valorization of urban life and acknowledgment of the emperor's supremacy are the most universal markers of what it meant to be Roman during the Empire, not temples to Jupiter Optimus Maximus, amphitheaters, the use of Latin, or even the diffusion of Roman citizenship.[53] Just as important as reinforcing a basis for cohesion of the immense Roman world, however, Hadrian's benefactions encouraged civic munificence, including the assumption of obligatory civic duties (now often termed liturgies), on the part of the municipal elites. His travels, ceaseless correspondence, and reception of embassies, often even his largesse itself, were mediated by cities' grandees, whose social and political standing was concomitantly advanced by their association with the emperor.

Hadrian's general laws affecting cities seem to have promoted civic pride. He introduced a *senatus consultum* that confirmed legacies could be left to any city in the empire (Ulp. *Reg.* 24.28).[54] He prohibited demolition of houses for the purpose of transferring their materials to another city (*HA,*

---

[51] See, e.g., the review article by Freeman 1993; Millett 1990; and Mattingly 1997. I avoid the older "Romanization" model, which has often been used, for example, in interpretations of Hadrian's changes of city status (see the end of chapter 3).

[52] See, e.g., Wallace-Hadrill 1988.

[53] Cf. Sherwin-White's discussion of "status Romanus" in the third and fourth centuries (1973, 451–60). As is clear in my discussion of city statuses in chapter 3, I feel less strongly than he about the importance of Roman citizenship in the second century.

[54] Johnston 1985: this followed a constitution of Nerva. The *SC Apronianum,* allowing cities throughout the empire to sue for *fideicommissa hereditatis* (*Dig.* 36.1.27), may date to Hadrian's reign (Talbert 1984, 446, #95).

Hadr. 18.2), evincing general concern for the physical appearance of cities.[55] He issued an edict (*CodJ* 10.40.7), according to which local citizenship was created by *origo* (normally descent from a male citizen of a town, e.g., *CodJ* 10.39.3), manumission by a citizen of the town, adlection, or adoption; status of *incolae* arose from the establishment of *domicilium* (place of residence) in a city (cf. Ulp. 1.2 ad ed., *Dig.* 50.1.1pr.).[56] Hadrian thus reaffirmed individuals' legal ties to towns, as he did when promoting a man to citizenship in a second town (chapter 4). Hadrian also gave legal privileges to decurions, which served to reward these town councillors for their service (*Dig.* 48.19.15).[57] Although he cannot be proved responsible for distinguishing Latin rights into "greater" and "lesser" Latin rights (*Latium maius* and *Latium minus,* with "greater Latin rights" awarding Roman citizenship to town decurions as well as magistrates),[58] his laws concerning legacies to cities and decurions' privileges may have boosted local benefactions by members of municipal elites.[59] The laws simultaneously increased the prestige of those who undertook municipal service and made it easier to benefit one's town materially. They facilitated the nexus of public service and public acclaim (often called "euergetism") that was characteristic of the Roman empire and essential to the health of cities and empire alike.[60]

Much more frequent and impressive than Hadrian's laws affecting all cities, however, were his direct interactions with individual cities outside of Rome: during Hadrian's twenty-one-year reign more than 130 cities received, in all, more than 210 marks of his favor. This book is the examination of those imperial interactions, divided according to general topics. As I show in chapter 2, the presentation of my evidence and methods, my ap-

---

[55] This notice fits with other laws against demolishing buildings, such as the *SC Acilianum* of 122 (*Dig.* 30.1.41, 43; cf. *Dig.* 18.1.52). See Lewis 1989; Boatwright 1987, 23–24; Murga 1976. Hadrian reveals similar aesthetic concerns in Coronea and other cities discussed below.

[56] Cf. Millar 1983, 80; cf. Nörr 1965.

[57] *Divus Hadrianus eos, qui in numero decurionum essent, capite punire prohibuit . . . verum poena legis Corneliae puniendos mandatis plenissime cautum est* (the deified Hadrian prohibited capital punishment of those who were decurions . . . but it was amply warned through mandates that they should be punished by the liabilities of the Lex Cornelia [by being deported]). See Garnsey 1970, 153–62.

[58] Cf. *CIL* VIII 14763 = *ILS* 6781; Gai. *Inst.* 1.96. *Latium minus* refers to the situation in which only magistrates receive Roman citizenship. Sherwin-White 1973, 255–56, 262–63, 414, and chapter 3, nn. 7 and 46 in this text. For the uncertain date and attribution of *Latium maius* and *minus:* Zahrnt 1989b, 179–80; Galsterer 1988a, 86; Langhammer 1973, 19–20.

[59] Johnston 1985, 110–12.

[60] The phenomenon is explored in depth in Veyne's masterful *Le Pain et le cirque* (see Veyne 1990), and by Gauthier 1985 (though for the Hellenistic period). I return to it in the following chapters.

proach has been largely determined by my sources. Romans celebrated Hadrian's municipal benefactions, whatever their guise, with the same words: *beneficium, indulgentia, euergesia,* and the like. Such undifferentiated terminology has persuaded me to examine comprehensively Hadrian's activities with cities outside Rome, rather than to concentrate exclusively on building donations or some other particular type of benefaction.

Chapter 3 addresses one of the most frequent forms of Hadrian's personal dealings with cities, at least in the Latin West: his changes of civic status. In my investigation I discuss the functions and political life of cities in Italy and the provinces during the empire, the roles of the municipal elite, and the interactions of cities and the central power in Rome. The chapter thus delineates, albeit along broad lines, life in cities throughout Hadrian's empire. In chapter 4 I discuss other local administrative and economic changes Hadrian brought about in various cities by, for example, holding a local magistracy in absentia, appointing a *curator aedium sacrarum* (supervisor of sacred buildings) or a *curator rei publicae* (supervisor of a city) to oversee a town's sacred buildings or finances, redistributing land, or adding to citizen lists or town councils. Chapter 5 complements chapter 4 by presenting the evidence for Hadrian's alterations of a city's status vis-à-vis its surrounding region or Rome itself. The material includes Hadrian's modifications of a city's territory, his determination of a city's taxes, revenues, or grain supplies, his promotion or ratification of festivals in a city, and his grants of various civic titles not marking a change of city status.

In chapter 6 I turn to Hadrian's construction or reconstruction of buildings and his engineering projects in various cities. Since my research points to almost one hundred Hadrianic structures in all, in this chapter I discuss only outstanding examples of the various types of construction he supported. In chapter 7 I examine three cities as case studies: Athens, Smyrna, and Italica. These are chosen for the wealth and detail of the data attesting the buildings and other benefactions they received from Hadrian, and their discussion allows me to address issues of planning, material, and technique. In chapter 8 I treat Antinoopolis, Colonia Aelia Capitolina, and other cities Hadrian created completely or largely *ex novo*. These provide the best opportunity to evaluate questions of urbanization and Romanization. The concluding chapter, chapter 9, brings together the rich evidence for Hadrian's personal interactions with cities throughout the empire, discussing the material chronologically and geographically, and emphasizing its significance for the Roman empire.

The title of my book reflects my ultimate aim, to illuminate the Roman empire of Hadrian's day rather than to focus on Hadrian himself. Hadrian provides the prism for my endeavor, thanks to the frequency, variety, and geographical spread of his municipal activity. His prominence in both title and book, moreover, indicates the difficulty of establishing the relative weights to assign to structure and agency in historical inquiries. Although Rome's structural realities were already in place—its ideology, mentalités, economy, geography, and the like—Hadrian maximized their potential. The evidence I have collected and assessed compels me to believe that Hadrian had a profound effect on the Roman empire, and particularly on its achievements of the second century: consensus, general internal peace, and expansion of urban amenities. Even if these benefited at most 20 percent of the population under Rome's sway, the proportion is greater than in any other preindustrial society. Those benefiting from Rome had a chance at values generally esteemed today: freedom within the law; access to culture; voluntary participation in social and religious ritual; a sense of one's place in society and history; the feeling that one's voice and actions matter and help determine one's fate. I know well that Rome's accomplishments were gained at a heavy price: Hadrian's war against the Jews abhorrently exemplifies Rome's ruthless suppression of nonconformists, and every city bolstered by his attention deprived others of revenues. Nevertheless, in the second century A.D. the benefits of Rome's rule seem to me to have outweighed the disadvantages. Hadrian's attention to the cities of the empire significantly influenced this generally positive effect, and the wealth of evidence amply repays close inquiry.

CHAPTER 2

The Sources

THE PRIMARY EVIDENCE for Hadrian's municipal benefactions comes from various literary and documentary sources, including inscriptions, coins, and papyri. At first sight the evidence is unpromising. In general, literary sources seldom mention this type of Hadrian's activity, as we shall see. In contrast, documentary evidence is plentiful, with more than two hundred inscriptions, coins, and papyri from recipient cities witnessing Hadrian's civic munificence. Yet these records offer no analysis of motivation or effect, and their representativeness is uncertain.[1] Moreover, their data is overwhelmingly positive. If the evidence is not simply incidental, such as when a later inscription notes reconstruction of something originally donated by Hadrian, it glorifies Hadrian's interest in the concerned city and ignores negative aspects and consequences. Failed petitions for Hadrian's help were not commemorated.[2] Archaeological and art historical evidence can also be too positive, as stylistic arguments and the desire to link a building or sculpture to a well-known figure have led many to attribute to Hadrian unidentified works that probably were given by local benefactors.[3] Despite such shortcomings, the assembled data provide the names of more than 130 cities that received attention from Hadrian himself. The cities span most of the Roman empire, and the attested types of imperial interactions are quite varied. Most meaningfully, the pattern of the evidence and the language used argue conclusively that Hadrian's benefactions were key to cities' life.

No ancient writer or document purports to catalogue Hadrian's municipal benefactions or to examine any particular type of them; only one, Aulus Gellius, offers any explanation of Hadrian's activity in this sphere, but incidentally (see below and chapter 3). My topic is not one Roman authors considered worthy of exposition and analysis, despite its significance to cities and individuals now so prominent on the inscriptions and coins remaining from throughout the empire. As Tacitus caustically implies (*Ann.*

---

[1] E.g., Keppie 1991, 30–35, hazards that the total number of Latin inscriptions surviving today is somewhat greater than three hundred thousand, out of an original total of perhaps six million, i.e., 5 percent.

[2] Millar 1977, 431–32, 436, 438–39, Bowie 1982, 37, and Reynolds 1978, 121, note the rarity of records of unsuccessful embassies and unfavorable imperial decisions.

[3] The "Traianeum" in Italica, Spain, not documented other than by archaeology, is the apparent exception to this rule, and will be discussed in chapter 7.

13.49.1), items about municipal life were not deemed appropriate to history: they offered little of moral, political, or military significance to the Roman historian. Histories of the imperial period, such as those of Tacitus and the later books of Cassius Dio, covered the emperor and his court, the senate, Rome, and military affairs (cf. Cass. Dio 53.19). Hadrian's dealings with a city might be noted when related to one of these subjects, for example, his foundation of Antinoopolis at the spot where his beloved Antinoos had drowned in the Nile (Cass. Dio 69.11.2–4). Tellingly, even this note is overshadowed in the excerpted history, for Cassius Dio or his eleventh-century compiler, Xiphilinus, attends with greater detail to the superstitions, sentimentality, and credulity Hadrian disclosed by his posthumous honors for Antinoos.

Historiographical bias has effectively silenced information presumably reported in the documents and writings to which the extant authors turned. These included the *populi diurna acta* (gazette of public business) and the *acta senatus* (proceedings of the senate), published speeches by the emperor and other eminent men, family records, and individual journals.[4] An emperor's reaction to municipal disaster would probably have been noted at least in the *acta senatus*, since embassies from afflicted cities were often heard in the senate,[5] and imperial alleviation of calamities was a sign of a good ruler (cf. *HA, Hadr.* 21.5).[6] But as Cassius Dio complains (54.23.8), a complete list of cities applying for aid after disasters would be endless. Details of such routine business were generally omitted by ancient historians as inconsequential.

Cities turned to the emperor for myriad reasons, which they and their representatives certainly did not consider trivial.[7] The incessant business of imperial response to petitions, from ambassadors and others approaching the emperor wherever and by whatever means they could, has been recorded in two main ways.[8] In biographies and other depictions of the emperor, imperial responses to petitions are noted as a way to adumbrate

---

[4] For the *acta senatus* and other documentary sources for historians, see Talbert 1984, 308–34.

[5] Cf. ibid., 262, 329, 414–15. *ILS* 6772 = *CIL* X 7507, for instance, is a Sicilian dedication to a Postumus who, among other benefactions to his city, voluntarily undertook an embassy to Hadrian and the senate.

[6] Leopold 1986; Kloft 1970, 118–20; Millar 1977, 422–24. L. Robert, *BCH* 102 (1978): 401, discusses some epigraphic instances.

[7] True also for individuals and groups such as the Dionysiac artists; cf. chapter 5. Types of individual petitions addressed to Hadrian are illustrated in the *Sententiae et epistolae divi Hadriani*, in the *Corpus Glossariorum Latinorum* (ed. G. Goetz), III.31–37, although the compilation is probably fictitious in particulars.

[8] Williams 1967 argues that Hadrian tried to discourage unnecessary embassies (cf. Plut. *Mor.* 815a). Bowie 1982, 36–38, notes that about two hundred embassies are attested from Greek cities to emperors from the Flavians to the mid third century.

the ruler's *civilitas* (approachability) and *liberalitas* (generosity).[9] Second, the interested parties frequently commemorated a successful petition publicly, installing its epigraphic record in a public setting that was often embellished architecturally or with sculpture. Some of these records seem to have passed into the literary tradition via Pausanias, Philostratus, and other writers. Extant inscriptions document other memorials. Although most such commemorations have surely perished in the lime kiln or by some other means, public records could not be patently false. Even though their vocabulary is often inflated, imprecise, and open-ended, they are always significant as public statements.[10] But I examine first the literary evidence, which often purports to reveal motivation.

LITERARY SOURCES

The literary sources for Hadrian's principate are less numerous and less extensive than those for earlier reigns, and the few we have offer particular problems. Most obviously, we lack a continuous historical narrative. Even Cassius Dio's *Roman History* survives for Hadrian's reign mainly in the discontinuous and selected epitome of Xiphilinus, a jurist, monk, and ultimately patriarch of Trapezus in the eleventh century. Xiphilinus's rather erratic selection of Cassius Dio's material was determined by personal concerns. His religious interests, for example, lie behind the relatively full coverage of the Third Jewish Revolt (also known as the Bar Kokhba War) in Judaea in 132–35, which includes notice of Hadrian's foundation of Colonia Aelia Capitolina and his building of a temple to Jupiter over ruined Jerusalem (69.12.1).[11]

Cassius Dio himself composed his *Roman History* in Rome probably during the 220s, to cover events from Rome's foundation to his own day.[12] He makes little reference to his sources. Most of what remains of the book devoted to Hadrian's principate, book 69, revolves around Hadrian's personality and moral qualities as revealed in his actions and his interactions with the leading men of the time. It provides little chronology or deep analysis. F. Millar has posited that Cassius Dio compiled much of this information from stories common among Rome's elite, perhaps augmenting his narrative with copies of Hadrian's reports to the senate concerning the

[9] Wallace-Hadrill 1982, 35, 43–44, though noting that literary sources pay scant attention to imperial reactions to petitioners, a topic fundamental to Millar 1977. For *liberalitas*, see n. 6 above.

[10] Williamson 1987; Corbier 1987; Beard 1985; Bowman and Woolf 1994, 1–16.

[11] Millar 1964, 2–3, 5–27, 68; P. A. Brunt, "On Historical Fragments and Epitomes," *CQ* 30 (1980): 488–92.

[12] Barnes 1984.

Third Jewish Revolt.[13] Although as a senator Cassius Dio is hostile to Hadrian, he seems quite familiar with the period; he refers twice to Hadrian as a source (66.17.1, 69.11.2),[14] once to a letter written by Hadrian (69.17.3), and once to the "truthful" account of the death of Trajan, which Cassius Dio's father had heard as governor of Cilicia in 117 (69.1.3).[15] Millar remarks that Cassius Dio often recounts in a trivial context items of considerable historical import (e.g., 69.4.1–5).[16]

Cassius Dio's focus on Hadrian's personality and its effects on Rome's elite apparently led him to overlook much we would now like to know. It seems dubious that he detailed Hadrian's dealings with cities. The most extensive passage relating to my purpose, 69.5.2–3, is quite generalized: "[Hadrian] aided the allied and subject cities most munificently. He had seen many of them,—more, in fact, than any other emperor,—and he assisted practically all of them, giving to some a water supply, to others harbours, food, public works, money and various honors, differing with the different cities."[17] Although Cassius Dio here lists six different types of benefactions from Hadrian to allied and subject cities, ranging from aqueducts to money, one type is simply termed "honors," and no cities are identified.

More information comes from the biography of Hadrian in the *Historia Augusta:* this is, for example, the most detailed literary source for Hadrian's travels, often remarking on imperial favors given during a trip (*beneficia* and *largitiones* in Campania, *HA, Hadr.* 9.6; *liberalitates* in Gaul, 10.1; I return to this vocabulary later in the chapter). Hadrian's biography is agreed to be one of the most veracious in the *Historia Augusta.*[18] The late-fourth-century author of the collection styles himself a biographer like Suetonius rather than a historian like Tacitus (*HA, Prob.* 2.6–7). In the *Life of Hadrian*, however, he includes more historical facts and events outside Rome than did Suetonius in his *Lives,* even though sharing the earlier biographer's aim of characterizing the emperors by instances of virtues and vices.[19] In the *Life of Hadrian* in the *Historia Augusta* we find, for in-

[13] Millar 1964, 61–72, esp. 62–63. Less cautious about Cassius Dio's sources, Baldwin 1985, 197, claims as Hadrian's words part of Dio's report of the Jewish revolt (see chapter 8), and 69.16.3, Hadrian's public refusal to bow to the mob.

[14] Millar 1964, 34: Hadrian and Augustus are the only earlier writers Cassius Dio unambiguously quotes by name.

[15] Baldwin 1985, 197, implausibly considers as only a literary topos Cassius Dio's crediting of "pertinent and confidential fact" to his father.

[16] Millar 1964, 66.

[17] Loeb translation by E. Cary, *Dio's Roman History,* ed. T. E. Page (Cambridge, MA, 1961), VIII:435.

[18] Honoré 1987 reasserts the general worth of the *Historia Augusta.* See also Callu et al. 1992, I.1:vii–lxxiii, and *HA, Gord.* 21.4.

[19] Wallace-Hadrill 1983, 137–38, 143, notes Suetonius's dearth of information on Italy and the provinces.

stance, a detailed list of municipal and regional magistracies assumed by Hadrian, juxtaposed with the generalization that "in almost every city Hadrian both built something and gave games." But the approving passage cites as examples only Athens and Rome, and the latter so as to suggest Hadrian's extravagance in posthumous honors for his mother-in-law, Matidia, and for Trajan:

> *In Etruria praeturam imperator egit. Per Latina oppida dictator et aedilis et duumvir fuit, apud Neapolim demarchus, in patria sua quinquennalis et item Hadriae quinquennalis, quasi in alia patria, et Athenis archon fuit. In omnibus paene urbibus et aliquid aedificavit et ludos edidit. Athenis . . . Romae post ceteras immensissimas voluptates in honorem socrus suae aromatica populo donavit, in honorem Traiani balsama et crocum per gradus theatri fluere iussit. (HA, Hadr. 19.1–5)[20]*

The more specific information about Hadrian's activities outside of Rome has been corroborated by inscriptions, and the more generalized statement of his generosity reflects the unusual extent of Hadrian's liberality to cities. As this instance shows, Hadrian's biography provides reliable information for my investigation.

The fourth-century *Epitome de Caesaribus*, which presents thumbnail sketches of the Roman emperors with a focus on their moral qualities,[21] notes Hadrian's famed largesse to cities among his virtues. Hadrian's civic munificence epitomizes his indefatigable exertions as emperor. While traveling through all the provinces, Hadrian "restored all the cities" with an attendant corps of builders and architects of all types: "*immensi laboris . . . cum oppida universa restitueret . . . namque ad specimen legionum militarium fabros perpendiculatores architectos genusque cunctum exstruendorum moenium seu decorandorum in cohortes centuriaverat*" (*Epit. de Caes.* 14.4–5).[22] Writing two centuries after the fact, the epitomizer focuses on Hadrian's physical restoration of cities, an intervention much needed in the

---

[20] (In Etruria he held the praetorship [of the Etruscan League] while emperor. Throughout the towns of Latium he was "dictator" and "aedile" and "duovir," [he served] in Naples as "demarch," in his own ancestral town as [duovir] quinquennalis, and similarly as [duovir] quinquennalis in Hadria, as if in another ancestral town, and he was "archon" in Athens. In almost every city he both built something and produced games. In Athens[, . . . a]t Rome, after other unrestrained luxuries in honor of his mother-in-law he gave incense to the people, [and] in honor of Trajan he ordered balsam and saffron to flow down through the steps of the theater.) See Callu et al. 1992, 120–21nn. 183–88 ad loc.

[21] Schlumberger 1974, 233–36; Syme 1968, 104–6.

[22] ([A man] of immense toil . . . when he restored all the towns . . . for in the likeness of military legions, he had ordered into cohorts builders, measurers, architects, and every type of person involved in building or decorating walls.) Brunt 1980, 83, suggests that that the unusual *perpendiculatores* should be understood as *mensores*, "surveyors" or "architects."

fourth century.[23] The brief notice offers no specific instances of Hadrian's municipal benefactions, but its unusually detailed list of builders and decorators may be drawn from some particularized and trustworthy source. (I return to this passage in chapter 9.)

A few other instances of Hadrian's interventions with cities are found in Philostratus's *Lives of the Sophists,* where they appear not so much to illustrate traits of Hadrian as to denote the power rhetorical skills and intellectual acumen garnered for sophists.[24] Philostratus provides many specifics about Hadrian's benefactions to Smyrna, for which he claims the great sophist Polemo was instrumental (*VS* 530–31; as we shall see in chapter 7, an inscription bears him out). Similarly, he details Hadrian's aid to Alexandria Troas so as to adumbrate the sway and personality of Herodes Atticus and his father, who interceded with Hadrian for the city (*VS* 548; see chapter 6). Although these striking examples may imply that sophists were vital mediators for imperial benefaction, this was not the case even during the reign of Hadrian, a Greek enthusiast.[25] Philostratus wrote his work only some two generations after Hadrian, when these instances were still fresh in the memories of cities and the sophists' descendants; furthermore, for Smyrna he probably also drew information from some monument raised there by Hadrian's benefaction.[26]

This latter source of knowledge, local records and recollections, must account for the information provided by Pausanias, who notes eight different cities as recipients of Hadrian's generosity. This author wrote his description of Greece between ca. 155 to sometime between 175 and 180, a generation or two after Hadrian's death.[27] He generally restricts himself to describing monuments in old Greece (mainland Greece, up into the third century B.C.), and his main interests are in cults and the offerings and works of art associated with them. He is favorable toward Hadrian, whom he depicts as a thoroughgoing benefactor to "all" Greek and barbarian

[23] Johnston 1985, 124; Ward-Perkins 1984, 14–37.

[24] For this overriding aim of Philostratus's *Lives,* see Bowie 1982, 29, and Swain 1996, 396–400. It is clearest in the case of Favorinus of Arles, who, unsuccessfully, sought to have Hadrian exempt him from holding the imperial flaminate at the concilium of Narbonese Gaul (Bowersock 1969, 35; Gleason 1995, 146–47; cf. *HA, Hadr.* 15.12–13). Philostratus concludes that Favorinus's continued popularity with Hadrian reflected "more to the credit of Hadrian who, although emperor, disagreed on terms of equality with one whom it was in his power to put to death" (*VS* 489). References to Philostratus's *Lives of the Sophists* will be given in this form throughout, with page number from the Olearius edition.

[25] In his reassessment of the relative merits of the historical and literary importance of the sophists, Bowie (1982, esp. 32–38) notes that only a very few of the identified ambassadors from Greek cities are sophists.

[26] Swain 1991; Bowie 1982, 52n. 67.

[27] Habicht 1985, 10–11.

cities (1.5.5, 1.36.3).[28] Some of the gifts Pausanias details, such as the stoa
Hadrian had built and inscribed with his name at Hyampolis in Phocis,
were to cities that have left little trace in the archaeological record, and
which even Pausanias marks as impoverished (10.35.6). Writing from personal observation, Pausanias is usually trustworthy, especially in his remarks
about noteworthy monuments.[29]

Some of the information offered by the sixth-century chronicler John
Malalas seems reliable, especially the reports on Hadrian's patronage to
Malalas's native city, Antioch.[30] These latter notices apparently come from a
"City Chronicle" of Antioch and other records Malalas could consult in his
(presumable) office as a middle- to upper-echelon imperial bureaucrat at Antioch.[31] Malalas adheres to the conventions of imperial biography and *patria*
(fatherland) literature, with the latter's emphasis on the foundation of cities
and on statues, and he is fascinated with earthquakes.[32] Yet Malalas's text is
quite difficult, his citation of epigraphic and other sources often illusory, and
some of his reports, especially those on matters outside of Antioch, untrustworthy.[33] Each piece of his Hadrianic data needs to be examined carefully.
For example, his report that Hadrian rebuilt the Colossus of Rhodes is complete balderdash, whereas his discussion of Hadrian's restoration of Cyzicus's
temple to Zeus contains some useful information among its exaggerations.[34]

Closer to Hadrian's day, and much more dependable, are three other
witnesses: Aulus Gellius, Arrian, and Fronto. Gellius reports Hadrian's re-

---

[28] Arafat 1996, 35 and passim; Swain 1996, 330–33, 348–49.

[29] Habicht 1985, e.g., 4, 63, 95; Swain 1996, 332. While discussing Hadrian's buildings
in Athens, Pausanias does not progress topographically, and sometimes gives imprecise individual descriptions: Wycherley 1959 and 1963. See chapter 7.

[30] Other material, presented even more incidentally by various late authors, similarly needs
individual evaluation. For instance, Christian and Byzantine sources term "Hadrianeion" two
buildings in Caesarea and Tiberias. Yet none credits Hadrian directly for the buildings, which
could have been raised in his honor, or the names of which these late sources may have sur-
mised from nearby inscriptions bearing his name. I plan to return to these buildings in a future article.

[31] His official position may have been that entitled *comes Orientis:* Moffatt 1990; Jeffreys,
Jeffreys, Scott et al. 1986, xxii–xxiii; E. Jeffreys, "Malalas' World View," in Jeffreys, Croke,
and Scott 1990, 55–56; and B. Croke, "Malalas' Sources," in Jeffreys, Croke, and Scott
1990, 201–5.

[32] Moffatt 1990, 96–98; Jeffreys, Croke, and Scott 1990, 58, 155–60, 209. Malalas uses
earthquakes to illustrate imperial generosity and as chronological markers.

[33] Jeffreys, Jeffreys, Scott et al. 1986, xxvi–xli, 147; "Language of Malalas" and "The
Transmission of Malalas' Chronicle," in Jeffreys, Croke, and Scott 1990, 217–312, cf.
200–1.

[34] Malalas's report that Hadrian restored Rhodes's colossal statue of Helios (XI 279.18)
is unreliable (see Strabo 14.2.5; cf. Weber 1907, 143–44). Hadrian's restoration of one of
the seven wonders of the world would have been related by other sources, had it occurred.
Malalas had earlier noted that an earthquake afflicted Rhodes in 115, on the same night that
Antioch was similarly devastated (XI 275.8); the information about Rhodes follows his account of Hadrian's generous reaction to an earthquake in Cyzicus (which included building

sponse, in the senate, to requests from Italica, Utica, and other *municipia* to be raised to colonial status (16.13; the speech in indirect discourse is now called the *de Italicensibus* and will be discussed in detail in chapter 3). In all the *Noctes Atticae,* composed ca. A.D. 170–90,[35] Gellius names Hadrian only four times, once as a chronological reference (11.15.3), once to cite a ruling of his (3.16.12), and twice to recognize approvingly Hadrian's bookishness (13.22.1, 16.13). The *de Italicensibus* is one of these latter instances. Gellius adduces the speech not to explain Hadrian's interactions with *municipia* and *coloniae,* but to exemplify his major complaint that modern grammarians are ignorant of the older, more proper uses of words they discuss, in this case *municipes* and *municipia*.[36] Despite Gellius's focus, the passage contains valuable information about the juridical status of cities, the means by which cities' status could be raised, and the hearing of municipal matters in the senate and by the emperor.[37]

L. Flavius Arrianus, who served Hadrian as imperial legate of Cappadocia from A.D. 131 to 137 or early 138, similarly provides brief but notable information in the *Periplus,* a work he dedicated to Hadrian ca. 132. He illuminates Hadrian's benefactions to Trapezus (*Perip. M. Eux.* 16.6, 1.4; see chapter 6).[38] The extant *Periplus,* a Greek literary treatise of unique form, incorporates some of the information Arrian originally dispatched in Latin, as governor, to the emperor (cf. *Perip. M. Eux.* 6.2, 10.1).[39] Here we glimpse another means by which imperial favor might be bestowed on a town: through the intermediary of the governor of the province (its senatorial proconsul, equestrian legate, or the like), who brought to the emperor's attention various problems of the cities in his jurisdiction. Such intercession is well known from the letters passed between Pliny and Trajan.[40]

Another contemporary of Hadrian, Fronto, corroborates Hadrian's mu-

---

the large temple [of Zeus], "one of the wonders," surmounted by a bust of himself with an inscription that "remains to today," XI 279.16). Malalas may have misunderstood his source: the correct information seems to be in the *Chronicon Paschale* (1.476.6–7; cf. 1.464.13–14), which notes for A.D. 130 [128] that Hadrian relocated the Colossus of Nero at Rome closer to the new Temple of Venus and Roma and transformed it into a statue of the sun (cf. *HA, Hadr.* 19.12–13). Halfmann 1986, 201, accepts Malalas's notice uncritically, but see H. Maryon, "The Colossus of Rhodes," *JHS* 76 (1956): 68–86, and D. E. L. Haynes, "Philo of Byzantium and the Colossus of Rhodes," *JHS* 77 (1957): 311–12. For Cyzicus, see chapter 6, n. 111.

[35] Holford-Strevens 1988, 12–19.

[36] Ibid., 128–29. Gell. *NA* 10.20 is another such complaint.

[37] For its derivation from Hadrian himself, see Grelle 1972, 85–88. Gellius's text is reproduced in the appendix to chapter 3.

[38] Mitford 1974, 162, imprecisely claims Hadrian ordered two monuments at Trapezus, the Temple of Hermes and Philesios and the statue of Hadrian.

[39] Stadter 1980, 9–14, 32–41.

[40] Reynolds 1988, 43; Sherwin-White 1966.

nicipal generosity even as he belittles the emperor. He notes that "one can see monuments of [Hadrian's] journeys in many cities in Asia and Europe, many of all types including tombs built of stone" (*eius* [Hadrian] *itinerum monumenta videas per plurimas Asiae atque Europae urbes sita, cum alia multa tum sepulcra ex saxo formata: Princ. Hist.* 11, p. 209 VDH).[41] The statement figures in a passage condemning Hadrian for having renounced Trajan's military conquests, so as to fritter away time traveling and building. The specific reference to tombs has been construed as insinuating that Hadrian drove many to death while he toured the provinces,[42] but this inference ignores the numerous tombs of heroes Hadrian restored (see chapter 6). Although Fronto's unhappy personal relationship with Hadrian accounts largely for the tone of this and other disparagement of the emperor in his writings,[43] also resonating here is the scorn with which many Roman authors viewed matters outside of Rome.

DOCUMENTARY EVIDENCE

The bias against municipal affairs was not shared by most inhabitants of the many provincial and Italian cities under Roman rule. These individuals' horizons usually coincided with those of their hinterland or surrounding region, and events affecting their cities were matters of great interest. The bulk of our data on Hadrian's municipal activities originates in these cities and not in Rome. Most of my evidence is epigraphic, although some comes from coins, papyri, and legal texts. Various archives in Rome and provincial cities, and monuments in individual beneficiary cities, once recorded Hadrian's responses affecting city status, city boundaries, state expenditure, the foundation of a colony, and the like. The same repositories and commemoration awaited Hadrian's more spontaneous decisions regarding cities. Since whatever archives there were in Rome and other cities have now mostly disappeared,[44] much of the evidence for Hadrian's municipal interactions comes from cities hailing his liberality in inscriptions or on coins, and it is dependent on chance preservation and publication.[45] As pointed out at the beginning of this chapter, the evidence clearly is skewed toward successful appeals to Hadrian. Despite its often conventional nature, it is invaluable to my study.

[41] Text from the Teubner edition of M. P. J. Van Den Hout, *M. Cornelii Frontonis Epistulae* (Leipzig, 1988).

[42] Champlin 1980, 94–96; Davies 1968, 94–95.

[43] Champlin 1980, 81, 94–96.

[44] Posner 1972, 186–205; Martín 1982, 282–84; Reynolds 1988, 33. The municipal archive at Orange was (partially) preserved because it was recorded on stone rather than bronze or parchment: Piganiol 1962; F. Salviat, "Orientation, extension et chronologie des plans cadastraux d'Orange," *RAN* 10 (1977): 107–18.

[45] See nn. 1 and 10 above; cf. MacMullen 1982.

The documentary material can be classified in six major groups. The first two I term "official," since the records were made in accordance with imperial decisions or municipal decrees. This tends to be the most positive and positivistic evidence: only what was successful is commemorated, and only in flattering terms. A third group records, purposefully or incidentally, Hadrian's delegation of authority to an individual to oversee a municipal concern. The fourth group comprises building inscriptions referring to constructions or reconstructions, and/or architectural ornamentation: these inscriptions, like the "official" documentation, furnish unqualified claims, but this time of patronage. The fifth group is chance data in the treatises of the *agrimensores* (land surveyors), papyri, and legal texts. The sixth group, mainly relevant to Hadrian's change of a city's status and his promotion of city festivals, comes more indirectly from inscriptions and provincial coins.

The first group of inscriptions and papyri, some forty examples, are those raised by order of Hadrian himself or by the benefiting community to commemorate and ratify an imperial decision. These include Hadrian's imperial proclamations or edicts (*diatagma*), his letters and responses to petitions to the emperor (*epistolai, epistula, rescripta*), and (less frequently) his replies to persons or groups of low status (*subscriptiones*), his general orders to governors or legates (*mandata*), and judgments he delivered at the conclusion of cases heard before him (*decreta*).[46] Hadrian's words have been preserved at times alone, and at times with other pertinent information.[47] Many of his letters fall into obvious groups, such as acknowledgments of good wishes, confirmations of various privileges previously granted to poleis, and responses to boundary disputes (both latter types discussed in chapter 5), and I cite his correspondence according to its recent publication in J. H. Oliver's posthumous *Greek Constitutions of the Early Roman Emperors from Inscriptions and Papyri*.

Julius Caesar and Augustus had established the expectation that Roman emperors were to be eloquent and persuasive orators and writers, and literary references and the texts of imperial pronouncements themselves show that most emperors undertook these tasks seriously and personally.[48] Hadrian was famed for responding personally to all requests (*HA, Hadr.* 20.7). He composed his own speeches, many of which he published.[49] Al-

---

[46] These official pronouncements are often called "constitutions," although "a constitution is strictly not a type of document but any utterance, oral or written, of an emperor, which can be taken as binding precedence in law (Gaius i.5; Ulpian, *Dig.* i.4.1.1)": Williams 1976, 67n. 1. Cf. Crawford 1988, 133; Mourgues 1987, 80–81, esp. n. 17.

[47] In general, see Oliver 1989, 1–24.

[48] Millar 1977, 203–72; Williams 1976; Williams 1979.

[49] For his speeches, see *HA, Hadr.* 20.7 and Charisius *Gramm.* I 222, 21. Hadrian allegedly composed some of Trajan's speeches: *HA, Hadr.* 3.11. Alexander 1938 collects Hadrian's pronouncements, pointing out that they convey "the impression of an extremely reticent man who is always at work . . . [with a] certain amount of vanity . . . he imagines he

most every oration has perished, but Hadrian's proclamations reveal him to be humane, yet dispassionate, and a man who consistently strove to be on top of every situation.[50] Although he avoids laying down detailed rules that must be strictly applied in all instances, he repeatedly cites parallels and precedents in justification of his decisions, offering the semblance of uniformity.[51] In numerous instances Hadrian's rulings mark innovations, as when he rescinded in 121 the rule that only Roman citizens could lead Athens's Epicurean school (Oliver, #73, cf. #74). Such innovations are expressed in the larger context of Hadrian's habitual marks of respect for the past, a context particularly obvious in his work at Athens and Cyrene.[52] Still clearer traits of Hadrian's pronouncements are the emphasis on his own generosity, and his authoritative stance.[53]

Even when examined individually, Hadrian's official statements reveal his overwhelming dominance in the Roman world and its cities. A good example of this comes in the Oenoanda inscription,[54] a document I return to in chapter 5 for its details on games. The huge inscription (117 lines, on a stone 187 cm high × 25 deep × 105 wide) concerns festivities established in this Lycian city (under the authority of Termessos, now in southwestern Turkey). It records that C. Iulius Demosthenes, a local magnate, instigated, organized, and endowed a competition to be celebrated every four years with music and drama. Hadrian endorsed the games and approved the penalties Demosthenes had set for shirking or infracting their rules. The document gives a more nuanced reality to the biography's statement that Hadrian "produced" or "brought about" games in almost every city (*ludos edidit, HA, Hadr.* 19.2; see above and chapter 5): Hadrian simply sanctioned competitions and rules established by a local sponsor. But just as important as its quantification of Hadrian's involvement is the emphasis the inscription accords him. The copy of Hadrian's letter, dated 24

---

would note any irregularity . . . not devoid of feelings" (172). Martín 1982, 258–62, argues unconvincingly for little personal imput from Hadrian in official proclamations.

[50] See, for example, Oliver, #70 (= Smallwood, #333; cf. Williams 1976, 72–73), Hadrian to Q. Rammius Martialis in A.D. 119 on the rights of children of soldiers; Smallwood, #328, Hadrian's address to the army at Lambaesis in A.D. 128.

[51] For example, when the original size of Aezanite landholdings could not be determined during Hadrian's settlement of land disputes in Aezani (*MAMA* IX 8 and 9, and references at p. 178 for P1–5; see *MAMA* IX, p. xxxix), Hadrian simply had measurements calculated according to the mean of landholdings in neighboring towns. Hadrian's reign marks greater standardization in imperial constitutions, laws, and rescripts, which reached a "normative efficacy": Bauman 1980, 169–71.

[52] Alexander 1938, 173.

[53] As in Smallwood, #445 lines 10–11, 454b, 333; see Williams 1976, 72–73, 69–70. Williams notes Hadrian's "confidence in his own ability to assess a witness' character from face-to-face questioning," and his occasional outbursts of impatience and anger.

[54] Wörrle 1988; cf. S. Mitchell 1990.

August 124, leads off the text. Its two opening lines, with Hadrian's titles and the beginning of his salutation, are cut into the molding above the *titulus* (the smoothed surface on which the text is inscribed). Their letters are larger than those used elsewhere in the inscription. Given the enormous size of the inscription, the first two lines may have been all that most people read.[55]

Visually and symbolically, Hadrian heads the record of Demosthenes' foundation at Oenoanda. This was a benefaction made by Demosthenes, but in its commemoration this local magnate appears secondarily, as an intermediate between the imperial power and his own city and region. Similarly, most of the other inscriptions of this group give the impression that the emperor himself initiated the action recorded. Although details in the texts often disclose that Hadrian's decision was reactive rather than spontaneous,[56] this type of inscription affirms the emperor's centrality in the ideology of municipal benefaction.

The second group of inscriptions, those erected by local authorities in gratitude to Hadrian, offers fewer specifics. Most often short texts with monumental lettering, they are sometimes found on a statue base (e.g., *AE* 1949, 55). Others were once displayed on a wall, as in Ostia (*CIL* VI 972 = XIV 95 = Smallwood, #476). In most cases no secure identification of Hadrian's activity can be made, since the terminology used, *indulgentia* and *liberalitas* in Latin, *euergesia* and *ktistein* in Greek, and the like, reflects on the emperor's benevolence, "the expression of his majesty," rather than designating a specific gift.[57] In the case of the Greek inscriptions with *ktistes*, added difficulties are caused by the original technical meaning of the word, conventionally used to denote a city-founder.[58] Yet the multivalence of the words employed in commemorating Hadrian's municipal benefactions (cf. above, on the *HA, Hadr.*) buttresses my main point: what mattered to these cities and authors was the fact that Hadrian attended positively to a city, not the particular configuration his attention took.

H. Cotton's investigation of *indulgentia* (indulgence), for example, shows that by the time of Trajan this word was used in connection with imperial favors of many different types.[59] Although it is found with grants of

---

[55] Wörrle 1988, 1–2; the letters of the first two lines measure ca. 1.5 cm, elsewhere ca. 1.0–1.2 cm.

[56] As is generally true for the imperial correspondence (Oliver 1989, 1), further corroborating Millar's thesis (1977). Mitchell 1993, I:220, however, notes that Demosthenes chose to endorse only cultural contests, rather than including athletic ones (as elsewhere in southwest Asia Minor), perhaps because he was influenced by Hadrian's well-known tastes.

[57] For "the expression of the emperor's majesty," see Veyne 1990, 347–80.

[58] Follet 1992 surveys dedications and honorary and building inscriptions mentioning Hadrian as *ktistes* or *oikistes*, concluding that in spite of a partial semantic overlap, *ktistes* was used in a more material sense (e.g., construction), whereas *oikistes* mainly alludes to population.

[59] Cotton 1984, esp. 252–58; cf. Corbier 1977. See also chapter 5, n. 15.

personal promotion or Roman citizenship, *indulgentia* and the verb *indulgere* additionally and frequently designate imperial permission to a town to construct some building,[60] imperial funding for a building project,[61] imperial favors to town councils,[62] and imperial changes of city status.[63] A good example of the use of *indulgentia* in the Hadrianic municipal inscriptions comes from a fulsome dedication to Hadrian from the *colonia Ostia conservata et aucta omni indulgentia et liberalitate eius* (Ostia, the colony, preserved and increased by his every indulgence and generosity: *CIL* VI 972 = XIV 95, A.D. 132/133).[64] The phrase does not let us determine what form Hadrian's largesse took, or even if actual benefactions were handed over.

Liberalitas (generosity) appears in the Hadrianic inscriptions generally as a synonym for *indulgentia,* as in the above couplet from Ostia, though with more material connotations.[65] *Beneficia* (benefactions, favors), twice in the Hadrianic inscriptions, points more to the tangible results of the emperor's favor than to the attitude or activity causing that favor (and see chapter 5).[66] The specialized meanings these words could intermittently assume should not mask the fact that such vocabulary was used precisely because it was polyvalent. It simultaneously connoted the emperor's moral virtues, his absolute control of politics and law, and the acts he undertook with this power.[67]

The Greek vocabulary used in inscriptions to commemorate Hadrian's municipal favors often employs derivatives of *euergetein,* "to do a good deed," a common euphemism in the Greek world since the Hellenistic pe-

---

[60] Pliny *Ep.* 10.23.1, 10.24; 10.70.1; 10.90.2; cf. *CIL* III 14120 = *ICret* IV 333, A.D. 169.

[61] *CIL* XI 3309, Trajanic.

[62] Pliny *Ep.* 10.112.1, cf. *CIL* XIV 2101 = *ILS* 5686 (early third century).

[63] Pliny *Ep.* 10.92, used with *beneficium* as *beneficio indulgentiae.* Cotton 1984, 257, includes Ostia in this group on the grounds of *CIL* VI 972 = XIV 95, A.D. 132–33, the Ostian dedication to Hadrian cited below, although there is no evidence that Hadrian changed the status of the colony.

[64] The other two Hadrianic examples of *indulgentia* are from Colonia Canopitana (*CRAI* 1979, 404–7), and from Uthina (*ILS* 6784: *Uthina ex [Africa] indulgentia eius au[cta et conservata]*), both discussed in chapter 5 at n. 15 and following.

[65] Ostia, as above; Caesena, Italy: *Atti e memorie, Deputazione di Storia Patria per la Romanga* 10, 1958–59, 281–85 (fragmentary); Signia, Italy: *CIL* X 5963; and Dyrrachium, *CIL* III 709, from A.D. 222–35. For *liberalitas,* see Kloft 1970, passim, and Cotton 1984, 262. In connection with the emperors and their apparently limitless resources, *largitio* (used in *HA, Hadr.* 9.6, referred to above) does not always retain its pejorative sense as the depraved version of *liberalitas:* Kloft 1970, 40–43, 146–49; cf. Cic. *De off.* 2.52.

[66] E.g., *ILS* 315 = *CIL* III 7282, a dedication from Alexandria Troas to Hadrian *ob multa beneficia quae viritim quae publice praestitit* (because of the many benefactions he offered both to individuals and to the general good), and *CIL* III 7283 = 6102, from Pisidian Antioch, A.D. 131–32. Cf. Cotton 1984, 261; and chapter 5 of this volume.

[67] Carrié 1992.

riod at the latest.[68] *Ktistes* (founder) also appears in many Greek inscriptions as an epithet for Hadrian, frequently coupled with *euergetes* (benefactor), *soter* (savior), *oikistes* (founder), or some other epithet.[69] Although the literal meaning of *ktistes* is city-founder, by Hadrian's day the term was often used as the inflated equivalent of *euergetes*.[70] The importance in Greece and Asia Minor of neocorate temples, temples to the imperial cult discussed in chapter 5, meant that *ktistein* (to be a founder) also designates imperial permission to establish such a temple in a city there.[71] As in the Latin West, it is impossible to limit the terminology to precise meanings. Moreover, the plethora of honorific inscriptions to Hadrian in the Greek East, in part due to his establishment of the Panhellenion, warns that at least some of these originated in more general gratitude, or in hopes for imperial favor.[72]

Two cases, Gabii in the Latin West and Megara in the Greek East, validate my cautious treatment of inscriptions employing such vague terminology, which I accept only when corroborated by other evidence. From Gabii the local decurions' acclamation of Hadrian and Sabina as the "enrichers of the town" (*locupletatoribus municipii, CIL* XIV 2799), is justi-

---

[68] This is the starting point of P. Veyne's monumental *Le Pain et le cirque. Sociologie historique d'un pluralisme politique* (Paris, 1976), translated in 1990 into English, and of Gauthier 1985. For the translation of the Greek *euergesia* as *beneficium*, see the bilingual inscription at Delos, *ILLRP* #363, cited by Veyne 1990, 347. Nicols 1990, 81 and n. 3, notes the frequent use of traditional Hellenistic titles for Roman magistrates in the late Republic and early Empire; cf. A. D. Nock, "Soter and Euergetes," in *Essays on Religion and the Ancient World*, ed. Z. Stewart (Cambridge, MA, 1972), II:732–33.

[69] Kyme, *IKyme* ##22, 23 (= *IGR* IV 1301); Elaia in S. Aeolis: *IGR* IV 268; Myrina, *IGR* IV 1174; Phocaea, *IGR* IV 1319, 1320; Pergamum, *IPergamon* ##364–74; Aedepsus in Euboea, *IG* XII.9 1234; Sparta, *IG* V.1 404 and 405; Tegea, *IG* V.2 128, 129; Megalopolis, *IG* V.2 533; Thespiae, *IG* VII 1841; Thasos in Thrace, *BCH* 1932, 285; Megara, *IG* VII 70 and 72; Samos, *IGR* IV 986; Klazomenai, *IGR* IV 1551. See also n. 58 above.

[70] Nörr 1966, 10n. 6; L. Robert, in *EtudAnat* (1937): 228n. 3, *Bull.Ep.* 1974, #404, and in *Hellenica* IV, 116ff; Galsterer-Kröll 1972, 78n. 172. Hadrian's actual city foundations are discussed in chapter 8. The emotive impact of such words in Hadrian's day is demonstrated in his exhortation to the Cyrenaeans, "to come together and repopulate your city [after the Jewish revolt of 115] and become not only residents, but also founders [*oikistas*] of your fatherland" (Reynolds 1978, 113, lines 29–30).

[71] Mitchell 1987, 343–44, and Price 1984b, 259, on Philadelphia, citing *IGR* IV 1619, from the reign of Caracalla.

[72] See the numerous inscriptions in Le Glay 1976, and those discussed by Benjamin 1963; cf. Spawforth and Walker 1985 and 1986. I thus reject the case of Mytilene, for example: *EE* 2 (1875):12 (base or marble basin): "A thank-offering to Emperor Traianus Hadrianus Caesar Augustus, Eleutherius, Olympius, Zeus, founder" (*ktistes*; A.D. 132–37), and that of Klazomenai, *IGR* IV 1551: "for Emperor Caesar Traianus Hadrianus Olympius, the New Sun, founder" (*ktistes*). The latter seems simply an effusive dedication to Hadrian on the occasion of his visit to nearby Erythrae, where Antonia Tyrannis Iuliane, as agonothete, produced games with the Sacred Thymelic Guild.

fied by two other inscriptions, which testify to Hadrian's donation of an aqueduct and his restoration of some structure in Gabii's archaic sanctuary of Juno (*CIL* XIV 2797 and *AE* 1982, 142).[73] Similarly in Megara, independent evidence substantiates the city's inscriptions honoring Hadrian as *ktistes* (*IG* VII 70, 72, cf. 71). Pausanias describes the general wretchedness of Megara in his day by calling its citizens "the only Greeks not even the emperor Hadrian could make more prosperous" (1.36.3). He later notes that Hadrian rebuilt in white marble Megara's Temple of Apollo (1.42.5), and that this emperor enlarged Megara's Scironian road (1.44.6). These details vindicate his previous allusion to Hadrian's favor, and doubtless account for Megara's honorific decrees. Regardless of the extent of benefaction to this city, however, these reconstructions do not legally constitute a founding or refounding of Megara, and there is no evidence of Hadrian's having changed Megara's civic status.

My third type of documentary evidence includes the inscriptions witnessing Hadrian's delegation of authority to another to oversee some project in a city. Veyne has neatly pointed out the lack of any real conceptual difference, either in the ideology of the emperor or in the understanding of the Roman populace, between imperial favors emanating from the emperor's legal and constitutional powers and those granted through caprice or spontaneous generosity.[74] This third category includes the engineering projects undertaken by the army and its commanders that were evidently sanctioned by Hadrian (as at Sarmizegetusa, where the inscription on an aqueduct built by the agency of [*per*] Hadrian's legate Cn. Papirius Aelianus begins with Hadrian's name in the ablative, *CIL* III 1446). Other inscriptions record individuals appointed by Hadrian as *curatores* (overseers) for various cities or as *curatores* for special projects in a city, and individuals who performed tasks or gave something to their city with special permission from Hadrian.[75] The extraordinary commissions are treated in chapter 4.

A fourth type of documentary evidence comprises building inscriptions. On many of these Hadrian's name appears in the nominative. His donation is sometimes specified in the inscription, as the aqueduct at Gabii (*CIL* XIV 2797) or the arch at Quiza (*CIL* VIII 9697 = 21514); often it can be inferred from the inscription's wording, as at Altinum (*CIL* V 2152), or from its being carved in an architrave, as in Nicomedia (*TAM* IV 10). Into this classification fall inscriptions commemorating a later emperor's completion or restoration of a project initiated by Hadrian. In Puteoli and

---

[73] Brick stamps of A.D. 123 corroborate the lacunose donor inscription: see chapter 6. On the other hand, the "Curia Aelia Augusta" in Gabii (*CIL* XIV 2795, line 5) does not have to be a donation of Hadrian, nor does the "Balineum Hadrianum" of Bithynian Apamea (*CIL* III 6992 = *ILS* 314, line 6, A.D. 128–29).

[74] Veyne 1990, 347–55.

[75] As in Italian Aeclanum, *CIL* IX 1414 = *ILS* 5877.

Ostia, for example, Antoninus Pius completed works begun by Hadrian (*CIL* X 1640 and 1641, and *ILS* 334 = *CIL* XIV 98),[76] and at Dyrrachium, Severus Alexander restored an aqueduct Hadrian had donated to the town (*CIL* III 709).

This group also includes the many epigraphic records of Hadrian's restorations, which I accept even while realizing their possible deceptions. One type of imposture may be exemplified in the famous bilingual inscription from Kyme (*IKyme* #17). This inscription records the settlement, in 27 B.C., of litigation caused by the private purchase of a sanctuary of Dionysus during the disturbances at the end of the Republic. The part relevant to my purposes comes from the section quoting a letter sent by the governor of Asia to Kyme's magistrates in 27: he orders them to investigate the truth of a declaration that the sanctuary is indeed privately owned, and, if true, to see to it that the individual is made both to accept the price offered and to return the property to the ownership of the god.[77] Once restored to the god (that is, to public domain), he continues, the sanctuary is to be inscribed *Imp. Caesar deivei* (sic) *f. Augustus restituit* (the Emperor Caesar Augustus, son of a god, restored [this]).[78] If solely the inscription the governor ordered carved on the sanctuary survived, rather than the record of the whole dispute and its settlement, we would surely assume that Augustus was in some way responsible for rebuilding the sanctuary.[79] S. Mitchell has used this inscription to warn against unconditional acceptance of epigraphic evidence for imperial building and rebuilding.[80]

In a similar vein, E. Thomas and C. Witschel have recently examined Roman rebuilding inscriptions from the Latin West, compellingly arguing that such inscriptions should neither be taken at face value nor be dismissed as meaningless bombast. Rather, they were "non-denotative." In many cases archaeological evidence belies the grandiose claims emblazoned on the building. At the same time, however, such inscriptions consciously marked the building as "a historic monument" that signified awareness of time, change, and the importance of the present.[81] Hadrian's restoration inscriptions are vital to my investigation, even if the "restoration" is only an imperial legal decision (as in Augustan Kyme) or simply the addition of

[76] Also in the dubious example from Firmum Picenum, *CIL* IX 5353.

[77] Sherk 1969, 315, commenting on this inscription, which he publishes there as #61.

[78] On the stone is found actually . . . *in eo inscreibatur Imp. Caesar Deivei f. Augustu[s] re[sti]-[tuit]* (*IKyme* #17, lines 19–20).

[79] N. Charbonnel, "À propos de l'inscription de Kymé et des pouvoirs d'Auguste dans les provinces au lendemain du règlement de 27 av. n.è," *RIDA* 26 (1979): 214–15.

[80] S. Mitchell 1987, 343–44.

[81] Thomas and Witschel 1992. This theory helps elucidate *HA, Hadr.* 19.10, the statement that Hadrian restored the name of the original patrons on buildings he reconstructed. This latter practice (evidenced in the Pantheon, for example) could work only in Rome, which was permeated by the emperor's presence (contra, Willers 1990, on the Arch of Hadrian in Athens).

marble ornament (such as Hadrian's renovation of Capua's amphitheater, *CIL* X 3832). Such acts were monumental signifiers of Hadrian's favor to the city, and they fit with the promotion and renewal of the past so prominent in most of his municipal activity.

My fifth category of documentary evidence is provided by the treatises of the land surveyors, by papyri, and by legal texts. Elsewhere I have discussed in detail the six references the *Liber Coloniarum* makes to Hadrian,[82] and I am ever more dubious about this testimony for Hadrian's centuriation and assignment of cities' land (see chapter 4). Papyri primarily elucidate Antinoopolis in Egypt, one of Hadrian's rare city foundations (chapter 8). The generalized legal texts relating to Hadrian's municipal activity have been cited in chapter 1, and will recur sporadically in the following chapters.

The sixth and final classification of my documentary evidence is that provided by the names of cities and their festivals, as recorded in inscriptions and coins from the cities or games' victors. When the title of a *colonia* or a *municipium* incorporates the adjectives *Aelius, Aelius Hadrianus, Aelius Hadrianus Augustus,* or *Aelius Augustus,* the city's status thus documented is considered as due to Hadrian, and a change from a previous civic status.[83] This spare testimony does not help explain the reasons or effects of the change of civic status. Ascertaining the city's title itself can be difficult, for it is often abbreviated to only a few letters or the text is lacunose.[84] In the following chapter I use such epigraphic evidence, Gellius's *de Italicensibus,* legal information on city status, and comparative material from other periods to arrive at more than thirty "Hadrianic" colonies and municipalities in the Latin West and, more interestingly, to delineate daily life in the varied cities of the Roman empire during Hadrian's principate.[85]

Similarly tantalizing are the names of cities' festivals recorded on coins and inscriptions, mainly in the Greek East. This is the only area in which cities struck their own coins during Hadrian's period, and civic festivals are characteristic of the cities here, but rare in the Latin West. In the Greek East the right to strike its own coins marked a city's high standing, and the legends on provincial coinage are key sources for local history.[86] Yet as we see in chapter 5, we can draw only limited conclusions from local coins' record of "Hadrianeia" games, for example. The most we can say un-

---

[82] Boatwright 1989, 242–44.

[83] Galsterer-Kröll 1972, 50, 77–78, 90–92.

[84] Ibid., 78, 85–87.

[85] In chapter 5 I discuss the cases in the Greek East where a city's assumption of some form of Hadrian's name does not denote a change of civic status.

[86] See, e.g., Millar 1990, 8, on coins of Colonia Aelia Capitolina; J. Robert and L. Robert, *Hellenica* XI–XII, 56, 59–60, on the right to strike coinage in Stratonicea-Hadrianopolis. In general: Harl 1987, 21–30; Burnett, Amandry, and Ripollès 1992, 1–54; Crawford 1986.

equivocally is that the city striking such coins wished to display its link, real or merely desired, to Hadrian.[87]

The central importance of Hadrian to the vitality and activity of Roman cities emerges more clearly from the documentary than from the literary evidence. This is due both to the enthusiasm with which cities welcomed his interest in them, and to the bias of imperial historians against municipal affairs. According to the compiled evidence, however, Hadrian's favorable recognition of a city was intrinsically more important than the particular form it took. The imprecision of the terminology used in referring to his benefactions, and the visual and semiotic primacy of his name and titulature on most inscriptions that do remain, urge us to view Hadrian's municipal interactions as a whole and within the wider context of the ideology and functioning of the Roman empire.

[87] Imperial coinage is less helpful for my purposes. Hadrian's "restitutor" series mostly concerns regions and provinces (Achaea, Arabia, Asia, Bithynia, Hispania, the Gauls, Italia, Libya, Macedonia, Phyrgia, and Sicilia), naming only two cities, Nicomedia and Alexandria: *BMC, Emp.* III, p. clxxxiii, and *RIC* II, p. 466.

CHAPTER 3

Changes of City Status and Their Impact on City Life

I BEGIN my discussion of Hadrian's municipal interactions with his changes of city status: these are his second most frequent type of such activity, but their significance has been elusive. By the second century A.D. Rome had largely ceased settling new *coloniae* (colonies) in Italy and the provinces. Beginning in the late Republic, "new" colonies and *municipia* (municipalities) could be established by administrative fiat from Rome, rather than with citizens whom the Roman government settled on appropriated land that had formerly been unoccupied or whose former inhabitants had been displaced. During the Empire a stroke of the pen, so to speak, rather than a group of intrusive newcomers was often responsible for changing (or sometimes simply ratifying) an existing city's internal juridical and political organization, as well as its relationship with the central power of Rome. This administrative procedure was widespread after Hadrian's reign, and Hadrian's veteran colonies, Colonia Aelia Capitolina (in Judaea) and Colonia Aelia Mursa (in Pannonia), are the last new colonial settlements in the history of Rome.[1] (For these and Hadrian's other new city foundations, see chapter 8.)

Although mere changes of city status occurred fairly often during the principate, when they were an imperial prerogative and *beneficium*,[2] Hadrian affected more cities in this way than any of his predecessors save Augustus, and his new municipia are particularly numerous.[3] Reliable evidence argues that Hadrian confirmed eleven "new" Hadrianic colonies and

---

[1] A basic bibliography includes: Kornemann 1900; Kornemann 1933; Sherwin-White 1973; Salmon 1970; *DizEpig* II:415–58, s.v. "colonia"; Langhammer 1973, 12–22; Keppie 1983; Levick 1967. See also chapter 8, n. 4. The modern term *titular colonies* is often used when speaking of "new" colonies established simply by administrative fiat. I do not discuss changes of city status during the Republic and the Augustan period.

[2] Kornemann 1900, 568–69, 565; *Dig.* 47.21.3.1 (Callistratus 5 cogn.); Millar 1977, 409. See chapter 5, n. 2.

[3] Zahrnt 1991 counts for Hadrian nine colonies and twenty-one municipia, in contrast to the eleven colonies and two municipia of Trajan. He sees an equally sharp distinction between the high numbers of Hadrian's "new" municipia and the low ones of the Julio-Claudians and Flavians. Zahrnt does not include Italian colonies in his totals. Gascou 1972, revised and expanded in Gascou 1982, provides tallies for North Africa from Caesar to the fourth century. I disagree with some details, but his general numbers buttress Hadrian's prominence in this sphere.

twenty-one "new" Hadrianic municipalities. He also seems to be responsible for two more circumscribed changes, one of the internal organization of an existing double community (a Roman colony in the Greek East and its "twin" indigenous polis), and the other of the personal rights of a city's political elite (by a grant of *Latium maius;* see below).[4] Hadrian's thirty-four changes of city status affected about a quarter of the total number of cities witnessing his personal intervention.

In addition to being statistically significant, Hadrian's changes of city status bear directly on two central topics of this book: the dissemination of norms by Rome, the central power; and the delicate balance between an emperor's encouragement of local autonomy and the manifestation of his preeminence. According to a passage in Aulus Gellius's *Noctes Atticae* that is the single most extensive text relating to Hadrian and city status, Hadrian expressly preferred that cities retain their age-old traditions, what we today might call their cultural diversity, rather than become mere facsimiles of Rome (*NA* 16.13.1–9; text and translation in the appendix to this chapter). Yet this predilection seems to contradict the increasing resemblance of cities to Roman models, discernible in extant city charters (local constitutions), municipal careers and legislation, and local architecture and art.

Various data attest Hadrian's changes of city status, but none of the cities whose status Hadrian changed has yet provided a municipal charter, conceivably the only unequivocal witness to his impact. In most cases Hadrian's act is apparent in the inclusion of some form of his name in the titles of towns (see chapter 2 at n. 83). Less often inscriptions name Hadrian *conditor municipii* or *conditor coloniae* (founder of the municipality, founder of the colony), although only one inscription, *AE* 1949, 55, from municipium Aelium Choba (Mauretania), contains both the acclamation of Hadrian as *conditor municipii* and the Hadrianic title of the city.[5] Personal nomenclature in other cities suggests that they received colonial status from him.[6] More vaguely, Hadrian's biography refers to widespread

---

[4] In a future article I will return to the difficult question of Hadrian's interactions with *canabae.*

[5] In general on the Hadrianic *conditor* inscriptions, see Galsterer-Kröll 1972, 78. Hadrian is hailed as *conditor municipii* in Althiburos, Avitta Bibba, Choba, Turris Tamalleni, and perhaps at Ilugo (see references in text and below, at nn. 10 and 20); at Turris Tamalleni his title *conditor municipii* (*CIL* VIII 83) is not corroborated by an attested name change for this city with only three inscriptions in *CIL* VIII. Hadrian appears twice as *conditor* of a colony, in Mursa (*CIL* III 3279, *conditori suo*) and Parium (*CIL* III 374 = *ILS* 320 = *IParion* #8, with its near twins (*IParion* ##7, 9), although Hadrian did not refound Parium, but only enlarged its territory: Zahrnt 1988b, 239–42. The new evidence from the lex Irnitana contradicts Millar's contention (1977, 406) that the phrase *conditor municipii* is meaningless for changes of city status.

[6] The nomen Aelius and/or the tribal affiliation Sergia, Hadrian's own tribe, can denote enfranchisement by Hadrian of inhabitants who formerly held peregrine (non-Roman) sta-

grants of Latin rights (*Latium*) to cities (*civitates*) as among the positive
acts of Hadrian's reign (*HA, Hadr.* 21.7). This reference is complicated by
the innovation, in the early second century A.D., of "greater Latin rights"
(*Latium maius*). By this award Roman citizenship was conferred not only
on magistrates (as previously in towns granted Latin rights), but also on
decurions.[7] Although the biography identifies no city receiving a grant of
Latin rights from Hadrian, such rights pertained to citizens of municipia.
As we shall see, Hadrian may have granted *Latium maius* to Gigthis (Africa
Proconsularis), and he may have given a municipal charter specifying Latin
rights to Ilugo (Baetica). Finally, Gellius names two cities in his passage on
municipia (see below).

   Overall, outside of Gellius's passage the meager data furnish few clues as to
the motivations and effects of Hadrian's activity. To help ascertain the meaning of Hadrian's changes of city status, I turn to comparative material: other
city charters and epigraphic testimony for municipal politics and law during
the principate. This information illuminates the functions and political life of
cities in Italy and the provinces, particularly the roles of the municipal elite, and
the interactions of cities with the central power in Rome. As we shall see, from
the end of the Republic such material shows increasing assimilation to Roman
models. Yet Hadrian's valorization of local traditions helped negotiate the
growing standardization by ostensibly offering municipal elites a choice:
Roman norms or their own conventions. Ultimately there was little difference:
during the second century, local culture and individual ancestries were exalted
even as political and legal procedures were standardized. Additionally, the city
charters illuminate how the emperor's interference in municipal life, in this case
through a change of city status, paradoxically encouraged local rule.

   The thirty-four communities whose civic status and constitutions evidently changed at Hadrian's directive are listed below.[8] An asterisk denotes
a city not yet localized and/or with an uncertain name:[9]

---

tus: cf., e.g., Grelle 1972, 200–2. For individuals adopting the nomen of the patron responsible for granting them citizenship, cf. Caes. *BGall.* 1.47; for adoption of imperial tribe, Kubitschek 1889, 138n. 201, 237n. 345, 272. Yet not every city with the tribe Sergia was
founded by Hadrian, not every city with some form of his name received a change of city status from him, and the pseudotribe Aelia is useless for determining city status: Galsterer-Kröll
1972, 85–98; G. Forni, "Il tramonto di un'istituzione. Pseudo-tribù romane derivate da so-
prannomi imperiali," in *Studi giuridici in memoria di A. Passerini* (Milan, 1955), 115.

   [7] This distinction is discussed later that century by Gaius (*Inst.* 1.96) and witnessed by inscriptions (*ILS* 6780, 6781; below at n. 46 and following). See Sherwin-White 1973, 255–
56, 262–63, 414.

   [8] My list is based on the works of Galsterer-Kröll and Zahrnt, with discrepancies as noted.

   [9] I omit discussing other Hadrianic changes in city status, presumable from Galsterer-
Kröll's list or assumed in other sources, but cogently refuted by Zahrnt: Thisiduo, Africa Pro-
consularis (Zahrnt 1989b); Avennio and Dinia, Gallia (Zahrnt 1988b, 229–33); Parium, Asia
(Zahrnt 1988b, 231, 239–42); Parlais, Galatia (Zahrnt 1988a, 231); "Flaviopolis," near
Hexamilion on the Thracian Chersonese (Zahrnt 1988b, 237–39); and Selinus, Cilicia

7 coloniae and 10 municipia in Africa Proconsularis (colonies in Bulla Regia, Lares, Thaenae, *Thapsus, Uluzibbira, Utica, and *Zama Regia; municipia in Abthugni, Althiburos, *Avitina, Avitta Bibba, Bisica Lucana, *Chlulitanum, *Thambes, Thizika, Thuburbo Maius, Turris Tamalleni);[10]

1 colonia and 1 municipium in Mauretania (Tipasa; Choba);[11]

2 coloniae in Italy (Aeclanum and Formiae);[12]

2 municipia in Noricum (Cetium and Ovilava);[13]

2 municipia in Dacia (Drobeta and Napoca);[14]

2 municipia in Pannonia (Carnuntum; Aquincum);[15]

(Zahrnt 1988b, 245–46). I do not accept Colonia Canopitana as the Hadrianic colony Beschaouch (1979) assumes on the basis of a boundary stone issued with Hadrian's authority, nor do I find compelling the postulate that Colonia Arcensium was Hadrianic, made by Teja 1980, 1107 (referring to *ILS* 1403).

[10] Thapsus (Ael. T[h]apso), Avitina (Ael. Avit[——], and Thambes (Ael. Tham [——]) are new additions. Although these three cities cannot be located or even clearly identified, their existence as Hadrianic foundations is argued from the AEL of their names on two military lists of the late second(?) century: Dupuis 1992, 129–30, cf. Le Bohec 1989, 197–201, no. 8, and 216–21, no. 22. Evidence for the others: *CIL* VIII 25522: colonia Aelia Augusta Bulla Regia; *CIL* VIII 1779: colonia Aelia Augusta Lares; *CIL* VI 1685 (A.D. 321): Colonia Aelia Augusta Mercurialis Thaenitana; *AE* 1940, 64: colonia Aelia Uluzibbira Africa; *CIL* VIII 1181: colonia Iulia Aelia Hadriana Augusta Utika, and Gell. *NA* 16.13; *CIL* VI 1686 (A.D. 322): colonia Aelia Hadriana Augusta Zama Regia; *CIL* VIII 23085, with *ILAf.* 71: municipium Aelium Hadrianum Abthugnitanorum; *CIL* VIII 27769 and 27781, *AE* 1913, 45: municipium Aelium Hadrianum Augustum Althiburitanum, cf. *CIL* VIII 27775, a fragmentary dedication to Hadrian, *conditori municipi*; *CIL* VIII 1177 and *ILT* 672: municipium Aelium Avitta Bibba, cf. *CIL* VIII 799, fragmentary dedication to Hadrian, *conditori municipi*; *CIL* VIII 12292: municipium Aelium with *CIL* VI 1401: municipium Aelium ?Hadrianum Augustum Bisica; *CIL* VI 1684 (A.D. 321): municipium Aelium Hadrianum Augustum Chlulitani; *ILAf.* 432: Municipium Aelium Thizika; *ILT* 699 and *ILAf.* 277: Municipium Aelium Hadrianum Aug. Thuburbo Maius; *CIL* VIII 83: *[Divo] Hadriano conditori municipi*, from Turris Tamalleni.

[11] *AE* 1958, 128: Colonia Aelia Augusta Tipasensis; *CIL* VIII 8375: municipium Aelium Choba, and *AE* 1949, 55: dedication to the Deified Hadrian, the founder of the municipium (*Divo Hadriano conditori municipii*), by the municipal citizens (*municipes*) of the municipium Aelium Choba.

[12] *CIL* IX 1111 (A.D. 166–67), lines 10–11, [Colonia] Aelia [Aug. Ae]cla[n]um; *CIL* X 6079: Colonia Aelia Hadriana Augusta Formiae. Zahrnt 1988b, 249, focusing on provincial colonies, omits these.

[13] *CIL* III 5630 = *ILS* 7112, 5658, 5663: Municipium Aelium Cet(iensium) or Cet(ium); *CIL* III, p. 1841, *CIL* IX 2593: Municipium Aelium Ovilaris. Zahrnt 1988b, 233, convincingly disallows changes of city status attributed to Hadrian at Solva and Aguntum (Noricum).

[14] *AE* 1905, 110, cf. *AE* 1914, 117, and *CIL* III 8129 = *IMS* II 75: Municipium Hadrianum Drobense; *CIL* III 14465 = *ILS* 7150, and *CIL* VIII 3021: municipium Aelium Hadrianum Napoca. Zahrnt 1988b, 234–37, convincingly rejects the purported Hadrianic "colony" at Malva, Dacia.

[15] *CIL* III 4554: Municipium Aelium Karnuntum; *CIL* VI 1057 line 17, with *AE* 1953, 14: Municipium Aelium Aq(uincum). Some city changes in Pannonia credited to Hadrian

1 municipium in Moesia Superior (Viminacium);[16]
1 municipium in Raetia (Augusta *Vindelicum);[17]
1 municipium in the Thracian Chersonese (Aelium Coela);[18]
1 colonia in Baetica (Italica);[19]
1 municipium in Tarraconensis (Ilugo);[20]
1 altered city status in a double community in Galatia (Iconium);[21]
?1 grant of *Latium maius* in Africa Proconsularis (Gigthis).[22]

Totals are:

11 coloniae (7, Africa Proconsularis; 1, Mauretania; 2, Italy; 1, Baetica);
21 municipia (10, Africa Proconsularis; 1, Mauretania; 2, Noricum; 2, Dacia; 2, Pannonia; 1, Moesia; 1, Raetia; 1, Thracia; 1, Tarraconensis);

---

have been rejected, such as at Siscia: Zahrnt 1988b, 233. I am doubtful of many Pannonian municipia attributed to Hadrian by A. Mócsy: Municipium Iasorum (Mócsy 1968, 1004, and Mócsy 1974, 143n. 121, noting merely that the one known decurion of Municipium Iasorum received Roman citizenship from Hadrian); Municipium Mogentiana (pseudo-tribe Aelia, *CIL* III 15188[4]); Municipium Cibalae (one decurion received citizenship from Trajan, *CIL* III 3267); Municipium Mursella (a local official had a wife named Ulpia Finita, *CIL* III 4267; Mócsy 1962a, 598–99); and Municipium Bassiana (a decurion with citizenship from Hadrian, *AE* 1965, 303) and Municipium Ulpianum (the decurions so far attested in the town are Ulpii and Aelii): Mócsy 1974, 143–45. A. Birley has also suggested to me that Municipium Halicanum was Hadrianic: cf. S. Soproni, "Municipium Halicanum," *Folia Arch.* 30 (1979): 91–98 (non vidi).

[16] *CIL* III 1654, 1655, 8102: municipium Aelium Viminacium. *AE* 1980, 786, witnesses a new road from Viminacium south to Dardania, begun by Trajan but finished by Hadrian between 119 and 138.

[17] For the uncertain final element of the town's name, municipium Aelium Augustum (?Vindelicum), see Zahrnt 1988c, with references including *AE* 1980, 661, *CIL* III 5800, *AE* 1972, 359, and *CIL* VI 32840.

[18] Lines 11–13 of *AE* 1924, 82 (= *IEphesos* VII.1 #3048), probably Hadrianic.

[19] *CIL* II 1135, XI 2699, XII 1856, *AE* 1908, 150 = *AE* 1952, 121 (= *Hispania Antiqua Epigraphia* 1–3 [1950–52]: #348), *CILA* 343 = *AE* 1982, 520, *CILA* 342 = *AE* 1983, 520, and *CILA* 344: Colonia Aelia Augusta Italicensium; cf. Gell. *NA* 16.3.4.

[20] *CIL* II 3239 = *AE* 1902, 1 = *EE* IX 125 = *ZPE* 79 (1989): 175 (after A.D. 128). Zahrnt 1989a argues that Hadrian gave the municipal charter to Ilugo, which had received "Latin rights" from the Flavians; in correspondence, Hartmut Galsterer has kindly informed me of his doubts about the argument. See also González 1986, 202–3, on chapter 21 of the Flavian municipal law.

[21] Iconium, an Augustan colony, was long thought to have been "recolonized" in some fashion by Hadrian, but its changed titulature in Hadrian's reign reflects rather the amalgamation of the indigenous community, which had been allowed to maintain itself as a polis, with the juxtaposed Augustan veteran colony: S. Mitchell 1979. See *CIL* III 12136, almost identical to an inscription photographed and discussed by B. Pace, *ASAA* 6/7 (1923–24): 347, fig. 4, but cf. Zahrnt; *CIL* III 12137; *ILS* 9414; coins referred to by Zahrnt 1988b, 242–45.

[22] *CIL* VIII 22707 = *ILS* 6779, together with *CIL* VIII 22737 = *ILS* 6780, and *ILT* 41, although not unequivocal proof that it was Hadrian who conferred *Latium maius* on Gigthis, have been argued strongly to be so by Zahrnt 1989b. See below.

1 grant of colonial status to the peregrine community twinned with
an Augustan Roman colony (Galatia);
?1 grant of *Latium maius* (Africa Proconsularis).

Although new epigraphic finds may change the numbers above, some features can be discerned. Typologically, there are more municipia than coloniae.[23] City status bears no observable relationship to the variety, density, and/
or extent of civic and other structures, as far as can be discerned in the archaeological record. Although specifics are lacking for these cities' population and
territorial extent, they have presumable populations ranging from less than
5,000 to more than 20,000, the same range as the majority of Roman cities.[24]
Geographically, the phenomenon of Hadrian's changes of city status is almost
completely restricted to the Latin West, and it is particularly prominent in
North Africa (twenty-one cities) and the Danubian region (nine cities).[25]

In the Greek East, Hadrian was responsible only for granting Roman citizenship to the peregrine (not Roman citizen but free) citizens of the polis
twinned with the Augustan colony at Iconium, and for the establishment
of a municipium in the Thracian Chersonese.[26] The infrequency of this
type of intervention corresponds to a more widespread scarcity of Roman
municipia and coloniae in the Greek East, a phenomenon accounted for by
the more urbanized nature of the region. The relative density of cities enabled Rome to maintain control by tying existing poleis to itself by means
of various separate or provincial treaties, and, in keeping with local traditions, by recognizing new urban conglomerations as poleis rather than municipia or coloniae.[27] (I return to the creation of new poleis in chapter 8.)
The illusion that poleis had greater autonomy, at least in internal affairs, is
underscored by their use of Greek, rather than Latin, for most public inscriptions.[28] In contrast, both coloniae and municipia used Latin for most
of their public business and were tightly bound to Rome, although in different ways.[29]

---

[23] A point stressed by Zahrnt in his article on Colonia Aelia Capitolina (1991).

[24] Against associating changes in city status with level of "urbanization," wealth, strategic
importance, or the like, see B. D. Shaw, "Archaeology and Knowledge: The History of the
African Provinces of the Roman Empire," *Florilegium* 21 (1980): 37–38, and Broughton
1929, 156. For city population in the Roman world, see Duncan-Jones 1982, 259–77.

[25] The distinction of North Africa may be illusory, for cities here were fond of civic titles
(Galsterer-Kröll 1972, 86).

[26] Most changes in poleis, such as the designation of one as metropolis, are treated in chapter 5.

[27] In general, see B. Levick, "Urbanization in the Eastern Empire," chapter 12 of Wacher
1987, I:329–44, and the survey by A. H. M. Jones 1940, chapter 1, pp. 1–26.

[28] *AE* 1924, 82 = *IEphesos* VII.1 #3048, in Greek, was raised by the regional group of
the Chersonesitai, on decree of the municipium Aelium Coela.

[29] Other forms of communities, such as *vici* and *praefecturae,* were also found in the Latin
West: A. Poulter, "Townships and Villages," chapter 14 of Wacher 1987, I:388–409. For

Hadrian's own words help elucidate those ties and his opinion of the two city types. Part of a speech the emperor presented to the senate is preserved by Aulus Gellius (*NA* 16.13.1–9), who adduces it in order to clarify the original definitions of *municeps* and *municipium* (for text and translation, see the appendix to this chapter).[30] According to Gellius, Hadrian was moved to speak by surprise when some long-established municipia, including Utica and his own ancestral town, Italica,[31] requested him to change their city status to that of colony (16.13.4). Hadrian's reported words, together with Gellius's comments, draw the following distinctions between municipia and coloniae: although citizens of municipia (*municipes*) could enjoy their own laws and rights and had access to Roman "privileges" (such as serving in the legions and not among the auxiliaries), they were otherwise free from Roman law and obligations. In contrast, citizens of colonies had to assume all Roman laws and institutions rather than ones of their own making (16.13.6–8). Apparently concurring with Hadrian's unconventional view, Gellius holds that colonies are not better off than municipia (*meliore condicione*, 16.13.3).[32] Remarking that colonies were in fact more subordinate to Rome, Gellius ascribes the misconception of colonies' greater prestige both to Rome's overwhelming majesty and to the increasing oblivion of traditions in municipia (16.13.9).

The passage apparently explains both why communities receiving municipal status from Hadrian outnumber those receiving the status of colonia (21 to 11) and how at least some communities managed to change their city status, by means of embassies to the emperor.[33] That both Italica and Utica are attested as "new" Hadrianic colonies, despite Hadrian's surprise at their request and his reported preference for municipia, cautions against assuming a Hadrianic policy of establishing municipia.[34] No evidence sug-

---

Rome's earlier co-option of urban centers, see also Keay 1992. For the use of Latin for public business and its effects on the survival of vernacular languages, see Brunt 1976 and Millar 1968.

[30] Grelle 1972, 72–80, would date the speech between 118 and 121. One contention of Gellius, that in his day the terms for various city statuses were loosely used, is buttressed by the many second-century inscriptions from North Africa employing the term *respublica* interchangeably with *colonia* and *municipium*: Gascou 1979. See also Mócsy 1962b, *Dig.* 50.1.1, and Millar 1983, 80. Pliny the Elder's difficult nomenclature for cities is discussed by Desanges (1972).

[31] See Millar 1977, 408. Italica and Utica had long been municipia, Italica at least from the time of Augustus and Utica by a grant from Octavian in 36 B.C.: Caballos Rufino 1994, 61–64; Gascou 1972, 120–22.

[32] Scholars often refer to the cited petitions of Italica, Utica, and other municipia when echoing Gellius's statement that coloniae were thought more illustrious during the Empire: e.g., Kornemann 1900, 513.

[33] Parts of the passage refer to conditions of the middle and late Republic, and parts to the second century A.D.: see Sherwin-White 1973, 376.

[34] The lack of evidence for such a policy is key to Millar's remarks on city statuses (1977, 408). For the assumption, see, e.g., Grelle 1972, 80–84, 103–12, 124–30, 149–53.

gests that Hadrian forced communities to retain ancestral laws and customs. Instead, he made clear his preference for long-standing traditions. His seemingly spontaneous speech in the senate publicized his appreciation of local culture, and his grants of municipal status must have similarly affirmed the importance of communities' traditions.[35]

The underlying question concerns the extent of diversity the nominally different civic constitutions brought to political and social patterns in municipia and coloniae in the early second century A.D. To answer this, I turn to detailed comparative evidence. My task is facilitated by the discovery in 1981 of the "lex Irnitana," six of presumably ten bronze slabs on which was originally inscribed the town charter of the Roman municipium now called Irni. The inscription adds to the information of the more fragmentary leges Salpensana and Malacitana, the other particularized examples of the Flavian municipal law likewise found in southern Spain.[36] The Flavian municipal law can be compared with the colonial charter of the Colonia Genetiva Iulia Ursonensis (Urso), a Caesarian colony also in southern Spain. Urso's civic charter, known as the lex Coloniae Genetivae Iuliae, was originally composed in 44 B.C., but was copied and revalidated in the Flavian period.[37] Other comparanda are the republican town charters in Italy,[38] and legal, epigraphic, numismatic, and literary sources for municipal life.[39] The data provide a good picture of municipia and coloniae, and reveal that by the end of the first century A.D. there were few constitutional

[35] The chronology of Hadrian's grants of city status is most uncertain. The *de Italicensibus* may date to 118–21 (see n. 30, above), and Italica and Utica could scarcely have been granted colonial status at the time of, or immediately after, its apparent rebuff of their requests. It is dubious that all the scattered changes in North Africa came during Hadrian's voyage of 128 to Africa, as suggested by Romanelli 1959, 338–43, or that all the city changes Mócsy (1974, 139) attributes to Hadrian in Pannonia occurred during Hadrian's visit in 124.

[36] González 1986, with Lebek 1993, 159–60; lex Salpensana: *CIL* II 1963 = *ILS* 6088 = Abbott and Johnson 1926, #64, pp. 369–74; lex Malacitana: *CIL* II 1964 = *ILS* 6089 = Abbott and Johnson 1926, #65, pp. 374–81 = Lewis and Reinhold 1990, II:#64. Smaller fragments of this law have been claimed from four other sites: González 1986, 150 (but most do not accept his contention that the "Fragmentum Italicense," *FIRA* #31, is from Italica); Fernández Gómez 1991.

[37] Dessau, ad loc. in *ILS* 6087, cf. Gabba 1988. The charter from Urso (the lex Col. Gen., also known as the lex Ursonensis) is also published as Abbott and Johnson 1926, #26, pp. 300–317 = Lewis and Reinhold 1990, I:#162, pp. 453–61 = Crawford 1996, #25, pp. 393–454.

[38] The Lex Tarentina (ca. 88–62 B.C.): *CIL* I² 590 = *ILS* 6086 = Abbott and Johnson 1926, #20, pp. 282–84 = Lewis and Reinhold 1990, I:#162, pp. 446–48 = Crawford 1996, #15, pp. 301–12; and the Tabula Heracleensis (45 B.C.): *CIL* I² 593 = *ILS* 6085 = Abbott and Johnson 1926, #24, pp. 288–98 = Lewis and Reinhold 1990, I: #162, pp. 449–53 = Crawford 1996, #24, pp. 355–91.

[39] Liebenam 1900; Langhammer 1973; Stahl 1978; Mackie 1983; Jarrett 1971. The legis Lauriacensis Fragmenta are published in Bruns⁷ 159, #33a; new fragment in *AE* 1953, 124, re-edited by Crawford in González 1986, 241–43.

differences either among individual municipia, or between municipia and coloniae.[40] Moreover, in many ways these two types of city organization resemble the typical structure of a polis, which helps explain the Romans' preference for poleis in the Greek East.

Municipia, coloniae, and poleis alike were characterized by a tripartite political organization: magistrates in collegial boards, an advisory council, and a voting and legislative assembly of citizens. All male citizens of municipia, coloniae, and poleis could participate in local political life, and local citizenship, open only to the freeborn or legally freed, was determined by birth to local citizen parents who had been married legally and bindingly, by adoption or manumission by local citizens, or by a special decree of the local council, now called "adlection."[41] Yet in all three types of cities, only a small segment of the inhabitants actually wielded political power, perhaps at most only 10 percent of a town's population.[42] These exceptional individuals, who constituted what is now often called the "curial class" or municipal elite, had the requisite property and social standing to be elected to city magistracies and priesthoods and to serve in the *curia* (town council) as *decuriones* (town councillors, henceforth called decurions).

Evidence from Spain, North Africa, the Greek East, and elsewhere discredits the suggestion sometimes made, that the institution of *Latium maius* in the early second century was aimed at inducing more qualified individuals to assume the responsibilities of local government, including financial ones, in municipia. Although some cities had difficulty filling town councils and magistracies earlier in the century, through the end of the second century most cities of all types disclose considerable zeal on the part of citizens to assume positions of civic responsibility.[43] Such positions were not rewarded financially, but they carried great prestige and authority. In-

---

[40] Crawford 1988, 128, holds that municipal charters of all types were "of course increasingly uniform from the Flavian period, at any rate in the West."

[41] The extant Flavian municipal law does not define *municeps:* Galsterer 1988a, 90. For Hadrian's law on local citizenship, see chapter 1, at n. 56. Citizens of a town usually shared the same tribe. See Nörr 1965; Berger 1953, 613, s.v. "origo"; *DizEpig* I:414–16, s.v. "adlectio." Adlection came about through a town's decurions, magistrates, or (less often) an emperor who, presumably upon request from the town, could adlect as a new citizen of that town a citizen of another town; see the last section of chapter 4.

[42] Duncan-Jones 1982, 283–87.

[43] The third- or early-fourth-century inscription from Tymandus in Pisidia, calling for fifty decurions to sit in the council of this newly established city, expresses fervent hope that the numbers will be increased quickly (*ILS* 6090 = *CIL* III 6866 = Abbott and Johnson 1926, #151, pp. 488–89). See Stahl 1978, 22–23; Langhammer 1973, 19; and Spitzl 1984, 35–36. Those who would see an ulterior political and financial aim for the institution of *Latium maius* include Seston 1962 and Sherk 1970, 79–80, referring to *AE* 1961, 156 (A.D. 187), *CIL* V 961 (unknown date), and *CIL* X 5670 (speculative restorations). See also chapter 1, at n. 24.

dividuals voluntarily paid a sum of money upon their election (the so-called *summa honoraria*), and while in office contributed money for their cities' needs by means of what are called *munera* and *leitourgiai* (both words with the double meaning of "public duties" and "public gifts," henceforth called liturgies). As mentioned in chapter 1, in the phenomenon now known as euergetism members of the municipal elite received recognition and acclaim in return for their money, time, and effort. On the local scale they mirrored the activities and status of the emperor himself.[44] In the wider context, they were most often the individuals the emperor used as intermediaries, and lauded publicly, when he dealt with cities.

Inscriptions, literature, and visual arts put members of the municipal elite individually and as a group at the head of processions, in the most conspicuous and best seats at spectacles, as the primary recipients of distributions, and as the major actors in sacrifices. During their tenure of office, a town's *duoviri* and *aediles* (the titles of magistrates in colonies and many municipia; see below) had special attendants and wore the *toga praetexta* (the white garment marking Roman citizenship, in this case adorned with a purple border).[45] These men were proud of their status, and inscriptions repeatedly proclaim their magistracies, priesthoods, and public salutations and honors.

The analogous social and local political standing of the curial classes in colonies and municipalities was reflected by the general parity of their political standing vis-à-vis Rome. By Hadrian's day both groups were Roman citizens. In colonies all citizens held Roman citizenship by virtue of the "colonial" status of the town. In municipalities all magistrates held Roman citizenship by Latin rights (*ius Latii*), and by the early-second-century innovation of *Latium maius,* men who served as decurions received Roman citizenship.[46] The privilege of Roman citizenship, shared by the curial class in colonies and most municipalities alike, helped ally this elite with Rome. This is apparently the demographic group that imitated Roman customs, trends, and styles most rapidly and faithfully.[47] Such assimilation is understandable in light of this group's function as mediators between Rome

---

[44] See chapter 1, n. 60; Liebenam 1900, 360–430.

[45] Lex Col. Gen., chapter 62. Livy, 34.7.2–3, notes that magistrates could be cremated in their togas. Decurions had privileges such as free water and public gifts: Garnsey 1970, 153–72.

[46] This was not true in poleis. Braunert 1966 shows that the conferral of *ius Latii,* Latin rights, on a town or towns granted personal rights to individuals. A subsequent grant of city status was needed formally to alter the town's relationships with the Roman authorities, according to Zahrnt 1989b; Grelle 1972, 151–53; and Le Roux 1986. Magistrates (and their parents, wives, children, and grandchildren) received Roman citizenship only after their office: *ILS* 6088, chapter 21 (lex Salp.); lex Irn., chapter 21, with González 1986, ad loc., 202–4.

[47] Brunt 1976; MacMullen 1984; Millett 1990.

and its subjects. Members of the curial class hosted Roman governors, legates, other officials, and their entourages in the provinces, and went to Rome themselves for embassies and other matters. In turn, at home they often served as the mouthpiece of Rome. Roman furnishings, styles, decoration, and deportment helped establish their authority as Rome's representatives and may have eased their work of administering the empire in its particulars.

Magistrates in cities throughout the Roman empire had numerous local duties. The magistracies of the Latin West were usually divided into two collegial boards. The chief magistrates had various titles, but in many cities were called *duoviri* (or *duumviri, IIviri,* "two men," hereafter called duovirs) or *quattuorviri* ("four men"); the lower magistrates were often called aediles. Both boards had juridical and financial powers that extended their authority to the town's religious life. The duovirs, or their equivalents, summoned and presided over the council, assembly, and legal courts, with a wide-ranging but not absolute jurisdiction.[48] Periodically the top officials had to conduct the census and farm out public contracts. The magistrates elected in these years apparently had special prestige befitting the importance of their duties, which were essential to Rome's revenues.[49] (See further in chapter 4.) Aediles were in charge of the corn supply, sacred buildings and sacred places, the town, roads, districts, drains, baths, the market, inspection of weights and measures, and the watch. In Irni, according to the lex Irnitana, aediles had powers of jurisdiction equal to those of duovirs.[50] In some cities officials subordinate to the duovirs and known as *quaestores* (financial officials) collected, spent, kept, administered, and looked after the city's funds, but elsewhere such functions were handled by the duovirs and aediles.[51] All magistrates had to be freeborn and of good repute; they also had to meet a property qualification and had to be at least twenty-five years old.[52]

---

[48] For instance, it did not include any *actiones famosae,* legal actions in which the condemnation of the defendant involved *infamia* (see below), unless both parties agreed to a local trial: lex Irn., chapter 84; cf. González 1986, 228, and a fragment of the lex Col. Gen. that has been republished by Crawford in González 1986, 239–41.

[49] Liebenam 1900, 256–57; lex Malac., chapter 63 (missing from the lex Irnitana and the lex Salpensana). These officials were termed *IIviri quinquennales, IIviri iure dicundo,* or the like.

[50] González 1986, 200–202, on chapter 19; Galsterer 1988a, 80–81; Liebenam 1900, 263–65.

[51] The quaestorship was not a universal magistracy: *Dig.* 50.4.18.2, cf. Liebenam 1900, 265–66; González 1986, 201–2, on chapter 19 of the Flavian municipal law.

[52] At Irni the property qualification was the same for magistrates and decurions, more than 5,000 HS: lex Irn., chapter 86, with González 1986, 215; age qualification in lex Irn., chapter 54, with González 1986, 215–16, cf. Liebenam 1900, 268–69. In North African epitaphs duoviri are generally in their early thirties, corroborating the *cursus honorum* usually presumed: Jarrett 1971, 516–18. Magistrates of Flavian municipia received Roman citizenship upon laying down their office; see n. 46 above.

A deliberative and advisory body of citizens, in Latin called the *ordo decurionum* (local senate of decurions), consulted with the magistrates and passed resolutions concerning offers of the position of town patron and of local citizenship, embassies, seating at spectacles, public buildings and distributions, religious spectacles, and demolition of private buildings.[53] They, rather than the magistrates, were the true governing body.[54] They had to meet a certain property qualification, have freeborn standing, and be at least twenty-five years old (*Dig.* 50.4.8).[55] Although local senates generally comprised one hundred councillors in towns of substantial size, higher and lower figures are also found. The municipium Irni had only sixty-three decurions, "the number by the law and custom of this municipium before the passage of this statute" (chapter 31; a clear example of the retention of pre-existing customs). On specific matters a quorum was necessary for the council's decrees to be binding.[56] The council's numbers were maintained, apparently, by co-option.[57]

The local citizenry, called collectively *populus, municipes, coloni,* or the like, was divided into voting units or wards (often called *curiae*). The citizens in assembly voted on matters of public finance, on offers to the emperor of honorary duumvirates, and perhaps on public acclamations and denunciations.[58] Their functions are instanced by a decree of Choba's *mu-*

[53] See lex Irn., chapters 61–62, 79, 82, 19, with González 1986, 208–9; lex Col. Gen., chapter 75, with Galsterer 1988a, 84. Lex Irn., chapter 29, reveals that in some cases the council also oversaw guardianship.

[54] Galsterer 1988a, 86: the "growing accretion of importance to the town council . . . took place in parallel with, and not uninfluenced by, the increasing predominance of the Roman Senate in relation to the popular assemblies and magistrates from the beginning of the Principate on." Talbert 1989 compares the procedures of Urso's council and Rome's senate.

[55] Although the lex Col. Gen., chapter 105, specifically allows freedmen to become decurions, apparently as in other transmarine colonies founded by Caesar with freedmen colonists, the lex Visellia of A.D. 24 abrogated this dispensation: *DizEpig,* 2nd ed., II:1525, s.v. "decuriones."

[56] Nicols 1988. Duncan-Jones (1982, 283–87) postulates norms of one hundred members and thirty members, respectively, in large and small cities in the Latin West. Translation of lex Irn. from González 1986, 185. Quorums in councils varied in the municipia and Colonia Genetiva Iulia according to matters under discussion (e.g., lex Col. Gen., chapters 97, 130, cf. González 1986, 209).

[57] Magistrates were usually chosen from among the decurions (lex Irn., chapter 21; lex Col. Gen., chapters 101, 105). Athough the Flavian municipal law (lex Irn., chapter 51) foresees eventualities in which the duoviri would have to fill the curia by selecting as decurions eminent citizens who had not yet served as magistrates (cf. Spitzl 1984, 32–35), Galsterer 1988a, 81–82, points out that the missing preceding chapter must have treated procedures for the normal circumstances of sufficient candidates.

[58] For the voting wards or *curiae,* see lex Irn., chapter L (and González 1986, ad loc., 214); Liebenam 1900, 214–16; Spitzl 1984, 38–39; for their role in elections, lex Irn., chapter 51. González 1986, 204–5, on chapters 24 and 79, notes the scant information in the lex

nicipes raising an impressive statue of Hadrian, hailed as *conditor municipii* (founder of the town), and by the allocation by Gigthis's *populus* of funds for a statue of M. Servilius Draco, who had obtained *Latium maius* for Gigthis.[59] During the first century of the principate and even later, the town assembly also elected the local magistrates.[60] In poleis the duties of councils and popular assemblies correspond to those described above, although evidence from Ephesus and elsewhere implies that assemblies in cities of the Greek East exercised more functions than their counterparts in the West.[61]

Citizens and noncitizens alike had political rights, privileges, and liabilities in their cities. Although men sometimes left their home towns to live in Rome or another city or to join the army, they remained citizens of their town of origin (*origo*, sometimes also termed *patria* or *domicilium*). This local citizenship was the basis of their political identity, and, whether at home or abroad, they were subject to duties to their town.[62] If they qualified for equestrian or senatorial status or enlisted in the army, by Hadrian's day they were part of a legally privileged group called the *honestiores* (the "better" or "more honorable" men, those who had held *honores,* or elective positions).[63] The immediate families of the local magistrates and decurions were privileged as well, as seen most obviously in families' automatic enrollment as Roman citizens when husbands or fathers received Roman citizenship by Latin rights. Sons of decurions were designated as *praetextati* (those granted the privilege of wearing the *toga praetexta*), and

---

Irnitana on the assembly's actual duties. Although González rightly observes (1986, 204–5) that Jacques 1984, 407–22, confuses formal and informal involvement of the assembly, Jacques's list furnishes examples of assemblies voting formally on public expenditures. Add *ILAlg.* I:1295 (from Thubursica Numidarum), recording a joint vote of *ordo* and *populus* for an honorary statue. Murga 1985 exhaustively surveys the *municipes* as known from the charters.

[59] *AE* 1949, 55; *ILS* 6780.

[60] Lex Irn., chapter 50; lex Malac., chapters 51–59; lex Col. Gen., chapters 101, 132. Lewin 1995, 15–85, collects the varied evidence for the continuing importance of municipal assemblies through the Severan period, particularly as they exercised pressure for honors and ratified proposals.

[61] Rogers 1992, 224–28, citing decrees of the Ephesian demos concerning water supply and public building.

[62] Eck 1980; Chastagnol 1977; Berger 1953, 441 and 613, s.vv. "domicilium" and "origo." Absence from towns caused local difficulties because of missed liturgies and munera: Millar 1983, 87–91. Except for the fragmentary lex from Lauriacum, our extant charters predate the distinction of citizens into *honestiores* and *humiliores* in the early second century. In this section I use the term "privileged" quite generally; see next note.

[63] Langhammer 1973, 33–40, includes in this group senators or *viri clarissimi, equites,* decurions, Augustales, soldiers, and veterans; cf. Garnsey 1970. The creation of this privileged group, which by including military men transcends local ties, potentially weakened the importance of town citizenship and municipal liturgies.

could enter the local council house even when younger than twenty-five, the legal age of admission.[64] Wives and daughters formed the group from which the towns' public priestesses were chosen, just as the men in their families served as public priests.[65] The extant charters carefully regulate the choice of patrons, powerful individuals (often from outside the town) who agreed to local ties and obligations.[66] In all the practices and customs listed above, no essential distinctions between coloniae, municipia, or poleis can be discerned. Privilege and status were relatively rare and were institutionalized by means of property and age qualifications.

In coloniae and municipia alike (and in poleis), in Hadrian's day inhabitants with inferior standing included *incolae* ("resident aliens"), freedmen and freedwomen, "attributed" persons (individuals from territories put under the control of another city; cf. chapter 5), slaves, and individuals marked with *infamia*, a political and social stigma carefully regulated in Roman law.[67] In neither municipia nor coloniae could incolae run for local office, and in both they were also denied access to Roman law if they were not Roman or Latin citizens. They were subject to land taxes and had to take on the same duties as local citizens, such as providing five days of free labor and a yoke of oxen for the town's public building projects.[68] Freedmen in either type of town could participate in assemblies but were generally barred from public office;[69] on the other hand, the organization of the Augustales gave freedmen an alternative means to gain local repute.[70] Al-

[64] Cf. the Canusium album, *ILS* 6121 = *CIL* IX 338 (A.D. 223), and Jarrett 1971, 532–36.

[65] See, e.g., Bremen 1983, 236. The wives of citizens are specifically referred to in chapter 133 of lex Col. Gen., which applies to them the laws of the colony and of their husbands. For male priests, see Jarrett 1971, 522, 526–32.

[66] Lex Col. Gen., chapters 97, 130; lex Malac., chapter 61. See also Nicols 1979; Nicols 1990; Harmand 1957; Engesser 1955.

[67] Mackie 1983, 44–46, on *incolae; Dig.* 3.2, with Greenidge 1894 and Kaser 1956, on *infamia.*

[68] Chapter 53 of the Flavian municipal law stipulates that incolae who are Roman or Latin citizens, i.e., the most elite group, can vote in the municipium. Their impact was limited, however, because they were grouped together and incorporated into one of the town's existing voting wards (chosen by lot each election). Nonetheless, their ability to vote is one of the few distinctions now discernible between this type of town and coloniae: lex Malac., chapter 53, with Spitzl 1984, ad loc., 40–42. For other stipulations regarding incolae, see lex Irn., chapter 83; lex Col. Gen., chapter 98; *Dig.* 50.1.37 praef.; Liebenam 1900, 401–2, 417–30, with references. Mackie 1983, 45, suggests that female, but not male, incolae could take on local priesthoods.

[69] Treggiari 1969, 63–64. See lex Irn., chapter 54; in Urso, unusually, freedmen could serve as decurions (lex Col. Gen., chapter 105, and n. 55 above).

[70] Duthoy 1974; Duthoy 1976; Duthoy 1978; Duncan-Jones 1982, 284–87. That free men as well as freedmen occasionally served as Augustales increases the prestige of the group: A. Abramenko, *Die munizipale Mittelschicht im kaiserzeitlichen Italien. Zu einem neuen Verständnis von Sevirat und Augustalität* (Frankfurt, 1993) (non vidi).

though in both types of cities slaves and *infames* (those marked by *infamia*) had no political rights, slaves could be manumitted and thus gain the rights of freedmen,[71] and *infamia* could be remitted.[72] Overall, in terms of political rights, differences in city status seem to have affected the less privileged members of coloniae and municipia but little.

The civil laws and institutions of Flavian municipia strongly resemble their Roman counterparts in the Roman colony Genetiva Iulia (Urso) and in metropolitan Rome itself. The Flavian municipal law assumes that Latin *municipes* have institutions largely identical to fundamental Roman ones: *patria potestas, manus, mancipium,* rights of patron over freedman, manumission, *tutela, tria nomina,* and even tribal affiliation, although we cannot know if a Roman court of law would have recognized these institutions as valid.[73] The section of jurisdiction that assimilates the Latin *municipes* of Irni to Roman citizens in numerous ways (chapters 84–93) even culminates by stating that, in any matter not specifically treated previously, "the municipes of the Municipium Flavium Irnitanum should deal with each other . . . under the civil law under which Roman citizens deal or will deal with each other."[74] The "letter of Domitian," with which the Irni charter closes, regulates by Roman law all marriages.[75] The trend is clear. Menander of Laodicea, writing around 270, says that all cities were then governed according to the common laws of Rome (Men. *Rhet.* 202, 205). Although the legal codes show this to be an exaggeration, for local law and custom persisted through the third century (e.g., *CodJ* 8.48.1), Menander correctly reflects the principate's gradual assimilation of local law to that of Rome.[76]

Knowledge of, and adherence to, Roman law were generally assumed in municipalities. One means by which Roman law was made public knowledge in the provinces is clear in chapter 85 of the lex Irnitana, which specifies that local magistrates exhibit in public every day, for most of the day,

---

[71] E.g., Giménez-Caudela 1981.

[72] Greenidge 1894, 177–85.

[73] Lex Irn., chapters 21 and 86, 22, 23, and 96, 28, 29, 86: it is unclear whether these institutions were recognized as valid in a Roman court of law. See Hanard 1987 and Mackie 1983, 207–9.

[74] González 1986, 148–49, with translation of chapter 93 by Crawford, ibid., 198–99. Galsterer 1988b, 70, holds that these chapters are "best explained by assuming that [the citizens of the municipium Flavium Irnitanum] were living *de facto* under Roman law even if they were not citizens *stricto iure.*"

[75] See esp. Lebek 1993.

[76] See Nutton 1978, 213–16. S. Mitchell 1990, 188, remarks that the electoral laws of Oenoanda, as revealed in the stipulations for the choice of the Demostheneia's agonothete, "seem to correspond closely with *nominatio, potioris nominatio,* and *vacatio,* found in Latin municipal laws," and may go back to a lex Provinciae.

and in such a place that it could be easily read from ground level, the album (edict) of the provincial governor, and that they administer justice according to it.[77] Roman law, thus physically displayed in the heart of this municipium, served as the model for justice. Procedures detailed in the lex Irnitana are essentially those of procedures in metropolitan Rome although, as we saw above, the actual jurisdiction of local magistrates was more limited.[78] Nevertheless, the chapters of the lex Irnitana concerning institutions and law show that there was little legal difference in civil matters between *cives Romani* and *cives Latini*, that is, between citizens in colonies and those in provincial municipalities.[79]

In legal matters and institutions, Hadrian's municipal charters also must have assimilated *municipes* to Roman citizens.[80] Yet we should not simply conclude that his grants of municipal and colonial status were due to a policy of "Romanizing" the empire, that is, of spreading Roman law and social institutions throughout the empire by establishing them in communities under Roman rule.[81] Without individual charters we shall never know what differences individualized the constitutions Hadrian confirmed for various municipalities, nor how great a change was felt in the smaller number of pre-existing communities he confirmed as colonies. In light of Hadrian's appreciation of local differences, which he avowed in the *de Italicensibus* and repeatedly manifested in interactions with cities, his municipal charters must have offered room for idiosyncrasies. We see in chapter 4, for example, the range of local titles Hadrian bore when he assumed the highest magistracies of various cities in absentia (cf. *HA, Hadr.* 19.1). At our great remove it may appear of little importance whether a town's top officials were called duovirs or quattuorvirs. To the inhabitants of the

---

[77] Cf. González 1986, ad loc., 230–31.

[78] Simhäuser 1989; Rodger 1990; Birks 1988. Johnston 1987 holds that a copy of the lex Iulia de iudiciis privatis was needed to understand all the provisions of the lex Irnitana. If so, the subordination of this "independent" charter to the rules and regulations of Rome was even more pronounced.

[79] See also Spitzl 1984, 3–8, 122; González 1986, 149.

[80] One fragment from the later municipal charter of Lauriacum seems to replicate jurisdiction of the Flavian municipal law: Crawford, in González 1986, 242–43.

[81] This is the view of Grelle 1972, although he also calls formative for this policy primarily Hadrian's commitment to pluralism, urbanization, and integration with Rome of the municipal upper classes, and secondarily his antiquarianism. Mócsy 1974 interprets Hadrian's city changes in the Danubian region, all grants of municipal charters, as part of a policy to Romanize this area. Gascou (1972 and 1982) links Hadrian's civic changes to a post-Augustan policy to urbanize and Romanize North Africa, generally attributing "promotions," from peregrine civitas to municipium or from municipium to colonia, to the economic importance and wealth of the community, the strategic interest of the site, and the level of "Romanization" (undefined). Less significant in his case-by-case analysis are other factors he discerns, such as the intervention of powerful patrons and the exceptional favor of the emperor (Gascou 1972, 12–13). Cf. n. 93 below.

second-century Roman empire, however, such distinctions were essential to civic pride and sense of self.[82]

Yet such distinctions must have been relatively cosmetic, as may have been the changes experienced in municipia and other communities Hadrian ratified as colonies. Inscriptions from Hadrianic municipalities and colonies disclose similar magistracies, and similar political and social groups. Further, the fragmentary third-century charter of the municipium Lauriacum (in Noricum) strongly resembles the Flavian municipal law:[83] we would expect that the intervening Hadrianic municipal charters also would be analogous. For Hadrian and others of his day, the principle of local diversity may have been at least as important as genuine variety among the laws and customs of cities in the Roman empire.

As remarked at the beginning of this chapter, the investigation of Hadrian's changes of city status can be used to illuminate the relations of Italian and provincial communities with the central power at Rome. Military reasons had been key when Rome first devised various city statuses: Roman citizens served in the legions, Latins served in Rome's auxiliary forces, and newly founded colonies served as armed outposts of Rome.[84] By 90 B.C., long before Hadrian's day, coloniae and municipia were equally subject to Rome's requests for military manpower. By the first century A.D., non-Roman citizens were joining the legions and receiving Roman citizenship upon enlistment, despite the fact that this more prestigious service, with its shorter and better-paid terms, had been restricted to Roman citizens during the Republic and into the Empire.[85] During the principate both types of communities seem to have undertaken conscription during Rome's emergencies, and both were equally responsible for the more usual local recruitment of volunteers.[86] By Hadrian's reign the burdens and privileges of military service were distributed equally among municipia and coloniae.

By this time, too, another early and fundamental distinction between colonies and municipalities had also been lost, colonies' freedom from land taxes and from tribute on persons and property. In 167 B.C. all Roman cit-

---

[82] See, e.g., Iconium's *princeps et IIvir primus coloniae* (most distinguished citizen and first duovir of the colony), M. Ulpius Pomponius Superstes: *ILS* 9414.

[83] For the charter from Lauriacum, see Crawford, in González 1986, 241–43.

[84] E.g., Levick 1967, 42–55; see works cited in n. 1 above.

[85] Grants of citizenship upon enlistment are discussed by Mann 1983, 51–66; Parker 1971, 169–72, dating the disappearance of different status for legionaries and auxiliaries to the reign of Hadrian; and Forni 1953, 103–18.

[86] See chapter 1, n. 23. Lex Col. Gen., chapter 103, also authorizes, by decree of a majority of the decurions, a duovir or praefectus to levy a local militia in an emergency. Galsterer 1988a, 85, suggests something similar was in the missing chapter 18 of the Flavian municipal law, which concerned duovirs' duties; cf. Hardy 1912, 47n. 110.

izens in Italy had been granted the *ius Italicum,* freedom from taxes on land, and later in the Republic the privilege was extended to Roman citizens in new colonies, regardless of location. *Immunitas,* freedom from other types of tribute, was also traditionally associated with colonies. But by Tiberius's reign such privileges were not automatically conferred even to colonies of new settlers, veterans, or others. During the principate colonies and muncipalities alike had to petition the emperor for these boons, which were seldom granted (see also chapter 5).[87]

From earliest times municipia and coloniae alike were generally autonomous in internal affairs, partly in compensation for supplying men for armed service. Despite their increasing services to Rome (detailed above and in chapter 1), through the Hadrianic period communities remained basically free from interference by the central government in local administration. Indeed, the Flavian municipal law is remarkable for the infrequency with which it mentions the emperor, the governor, and other direct representatives of Rome. The emperor figures actively only as a possible honorary holder of the local supreme magistracy, in this case a duumvirate, and even then it is expected that he nominate a praefectus to take his place in office if he accepts (lex Irn., chapter 24; below, chapter 4).[88] The governor of the province is mentioned but rarely:[89] he must authorize any town debt of more than 50,000 HS in any one year (lex Irn., chapter 80), he gives the final decision on the balance of decurions and other *municipes* in jury panels (lex Irn., chapter 86), and his edict must be displayed publicly and adhered to (lex Irn., chapter 85, mentioned above).[90] The lex Coloniae Genetivae Iuliae, in its Flavian redaction, specifically prohibits the colony Urso from adopting, choosing, or creating as patron any public man outside of Italy with *imperium,* and it controls closely the adoption of Roman senators or their sons as public guests, unless they be without *imperium,* and within Italy rather than abroad (lex Col. Gen., chapters 130–31).

Although the resulting picture may be illusory, its purport is important. The extant civic charters downplay the direct roles of the emperor, and of others with Roman *imperium,* in local affairs. Local affairs were local business, to be handled by towns' magistrates and decurions. Given Rome's dependence on its cities, however, this stance hinges on local compliance

---

[87] Ulp. *Dig.* 50.15.1; Bleicken 1974. Galsterer 1988b, 66, suggests that all Augustus's military colonies in Spain received *ius Italicum* and *immunitas;* Watkins 1983 speculates about such grants to post-Augustan colonies.

[88] The emperor also figures in the Flavian municipal law in oaths, e.g., chapter 87.

[89] According to Paul. *Lib.* 1, ed. *Dig.* 2.12.4 (early third century), the governor determines the periods during which local official business is to be postponed, but lex Irn., chapter K, has this matter decided by the decurions.

[90] Cf. Galsterer 1988a, 87; Johnston 1987, 64–65. Although it is unstated in the charter, the governor decides cases beyond local jurisdiction.

with Rome's instititions. The threat of Roman intervention, Plutarch's "Roman boots above our heads" (*Mor.* 814e), was always present. Yet the charters seem designed to minimize direct appeals to the emperor and other representatives of central Roman power.[91] As we see in chapter 5, one aim may have been to reduce the flood of imperial business. Another effect may have been less conscious. Embassies, carefully regulated (e.g., lex Irn., chapters F–I, lex Col. Gen., chapter 92), were the common but costly means of appeal to Rome.[92] They reinforced the importance of the curial class as mediators between local community and central government. Town patrons, another focus of the regulations, must also have been influential in relaying the concerns of a community to the central government. Here, too, we are dealing with men of local or regional importance, rather than delegates sent from Rome.[93] Thus the town charters reinforce the standing of the municipal elite, the men essential to the functioning of the Roman state.

Although the detailed extant civic charters predate Hadrian, the charters Hadrian established in his twenty-one municipia and eleven titular coloniae must have similarly minimized the direct involvement of central government in local jurisdiction and administration. Aulus Gellius's report implies that Hadrian advocated self-reliance for provincial and Italian cities. The sheer numbers of communities Hadrian recognized with city status, of whatever type and regardless of proximate cause, point to the emphasis he placed on local rule throughout his reign. That communities themselves valued such self-rule is clear from Gellius's passage and from the documented embassies requesting from Hadrian a change in their city status.[94] Yet the very fact that in Gellius's and Hadrian's day local autonomy was a privilege that had to be sought from the emperor himself reveals the overpowering might of the emperor and Rome. Gellius holds that assimilation of Rome was voluntary, encouraged by Rome's prestige. Hadrian's own privileging of local autonomy is demonstrated by his administrative interactions with cities, discussed in the following two chapters. Local autonomy may have been more apparent than real, but its championing by Hadrian and local elites furnished cities the measure of self-respect necessary for their voluntary assumption of their obligations.

---

[91] Galsterer 1988a, 87.

[92] Liebenam 1900, 353–57; Millar 1977, 375–85, cf. 394–456; Williams 1967.

[93] Cf. B. D. Shaw, "Archaeology and Knowledge," *Florilegium* 21 (1980): 37–38, who holds that "the connection between local and central political élites and the process of patronage" were key for changes of city status; Millar 1977, 493–509.

[94] A point well brought out by Sherwin-White 1973, 411–15, in his general treatment of changes of city status, which he sees as stepping stones from non-Roman (peregrine) status to full Roman status (cf., e.g., 262–65).

APPENDIX

Aulus Gellius, *Noctes Atticae* 16.13.1–9 (*"de Italicensibus"*)

Gell. *NA* 16.13.   1 'Municipes' et 'municipia' verba sunt dictu facilia et usu obvia, et neutiquam reperias, qui haec dicit, quin scire se plane putet, quid dicat. Sed profecto aliud est, atque aliter dicitur. 2 Quotus enim fere nostrum est, qui, cum ex colonia populi Romani sit, non se municipem esse et populares suos municipes esse dicat, quod est a ratione et a veritate longe aversum? 3 Sic adeo et municipia quid et quo iure sint quantumque a colonia differant, ignoramus existimamusque meliore condicione esse colonias quam municipia. 4 De cuius opinationis tam promiscae erroribus divus Hadrianus in oratione, quam de Italicensibus, unde ipse ortus fuit, in senatu habuit, peritissime disseruit mirarique se ostendit, quod et ipsi Italicenses et quaedam item alia municipia antiqua, in quibus Uticenses nominat, cum suis moribus legibusque uti possent, in ius coloniarum mutari gestiverint. 5 Praenestinos autem refert maximo opere a Tiberio imperatore petisse orasseque, ut ex colonia in municipii statum redigerentur, idque illis Tiberium pro ferenda gratia tribuisse, quod in eorum finibus sub ipso oppido ex capitali morbo revaluisset.

6 Municipes ergo sunt cives Romani ex municipiis legibus suis et suo iure utentes, muneris tantum cum populo Romano honorari participes, a quo munere capessendo appellati videntur, nullis aliis necessitatibus neque ulla populi Romani lege adstricti, nisi in quam populus eorum fundus factus est. 7 Primos autem municipes sine suffragii iure Caerites esse factos accepimus concessumque illis, ut civitatis Romanae honorem quidem caperent, sed negotiis tamen atque oneribus vacarent, ...

8 Sed coloniarum alia necessitudo est; non enim veniunt extrinsecus in civitatem nec suis radicibus nituntur, sed ex civitate quasi propagatae sunt et iura institutaque omnia populi Romani, non sui arbitrii, habent. 9 Quae tamen condicio, cum sit magis obnoxia et minus libera, potior tamen et praestabilior existimatur propter amplitudinem maiestatemque populi Romani, cuius istae coloniae quasi effigies parvae simulacraque esse quaedam videntur, et simul quia obscura oblitterataque sunt municipiorum iura, quibus uti iam per innotitiam non queunt.

Translation

1 "Municipes" and "municipia" are words easy to say and routine in their use, and by no means might you find anyone who says these things but who thinks he clearly knows what he was saying. But really it is something else, and the meaning is different. 2 For how many are there, generally, in our age who, although they might be from a colony of the Roman people,

might not say that they are a "municeps" and that their fellow townsmen are "municipes," which is nonsensical and far from the truth. 3 Thus, in fact, we are ignorant of municipalities [*municipia*], what they might be, and of what juridical status, and how far they differ from a colony [*colonia*], and we think that colonies are of a better station than municipalities. 4 About the delusions of this belief, which is so widespread, the deified Hadrian spoke most knowledgeably in the address he gave in the senate about the city of Italica [*de Italicensibus*] (whence he has his own descent), and he revealed that he was amazed because both the citizens of Italica themselves, and likewise certain other long-established municipalities (amongst which he names Utica), although they could use their own customs and laws, were very eager to be changed to the juridical status of colony. 5 He mentions, moreover, that the citizens of Praeneste had begged and implored the emperor Tiberius with the utmost fervor that they might be restored from the status of colony to that of municipality, and that Tiberius had granted this to them as a way of showing his thanks, because in their territory, near the city itself, he had recuperated from a grave illness.

6 And so, "municipes" are Roman citizens from municipalities, using their own regulations and laws, sharing only honorary duty with the Roman people—and from the assumption of that duty [*munus*] they seem to have gained their name—bound by no other compulsions or any other law of the Roman people, except some law that their citizenry has itself approved. 7 Indeed, we have heard that the citizens of Caere were the first to be made "municipes" without the right of voting, and that it was conceded to them that they might in fact receive the honor of Roman citizenship, but that they would nevertheless be free from its tasks and burdens, ...

8 But the relationship of colonies is something else; for they come into the Roman state not from abroad nor do they grow from their own foundations, but they are, so to speak, grafted from the Roman state and they have all the laws and institutions of the Roman people, not of their own determination. 9 Which status, all the same, although it is more exposed to constraint and less free, nevertheless is considered better and more preferable because of the greatness and majesty of the Roman people, whose little likenesses and reflections, so to speak, these same colonies seem to be, and at the same time, because the laws of municipalities are obscure and forgotten, out of ignorance they [the townsmen] can no longer use them.

Teubner Latin text, ed. C. Hosius (Stuttgart, 1959), translated by the author.

CHAPTER 4

Changes Affecting Cities' Daily Governance and Economy

CHANGES OF CITY STATUS, acknowledged as a mark of prestige for the city thus recognized, seem impersonal in comparison to the emperor's municipal acts examined in this chapter, his interventions in a town's daily life. These include Hadrian's assumption of a city's highest magistracy or priesthood (now called "eponymous" because official dates in the town were given by the name and title of the individual(s) holding the position); his appointment of men, most frequently termed *curatores,* to oversee specific tasks in a city; his organization or rearrangement of a city's territory; and his promotion of men to towns' citizen lists or councils. Such imperial acts, immediately affecting a city's daily management and economy, are witnessed by epigraphic and literary sources, including treatises of land surveyors. Although such manifestations of Hadrian's care touched Rome's subjects "where they lived" and were undoubtably important to both city life and the cohesion of the empire, they did not radically change cities' social, political, and economic structures. Instead, they seem to have reinforced existing institutions and local power hierarchies, ultimately strengthening the nexus of power and obligation connecting emperor and local elites.

ASSUMPTIONS OF CITIES' HIGHEST MAGISTRACIES (AND PRIESTHOODS)

Compensating for the emperor's physical distance from most cities and territories under his control, Augustus and his successors encouraged the idea that the Roman emperor cared intimately for his subjects. One means used by the *pater patriae* (father of the fatherland) to show personal concern for the urban inhabitants of the Roman world was his assumption of a town's highest magistracy;[1] another means, much less frequent, was his assump-

---

[1] Such magistracies were titled variously in Greek cities, with forty titles from the archaic period through the Roman one collected by Sherk 1990a, 1990b, 1991, 1992, 1993; see also *Bull. Ep.* 1991 ##161 and 373. For Italy, see A. Degrassi, *Scritti vari di antichità* (Trieste, 1971), 73–76, 79–80.

tion of a municipal priesthood. Politics and religion were inseparable in the Empire, when most priesthoods were integral to a man's *cursus honorum* (political career) and demanded no special expertise or behavior other than what served also to raise him politically.[2] Imperial acceptance of local magistracies and priesthoods reinforced the emperor's eminence at the top of Rome's political and social hierarchies. As highest civic magistrate, the emperor reproduced on the local scene his position as supreme magistrate and judge; as local priest, he replicated in situ his position as *pontifex maximus* and the accumulator of multiple religious positions in Rome. Neither honorary magistracies nor local priesthoods held by emperors have been investigated systematically, despite their bearing on the relations between emperor and city.[3] I therefore integrate discussion of Hadrian's activity in this field with a historical overview of the phenomenon, beginning with honorary magistracies.

Hadrian is attested most frequently among the numerous emperors who are known to have accepted a town's supreme position.[4] Inscriptions, coins, and the "Life of Hadrian" (see below) place Hadrian in this capacity in four Italian cities, Naples, Hadria, Ostia (at least twice by 126), and an unidentified town near Formiae; in Spain at one city, his ancestral town, Italica; in Greece at three, Sparta (in 127/128), Delphi (at least twice, probably sometime in 118–20, and in 125), and Athens (in 111/112 or 112/113, before his assumption of the throne); in the Black Sea region at two, Byzantium (twice, unknown dates) and Odessus; and in Asia at two, Cyzicus (twice, unknown dates) and Colophon.[5] According to the biography's passage reporting some of these positions (quoted below), Hadrian held others in Latin cities, and assumed the leadership of the Etruscan League as well.[6] In all, twelve cities are attested as nominally under Hadrian's local leadership for at least a year; in four, Ostia, Delphi, Byzantium, and Cyzicus, Hadrian seems to have assumed the chief position more than once. Hadrian also accepted the religious position of *prophetes* at Didyma, and

[2] E.g., Gordon 1990a, 196–97, and 1990c, 201–31.

[3] Liebenam 1900, 261n. 4, lists epigraphic and numismatic evidence, mostly for towns in the Latin West; Sherk 1993, 285–87, provides a list for Greek cities, with reference to Robert 1938, 143–50; cf. Münsterberg 1973, 80–81, and Burnett et al. 1992, 4. On praefecti of emperors and others in the Latin West, see Ensslin 1954, and Wilmanns 1873, 625–26.

[4] Cf. Robert 1938, 143–50. Detailed evidence for Hadrian's positions is discussed and noted later in this chapter.

[5] L. Robert, *BCH* 102 (1978): 522–28, has shown that a "wandering stone," which has been attributed to Dionysopolis and lists Hadrian as *hieromnemon* for the second time (*IG* XII.9 1260), is from Byzantium. A fallacious entry in the *Liber Coloniarum* (231 L: *Ardea oppidum. Imperator Hadrianus censuit*, below, nn. 116–17) led Liou 1969, 12–13, to assume that Hadrian held the quinquennial duumvirate in Ardea.

[6] Liou 1969, 12–16, 81–88, arguing also that Hadrian reorganized this league.

may have twice been the eponymous priest of Apollo in Cyrenaican Ptolemais.

The extant municipal charters specify the plentiful civic duties administered by cities' highest magistrates, whose activities ranged from mundane decisions about their town's material fabric to determination of its political standing and future. In the town charter of Urso, for example, the duovirs' mandate included overseeing physical aspects of the city, such as the introduction of corpses within the city's boundary (lex Col. Gen., chapter 73), demolition of buildings (chapter 75), and legislation concerning roads, ditches, and aqueducts (chapters 77, 99, 100). It also encompassed religious matters, such as arranging gladiatorial shows or dramatic spectacles honoring Jupiter, Juno, and Minerva (chapters 70, 126), and determining festal days, sacrifices, and religious personnel (chapters 64, 128). Urso's duovirs judged or otherwise oversaw the legal settlement of most local disputes (chapters 94, 96, 102, 105, 123), and they advanced proposals to the decurions about embassies, patrons, and "public guests" (chapters 92, 97, 130, 131).[7] Similar responsibilities are mandated for the duovirs in charge of the Latin towns affected by the Flavian municipal law.[8]

Countless municipal inscriptions substantiate such directives as they witness duovirs and other supreme local magistrates in action throughout the empire.[9] Although the Flavian municipal law reveals that town councils actually made the most important decisions (see my chapter 3 at n. 54), the highest municipal magistracies carried more prestige. A local office symbolized the political and social repute of a man, denoting his ability to command, direct, and win consensus. By the second century, individuals reaching these positions paid specified amounts to the city, the *summa honoraria* discussed with euergetism in my chapter 3 at n. 44.[10]

The number and diversity of local duties undertaken by towns' officials make somewhat astonishing the rubric in the Flavian municipal law about conferring the duumvirate on Domitian (chapter 24), for it implies that the transaction was nothing unique.[11] The rubric details the town council's procedure for the decision, anticipating that the emperor will select a single praefectus (superintendent) to govern in his stead. It corresponds with

[7] In Urso, perhaps unusually, the senior duovir or a praefectus also headed the town's militia (lex Col. Gen., chapter 103; see chapter 3, n. 86).

[8] See González 1986, for chapters 20, 25, 27–29, 31, A–H, K, L, 52, 63–66, 68, 71–73, 76–79, 82, 84–87, 89–90.

[9] Cf. Langhammer 1973, 62–147.

[10] Duncan-Jones 1982, 82–88. Oliver 1953, 964, and Sherk 1993, 283–85, note that naming a deity as a city's eponymous magistrate probably enabled the city to take the *summa honoraria* from the treasury of the deity's shrine.

[11] Hardy 1912, 86n. 12, remarks as an oversight that the law names only Domitian, and not succeeding emperors as well.

relatively abundant epigraphic and numismatic evidence for emperors named as eponymous magistrates in Roman cities. The practice is also instanced by the lengthy passage in Hadrian's biography referred to above (*HA, Hadr.* 19.1), the only pertinent literary source that mentions the phenomenon in any city other than Athens.[12]

Hadrian's assumptions of local positions fit established practice. Alexander the Great was the first of a handful of Greek and non-Greek kings who accepted eponymous magistracies in prominent cities such as Miletus, Athens, and Chios, holding the honors in absentia, with their duties delegated to another.[13] Late in the Republic a few ambitious Romans also took on municipal magistracies outside their towns of origin: after Caesar reestablished Capua as a colony in 58 B.C., Pompey and L. Piso separately served there as duovir. Both apparently performed duties in Capua itself (Cic. *Post red.* 11.29, *Mil.* 15, cf. *In Pison.* 11.25; *Pro Sest.* 8.19, cf. *In Pison.* 11.25).[14] But these are isolated cases. Only with Augustus's rise to power does the phenomenon appear frequently in the Roman world, and from this time on individuals thus honored were members of the imperial family or, much more uncommonly, persons closely connected to the emperor.

During the Empire the phenomenon is particularly noticeable in the Julio-Claudian era, and most frequent during Augustus's and Tiberius's reigns. Agrippa, Germanicus, Tiberius, Caligula, and others are named at least seventy-five times as duoviri (quinquennales) and other high magistrates on coins and inscriptions. At least thirty-eight cities, from Spain to Asia, received this distinction.[15] Augustus himself is outnumbered on this

---

[12] Sandwiched between a list of Hadrian's legal initiatives and a generalized one of his urban benefactions, it reads: *in Etruria praeturam imperator egit. Per Latina oppida dictator et aedilis et duumvir fuit, apud Neapolim demarchus, in patria sua quinquennalis et item Hadriae quinquennalis, quasi in alia patria, et Athenis archon fuit* (The emperor held the praetorship of Etruria. In the Latin towns he was dictator, aedile, and duovir, in Naples the demarchus, in his home town [Italica] the [duovir] quinquennalis, and similarly the [duovir] quinquennalis in Hadria, as if in another home town, and he was archon at Athens; *HA, Hadr.* 19.1). Athens has special connotations for its foreign magistrates, cultural, religious (see *HA, Gall.* 11, and Julian. *Or. in laud. Const.* 8), and political (see Philostr. *VA* 8.16).

[13] Robert 1938, 144: Alexander, Demetrius Poliorcetes, Antiochus I, and Mithridates, in Miletus; Antiochus I, *strategos* of the Aitolian League; Antiochus IV of Commagene and Rhoimetalkas, in Chios; Rhoimetalkas, and perhaps Cotys of Thrace, in Athens; probably Cotys in Callatis.

[14] These, the earliest examples I have found, are noted by J. Beloch, *Campanien. Geschichte und Topographie* (Breslau, 1890), 322, but unremarked in Frederiksen 1959.

[15] The honorary magistracies of Augustus, Gaius Caesar, Drusus II, Tiberius, and Caligula are cited in the following notes, where praef. and p. are abbreviations for praefectus/i, and quinq., quin., q.q., and q. are abbreviations for *quinquennalis/es*. Also known are: Agrippa, at Carthago Nova (quin., with two praef., Heiss 1870, 270, #13); Germanicus at Caesaraugusta (with praef., who appears alongside a duovir, Heiss 1870, 201, ##18–21, though Heiss, p. 210, implausibly interprets the legend *praef. German.* uniquely on a coin for the

list. In the long period from his rise to power as Octavian until his death, he is attested as municipal magistrate in five cities,[16] whereas Gaius Caesar is named as magistrate in at least six,[17] Drusus II (son of Tiberius) in ten

---

military title "praefectus Germanorum"), Regium Lepidum (*CIL* XI 969; Ensslin 1954, 1319) Hispellum (with praef., *CIL* XI 5289), Fulginiae (p. ex s.c. . . . quinq. pot., *CIL* XI 5224), Interpromium (with praef. quinquennalici iuris ex s.c., *CIL* IX 3044 = *ILS* 2689), and Priene (*IPriene* #142); Nero Caesar (son of Germanicus) at Brixia (with praef. IIvir. quinq., *CIL* V 4374), Aquinum (with praef. q.q., *CIL* X 5393 = *ILS* 6286), Praeneste (with praef. IIvir. q.q., *CIL* XIV 2995; Ensslin 1954, 1320, attributes to the emperor Nero), ?Pompeii (between A.D. 23 and 31, as per Castrén 1983, 105), and Utica (Burnett et al. 1992, ##731–32); Drusus (son of Germanicus) at Salonae (with p. quinq., who served likewise for P. Cornelius Dolabella, *CIL* III 14712 = *ILS* 7160), and Utica (Burnett et al. 1992, ##733–34); an uncertain Caesar, and Tiberius, at Aequiculi (with praef. quinq. for the two of them, *CIL* IX 4122 = *ILS* 2644); Germanicus and Drusus together at Praeneste (with one praef. "quinquennali ordine ex s.c." in their place, *CIL* XIV 2964), Aquae Flaviae (with praef. Caesarum bis, *CIL* II 5617 = I 2479; Ensslin 1954, 1317, attributes this to Nero and Drusus Caesar, sons of Germanicus), Acci (IIviri, Heiss 1870, 257, #12), and ?Carteia (IIIIviri, Heiss 1870, 332, #29, and 334); Nero and Drusus Caesar (sons of Germanicus) together at Formiae (with one praef. for their designated quinquennial duumvirate, *CIL* X 6101 = *ILS* 6285, the same man who was earlier praef. quinq. of Tiberius), Praeneste (with praef., *CIL* XIV 3017), Caesaraugusta (IIviri, O. G. Farrés, "La ceca de la Colonia Caesarea Augusta," *Ampurias* 13 [1951]: 69, 83–84, ##103–12), and Carthago Nova (quinq., Heiss 1870, 271, ##28–29); an unidentifiable son of Germanicus at Praeneste (with praef., *CIL* XIV 2965; Ensslin 1954, 1317, referring to *CIL* XIV 3017, attributes this to Nero and Drusus Caesar, sons of Germanicus, together), Bononia (with praef., *CIL* XI 701; Ensslin 1954, 1319, attributes this to Nero Caesar); Nero (emperor) at Luna (with praef., *CIL* XI 6955), Cures (with praef. Neronis Caesaris Aug., *CIL* IX 4968 = *ILS* 5543), and ?Pompeii (conjectured by Castrén 1983, 61 and 108). A praef. for T. Statilius Taurus, who oversaw Illyricum in 34/33 B.C., served as quinquennial duovir in Dyrrachium at an unknown date (*CIL* III 605); a p. quinq. served in Salonae in A.D. 16/17 for P. Cornelius Dolabella, governor of Dalamatia, *CIL* III 14712 = *ILS* 7160, and also served for Drusus, son of Germanicus; L. Arruntius was duovir, together with Octavian, at Pella (Imhoof-Blumer 1883, 86–87, #100; non vidi); Juba II and rex Ptolemy were duoviri in Carthago Nova (Heiss 1870, 269, ##5–7, and *CIL* II 3417), and for Pisidian Antioch, see also n. 25 below. So far I have no evidence for Lucius Caesar serving as an honorary magistrate. Dubious cases of other Julio-Claudians are at Urbino, *CIL* XI 6058, and Caere, *CIL* XI 3610.

  [16] As Octavian: Pella (q.q., with L. Ar[r]untius) (Imhoof-Blumer 1883, 87, #100; non vidi); as Imperator Caesar: Carthago Nova (quin. with two praef., Heiss 1870, 270, #12; since the two praefecti are the same as those for Agrippa (n. 15 above) and both simply titled praefecti on one coin (Heiss 1870, 270, #19), it may be that Augustus and Agrippa accepted honorary positions together: cf. Ensslin 1954, 1320, and for location, see Keppie 1983, 113n. 59; Ucubi, Baetica (with praef., *CIL* II 1558); ?Caesaraugusta (H. Cohen, *Description historique des monnaies frapées sous l'Empire romain communement appelées medailles imperiales,* vol. I, 2nd ed. [Leipzig, 1930], 175, ##13–15); Heraklea-by-Latmos (*OGIS* 459, for the fourth time); Miletus (*IMilet* I.3 #127, in 17/16, 7/6 B.C.).

  [17] Gaius Caesar: Baeterrae (with praef. pro IIviro, *CIL* XII 4230); Ulia, Baetica (with praef., *CIL* II 1534; Heiss 1870, 271, ##30–34); Carmo, Baetica (with praef. quattuorvirali [potestate], *CIL* II 5120, on p. xlii; non vidi); Eresus on Lesbos (*IG* XII, supp. 124); Priene (*IPriene* #142); Heraklea-by-Latmos (twice, *OGIS* 459).

or so,[18] Tiberius in ten,[19] and Caligula in five.[20] Occurrences cluster in southern Spain (six cities) and at Caesaraugusta, although this phenomenon may be due to the unusual appearance of local coinage in Spain until the reign of Caligula.[21] Carthago Nova, Acci, and Caesaraugusta all boast more than one honorary duumvirate held by a member of the Julio-Claudian house (six, two, and four, respectively).[22] Central and northern Italy are also well represented, with Julio-Claudians holding honorary magistracies in eighteen cities from Brixia and Hasta in the north to Pompeii and Paestum in the south.[23] More spottily represented are the Adriatic and Black Sea regions (three cities, and one), Macedonia and the Aegean (one, and one), the Greek East (five), and North Africa (one). To my knowledge no honorary municipal magistracies were ever held in Gaul.[24]

[18] Pisidian Antioch, twice (with praef. IIvir., *CIL* III 300 = *CIL* III 6843 = *ILS* 7201); Hasta (with praef. IIvir. q.q., *CIL* V 7567 = *ILS* 6747; Ensslin 1954, 1319, attributes this to Drusus, son of Germanicus); Volaterra (with praef., *ILS* 6598); Aquinum (with praef. q.q., *CIL* X 5393 = *ILS* 6286); Aricia (as dictator, proposing a decree, *EE* VII 1236); ?Pompeii (A.D. 20/21, conjectured by Castrén 1983, 104); ?Cyzicus (*JHS* 1904, 28n. 28; cf. Robert 1938, 146). For other positions held in tandem with relatives, see n. 15 above. Ensslin 1954 attributes two of these to others.

[19] Before A.D. 17, in Carthago Nova (quin. with praef., Heiss 1870, 270, #14); Demetrias (= *strategos* of the Magnesian Confederacy, *IG* IX .2 1115); Cnossus (with another; *Journal International d'Archeologie Numismatique* 2 [1899]: 93; non vidi); Callatis in Thrace (*SEG* XXIV 1026); Priene (?twice or thrice, *IPriene* #142); Miletus (*IMilet* I.3 #127, A.D. 8/9); Formiae (with praef. quinq., *CIL* X 6101); Aquinum (with praef. quinq., *CIL* X 5392 and *CIL* X 5393 = *ILS* 6286); after 17: Paestum (R. Garrucci, *Le monete dell'Italia antica* CXXIII [1885]: 25; non vidi). For his positions held in tandem with another relative, see n. 15 above.

[20] In Caesaraugusta (with praef. alongside a duovir, Heiss 1870, 202, #25–26, #31); Carthago Nova (quinq., Heiss 1870, 271–72, #30–34); Cyzicus (*IGR* IV 145 = *Syll.*³ 798); Priene *(IPriene* #142); Pompeii (in A.D. 33/34, praefectus with a colleague, *CIL* X 901 = *ILS* 6396 and *CIL* X 902; again in 40, praef. i.d. with a colleague, *CIL* X 904).

[21] But from the Spanish provinces, only the honorary magistracies in Acci, Caesaraugusta, and Carthago Nova are known from coins.

[22] At Carthago Nova, Augustus, Agrippa, Drusus II, Nero Caesar, Caligula, and Tiberius; at Acci, Germanicus and Drusus the Elder; at Caesaraugusta, C. Caesar, Germanicus, Drusus II, and Nero Caesar. Southern Spanish towns represented by a single honorary magistracy are Ucubi (Augustus) and Baeterrae, Ulia, and Carmo (C. Caesar). Both Juba and Ptolemy rex held honorary duumvirates at Carthago Nova. Other marks of favor by "Julio-Claudians" to towns in southern Spain include the patronate of young Tiberius at Carthago Nova (*ILS* 144) and the patronate of Agrippa at Gades (Heiss 1870, 350, #42–46).

[23] Hasta, Drusus II, and Aquae Flaviae, Germanicus and Drusus II together; Brixia, Nero Caesar; Regium Lepidum, Germanicus; Bononia, a son of Germanicus; Luna, Nero; Hispellum, Germanicus; Fulginiae, Germanicus; Volaterra, Drusus II; Interpromium, Germanicus; Aricia, Drusus II; Praeneste, Germanicus and Drusus II together, a son or sons of Germanicus, and Nero Caesar; Aquinum, Drusus II and Nero Caesar together, and Tiberius; Cures, Nero; Aequiculi, Tiberius and an unknown Caesar; Formiae, Tiberius, and Drusus II and Nero Caesar together; Pompeii, Caligula twice, and perhaps Drusus II, Nero Caesar, and Nero; Paestum, Tiberius.

[24] In the Adriatic Sea region Octavian and L. Arruntius served at Pella; Drusus (son of

Some cities saw repeated honorary positions; for instance, Augustus four times and C. Caesar twice accepted the position of *stephanephoros* (epony-mous magistrate) of Heraklea-by-Latmos (*OGIS* 459), and Augustus was stephanephoros of Miletus twice (*IMilet* I.3, #127). Pisidian Antioch boasts among its duovirs Cn. Domitius Ahenobarbus, P. Sulpicius Quirinius, and M. Servilius, as well as Drusus II, twice.[25] The appearance in one city of so many nonimperial men as duovirs is exceptional. Since all Pisidian Antioch's honorary duovirs were Tiberius's friends, protégés, or relatives by blood or marriage, B. Levick has suggested that Tiberius may have formed a special connection with the colony as early as 20 B.C. while traveling to Syria.[26] As is true with Antioch, many of the cities boasting Julio-Claudians and their close associates as honorary magistrates are Caesarian-Augustan colonies, but this is not always the case.[27] With the reign of Tiberius the honor gen-erally narrows to the emperor himself, although later a few imperial "princes" and even two imperial women are cited as holding municipal magistracies.[28]

From the fall of Nero through the reign of Constantine, emperors and, more rarely, imperial relatives continued to accept municipal magistracies. Although the overall incidence is more sporadic than it was in the Julio-Claudian era (with its thirty-eight cities and seventy-five instances), Ha-drian stands out for the frequency of his municipal positions. From A.D. 69 to 337 at least twenty-four cities experienced some forty-four instances of the emperor, or someone close to him, serving as their chief honorary mag-

---

Germanicus) and P. Cornelius Dolabella at Salonae; and Ti. Statilius Taurus at Dyrrachium. In the Black Sea region Tiberius served at Thracian Callatis. In Macedonia Tiberius served at Demetrias, and in Crete and Cyrene he served at Cnossus. In the Greek East Augustus served four times, and C. Caesar twice, at Heraklea-by-Latmos; Augustus and Tiberius at Miletus; C. Caesar, Germanicus, Caligula, and Tiberius (at least twice) in Priene; C. Caesar at Eresus on Lesbos; and Caligula and perhaps Drusus II at Cyzicus. In Africa Drusus II and Nero both served at Utica.

[25] Cn. Domitius Ahenobarbus, the father of Nero (with praef., *CIL* III 6809); M. Servil-ius and P. Sulpicius Quirinius (praefecti attested for both, *ILS* 9502 and 9503). For Drusus, see n. 18 above.

[26] Levick 1967, 81 n. 6. S. Mitchell 1987, 349, notes the "striking coincidence" of these honorary positions and the construction, between the reign of Augustus and A.D. 50, of a vast urban precinct for imperial cult.

[27] E.g., Priene, Heraklea-by-Latmos, Aricia, and Pompeii were not Caesarian-Augustan colonies.

[28] For examples, see n. 29 below. T. Mommsen, *Gesammelte Schriften* (Berlin, 1905), I:308 and n. 64, 324, speculates that Tiberius restricted honorary magistracies to the emperor alone as a way to preclude honors for Germanicus's family. I find implausible the sole later nonimperial man cited as holding an honorary duumvirate, Ti. Statilius Severus (perhaps iden-tifiable as the most prolific brickmaker of Hadrian's day). Although an honorary decree for M. Cornelius M.f. M.n. Publ. Iustus Acutianus identifies Acutianus as a praefectus of Statil-ius (*CIL* X 3910, probably from Cales), the order of Acutianus's inscribed offices and hon-ors and the lack of any qualifier (such as "quinq.") for "praefec. Ti. Statili Severi," argue against assuming that Statilius held a municipal duumvirate.

istrate. Hadrian is attested in thirteen cities, for at least eighteen positions.[29] Beyond the obvious difference in quantity, other changes from the earlier period are notable. Most dramatically, there was only one honorary magistracy in Spain, Hadrian's quinquennial duumvirate in Italica. This contrasts with at least eighteen instances in seven cities during the Julio-Claudian period. As counterweight, in the north Balkans and Black Sea area (opened with Trajan's conquest of Dacia), four cities boast emperors and imperial relatives as eponymous magistrates.[30] Byzantium had as its eponymous priest-magistrate, *hieromnemon,* not only Hadrian (twice),[31] but Trajan (three times), Faustina the Younger, and Bruttia Crispina (the wife of Commodus). In Italy honorary magistracies cluster around Rome or at ports, with Hadrian "serving" at Ostia, Naples, and Hadria (on the Adriatic Sea).[32] The absolute number, ten, of Italian cities represented from A.D. 69 to 337 is about half the eighteen of the Julio-Claudian pe-

---

[29] Vespasian, once at Berytus (with praef. imp. Vespasiani Caesar(is) Aug., *CIL* III 170); Titus and Domitian together, once at Interamna (with two quinq. [praef.], *CIL* X 5405 = *ILS* 6125, A.D. 73); Titus, once at Delphi (archon: *BCH* 1894, 96n. 13 = *Syll.*[3] 817 = *F.Delphes* III.4, 34); Domitian, once at Athens (eponymous archon: Philostr. *VA* 8.16, cf. *F.Delphes* III.2, 65 and *IG* II[2], 1996); Trajan, eight times, in six cities: Miletus (*IDidyma* #293); Byzantium (thrice, B. Pick, "Die Personen- und Göttername auf Kaisermünzen von Byzantion," *N.Z.* 27 [1896]: 31), Aricia (*CIL* XIV 2213 = *ILS* 3243, dictator, with praef.), Attidium (with praef. i.d. imper., *CIL* XI 5669 = *ILS* 2728); Arimium (with praef. IIvir. quinq., *CIL* XI 421 = *ILS* 6662); Vardagate (with praef. i.d. imper., *CIL* V 7458); L. Aelius Caesar, twice, once at Ostia (with praef., *CIL* XIV 376; cf. Meiggs 1973, 492–96) and once at Colophon (Robert 1938, 147–49); Antoninus Pius, four times in toto, at Mazara (Sicily, with praef. imp. Antonini IIviri, *CIL* X 7211), Sarmizegetusa, Dacia (with praef. q.q., *CIL* III 1497 = *ILS* 7133, though Ensslin 1954, 1320, attributes this to Commodus), and at Cyzicus (*IGR* IV 117) and Delphi (*Syll.*[3] 848); Faustina the Younger, once at Byzantium (Pick, 34–35); Commodus, twice, once at Puteoli (IIvir quinquen., *CIL* X 1648) and once at Athens (*Hesperia* supp. 8.282); Bruttia Crispina, wife of Commodus, once at Byzantium (*IApameia und Pylae* #114); Maximinus, once at Colophon (*Mt. S.* VI 105 (s); Streber *num.* 213); Elagabal, once at Anazarbus (*BMC, Lycaonia,* p. 34, #20); Alexander Severus, once at Tarsus (*BMC, Lycaonia,* p. 203, #214); Gallienus, twice, once at Athens (archon: *HA, Gall.* 11) and once at Traianopolis in Thrace (*IBulg* III 1567 = *IGR* I 759); Constantine, once at Athens (strategos: Julian. *Or. in laud. Const.* 8; Eunap. *V. Aed.,* p. 22). More uncertain are the cases of Sarmizegetusa, Dacia (with q.q. primo, *CIL* III 1503, perhaps referring to Antoninus Pius), Tridentum (Italy) (where only a praefectus is named; Wilmanns 2163); ?Titus as demarch in Naples, *IG* I 729); Trajan or Titus at Ostia (*CIL* XIV 4674–75); and ?Pertinax at Ostia (*NSc* 1953, #54).

[30] Byzantium, Traianopolis, Odessus, and Cyzicus, as opposed to the sole earlier instance of Callatis; Byzantium and Cyzicus repeat such honors.

[31] *SEG* XXVIII 562, and *IG* XII.9 1260: see above, n. 5, and Sherk 1991, 235–36.

[32] The only city in northern Italy thus represented is Vardagate, just south of Vercellae; Attidium in Umbria also seems anomalous. Ports: Ostia, Puteoli, Ariminum, Hadria, Naples, and Mazara (between Selinus and Motya in Sicily). Hadrian in Ostia: *Insc. Ital.* 13.1, pp. 203, 233 = Smallwood, #24; in Naples: *HA, Hadr.* 19.1, cf. *CIL* X 1496; in Hadria: *HA, Hadr.* 19.1.

riod. In mainland Greece the cultural centers Athens, Sparta, and Delphi display emperors and prominent individuals as their eponymous magistrates, with Hadrian at all three; this contrasts with the sole honorary magistracy held during Augustus's reign, at strategic Demetrias in Macedonia.[33]

Throughout the imperial period in the West, the municipal magistracy nominally held by the emperor himself was usually the highest in the city. This position occurred every fifth year and was associated with censorial powers, and its holder was often titled either *duovir quinquennalis* or *duovir iure dicundo*. Additionally, but less regularly, the emperor, "princes," and others seem to have accepted the lesser-status annual duumvirate or some other "supreme" position.[34] Yet in only one instance is there any suggestion that a member of the imperial family actually directed a town's daily administration. If the common interpretation of a fragmentary inscription (*EE* VII 1236) is correct, as "dictator" of Aricia Drusus II proposed a decree there, thus presiding in person over the local curia at least that day.[35] But this case, early and close to Rome, seems the exception that proves the rule. Emperors and their kin held municipal positions in absentia, with a praefectus representing them locally.

We do not know if all praefecti served without colleagues during honorary magistracies, although this seems true for praefecti of emperors (rather than of imperial relatives). Inscriptions to individual praefecti furnish most of our data; with their focus on the honored individual and the emperor, their silence about a praefectus's possible colleague(s) is inconclusive. The Flavian municipal law envisions Domitian's praefectus as sole duovir (chapter 24), and sole power accorded an imperial praefectus would correspond to the overweening authority of the emperor. Moreover, single praefecti are known to have served for double honorary duoviri: one praefectus is designated for Nero and Drusus II at Formiae (*CIL* X 6101 = *ILS* 6285), one served for Tiberius and a Caesar in Aequiculi (*CIL* IX 4122 = *ILS* 2644); and single individuals served for the joint appointments of Germanicus and Drusus II at Praeneste (*CIL* XIV 2964) and Aquae Flaviae (*CIL* II 5617 = I 2479). On the other hand, coins from Pella list Octavian and L. Arruntius as duovirs together, and ones from Cnossus show Tiberius and a local colleague as duovirs (*JAN* II 93). Coins from Carthago Nova display Agrippa and Augustus as co-duovirs, and Germanicus's praefectus alongside a duovir.[36] During Caligula's honorary du-

---

[33] For Hadrian's positions in Athens, Sparta, and Delphi, see nn. 53–55 below. More isolated are Vespasian's duumvirate in Berytus, and the magistracies of Elagabalus and of Alexander Severus in Anazarbus and Tarsus in Cilicia Campestris. For Berytus, see Millar 1993, 279–81, 527–28; for Cilicia Campestris in the third century, see Ziegler 1993.

[34] See nn. 15 and 29 above.

[35] Mommsen 1887, 978.

[36] See nn. 15 and 16 above.

umvirates in Pompeii, in 33/34 and 40/41 (i.e., before his rise to the throne), his praefectus ruled jointly with a colleague (*CIL* X 901 = *ILS* 6396 and *CIL* X 902, *CIL* X 904 = *ILS* 6397),[37] and in Interamna on the Liris two praefecti [quinq.] took the place of Titus and Domitian as the town's quattuorviri in A.D. 73 (the supreme magistrates in this town; *CIL* X 5405).[38] Finally, the fragmentary Ostian *fasti* (local calendar) may indicate that two praefecti served in Hadrian's stead in 126.[39]

Known praefecti were persons of local or at best regional eminence, and prefectures for an emperor were the summit of municipal honors.[40] Yet it is uncertain how praefecti were chosen. The Flavian municipal law has Domitian choose his own praefectus (chapter 24), perhaps the custom for imperial praefecti. Three earlier cases of a praefectus's selection by a local council refer to praefecti serving for a relative of the emperor, not the emperor himself.[41] It may be that the choice passed from city to the emperor involved during the reign of Tiberius,[42] when honorary municipal magistracies became generally restricted to the emperor (noted above). In some cases the praefectus had clearly attracted imperial attention elsewhere: Nero's praefectus in Luna, L. Titinius Glaucus Lucretianianus, had earlier been made IIvir quinquennalis of the town by dispensation of Claudius, to whom he also owed his position as *flamen Augusti* (municipal priest of the imperial cult; *CIL* XI 6955). Thus imperial favor to a city was manifested by the promotion of one of the city's inhabitants. The personalized nature of the phenomenon can be gauged by the iteration of prefectures. In Aequiculi, for example, Sabidius served first as praefectus of C. or L. Caesar, and then as praefectus of Tiberius when the latter was on the throne (*CIL* IX 4122 = *ILS* 2644); a Q. Decius Saturninus in Aquinum was praefectus of Tiberius before A.D. 14, then praefectus of Drusus II, and finally praefectus of Nero, son of Germanicus (*CIL* X 5392 and 5393 = *ILS* 6286).

Only a few interpretations of honorary municipal magistracies have been advanced. P. Castrén, noting Caligula's honorary duumvirates in Pompeii and

----

[37] Puzzlingly, the two nearly identical inscriptions witnessing Caligula's honorary duumvirate (33/34) do not identify as his praefectus the same governing magistrate.

[38] Interamna's local calendar includes other years in which all four positions of quattuorviri were not filled.

[39] Meiggs 1973, 512.

[40] E.g., C. Nicolet, "Tribuni militum a populo," *MEFR* 79 (1967): 64; R. P. Duncan-Jones, in *JRS* 67 (1977): 196.

[41] "According to the council's decree" (*ex s.c.*), qualifies Germanicus's praefectus at Interpromium, *CIL* IX 3044 = *ILS* 2689, the praefectus at Fulginae, *CIL* XI 5224, and the praefectus of Germanicus and Drusus II at Praeneste, *CIL* XIV 2964. The Flavian municipal law (chapter 25) specifies that serving as a nonimperial praefectus did not automatically grant Roman citizenship, showing that in municipalities of this era the praefectus for normal duoviri could be a noncitizen.

[42] Veyne 1990, 458n. 252.

conjecturing three other Julio-Claudian duumvirates there, holds that such events either denoted internal crisis in a city or complimented "heirs apparent" upon imperial recognition. His first explanation has little support and his second rests upon conjectural cases.[43] According to R. Sherk, the phenomenon begs the "interesting historical question" of whether the emperors actually were present at the appropriate time in the towns of their honorary duumvirates. He rightly answers in the negative (cf., e.g., Cass. Dio 69.10.1 on Italica, discussed below),[44] but his question highlights the general enigma of the phenomenon. L. Keppie comments, with surprise, that so far no evidence shows Augustus as honorary duovir in any of his Italian colonies, despite other data for Augustus's enduring links with cities he colonized.[45] P. Veyne sees the practice originating so as to manifest "sentimental relations between powers which, though unequal, were independent or at least autonomous,"[46] and R. P. Duncan-Jones and W. Eck have called the practice "little more than harmless flattery."[47] In contrast, S. Mitchell proposes that the appointment of emperors, or their family members, to municipal offices provided the occasion for imperial contributions to the town.[48] This is corroborated by Commodus's letter accepting the position of archon of the Eumolpidae at Eleusis (see below), although we cannot prove the correlation in Hadrian's posts.

As B. Liou notes, apropos of Hadrian's leadership of the Etruscan League, emperors could choose which positions to accept. Liou cites Hadrian's ancestral ties as responsible for his honorary magistracies at Italica and Hadria, the Italian city from which his family had emigrated to Italica, his philhellenism for those at Naples, Athens, and other Greek cities, his own and the era's archaizing emphasis on Latium and Etruria for Ostia and other Italian cities (as well as for the praetorship of the Etruscan League), and his celebrated curiosity, which apparently accounts for all the others. Liou also argues for the influence of *amici,* suggesting that Hadrian's interest in the Etruscan League was encouraged by friends and relatives with Etruscan connections.[49] Liou is right to point to a multiplicity of factors influencing Hadrian's acceptance of municipal magistracies, and the reasons he postulates can be expanded, in light of other information, for Hadrian's relations with cities. This leads to the related topic

[43] Castrén 1983, 60–61, 105–6, although all his three conjectured honorary duumvirates are "complimentary." Reviewing Castrén's book (in *JRS* 67 [1977]: 196–97), R. P. Duncan-Jones points out that the only evidence adduced for the "internal crisis" explanation is Caligula's duumvirate of 40/41.

[44] Sherk 1993, 285–88; cf. Halfmann 1986, 138.

[45] Keppie 1983, 112–13.

[46] Veyne 1990, 458n. 252.

[47] Duncan-Jones in *JRS* 67 (1977): 197; Eck 1979, 16n. 33.

[48] S. Mitchell 1987, 348–49; cf. Duncan-Jones 1982, 88n. 4.

[49] Liou 1969, 14–15. For specific evidence for these positions, see notes below.

of Hadrian and local priesthoods, and I finish this section by exploring the effects of Hadrian's municipal magistracies and priesthoods.

In Italica, Ostia, Athens, Sparta, Delphi, Cyzicus, and Neapolis, Hadrian's honorary position was only one of his many marks of favor to those cities. Here I treat the evidence briefly. Cassius Dio contrasts Hadrian's largesse to Italica with his failure to visit there while emperor, implying that the latter was perceived as a snub (Cass. Dio 69.10.1). If so, Hadrian's assumption of its quinquennial duumvirate (*HA, Hadr.* 19.1; no date) and his elevation of the town to the status of colony (discussed in chapter 3) may have been aimed at conciliation. The many Julio-Claudian honorary magistracies in southern Spain suggest as well that Hadrian was consciously emulating Augustus. Different considerations seem important for Ostia, for this city was ever more vital to Rome's provisionment after Trajan's harbor was built. Hadrian's honorary duumvirates there, the second of which was held by A.D. 126 (*Insc. Ital.* 13.1, pp. 203, 233 = Smallwood, #24), were prefigured by one held by Titus or Trajan (*CIL* XIV 4674–75), and followed in 137/138 by one held by his adopted son, L. Aelius Caesar (*CIL* XIV 376).[50] The economic and political importance of Ostia enhanced the prominence of this city of Latium Vetus.[51]

Hadrian's positions in Athens, Sparta, and Delphi are part of his renewal of the "classical" Greek world, discussed in chapter 7.[52] His predilection for Athens was demonstrated early by his assumption of its archonship in 111/112 or 112/113, five years before he came to the throne.[53] He visited Sparta twice, in 123/124 and again in 128/129, and his patronomate dates to yet a third year, 127/128.[54] Hadrian served as archon two times at Delphi, probably in 118–20 and in 125.[55] Other Greek cities in which Hadrian "served" locally also participated in the panhellenic movement of his day. Neapolis (Naples), whose Greek culture was celebrated during the Roman Empire, apparently revived its links with Sparta during the Hadri-

[50] Pertinax, too, may have assumed the duumvirate in Rome's port (*NSc* 1953, #54).

[51] The period in which emperors assumed the duumvirate at Ostia coincides with the increasing rise to the duumvirate of "new men" and men of freedman descent, a "social revolution" discussed by Meiggs 1973, 189–206.

[52] Cf. Spawforth and Walker 1985, 81; Spawforth and Walker 1986, 96 (citing *IG* V.1 32b.13–14, 33.5, 1314b.26; *SEG* XI 489.5). Sometime before A.D. 125, Hadrian had envisioned making Delphi the center of a new panhellenic league: see chapter 7, n. 12.

[53] *HA, Hadr.* 19.1; *CIL* III 555 = *ILS* 308 = *IG²* 3286 = Smallwood, #109; Phlegon, *FGrHist* 257 F 36.xxv, with Follet 1976, 29 (contending that he held the position in absentia), and Weber 1907, 15.

[54] Bradford 1986 and Cartledge and Spawforth 1989, 108–10; references to the patronomate are in n. 52 above.

[55] *Syll.³* 830, 836, with Flacelière 1971, 170–71, and S. Swain, "Plutarch, Hadrian, and Delphi," *Historia* 40 (1991): 318–30, esp. 322–24. He was also responsible for restorations in Delphi, perhaps of the area Pylaia, and he may personally have appointed the soldier Pudens as supervisor (*Syll.³* 830).

anic period.[56] Cyzicus dedicated two statues to Hadrian in the Olympieion at Athens, and saw its temple of Zeus rebuilt by Hadrian sometime after an earthquake in 120.[57] Thus these two Greek cities, even though our current evidence does not show them to be members of the Panhellenion, joined in the Greek revival Hadrian's reign fostered.

The increasing importance of Byzantium and Odessus in the second century, the result of Trajan's success in Dacia and the consolidation of Moesia, may help explain Hadrian's assumption of municipal magistracies in these two coastal cities.[58] Trajan had been *hieromnemon* (eponymous priest-magistrate) in Byzantium twice, and Tiberius, who had devoted much of his military career to the north Balkans, had earlier accepted Callatis's chief position, that of *basileus* (the only example of an honorary magistracy in the Black Sea region prior to Trajan). Although strategic considerations may have attracted Hadrian's attention to Byzantium and Odessus, in both cities the eponymous magistracy was in fact an eponymous priesthood. The more pronounced religious aspect of Hadrian's honorary positions in Byzantium and Odessus accords well with another honorary magistracy Hadrian is known to have accepted, that at Colophon.[59]

Colophon's eponymous prytanis served simultaneously as the eponymous official of Claros, the famed oracular sanctuary of Apollo Klarios. Although the annual magistrate did not have a direct role in the oracular pronouncements at the shrine, the sanctuary was under his supervision (as opposed to the "panhellenic" sanctuary of Delphi, for example, under the control of the Amphictyonic League), and the name of Colophon's eponymous prytanis heads the many inscriptions recording delegations and visits to the oracle. The prestige of the municipal position at Colophon and its intimate relationship with the shrine at Claros are demonstrated by the number of times Apollo himself is named as Colophon's prytanis.[60]

[56] Spawforth and Walker 1986, 92; cf. e.g., J. H. D'Arms, *Romans on the Bay of Naples* (Cambridge, MA, 1970), 142–52. For Hadrian's assumption of Neapolis's chief position of demarchus (date unknown), see *HA, Hadr.* 19.1, cf. *CIL* X 1496.

[57] Benjamin 1963, 81, ##178–79 (= *IGR* IV 138–39). Hadrian assumed Cyzicus's highest magistracy twice, with his second hipparchonship falling between 123 and 132: *SEG* XXXIII 1056, with Sherk 1991, 244–46, 286.

[58] Hadrian as *hieromnemon* twice in Byzantium (unknown dates): *SEG* XXVIII 562, and *IG* XII.9 1260 (see nn. 5 and 31 above); Hadrian as eponymous priest in Odessus (unknown date): *IBulg* I² 49, with Sherk 1992, 234–35.

[59] Hadrian as eponymous prytanis of Colophon (unknown date; the position simultaneously made him eponymous prytanis at Claros, under Colophon's management): Robert 1938, 147–49, with S. Şahin, "Epigraphica Asiae Minoris neglecta et iacentia," *EpigAnat* 9 (1987): 66–67, #16, and Sherk 1991, 241–42.

[60] Robert 1969; Robert 1954, 6–7, pointing out that there was probably not even a village at Claros; Lane Fox 1987, 168–200, for the oracle of Claros and its place in the religious developments of the second and third centuries. Colophon refers to "Colophon on the Sea,"

Hadrian's honorary magistracy at Colophon, even more than his eponymous magistracies at Byzantium and Odessus, reinforced his position
as guarantor of political and social order.[61] Just as when Apollo himself
took on the post, Hadrian as prytanis of Colophon was responsible for
the smooth operation of Claros's shrine, and he sanctioned its oracular
responses.

Hadrian went one step farther when he accepted, in 136/137 or the
following year, the position of prophetes at Didyma's shrine.[62] As at the
less acclaimed shrine of Apollo in Claros, in Didyma specialized cult attendants mediated between human and god.[63] The prophetes at each
shrine held an annual position, whereas other cult personnel had appointments for extended periods or for life.[64] At Didyma the prophetes was the
most important of all the cult attendants, with even more prestige than the
Milesian stephanephoros, whose name headed the shrine's inscriptions.[65]
The prophetes wrote up the oracle's responses and conveyed them to those
requesting them. He additionally administered the Great Didymaeia,
funding these games and directing assistants.[66] The position had more
specialized religious duties than the other eponymous magistracies Hadrian accepted in Byzantium, Odessus, and Colophon.

Hadrian's assumption of the role of Didymaean prophetes publicly identified him with "magic" and more unconventional types of Roman religion,
whose popularity had been growing from the end of the first century.[67]
D. R. Edwards has pointed out the importance of oracles and oracular pro-
cesses in individuals' and society's attempts to control the future, and how
often the imperial authorities judged such endeavors antithetical to Rome's
greater interests.[68] By associating himself with the oracles at Didyma and
Claros, Hadrian appropriated these powerful symbols to the imperial
power itself. He assumed the Didymaean position in absentia, for he spent

---

the ancient town of Notion resettled by those who fled ancient Colophon in the early third
century B.C. Cf. La Genière 1990, 107–10.

[61] L. Aelius Caesar's subsequent appearance as Colophon's prytanis (above, n. 29) may
have been one way in which he was marked out for the succession.

[62] *IDidyma* #494 = Oliver, #87, pp. 219–20.

[63] R. Martin, "Le Didymeion," in *La Civilisation grecque de l'antiquité à nos jours,* ed. C.
Delvoye and G. Roux (Brussels, 1969), 302–3; Robert 1969, 309–11.

[64] Robert 1969, 310; Sherk 1991, 248.

[65] Sherk 1991, 247–48. Other kings, emperors, and princes had figured at Miletus as
stephanephoroi: Alexander, Demetrius Poliorcetes, Antiochus I, Mithridates, Augustus, C.
Caesar, and Trajan (nn. 13, 16, and 29, above); and Trajan had accepted the position of
Didyma's prophetes (*IDidyma* ##318, 407).

[66] Sherk 1991, 248.

[67] Gordon 1990b, 238–40, remarks on "magic" in Roman religion. Levin 1989, 1606–
15, remarks on oracular shrines.

[68] Edwards 1996, 120–30.

his last years in Rome and Baia. His interest in magic and oracles, reportedly keen throughout his life, increased during his final protracted illness (Cass. Dio 69.22.1; *HA, Hadr.* 16.7, 25.1–4).[69] Yet we cannot simply attribute Hadrian's honorary priesthood at Apollo's shrine at Didyma to an idiosyncratic, morbid irrationality. The pragmatic Trajan had similarly been prophetes, perhaps in 101/102 (*IDidyma* ##318, 407). Moreover, Hadrian may also have been eponymous priest of Apollo at Ptolemais twice by some time after A.D. 131.[70] These positions concur with other demonstrations of Hadrian's special interest in Apollo, his rebuilding of Apolline shrines at Abae and Megara in Achaea, and his restorations at the oracular shrine of Claros.[71]

One aim of emperors' honorary priesthoods is acknowledged in the later record of Commodus's acceptance of a priesthood, that of archon of the Eumolpidae at Eleusis.[72] Like the Didymaean position of prophetes, Commodus's priesthood also entailed an expensive duty, probably that of *panegyriarches* of the Mysteries in Boedromion.[73] Commodus writes that he accepted the title of archon "in order that, if the secret rites of the initiation during the Mysteries receive some additional support, worship may be rendered to the goddesses in a more glorious and reverent manner even on account of [me], and in order . . . that I may not seem . . . to decline the practical obligation of the honor."[74] Acknowledging that his acceptance of the priestly position and his assumption of its financial obligations will increase the cult's reputation, Commodus deliberately sets an example for others. Hadrian may have done the same as prophetes in Didyma and in his other positions elsewhere.

That imperial assumption of honorary municipal positions had exemplary results seems plain from *CIL* X 6090 = *ILS* 6295, an inscription found near Formiae. A devoted friend erected this to honor L. Villius Atilianus, an equestrian and patron of the colony. Atilianus had given a gladiatorial show and remitted money promised him by the populace "in the same year in which Hadrian, the best emperor, undertook the honor of the duumvirate."[75] We cannot identify the town Hadrian served as hon-

---

[69] Champlin 1976. The Great Magical Papyrus records how Hadrian was given a demonstration in magic by the expert Pachrates, the prophet of Heliopolis: *PGM* I, #2, IV lines 2442ff; see Birley 1994, 195–96.

[70] Reynolds 1990, 65n. 2, publishes the fragmentary evidence.

[71] The restorations at Abae and Megara are discussed in chapter 6, at nn. 80, 97–98; that at Claros, in chapter 6, n. 87.

[72] After A.D. 182: Oliver, #206; A. E. Raubitschek, "Commodus and Athens," *Studies in Honor of T. L. Shear,* Hesperia supp. 8 (Princeton, NJ, 1949), 285.

[73] Oliver 1989, 418–19, construes *to ergon tes times* as "the practical obligation of the honor," a euphemism for a costly duty he identifies as that of the panegyriarch.

[74] Translation by Oliver 1989, 418.

[75] . . . *eo anno quo et optimus imperator Hadrianus Augustus etiam duumviratus honorem suscepit, CIL* X 6090 = *ILS* 6295, lines 12–14.

orary duovir and Atilianus as generous patron,[76] but of greater importance for my purposes is the obvious link of Hadrian's duumvirate to local euergetism.[77] The inscription incidentally discloses a practical consequence of an imperial eponymous magistracy: by giving something noteworthy during that year, a benefactor associated him- or herself with the emperor simply by virtue of the emperor's name and position, which dated the deed.

I doubt, however, that Hadrian or any other emperor consciously tried to bolster municipal giving in any particular city by assuming its chief magistracy. Nothing indicates rampant urban distress in cities thus honored. Moreover, the random geographical spread of the towns thus singled out at any one period, the absence of correlation between the phenomenon and times and areas of crisis, and the general lack of large-scale programs and "rational" economic initiatives in the Roman world all argue against such a hypothesis. On the other hand, the great number and widespread distribution of honorary municipal magistracies early in the principate indicate that Augustus and Tiberius recognized that the practice entailed little from the emperor or his kin even as it conspicuously honored the community. Titular magistracies and priesthoods must have been key in consolidating municipal support for the emperor and imperial house. They manifestly valorized local civic positions. Even if the emperor never visited the city, by accepting a local office he proffered the illusion that the imperial power was on almost the same level as local notables. Moreover, the variety of the municipal titles Hadrian assumed, bewildering to modern readers, underscores his sanction of local traditions. Yet imperial assumption of a city's highest magistracies and priesthoods also proclaimed at a local level an emperor's supreme position in the Roman world.

Alongside such ideological effects, the titular positions occasioned an extraordinary office in their cities, that of the praefectus, who took over the many tasks of chief municipal magistrates delineated above. Although all identified praefecti predate Hadrian, they indicate that local men customarily "stood in" for the emperor or other honoree. Such elevation of individuals to political and social eminence in their own towns coincides with other ways Hadrian encouraged self-government in Rome's cities.

---

[76] The inscription is attributed both to Formiae and to Minturnae (cf. Liou 1969, 13n. 3, referring to, e.g., Mommsen, *CIL* X 603, 1100), although neither city is part of the voting tribe to which Villius is attached.

[77] Although the inscription does not specify Hadrian as Atilianus's model for municipal generosity, we should probably assume that Hadrian, like other local magistrates in the second century, contributed a *summa honoraria* (see chapter 3).

APPOINTMENT OF CURATORES

To various cities the emperor might send as his representatives *curatores*, men he appointed to oversee a certain task within a city or to supervise more generally a city or group of cities. Imperial emissaries could guide entire regions or provinces, as Pliny in Bithynia-Pontus under Trajan, but we focus here on municipal curatores.[78] Eight municipal curatores of Hadrian are known, of whom one served successively in Tarracina, Ancona, and Narbo (Gaul), five in other Italian cities (Beneventum, Venusia, Trebula Mutuesca, Matilica, and Comum), one in Nicaea (Bithynia-Pontus), and one in Trapezopolis (Asia) (ten cities in all).

Three of these eight curatores were entrusted with specified tasks in their cities. Hadrian selected C. Ennius C. f. Firmus, a local man, to supervise the construction of baths in Beneventum (*curator operis thermarum, CIL* IX 1419); a [———] Patrocles to manage public building in his native Nicaea ([*epistates*] *ton ergon, MuseumIznik, #*56 = *ILS* 8867); and C. Neratius C. fil. C. n. C. pron. C. abn. Cor. Proculus Betitius Pius Maximillianus, of Aeclanum, to oversee public building in nearby Venusia (*curator operum publicorum, CIL* IX 1160 = *ILS* 6485). In Beneventum Ennius also held the positions of aedile, duovir iure dicundo, and quaestor; he was thus a man of local eminence, although otherwise unknown.[79] Hadrian's charge to [———] Patrocles, who had commanded two Roman cohorts, to oversee public building in Nicaea fits this equestrian's other high positions in his native city, his family's reputation there, and the historic situation of Nicaea's rebuilding after a calamitous earthquake of A.D. 120 (see chapter 6 at n. 46). Neratius Proculus was distinguished in his native Aeclanum and its vicinity. In addition to being Hadrian's special representative to oversee public building at Venusia, Neratius served in Aeclanum as quaestor, duovir quinquinnalis, patron, and flamen of the deified Hadrian. Further, he received a special appointment from Antoninus Pius to oversee city finances at Nola, and he had marriage connections to L. Neratius Priscus, the celebrated jurist of Trajan's and Hadrian's era from Saepinum.[80]

Hadrian's five other known municipal caretakers were *curatores rei publicae*, a less circumscribed position. T. Prifernius Paetus served as Hadrian's

---

[78] E.g., Sherwin-White 1966, 527–28. For road curatores, see *DizEpig* II:1334–35, 1337, 1340, s.v. "curator." Much of the following information on Italy is explored in greater detail in Boatwright 1989, 247–50, 263–65.

[79] Boatwright 1989, 263–65.

[80] Ibid., 240.

curator rei publicae in Trebula Mutuesca, apparently around 137 (*AE* 1972, 153). Besides holding numerous offices in his Sabine home, including that of patron, this senator performed brilliantly in Roman politics, reaching the consulship in 146 and the governorship of Dalmatia around 156–59.[81] C. Arrius Clemens, Hadrian's curator in Matilica (on the Aesis River between Umbria and Picenum), was equestrian rather than senatorial, but he too returned to his *origo* to serve as curator and patron in the 130s (curator rei publicae, *CIL* XI 5646 = *ILS* 2081).[82] Less is known about M. Ulpius Damas Catullinus, whom Hadrian appointed as curator (*epimeletes*) of Trapezopolis, Asia (*OGIS* 492).[83] Ulpius Catullinus is attested securely only in this inscription. Its other information, that he was an *asiarches* (priest of the imperial cult in the province of Asia), establishes him among the provincial elite of Asia but gives no clues about his town of origin.[84] He certainly benefited Trapezopolis, which honored him as founder and benefactor (*ktistes kai euergetes, OGIS* 492).

Hadrian's last two curatores rei publicae served in this capacity more than once during their long careers. L. Burbuleius Optatus Ligarianus was Hadrian's curator rei publicae successively in Tarracina, Ancona, and Narbo (*CIL* X 6006 = *ILS* 1066), three port cities flourishing in the second century.[85] Burbuleius's three curatorships have been dated to the period 125–28 and associated with his attested financial positions, suggesting that this senator was a financial specialist.[86] He seems either to have come from Minturnae or to have possessed land there, according him a regional prominence that helps explain his initial curatorship in Tarracina.[87] Finally, Hadrian appointed as curator rei publicae of Comum P. Clodius Sura, an equestrian who had held the same position for Trajan in the neighboring city of Bergomum (*CIL* V 4368 = *ILS* 6725 = *Insc. Ital.* 10.5 [1985] 157). Clodius seems to have hailed from Brixia, a city along an unidentified but important Roman road running east from Comum through Bergomum and Brixia to Verona and Vicetia.[88]

---

[81] Ibid., 248.

[82] Ibid., 250.

[83] The more usual Greek equivalent of *curator* is *logistes,* although the transliterated *kurator* is also found.

[84] Rossner 1974, esp. 137. She tentatively identifies Hadrian's curator with [M.?] Ulpius Damas . . . , archiereus of Asia (*IEphesos* VI #2067), a relative of Ulpia Marcella, archiereia of Asia (*IGR* IV 1225, 1254, cf. *CIG* 3507–8). Burton 1979, 468n. 10, argues that Catullinus and other asiarchs of unknown origin did not come from the cities they served as curators.

[85] Boatwright 1989, 249.

[86] Corbier 1974, 187–89.

[87] Eck 1979, 200; Boatwright 1989, 249.

[88] Boatwright 1989, 249–50.

What is known of Hadrian's eight municipal caretakers fits with the general understanding of specialized curatores and curatores rei publicae, with the one distinction that the Hadrianic curators do not seem as foreign to the cities they served as do later holders of such positions.[89] Augustus and subsequent emperors occasionally appointed Roman citizens to oversee specific tasks in various cities and, like [————] Patrocles in Hadrianic Nicaea, our earliest example is from the Greek East.[90] This type of limited commission, relatively rare, tended to go to municipal notables or equestrians, as is true for Hadrian's three curatores with defined tasks.[91] Curatores rei publicae were usually of higher status and a more general supervision, often documented as including construction projects.[92] Curatores rei publicae begin to be attested relatively frequently during Trajan's reign, increasing slowly until the reign of Marcus Aurelius, then more quickly up to the third century.[93] Most curatores rei publicae are documented in Italy, though many are found in the African provinces, some fewer in other provinces in the Latin West, and about forty in Asia.[94] The relatively small number of Hadrian's curatores rei publicae and their geographical distribution correspond to the history of the position.

Most of Hadrian's curatores rei publicae served in Italy (with one additionally serving in Narbonese Gaul), suggesting that they should be evaluated within an Italian context. About eighty of the 140 known curatores rei publicae of Italy (ca. 57 percent) are senatorial, with the other sixty equestrian or municipal men.[95] Of Hadrian's four Italian curatores rei publicae, two were senatorial (Prifernius Paetus in Trebula Mutuesca; Burbuleius Optatus in Tarracina, Ancona, and Narbo), and two equestrian (Ar-

[89] The bibliography on curatores r. p. is discussed by Sartori 1989; Jacques 1983, 401–5. For my purposes the most important works are Duthoy 1979, Burton 1979, Camodeca 1980, Jacques 1983, Jacques 1984, and Eck 1979, 190–246. To my knowledge I am the only one to mark the Hadrianic distinction of curators.

[90] See Brunt 1974a, 182–83. Fabricius, a citizen of Alexandria Troas who had perhaps already held the chief magistracy in the town, apparently was *praefectus operum quae in colonia iussu Augusti facta sunt* (placed in charge of the works that were undertaken in the colony by the order of Augustus) even while prefect of the cohors Apula, suggesting that he may have used the cohort in the constructions. See also MacMullen 1959, 211n. 30.

[91] Boatwright 1989, 263; T. Corsten, "Ein Baubeauftragter Hadrians in Nikaia," *Epig-Anat* 10 (1987): 113–14, supplies six comparanda for Patrocles from the Greek East, although without dates. See also *DizEpig* II:1334–35, 1337, 1340.

[92] Sartori 1989, 16.

[93] Burton 1979, 466–79, on possible first-century curatores r. p., and the notable transformation of the office in the late third century, after which the curator was a senior magistrate of the local community.

[94] Sartori 1989, 6–7; Burton 1979, 482–87, lists thirty-eight in Asia, of which Hadrian's Catullinus is third. The two earlier examples are somewhat dubious.

[95] Sartori 1989, 6–7.

rius Clemens in Matilica; Clodius Sura in Comum and earlier for Trajan in Bergomum).[96] Most curatores rei publicae, especially those of senatorial rank, were not from the cities they served in this capacity, but from about seventy to one hundred kilometers away, two or three days' travel.[97] This distance fits the slight information we have about tasks of curatores rei publicae, which as a rule were sporadic and merely approbatory.[98] When local men served as curatores, they often were patrons of their towns as well, as were Prifernius and Arrius Clemens.[99] Since Hadrian's curator in Trapezopolis is the first securely attested curator r. p. in the province of Asia, it is more difficult to establish his context. G. P. Burton argues that curatores r. p. in Asia were not local men, which may hold true also for Catullinus.[100]

Forcing the limited numbers of Hadrian's curatores rei publicae, and considering also his more specialized curatores, we may discern a more local aspect for Hadrian's curatores than indicated by the Italian statistics. Four of Hadrian's eight curatores were well-respected local men: they were no alien intrusions in the cities they oversaw at Hadrian's request.[101] No evidence suggests financial or political weakness in the ten cities they served: we cannot see them as dispatched to intervene in a local crisis.[102] Rather, Hadrian's commissions elevate the chosen men and the towns they "cared" for.[103] These conclusions buttress recent arguments that during the second and much of the third century curatores had limited functions and short tenures.[104] Hadrian's curatores correspond with his other interventions in municipal life throughout the empire. They signaled his personal interest in the towns but did not disrupt local patterns.

The data for Hadrian's curatores r. p. do not specify their tasks, some of which may be inferred from his existing correspondence with cities. His let-

---

[96] If we look at cities rather than individuals, more cities received senatorial than equestrian curatores rei publicae from Hadrian.

[97] Sartori 1989, 7.

[98] Ibid., 9–20; F. Vittinghoff, "Zur Entwicklung der städtischen Selbstverwaltung," in *Stadt und Herrschaft*, ed. F. Vittinghoff (Munich, 1982), 115.

[99] Yet in neither case can we determine chronological order. See Sartori 1989, 7, 16–17, for general comments. In contrast to Neratius Proculus, *curator operum publicorum* of Venusia, *curator kalendarii* of Nola, and patron of his city Aeclanum, both Prifernius and Arrius served Rome in a more than local or regional capacity.

[100] See nn. 84 and 94, above.

[101] Burbuleius's appointments as curator rei publicae of Ancona and of Narbo are the only Hadrianic curatorships not given to men of local or regional standing, but in these two ports outsiders must have been less unusual than in inland towns like Trebula Mutuesca.

[102] Sartori 1989, 5–6, discusses such interpretations of curatores.

[103] Philostratus later calls Dionysius of Miletus's "greatest honor" his appointment by Hadrian as "satrap [curator or procurator] over peoples by no means obscure": Philost. *VS* 524; cf. Keil, *Forsch. Eph.* III 133 #47: Dionysius *epitropos tou Sebastou*, cited in *PIR²*, D105.

[104] Cf. Sartori 1989, 6; see n. 93 above.

ters about minor sums of money or the extent of local jurisdiction may represent the type of problems curatores rei publicae would be appointed to oversee for the emperor.[105] For instance, sometime during his reign Hadrian responded to Prusa about a controversy over its hot springs (Oliver, #106):[106] the dispute likely involved financial questions, and is comparable to difficulties Pliny dealt with as Trajan's representative in Bithynia-Pontus.[107] In another letter, from Gytheion in the southern Peloponnesus, the Roman proconsul refers to Hadrian's injunction, or request, to protect an endowment to the city as a favor Hadrian had granted when petitioned by the city's embassy (Oliver, #90).[108] A third letter, presumed to be written by Hadrian to Sparta, adumbrates the frequency with which individuals petitioned over the heads of local authorities.[109] In it the author forbids appeals to him about trials for sums below a certain level and about trials not concerning capital cases or citizenship. Once an appeal was made, the process had to be completed (see Oliver, #91).[110] Burton and others have pointed out that the protection of funds and endowments is part of the few extant sections of Ulpian's treatise on the duties of curatores.[111]

Yet during Hadrian's reign even such responsive duties may not have been foremost in the appointment of curatores rei publicae.[112] The great majority of Hadrian's caretakers served towns in Italy, ones relatively close to Rome at that; nothing records their tasks. Hadrian's municipal curatores seem appointed to work with, not dictate to, the communities they served.

---

[105] Burton 1979, esp. 474–77, with references to the extant sections of Ulpian's treatise on the duties of the curator, and to epigraphic evidence.

[106] L. Robert, *Études anatoliennes* (Paris, 1937), 231; G. Daux, *BCH* 91 (1967): 476–77, pl. 16; R. Demangel, *BCH* 64–65 (1940–41): 288.

[107] Pliny and baths, perhaps hot springs: *Ep.* 10.39.5, cf. Sherwin-White 1966, 593 on *Ep.* 10.23; Pliny and financial matters: *Ep.* 10.37, 39, 43, 47, 77, 90, 92, 98, cf. 10.43, 10.32.

[108] See also Oliver 1953, 965. Cf. Pliny and Trajan on *fideicommissa* to cities, *Ep.* 10.75–76.

[109] A practice decried earlier by Dio Chrysostom and Plutarch: Dio Chrys. *Or.* 45.8, 47.18, 48.3, 9; Plut. *Mor.* 815A.

[110] Abbott and Johnson 1926, #121; Oliver 1970b. Millar 1977, 514n. 45, doubts that this inscription emanates from an emperor. The now fragmentary letter does not specify to whom appeals about major cases should be directed, but the cases it cites as worthy of appeal to higher authority are more or less those the Flavian municipal law holds above local jurisdiction (chapter 84; the law predates the full development of curatores r. p.). Burton 1993 discusses the evolution of ways of dealing with matters exceeding local jurisdiction.

[111] Burton 1979, esp. 474–77, referring to *Dig.* 22.1.33, 50.8.12.2, 50.12.1.

[112] Eck (1996) has argued that Hadrian's establishment of the *IV viri consulares* in Italy, an institution known only from the *HA*, Appian, and an inscription and usually presumed to have limited itself to juridical duties, in effect imposed governors on Italy, diminishing the traditional power of both municipal elite and magistrates in Rome (especially the praetors, consuls, and praefectus urbi). If Eck is correct, the low profile of Hadrian's curatores may have mitigated the hostility Hadrian's innovation presumably provoked.

They demonstrated the emperor's responsiveness to cities, even as they exalted the appointees themselves.[113]

ORGANIZATION OF A CITY'S TERRITORY

Hadrian's organization of a city's territory is a difficult subject, due to both the obscurity of the sources attesting this imperial activity and the dearth of evidence for its effects.[114] Although details, firm data, and unequivocal conclusions are elusive, as with so many other topics related to the Roman economy, the evidence underscores the infrequency with which Hadrian meddled with cities' internal affairs in this way.[115] Six purported instances come from Italy, and one from Aezani in Asia.

Hadrian and land division are mentioned six times in the *Liber Coloniarum,* a work compiled in the fourth century from treatises written in the Augustan period and later.[116] Most of the references can be discounted. Two are patently false.[117] Another notes that in Veii Hadrian ordered inscribed boundary stones to be substituted for boundary markers of *lignei sacrificales* (special wood used ritually; 221L). Hadrian's Veian activity exhibits archaic and ritual aspects, sanctioning rather than altering an earlier land division in this venerable city just northwest of Rome.[118] As so often, Hadrian manifests interest in a city without breaching its autonomy. A fourth report, that Hadrian assigned land in Lavinium in strips as Vespasian and Trajan had done (234L), is not supported by aerial photography or other marks of Hadrian's interest in the town. It can be dismissed as untrustworthy.[119]

According to the other two pertinent passages of the *Liber Coloniarum,* in Lanuvium Hadrian assigned to his *coloni* (colonists) land originally as-

---

[113] My conclusion coincides with, but was arrived at independently of, Woolf's 1990 remarks on the general increase of alimentary rates in Italy.

[114] Since presumable effects are basically limited to the town concerned, I treat this topic here (cf. boundary disputes, which changed the relationships of towns, in chapter 5). I omit the modern speculation that Hadrian centuriated land at Cyrenaican Apollonia (see chapter 8, n. 62).

[115] Another intervention seems of a different type: sometime after A.D. 119 Hadrian granted Dictynnaeum (Crete) money from the sanctuary of Dictynna to pave the road from the shrine to the city (*ICret* II.XI.6). Ephesus furnishes an earlier instance of imperial transfer of sacred moneys from a shrine to its town, when Augustus directed that the shrine of Artemis help fund a protective wall for the Augusteum (*ILS* 97): Alföldy 1991.

[116] In the following I refer to the edition of the *Liber Coloniarum* of Blume et al. 1848–52, using page number followed by L. Overviews of the treatise include Keppie 1983, 8–12; Toneatto 1983; and Chouquer et al. 1987.

[117] Hadrian in Hispellum and in Ardea, 224L, 231L: see Boatwright 1989, 242–43.

[118] See Boatwright 1989, 243–44, for discussion.

[119] Ibid., 244.

signed by Augustus to his veterans and the Vestal Virgins (235L); in Ostia Hadrian, Trajan, and Vespasian assigned to their *coloni* land in various shapes (236L). Although without confirmation, the two notices have some plausibility in light of Hadrian's demonstrated interest in these ancient towns of Latium.[120] Yet the general absence of Hadrian's tribe, Sergia, in the two cities implies that veterans he discharged, the most common meaning of *coloni* in this context, were not settled on land allotments at either spot.[121]

Although no identification of Ostia's imperial *coloni* has been made, R. Meiggs has suggested that Hadrian, and Vespasian and Trajan before him, assigned Ostian land (perhaps even imperially owned land) to imperial tenants in an attempt to redress a drain of farmers to Ostia.[122] The number of farmers at Lanuvium, a city said to have been in decline during the imperial period, may have needed bolstering as individuals and families migrated to Rome.[123] Yet N. Morley's recent work argues forcefully for the prosperity of Rome's suburbium in the first and second centuries of the Empire, and for the high value and intense usage of its land.[124]

If Hadrian assigned land in the territoria of the two towns, it may have been to the landless poor of Rome in a liberal gesture anticipated by Nerva though evidently further afield (Cass. Dio 68.2; Pliny *Ep.* 7.31.4; *ILS* 1019, 5750).[125] The propinquity of Lanuvium and Ostia to Rome would have enhanced the allotments' desirability for the Roman poor, since colonists would not have to move farther than a day's journey to their new holdings. But we are now in the realm of speculation, a dangerous place given the uncertain understanding of the Roman economy and of the interdependence of town and countryside.[126] We should be wary of ascribing Hadrian's purported land assignments at Lanuvium and Ostia to any

---

[120] For Hadrian's repeated tenure of the duumvirate of Ostia, see n. 50 above; for his baths in the city, see chapter 6 at n. 69. For his work at two ancient temples in Lanuvium, see chapter 6, at n. 92.

[121] Cf. Keppie (1984, 107), who notes that veteran settlement in Italy ceased after Vespasian.

[122] Meiggs 1973, 267.

[123] Morley 1996, 178–80. Lanuvium's antiquity and religious associations may also have attracted Hadrian's interest.

[124] Ibid., 83–107. His rough definition of Rome's "immediate hinterland," most of which lies within thirty kilometers of Rome, includes these two towns.

[125] See also Keppie 1984, 104–5.

[126] See, e.g., Millett 1991. Hopkins's 1978 theory that urbanization, the spread of civic culture, and rural impoverishment were concomitant does not apply to these long-established cities even if it is valid. Many colonization schemes failed because of colonists' reluctance or inability to farm, most notoriously Sulla's settlement of his "Corneliani" in northern Italy. Keppie 1984 details difficulties during the imperial period.

"economically rational" scheme of repopulating arable land near Rome.[127] The two isolated acts make little sense, given the high demand for land close to Rome. I would reject the two imperial land assignments, for their local effects would have altered patterns of land-holding, wealth, and status too profoundly.[128]

Significantly, Hadrian's recorded settlement of a long-standing land dispute at Aezani mentions no local citizens: his decision of 125–26 could have only upset the city's elite landowners. Working through Asia's governor, T. Avidius Quietus, and calling for a survey of Aezani's territory by imperial agents, Hadrian ordered immediate or even retroactive payment of taxes (or perhaps dues) by those who were occupying land declared sacred to Zeus some four centuries earlier (*MAMA* IX, pp. xxxvi–xxxvii, ##P1–P4).[129] Since the Aezanites could not agree on the dimensions of their city's land parcels (*kleroi*), Hadrian ruled that the size of an Aezanite *kleros* was to be the mean of land parcel sizes in neighboring cities (#P2, lines 5–6, #P3, lines 4–7). Though the decision may express a desire for fairness and predictability,[130] it transgresses the principle of local autonomy. Aezani is the exception that proves the rule: Hadrian's activity affecting the internal relations of communities tended to reinforce the political and social status quo. The municipal interactions of Hadrian grouped in this chapter conferred honor on towns and their citizens; they did not confirm local dependency on the emperor, as the land redistribution schemes the *Liber Coloniarum* ascribes to him would have done.

ADDITIONS TO CITIES' CITIZEN ROLLS AND COUNCILS

Besides city foundations and refoundations, discussed in chapter 8, we have a few rare instances of Hadrian's direct imprint on the political and social patterns of a city. An inscription from Tarraco honors M. Valerius Capellianus of Damania (Tarraconensis) who, by favor (*beneficium*) of Hadrian, was also made a citizen of Caesaraugusta (also in Tarraconensis). This Roman citizen served in every official position in both cities (thus rising to the councils of each town), and as imperial flamen (priest of the provincial imperial cult) in the provincial capital Tarraco (*CIL* II 4249). Capellianus possessed dual local citizenship, a rare but not unparalleled phenomenon

---

[127] For well-grounded criticism of notions of Italian economic crisis and imperial economic policies at this time, see Patterson 1987.

[128] I depart here from my conclusion in 1989.

[129] Cox et al. 1988, xxxvi–xliii, provide a convenient translation into English and commentary. The letters were edited earlier by Laffi 1971, 3–53, and are supplemented by three boundary stones, dated to A.D. 129, from Aezani (##P5 and C8, C9, pp. 4–6 of *MAMA* IX).

[130] Alexander 1938, 174, remarks on Hadrian's desire for uniformity.

in the empire.[131] More peculiar is that he obtained his second local citizenship through Hadrian. In general this honor was decreed by the local town council, and to my knowledge there is only one other instance of an emperor's involvement in such an adlection (*CIL* II 4277).[132]

Slightly less unusual was imperial involvement in a man's elevation to a political position in a town, although only two examples involve Hadrian.[133] Both, from Ephesus, are sea captains who had helped convey Hadrian and his entourage across the Aegean twice before A.D. 129.[134] Nearly identical letters from Hadrian to Ephesus's council and magistrates, inscribed on the wall of Ephesus's bouleterion (council house), attest Lucius Erastus and Philokyrios, two mercantile men who were not Roman citizens but probably Ephesian freedmen (Oliver, ##82 A and B = *IEphesos* V ##1487 and 1488).[135] Hadrian notes that each man always helped his city to the fullest extent of his position and that each helped transport Roman authorities, including himself. For our purposes the important part of the letters comes at their end. In both missives, Hadrian first remarks that the man under discussion desires to be made town councillor, then explicitly leaves the individual's review to the Ephesians, and finally promises to pay the sum associated with entry into Ephesus's council if the petitions are approved.

The letters underscore the delicacy with which Hadrian promotes the two sea captains, men whose banausic livelihood excluded them, by custom, from political and social prominence in a Greco-Roman city.[136] Featuring the men's benefactions to Ephesus and their repeated service to Roman leaders, Hadrian intimates future largesse from Erastus and Philokyrios. He stresses, however, that the decision is local, reiterating the stipulation that each applicant pass Ephesian muster: "I make the decision *yours; if* nothing is an obstacle to him, but he seems worthy of this honor, I will give the sum . . . " (lines 12–14; emphasis mine). Although no city may have dared reject imperial canvassing,[137] Hadrian expresses his sup-

---

[131] Mackie 1983, 79, 89–90n. 6; Sherwin-White 1973, 303–6; *CodJ* 10.40.7.

[132] *CIL* II 4277: C. Valerius Avitus, citizen of the municipium Augustobriga(?), was made a citizen of Tarraco by Antoninus Pius. See Mackie 1983, 90n. 6; *DizEpig* I:414–16, s.v. "adlectio/allectio"; cf. Pliny *Pan.* 37.3, Gai. *Inst.* 1.93–94. The freedman whom Hadrian appointed as magistrate of the *collegium fabrorum tignorum* (guild of woodworkers) at Praeneste (*quinq. perp. datus ab imp. Hadriano Aug. collegio fabr. tign.*, *CIL* XIV 3003 = *ILS* 6255), falls outside my civic focus.

[133] Cf. *CIL* XI 6955, a duovir quinq. at Luna, *creatus beneficio divi Claudii; CIL* X 1271, a decurion *[be]nefic(io) dei Caesaris* in Nola; Pliny *Ep.* 10.39.5, 10.112; Dio Chrys. *Or.* 45.7–10, 48.11; and Oliver, #156 = *IBulg* IV 2263 = H. W. Pleket, *Epigraphica*, vol. I (Leiden, 1964), #24. See also Millar 1977, 395, on changes in numbers of councillors by imperial order, *ILS* 6090, and Abbott and Johnson 1926, #151.

[134] For this interpretation, see Drew-Bear and Richard 1994.

[135] See also ibid., 742–44, on the text.

[136] Cf. Pleket 1984, 136.

[137] Compare Favorinus's remark about yielding to Hadrian, cited in chapter 1.

port for these two atypical *bouleutai* most discreetly and with a promise not to override the city's decisions.

CONCLUSIONS

Respect for municipal autonomy characterizes the activities discussed in this chapter. Hadrian's interventions affecting citizens of Rome's cities in their own cities, the center of their political and social life, tended not to disrupt existing patterns. Moreover, the three "outsiders" Hadrian promoted to urban elites at Caesaraugusta and Ephesus participated fully in the traditional duties and obligations of their cities: they served their towns politically and, apparently, materially by benefactions. Indeed, his public endorsements extol their municipal benefactions and service.[138] Overall, the evidence for Hadrian's municipal interventions with internal effects discloses a profound respect for cities' autonomy and their traditions.

---

[138] Another individual Hadrian singled out as exemplary for his home town is C. Iulius Quadratus Bassus, cos. suff. 105, who died while serving as governor of Dacia in 117/118. On Hadrian's orders Quadratus's corpse was brought back with full honors at state expense to his native city, Pergamum: *IAsklepieions* #21, pp. 43–44. Hadrian also provided negative examples, as noted in chapter 1 (cf. Cass. Dio 69.23.2).

CHAPTER 5

Civic Benefactions with Extramural Effects

A DISTINCT GROUP of Hadrian's municipal interventions altered a city's relations with a neighboring city or cities, ones farther afield, or even Rome itself. This group includes his modification of cities' territory, either by "giving" a city land distant from its contiguous holdings or by settling boundary disputes; his determination of a city's taxes, revenues, or grain supplies; his promotion or ratification of festivals in a city; and his grants of various titles not marking a change of city status (cf. chapter 3). Although economic issues were explicitly recognized in some cases, in general such interactions were understood as signifying the emperor's magnanimity and the city's standing. This is especially true when two or more such decisions affected the same city. Cassius Dio, for instance, demonstrates Hadrian's imperial largesse and particular esteem for Athens by citing his completion of its Olympieion, his personal direction of its Dionysia games, his establishment of new Panhellenia games, and his grant to the city of large sums of money, an annual grain dole, and "the whole of [the island] Cephallenia" (Cass. Dio 69.16.1–2).[1] Dio here lumps together measures modern economists would differentiate, just as he does when marveling that Hadrian's generous assistance to allied and subject cities included giving aqueducts, harbors, food, public works, money, and various honors (69.5.3). Likewise, Hadrian's biography states, "in almost every city [Hadrian] both built something and gave games" (*HA, Hadr.* 19.2).

Hadrian's engineering works and public buildings are so numerous that I treat them separately in chapters 6 and 7, but in this chapter I discuss the other types of his benefactions lauded above. I begin with Hadrian's involvement with cities' land, and in turn discuss taxes and revenues; competitive games and festivals; and names and titles.

LAND ATTRIBUTION AND SETTLEMENT OF BOUNDARIES

Determining cities' territories always fell to the Roman authorities. Grants of land or of revenues from land, as well as settlements of boundary disputes, were considered *beneficia* of the emperor if he was personally in-

---

[1] Follet 1976, 115, treats chronological implications of the passage. I depart from her interpretation in that I see Cassius Dio shifting focus from Athens to Rome immediately after the quoted passage.

volved in the decision.[2] The few instances of land settlement attributed to Hadrian himself reveal how seldom he engaged in such largesse, and how highly it was valued.[3] Hadrian personally attended to the territory of six, perhaps eight, cities. Five are in Achaea: Athens (Cass. Dio 69.16.1–2), Sparta (*SEG* XI 490, and below), and Coronea, Orchomenus, and Thisbe (Oliver, ##111, 113, 114). One city, Abdera, is in Thracia (*AE* 1937, 170 = Smallwood, #448; *AE* 1937, 171), and one, Parium, in Asia (*AE* 1938, 140, cf. *ILS* 320). The two more uncertain examples are Uthina (*ILS* 6784) and Colonia Canopitana, both in Africa Proconsularis (*CRAI* 1979, 404–7).[4]

Hadrian's "grants" of land to Athens and Sparta are relatively clear, albeit both with difficulties. Their singularity reflects the importance Hadrian accorded these two cities as he cultivated the glorious Greek past and encouraged the Panhellenion.[5] Yet Cassius Dio's claim that Hadrian gave (all of) the island Cephallenia to the Athenians (69.16.2) cannot be accepted at face value. Pliny's earlier designation of this island, west of the Gulf of Corinth, as "free" (*libera*, *HN* 4.54) shows that it was not part of the imperial fiscus in his day. As late as 131/132 Pale, the westernmost of Cephallenia's four major cities, proclaimed itself "free and autonomous" in a dedication to Hadrian in Athens's Olympieion (*IG* II² 3301). Hadrian apparently granted Athens the revenues from some part of, rather than from all, the island. Although he did not place Cephallenia entirely under Athenian control, the abnormality of any land grant in his day may account for the exaggeration of Cassius Dio's report.[6]

---

[2] Alföldy 1991, 160–61; Mommsen 1887, 1126–29. Although in his definition of *beneficia* Mommsen includes freedom from taxation, I treat this separately below.

[3] I omit as outside the scope of this book Hadrian's demarcation of imperial holdings in Cemenelum, Gaul (*AE* 1981, 600), of the border between Thrace and Moesia (*AE* 1985, 733, cf. *ILS* 5956), and of imperial timberlands in Lebanon (e.g., Smallwood, #457, and Breton 1980, with R. Meiggs, *Trees and Timber in the Ancient Mediterranean World* [Oxford, 1982], 85–87).

[4] In the records of boundary disputes settled by an official "on the authority of Hadrian," the agency of the legate, not Hadrian, is paramount, so I omit them; see, e.g., *Syll.*³ 827c = Smallwood, #446, from Delphi; *ILS* 5947a = Smallwood, #447, from Lamia, Achaea; *MAMA* V 60, between Dorylaeum, Asia, and Nicaea, Bithynia: cf. H.-G. Pflaum, "Légats impériaux à l'intérieur de provinces sénatoriales," in *Hommages à A. Grenier,* ed. M. Renard (Brussels, 1962), III:1236–37; *PIR*² J 573; Halfmann 1979, 151–52, #62; *AE* 1939, 160, cf. *ILS* 5977–80, from Cirta, possibly connected with the Trajanic reorganization of territory and judicial status proposed by Gascou 1972, 111–15; and the mutual boundary of the Sacilienses, the Eporenses, and the Solienses near Corduba, *AE* 1913, 3, a better reading of *CIL* II 2349 = *ILS* 5973.

[5] See chapter 7 and, e.g., Cartledge and Spawforth 1989; Alcock 1993, 152, 162–64, who notes that Hadrian's largesse enabled cities to survive economically. Calandra 1996, 84, sees Hadrian's gift to Athens of Cephallenia ("Cefalonia") simply as emulation of Antony's earlier donation to Athens of Aegina, Ceos, Eretria, and three other small islands.

[6] Day 1942, 188.

The evidence is even more oblique for Hadrian's land grants to Sparta. Four allusive inscriptions have been reconstructed to suggest that Hadrian handed over to Sparta's jurisdiction three land masses: Caudus, a small island off the southwest coast of Crete; Coronea, a small but prosperous Messenian port with a fertile hinterland (both "given to Sparta" in the 120s); and the island of Cythera, southeast of Sparta (given to Sparta in 136). The first two "gifts" are attested epigraphically by the presence in them of Spartan *epimeletai* (supervisors). The third is documented by Sparta's revival of the title of "Cytherodices" ("judge of Cythera"), a title held by Spartan governors of the island in Sparta's heyday (Thuc. 4.53).[7] The sparse Spartan testimony lacks even the slight economic context Cassius Dio's passage accords the grant of Cephallenia to Athens. It reflects instead Sparta's erstwhile hegemony over Caudus and other parts of the Peloponnesus, evoking the heyday of Sparta's power.[8] These two *beneficia* demonstrate Hadrian's munificence and his high esteem for the recipient cities.

Inscriptions from Abdera (Thrace) illustrate the welcome accorded Hadrian's territorial grants by their beneficiaries (*AE* 1937, 170 = Smallwood, #448; *AE* 1937, 171). Calling itself "the City of the Hadrianeian Abderans," Abdera gratefully raised dedications to Hadrian because "by means of his divine providence" their boundaries were extended to the river Nestor and they recovered ancestral land. The inscriptions, apparently set up on the new frontiers themselves, assimilate Hadrian to Zeus Ephorios, Zeus of the Frontiers.[9] In this case the favored city casts Hadrian's benevolence as divine. In their extravagant language, the inscriptions underscore the indebtedness of Abdera to the emperor. Further, by using religious terminology in the record of a political act, the Abderans may have aimed at raising the decision beyond reversal.

Other epigraphic evidence for this type of activity, although less effusive, underscores the passions aroused by cities' land. Three nearly identical Latin inscriptions from Parium, an important port on the Turkish Hellespont, are dedicated to "Hadrian, Jupiter Olympius, the founder of the

---

[7] Cartledge and Spawforth 1989, 108–11, for the gifts, citing *SEG* XI 494, *IG* V.1 34 .11 (*SEG* XI 479), *IG* V.1 36.24–25 (*SEG* XI 480); *IG* V.1 44.7–8 = *SEG* XI 486.7–8, *SEG* XI 495. The three "gifts" would resemble the earlier *adtributio,* by which a community outside the proper territory of another, dominant community, is combined administratively and juridically with the second: Laffi 1966, 87–98.

[8] Cartledge and Spawforth 1989, 108–11; they try to establish an economic context but note that "there is no evidence to suggest that [Sparta's revenues] were in an especially parlous state at the time." Other allusions to Sparta's ancestral laws are found in Hadrian's letter to Cyrene, discussed in chapter 8.

[9] L. Robert, *BCH* 102 (1978): 441–42; *Bull.Ep.* 1972, 270. "Mestor" is inscribed incorrectly on the stone for Nestor, the nearby river. The more complete *AE* 1937, 170, differs in details from *AE* 1937, 171, which lacks Hadrian's assimilation. Hadrian may have similarly defined the borders between Apamea and Apollonia (which were the borders between Asia and Galatia): Robert 1963, 358–59n. 3.

colony" (*conditor col[oniae]*, *IParion* ##7–9).[10] Their text is echoed on an inscription found in the 1930s at Hexamili, on the upper neck of the Thracian Chersonese across the Propontis (*AE* 1938, 140). Arguing persuasively that its findspot is original to the latter inscription, Zahrnt contends that these texts did not commemorate some "refounding" by Hadrian of the Augustan colony at Parium. Rather, the emperor attributed to Parium land on the Thracian peninsula across from it, and in gratitude Parium erected multiple corresponding dedications to Hadrian in the city itself, its contiguous territorium, and its newly acquired tract across the straits.[11] An abbreviated H appears as part of Parium's name on coins struck from Pius's reign into that of Gallienus, suggesting that the city assumed the honorific name "Hadriane."[12]

Less satisfactory evidence has suggested to some that Hadrian granted land to Uthina and demarcated land in Colonia Canopitana, two cities in North Africa. From the Roman Forum comes a lacunose dedication to an emperor in his thirteenth year of tribunician power, erected by Uthina "increased [and preserved] by his indulgence" (*indulgentia eius au[cta et conservata]*, *CIL* VIII 2427 = *ILS* 6784). Because the reconstructed inscription echoes a dedication Ostia raised to Hadrian in 133 (*CIL* XIV 95 = VI 972 = Smallwood, #476), C. Hülsen and others conjecture that the emperor responsible for Uthina's gain is Hadrian. This would date Uthina's inscription to 134.[13] Hadrian's "indulgence" also appears on an unusual Hadrianic boundary stone from Colonia Canopitana, a town some fifteen kilometers northeast of Uthina. Headed "In accordance with the indulgence of Hadrian," the inscription marks three thousand feet of (from?) the "league" or territory of Colonia Canopitana (*Ex indulgentia Hadriani*, *CRAI* 1979, 404–7). It is unclear if this stone marks some donation by Hadrian of land (from imperial property?) to Colonia Canopitana or a simple settlement by him of boundaries between the community and one of its neighbors.[14]

---

[10] *IParion* #8 = *ILS* 320 = *CIL* III 374 = Smallwood, #491. Only a few minor differences distinguish the Thracian inscription cited below from the three of Parium, which themselves differ but slightly.

[11] Zahrnt 1988b, 239–42; cf. Robert and Robert, *Hellenica* IX, 88–89. See also chapter 3, n. 5.

[12] Zahrnt 1988b, 241–42; W. Wroth, *British Museum Catalogue of the Greek Coins of Mysia* (London, 1892), p. 102, #83; pp. 104–9. As we see at the end of this chapter, Hadrian's permission was not required for such a name change.

[13] E.g., C. Hülsen, *RömMitt* 1901, 96; Gascou 1982, 186. For refutation of the suggestion that the "increase" was made by joining the Roman colony there to an indigenous *civitas* supposedly living next to it, see P. Quoniam, *RE* 9.A.I (1961): 1178, s.v. Uthina; and, with different arguments, Gascou 1982, 186.

[14] If a boundary dispute, it can be compared to *AE* 1936, 137 (cf. *CIL* VIII 7084–88), a boundary stone in Madauros, Numidia. This baldly states: *Ex auct(oritate) Imp. Caes. Tra-*

As we saw in chapter 2, the specific language associated with imperial generosity at this time does not denote any particular type of benefaction. Nothing attests that the emperor to whom Uthina raised a dedication at Rome had granted land to this African city; although the emperor in question may be Hadrian, he does not have to be.[15] Yet lavish acknowledgments of Hadrian's liberality were more than mere rhetoric: their fervor and frequency reflect how essential imperial munificence was in mediating Roman political, economic, and social relationships.

Interchange between emperors and cities about land is incidentally but tellingly depicted in a dossier of letters from Coronea, Boeotia. The major topic is an engineering project to control flooding of Lake Copais (described in chapter 6), which evidently triggered land and tax disputes between Coronea and its neighbors, Orchomenus and Thisbe.[16] In one missive Antoninus Pius writes to the Coroneans about a recurring conflict over lands mutually claimed by them and their southern neighbor Thisbe: apparently even after Hadrian had judged the lands Coronean and Pius had reaffirmed the decision, the Thisbeans grazed animals on them without paying pasturage fees (A.D. 154/155; Oliver, ##113, 114). Pius displays some impatience as he appoints the proconsul to see to a speedy resolution of the lengthy dispute, which "affords cause and occasion to your cities [for strife and] rivalry."[17] The Coronean letters illuminate the seemingly intractable nature of boundary disputes, as well as suggest their financial impact on a city's revenues through fees and the like. In this, the letters match other information on boundary disputes of the period (e.g., Smallwood,

---

iani Hadriani Aug. agri accept. [———] separa. (other side:) *A P C.* An undated dedication to the numen of the Lares Aug. by a *disp(ensator) regionis Thurb. Maius et Canopitan.* (imperial steward of the district Thurburbo Maius and Canopitana, *ILAf.* 246) suggests extensive imperial lands in the region. I am not convinced by Beschaouch 1979 that the phrase *ex indulgentia* cannot refer to settlement of a boundary dispute and thus attests Hadrian's grant of colonial status to Canopitana: *ILS* 5960, similarly beginning *ex indulgentia,* marks the limits assigned to the Numidians by Hadrian's procurator in Mauretania. See Gascou 1982, 186–87.

[15] No evidence supports interpreting Ostia's claim to be "preserved and increased by Hadrian's indulgence" as anything more than magniloquent gratitude for other benefactions from him (see chapter 2, n. 59 and following, and chapters 4, 6). In the fourth century *indulgentia* connotes remission of taxes or remittance of punishments, and *munificentia* or *liberalitas,* attributions of vacant land: Carrié 1992, 418–19.

[16] From its probable placement in the dossier, the lacunose Oliver, #111, appears to have been from Hadrian to the Coroneans. Its first part mentions an engineering project, most likely that discussed in the earlier letters, and it ends by announcing that the emperor charged the proconsul to enforce his prior prohibition of the Orchomeneans to collect taxes, presumably ones levied on former floodplains rendered arable and claimed by both Coronea and Orchomenus.

[17] Translation Oliver 1989, 269. The dispute continued, apparently to be settled by Pius later in A.D. 155: Oliver, #116.

##446, 447). With this background one can better understand the Ab-
derans' praise of Hadrian, "Zeus of the Frontiers," whose "divine providence" led him to settle land problems in their favor.

INVOLVEMENT WITH TAXES; BESTOWAL OF REVENUES AND GRAIN

The central government exacted from citizens and others in its cities taxes
in many different forms, from annual or recurrent taxes such as poll taxes,
taxes on land, or *portoria* (tolls), to miscellaneous and extraordinary levies
such as the "crown tax," the "spontaneous" contribution of money expected from cities at imperial accessions.[18] The cities were responsible for
collecting taxes for Rome in addition to ones for their own use.[19] Although
the details of Roman finances are still unclear,[20] there can be no doubt that
taxation was resented. Communities and individuals alike eagerly pursued
and wildly appreciated tax remissions and exemptions, which were possible
only through the emperor.[21] Hadrian's remission in 118 of tax arrears and
taxes upcoming for the next ten years was widely publicized, and Duncan-
Jones now suggests that it helped spur local spending during Hadrian's
reign (see chapter 1, at n. 32 and following). Yet remission of taxes in the
provinces reduced imperial revenue, and the treasury was drained by imperial *congiaria* (handouts) at Rome, building programs, and other celebrated
acts of generosity (Pliny *Pan.* 41.1).

The infrequency with which Hadrian seems to have granted specific tax
remissions or exemptions after his initial, spectacular act of generosity in
A.D. 118 may be due to his understanding of their economic import.[22]
Hadrian had publicly detailed the state's financial difficulties even while re-

---

[18] Neesen 1980, with Brunt 1981; Corbier 1991. We may have evidence of a new tax imposed by Hadrian, if Oliver is right in assigning to Hadrian his #56. This, probably addressed
to the Lyncestae of Macedonia, orders that the costs of paving a military road in the region
(the Via Egnatia?) be shared by the Lyncestae ($\frac{2}{3}$) and the nearby Antani ($\frac{1}{3}$). See also L.
Robert, *REG* 47 (1934): 33.

[19] See Corbier 1991, 229–30. A splendidly detailed example of local taxes in a Roman city
during Hadrian's reign is the "Tariff of Palmyra": Levick 1985, 89–95, #82; Matthews 1984;
Zahrnt 1986. Its record reveals final Roman say over local tax collection (cf., e.g., Levick
1985, #81, pp. 88–89, and A. H. M. Jones 1940, 135, 244–47).

[20] In Brunt's words (1990, 386), "Our ignorance of Roman finances . . . is profound."

[21] Millar 1983.

[22] Cf. Augustus's explanation to Samos in 31–27 B.C. of why he would not grant them
immunity: "For it is not right for the greatest privilege of all to be granted at random and
without cause. . . . It is not the money that you pay for tribute which concerns me, but I wish
the most prized privileges to be given to no one without suitable cause" (Reynolds 1982,
#13). His express mention of money directly reveals his awareness of the financial conse-
quences of such grants.

mitting the crown tax for Italy and lowering it for the provinces (*HA, Hadr.* 6.5). Only one inscription substantiates this report of lowered crown taxes for provincial cities. A fragmentary letter from Hadrian to Astypalaea is often interpreted as sanctioning a reduction or remission of the crown tax the city owed at his accession (A.D. 118; Oliver, #65 = Smallwood, #449b).[23]

In contrast, all Hadrian's other references to tax remissions or immunities confirm previous exemptions of imperial taxes rather than conferring new privileges.[24] For example, in A.D. 119 Hadrian specifically confirmed Aphrodisias's exemption from the Asian tax on nails (a tax not attested before the discovery of this inscription), even as he noted his prior confirmation of the "freedom and autonomy" previous emperors and the Roman senate had granted the city (Oliver, #69).[25] Although "freedom and autonomy" probably included immunity from taxation, that Hadrian subsequently had to stipulate Aphrodisias's exemption from one particular tax reveals how precarious the general privilege was.[26] Similarly, his other references to tax immunity are to confirmations, not new grants. In a letter to Delphi in 118 he ratified grants of previous emperors, including "freedom and autonomy" (Oliver, #62, lines 8–10). Astypalaea, a small Aegean island, similarly saw its "freedom [and autonomy]" confirmed by Hadrian (Oliver, #64, A.D. 118),[27] as may have the community tentatively identified as Samos, which received a letter possibly written by Hadrian (Oliver, #107). In all three cases the emperor acknowledges the cities' joyous acclamation of his accession, evidence Millar has used in depicting urban fervor in the Greek East at tidings of a new emperor.[28] The rejoicing must have been been doubled upon hearing that earlier tax immunities were expressly confirmed.

[23] I find perplexing the last phrase extant in Hadrian's letter to Astypalaea: "[From] your decree, I learned . . . not how much [the money offering] was nor how long ago you had begun to pay it." Would not these two facts be obvious, if the discussion concerned a customary contribution? Cf. Larsen 1938, 458n. 28, and Millar 1997, 429n. 58. When Severus Alexander declared a remission of the crown tax for all the cities in Italy and the provinces, he cited as examples only Trajan and Marcus Aurelius (*Select Papyri* #216, rev. ed. in *Archiv für Papyrusforschung* 14 [1941]: 44–59, A.D. 222).

[24] Like Titus, Domitian, and Nerva before him, Hadrian issued an edict upon accession confirming the grants of his predecessors: *Dig.* 27.1.6.8. Suet. *Tit.* 8, cf. Cass. Dio 66.19.3 and 67.2.1; Pliny *Ep.* 10.58.3 and 10.58.7–9; and Millar 1977, 413–18, note emperors' renewals and grants of *beneficia* upon accessions.

[25] L. Robert, *BCH* 107 (1983): 509–11: the "use of iron" also mentioned in the letter is the exploitation of iron ore found in Aphrodisias's territory.

[26] Reynolds 1982, 116–17; Millar 1977, 429; cf. Bernhardt 1980.

[27] = *IGR* IV 1031c = *Syll.*[3] 832 = Smallwood, #449a.

[28] Millar 1977, 418, highlighting the "constant challenge" of cities' rights and duties by their neighbors, "in which the evidence of an up-to-date imperial reaffirmation could be of crucial importance."

In addition to Hadrian's letter to Aphrodisias attesting the Asian nail tax (Oliver, #69), a few other inscriptions document Hadrian's dealings with specific taxes and exactions. A long imperial rescript at Pergamum, attributed to Hadrian on the basis of its lettering and use of the imperial "we," has been dated to A.D. 129 on its presumed connection with Hadrian's visit to Ephesus in that year (Oliver, #84 = Smallwood, #451).[29] The rescript, couched as a response to Pergamum about matters conveyed by its ambassador, narrates the imperial hearing of a dispute concerning the concessionaires of Pergamum's public bank (the *trapezitai*). As the rescript moves from charge to charge, it reveals imperial concern to see that all parties abide by an earlier contract and by just standards. The emperor asserts his intent to preserve tax revenues for the city, to ensure that fish dealers not be overcharged while changing monies, to keep prices down during festivals, and to prevent abuses of power by the *trapezitai*. The inscription now breaks off while discussing the local composition of the jury to try abuses.[30] In a long letter to Delphi on various matters (A.D. 125; Oliver, #75), Hadrian incidentally reveals that a community could pay a lump sum to obtain in perpetuity the rights to a harbor and pasturages (i.e., without further fees).[31] In both cases the exactions under discussion are local ones, whose revenues went to local authorities.

In a letter of A.D. 127 (Oliver, #79), Hadrian grants to Stratonicea-Hadrianopolis the taxes from the rural area, as is "only just and necessary to a recently established city" (see also chapter 8). Again the financial information is frustratingly vague. Scholars have suggested both that revenues from imperial land in the neighborhood were granted to the city to support its growth, and "that Hadrian was granting the city the right to levy new direct (or indirect) taxes on its territory," which would remain with the city rather than be funneled to the central government.[32] An inscription from Eleusis may document a ruling by Hadrian about a sales tax on fish (Oliver, #77). The "Fish Tax" decree, attributed to Hadrian only on the basis of its letter forms, exempts the fishermen of Eleusis from Athens's two-obol tax while selling at Eleusis, and entrusts to the court of the Are-

---

[29] Oliver 1989 ad loc., p. 213. The inscription is also published as *IGR* IV 352 = *OGIS* 484.

[30] The bibliography is extensive: see Broughton 1938, 892–95; Bolin 1958, 238–43; D. MacDonald, "The Worth of the Assarion," *Historia* 38 (1989): 120–23; Harl 1996, 114, 116, 209, 259. Macro 1976 calls the imperial resolutions "measured and benign."

[31] Column II, lines 31–40, of Oliver, #75. In another letter to Delphi, now too fragmentary to reconstruct, Hadrian mentions the Amphictyons and finances several times (Oliver, #76).

[32] Broughton 1934, 222–23; Burton 1993, 17–18, respectively. According to Millar 1977, 426, this is more likely a request for the right to raise certain indirect taxes on the land than for a remission, or even diversion, of Roman indirect taxes.

opagites in Athens the control of profiteering by vendors.[33] The fragmentary decree offers some parallels to Hadrian's dealings with other local taxes: as in Delphi, Stratonicea-Hadrianopolis, and Pergamum, although Hadrian intervenes in the dispute, he reaffirms local authority to collect and supervise local imposts. Millar uses this and other evidence to emphasize that cities needed imperial assent even for changing internal taxes.[34]

One last intervention, Hadrian's Oil Decree at Athens (Oliver, #92), also illustrates Hadrian's influence on local finances. A long inscription, now heavily weathered, decorates the jamb of the main entrance to the "Roman Agora."[35] With a terminus post quem of 126/127, it regulates the sale of olive oil produced in Attica.[36] In two places the law refers to Hadrian himself: he is to be informed if an oil merchant is denounced after sailing away without making a formal declaration; less unusually, he and the proconsul are named as those who receive appeals (Oliver, #92, lines 46–47, 55–56).

Oliver compares the Oil Decree to the rescript to Pergamum about exchange rates (Oliver, #84), holding that their common purpose was to demonstrate the coincidence of local and Roman law in the matters under dispute.[37] Yet, in contrast to the other laws and epistles I have discussed, the text from Athens attests an unusually high level of Hadrian's involvement. The other rescripts relegate problems either to local authorities or to appointees from Rome,[38] whereas the Athenian Oil Decree twice defines Hadrian as arbiter. Hadrian's greater attention to the matters covered by the Oil Decree may pertain to his purported revision of Athens's ancestral laws.[39] At Athens Hadrian assumed the role of *nomothetes* (law-

---

[33] Most scholars presume the decree was impelled by the possibilities of food shortages at Eleusis during the celebration of the Mysteries, when the sanctuary became extremely crowded: Graindor 1934, 127–29; Oliver 1989, ad loc., pp. 194–95.

[34] Millar 1977, 426–27.

[35] *IG* II² 1100, re-edited by Oliver 1953, 960–63; see also Graindor 1934, 74–79; Day 1942, 189–92; Follet 1976, 117 and my chapter 7, appendix 7.5.

[36] Olive growers must deliver to Athens one-third of their olive oil, except the producers on the former estates of Hipparchus, who may deliver only one-eighth; growers must make formal declarations about their produce, its export, and their buyers; the merchants must declare in writing how much they are exporting from each producer. Violations under a certain value are to be reviewed by Athens's council, ones over that value by Athens's council and demos together. Informers are encouraged by the award of half the value of disputed oil upon a conviction. At the end of what survives, the text lays out judicious arrangements about surplus production and protections of current market prices. See Oliver 1989, ad loc., pp. 237–38.

[37] Oliver 1989, 236. In Oliver, #75 lines 37–40, Hadrian promises Delphi an investigation of Amphictyonic decrees that differ with one another or with Roman law.

[38] Cf. the general absence of the emperor in the Flavian municipal decree, discussed in chapter 3 at n. 91.

[39] Vers. Arm. *Ab Abr.* 2137 (A.D. 121); Hieron. *Ab Abr.* 2138 (A.D. 122); Eus., ed. Helm, p. 198, Sync. 659, 9, cf. Hieron. *Chron.*, ed. Helm, p. 592 (Graindor 1934, 30–32): Plácido

giver), an epithet accorded him in Megara and Cyrene.[40] Hadrian's unusual concern with Athens's laws shows yet again his deep interest in Athens.

This interest is borne out as well in Hadrian's supply to Athens of the annual grain dole Cassius Dio notes (69.16.2).[41] Other than Rome, only Athens had an annual, imperially funded grain supply: Hadrian's benefaction to this provincial city was unique.[42] Although a few cities besides Rome and Athens had their grain supply personally attended to by an emperor, of these only Ephesus and Tralles also benefited from Hadrian.[43]

According to an inscription (*IEphesos* II #274 = *Syll.*[3] 839 = Smallwood, #494), in A.D. 129 Hadrian granted Ephesus permission to buy Egyptian grain. A separate letter sent by an unknown second-century emperor to the Ephesians throws some light on this city's purchase of Egyptian grain, a commodity normally monopolized by the Roman government (*IEphesos* II #211).[44] Now beginning with a reference to the magnificence

---

1992. Some change in Athenian law during this period seems reflected in *IG* II² 1104, the law concerning defaulting debtors (Follet 1976, 117n. 7, and Geagan 1973), and in the reorganization of the Athenian bureau of the *opisthodomos* (Follet 1976, 117n. 8; Oliver 1965, 126–29).

[40] Megara, *IG* VII 70, 72; Cyrene, *SEG* IX 54 = *SEG* XVII 809. Follet 1976, 116–25; Oliver 1989, 238; A. P. Christophilopoulos, *Athèna* 69 (1967): 17–53; Weber 1907, 91, 165–66, 180; *Bull.Ep.* 1960, #438. Hadrian's image as lawgiver is also alluded to by *Orac. Sibyll.* 12.173–74. The high level of Hadrian's interest in the Oil Decree resembles his involvement in Cyrene's refounding, discussed in chapter 8.

[41] It has been suggested, more or less explicitly, that Hadrian was responsible for establishing an alimentary scheme in Athens: Woolf 1990, 227; Alcock 1993, 113. If so, this would be the only imperial alimenta established outside of Italy other than Hadrian's program for citizen children in Antinoopolis (for which see chapter 8 at n. 131). Yet the current evidence, an acephalous inscription probably from the Athenian Agora (*IG* II² 2776), does not definitively attest an alimentary scheme in Athens, much less Hadrian's responsibility for it: Miller 1972 (suggesting that the inscription recorded the financing of an endowment for the "University of Athens"); cf. Day 1942, 221–35.

[42] See, e.g., Spawforth and Walker 1985, 90, who attractively connect the annual supply to Athens's new importance as the head of the Panhellenion. Only this brief mention in Cassius Dio documents the annual supply. Constantine later granted Athens an annual grain dole: Julian *Or. in laud. Const.* 8.

[43] For the possibility that Hadrian provided Cyrene with a donation of grain, see chapter 8, n. 47. Although *ABSA* 26 (1923–25): 163 A 10 has suggested to some that in the 120s Hadrian authorized a Spartan to import Egyptian grain to Sparta (Cartledge and Spawforth 1989, 152–53; Halfmann 1986, 138–39), this seems most dubious in light of the inscription's silence about Hadrian: Garnsey 1988, 256. Garnsey 1988, 234, notes Hadrian's general ruling that only those who invested "the greater part" of their resources in the service of the annona could enjoy immunity from municipal liturgies.

[44] Wörrle 1971, with Robert and Robert, *BCH* 107 (1983), #465. Garnsey 1988, 255, translates part of the latter letter. Wörrle 1971, 340, advances other possibilities for the imperial author.

of Ephesus and the multitude of its inhabitants, the fragmentary inscription promises that if a surplus of Egyptian grain is produced that year, Ephesus will be among the first cities, after Rome itself, to be allowed to receive some of the surplus. M. Wörrle argues from this and other evidence, including the inscription from Tralles discussed below, that *IEphesos* II #274 does not record a "gift" of grain (as Hadrian's annual grain supply to Athens seems to be). Rather, it records imperial permission to Ephesus to buy Egyptian grain, a product under direct Roman control.[45] Similarly, in A.D. 127 nearby Tralles was allowed to buy sixty thousand modii of Egyptian grain through the money and agency of A. Fabricius Priscianus Charmosynus, a local grain commissioner who had gained the favor of Hadrian (*ITralleis und Nysa* #80 = *CIG* 2927).[46] Since the temporary grants were merely provisional, the inscriptions seem to commemorate Hadrian's interest in the welfare of Ephesus and Tralles rather than particular boons.

All the benefactions discussed above involve Hadrian's donations of goods in kind, or his sanctioning or remitting local taxes. It is hard to imagine how he would or could have "given money" outright to various cities.[47] Yet Cassius Dio and others recount gifts of money to Athens and other cities, at times even citing sums. It may be that in some cases actual money was transferred to a city while in others the sources refer to the value of what was built or achieved with imperial subventions. The first scenario seems to have prevailed at Alexandria Troas, where an aqueduct Hadrian was financing was denounced as exhausting the tribute of five hundred cities after its costs had reached seven million drachmae (Philostr. *VS* 548).[48] The second seems to be true for Hadrian's gift of ten million drachmae to Smyrna "in a single day," which the great sophist Polemo arranged: Philostratus, who provides this information, then immediately lists the buildings constructed with the sum (Philostr. *VS* 531, cf. *VS* 533, cf. *IGR* IV 1431). (The two benefactions are discussed in chapters 6 and 7.) The infrequency of actual figures in the data for Hadrian's municipal

---

[45] Wörrle 1971, 335–37.

[46] Ibid., 335. Garnsey 1988, 256, speculates that Hadrian's freedman Phlegon of Tralles was somehow involved. Halfmann 1986, 138–40, 204, proposes that Hadrian was traveling through Tralles in A.D. 127. *CIL* III 444 may record a gift(?) from Hadrian in 128–30 to the Romans(?) living at Tralles. The Romans living at Tralles, collectively, were partly responsible for the inscription dedicated to the Hadrianic grain commissioner.

[47] MacMullen 1959, 210, is more dubious about imperial gifts of cash than Mitchell 1987, 344, or Millar 1977, 420–34. The topic is bedeviled by the controversial extent of Rome's monetarization (its use of actual bullion and coined money rather than goods in kind): Howgego 1994; Whittaker 1990; Duncan-Jones 1990; Lo Cascio 1981; Crawford 1970.

[48] See S. Mitchell 1987, 346–47. This would generally fit the model of taxation and expenditure proposed in Hopkins 1980.

interactions suggests that he strongly preferred benefactions that were not simply financial outlays. This inference accords with the fiscal prudence implied by the rarity of Hadrian's tax remissions and exemptions.

COMPETITIVE GAMES AND FESTIVALS

Hadrian's promotion of a city's agonistic (competitive) games is one benefaction not entailing imperial expenditure yet promising much for a city's status and well-being.[49] Festivals featuring gymnastic, equestrian, musical, and/or dramatic competitions characterized life in the Greek East, where almost every city seems to have staged at least local games.[50] The evidence for Hadrian's association with festivals, which I have compiled for twenty-one cities, runs the gamut. For some cities, such as Smyrna (see chapter 7), Hadrian's involvement is well documented on many levels and even linked to construction or reconstruction of imperial cult temples. For others, however, only coins, victors' honorific epithets, or enumerated prizes witness a game's "Hadrianic" title: we thus hear of the Hadrianeia Philadelphia games of Alexandria, and the Olympia Pythia Hadriana games of Tralles, for instance.[51] As is true for cities with "Hadrianic" titles in the Greek East, discussed at the end of this chapter, we cannot be certain that Hadrian personally intervened with the city in some way to occasion the name change. In every case, however, cities apparently promoted their "Hadrianic" games in order to suggest a link to the emperor himself. In turn, Hadrian seems to have recognized games' cultural significance, and especially their functions of weaving the routines of Roman city life together with the figure of the Roman emperor.

Greek games during the imperial period were divided into two major types. Somewhat less prestigious were games known as "themides" (or "agones themateitai"), in which victory conferred a cash prize (*thema*);

[49] I have not found any evidence that emperors contributed materially when sanctioning new games, as suggested by S. Mitchell 1990, 191.

[50] The history of such games has still to be written, despite much recent interest in the subject. Fundamental are Price's anthropological treatment of imperial cult festivals (1984b, 102–7 and passim); S. Mitchell 1993, I:217–25; S. Mitchell 1990; Spawforth 1989; Robert 1984; Pleket 1975; Wörrle 1988; Ziegler 1985, 9–12.

[51] S. Mitchell 1993, I:218–19, notes the limitations of the ancient evidence. The two forms, *Hadrian(e)ia* and *Hadriana,* appeared interchangeably, at least at Smyrna: Robert 1977, 29. Partial lists are found in Le Glay 1976, 358–64; Lämmer 1967, 39; Moretti 1953, 275; Stengel, *RE* VII.2 (1912): 2165, s.v. Hadrianeia. The third-century date of many attested titles underscores the longevity of the prestige associated with Hadrian's name and civic munificence. On double or multiple titles for games, see Price 1984b, 103–4; Ziegler 1985, 10–11. I omit discussion of Oliver, #74, a fragmentary letter from Hadrian to Delphi that mentions games.

these were staged annually, biennially, or every four or eight years. The more acclaimed "sacred" or "sacred crown" festivals (the "agones hieroi kai stephaneitai") entitled winners to a "sacred crown," which was dedicated to the gods.[52] Sacred crown games were held at two- or four-year intervals, with the most eminent ones held every four years. (This group is often called "penteteric," after their Greek name derived from the inclusive reckoning of their occurrence.) These had the éclat of the four great festivals of the renowned "ancient circuit" of Olympia, Delphi, the Isthmus, and Nemea, specially emulating the prominence of Olympia and Delphi, and their celebrations were staggered so as not to clash.[53] Despite some differences, local and sacred crown games corresponded in many ways. Both might last several days. Their comparable promise of glory and money attracted traveling professionals, mainly from the guilds of performing artists and of athletes discussed below, as well as local contestants.[54] Both could include equestrian events, gymnastic competitions such as foot races and wrestling, and contests of musical, theatrical, and poetic performance.[55] Finally, sacred crown festivals needed imperial sanction but, as with the Demostheneia discussed below, some themides are also attested as approved by the emperor.[56]

Agonistic games served many functions in the Greek East. They reenacted and reconfirmed the grateful acceptance of the emperor and Rome by the cities staging the games. The inscription recording the foundation of C. Vibius Salutaris at Ephesus, for example, specifies that costly statues he donated be paraded through the city and exhibited in the theater during Ephesus's penteteric games and the imperial cult festivals, as well as during other more traditional Ephesian religious celebrations (*IEphesos* Ia #27, lines 48–56, 202–14, 554–60). His statues represented Trajan, Plotina, the Roman senate, the Roman equestrian order, and the Roman people; also portrayed were Augustus, Artemis, the city of the Ephesians, and Ephesus's demos, six tribes, boule, gerousia, and ephebeia (elders' or-

---

[52] A. H. M. Jones 1940, 185, 343n. 56, suggests that their victors (called "hieronikai") were also entitled to substantial privileges in their native cities, including immunity from local liturgies. By the later second century, the highest-ranking sacred games were known as "hieroi kai eiselastikoi": Spawforth 1989, 193–94. See below, n. 69.

[53] For their schedule, see Pleket 1973; Robert 1984, 44; S. Mitchell 1993, I:219. For the "ancient circuit," see, e.g., Robert 1984, 36; Spawforth 1989, 193.

[54] Robert 1984, 42–43; S. Mitchell 1993, I:218, with evidence for money prizes also at the sacred games.

[55] See references in n. 54 above, and Robert 1984, 36; S. Mitchell 1990, 189.

[56] Robert 1984, 38, noting that the senate could join the emperor in authorizing games; L. Robert, *CRAI* 1982, 228; Wörrle 1988, 175–82; S. Mitchell 1993, I:221. Cyrene requested permission from Antoninus Pius to establish games: see chapter 8, n. 53.

ganization and youth organization).[57] The images of the Roman imperial family and state head the list, and they can be presumed to have led off the processions. Dating from A.D. 104, the text shows the convergence of "Roman" and local elements during urban rituals in the Roman Greek East.[58]

The record of the theatrical festival established by C. Iulius Demosthenes of Oenoanda (Lycia) in 124/125, which was ratified by Hadrian himself (see chapter 2 at n. 54 and following), registers not only competitions, prizes, personnel, and processions, but also the civic priest and priestess of the emperors and the imperial image of Hadrian on the crown worn by the agonothete (president of the games).[59] Again the ties to Rome and the emperor are tangibly expressed. Oenoanda's account delineates the civic elite mediating the exchange: the benefactor Demosthenes, the officials of the imperial cult, and the impresario of the festival that bore Hadrian's imprint. Analogously, at the opening of local themides and of more prestigious games the reigning emperor, deified emperors, and the imperial house were regularly lauded in prose and/or poetry.[60] In turn Roman emperors, including Hadrian, accorded various privileges to the guilds of performers who traveled from festival to festival, although Roman favor to these groups had begun already in the late Republic (see below).

Further, games associated with neocorate temples (provincial temples for the imperial cult, such as that in Smyrna discussed in chapter 7 at n. 64) enabled regional relations to be worked out and displayed as an entire province or conventus (regional assembly) met in honor of the imperial house.[61] Of critical importance for a city was its position in the provincial hierarchy, as we saw above in the imperial letter promising Ephesus that it will be "among the first" after Rome to purchase surplus Egyptian grain. Designation as "neocoros"—a city where the provincial cult and temple of the emperor were located—was eagerly pursued. A city's classification as neocoros apparently entailed the building or rededication of a temple there, as well as the establishment of "sacred" games for the imperial cult.[62] When, in the 80s, more than one

[57] *IEphesos* Ia #27; see Rogers 1991, 34n. 67. Rogers reproduces and translates the inscription in his appendix 1, pp. 152–85.

[58] See Rogers 1991, passim. My interpretation here differs from that of Rogers, who views Salutaris's prescribed rituals as reaffirming Ephesus's Greek identity in resistance to the city's "Romanization."

[59] Wörrle 1988, 258; S. Mitchell 1993, I.210n. 73, contra Rogers 1991, 190.

[60] For performers such as *theologoi* and *hymnodoi,* who praised the emperor in prose and poetry during games, see Price 1984a, 90, and the bibliography collected by Petzl 1987, p. 76, ad *ISmyrna* II.1 #594, lines 2–4.

[61] Burrell 1981; Hanell 1935; Friesen 1995, heavily indebted to Price 1984b; S. Mitchell 1993, I:221.

[62] *ISmyrna* II.1 #697, lines 36–38, and Petzl's references ad loc. (1987, pp. 195–96).

city in a province began to be recognized as neocoros by the Roman emperor and the senate, cities jostled for the right to have their representatives march first in the processions associated with provincial games. This order, too, seems to have been determined by Rome.[63] Competitive games associated with festivals divulge Rome's regulation of a framework, intimately connected with imperial worship, for "negotiating, shaping, and proclaiming" regional and imperial relationships.[64]

Yet games in the Roman Greek world should not be seen simply in political terms, even if Augustus and subsequent emperors demonstrably saw their utility in promoting imperial cult.[65] The numerous inscriptions pertaining to festivals and competitors reveal other aspects of agonistic games, ones reflected in the literature, art, and architecture in the Greek East of this period. Games exalted local traditions and history, a balance to the unavoidable, daily concession of Rome's supremacy. At the same time games promoted, through open competition, a shared culture based on common literature, music, and rituals. My first point is clear in the list of statues Salutaris had paraded at Ephesus's festivals. Statues representing Rome come first, but the following statues, which personify aspects of Ephesus's self-rule and history, are more numerous. My second point is reflected in the Demostheneia, which staged competitions for interpreters of classical comedy, for interpreters of classical tragedy, and for citharists. The overall scheme of the Demostheneia resembles that known for the musical and dramatic parts of festivals at Aphrodisias, Corinth, Thespiae, and elsewhere.[66] Games in the Greek East afforded individuals and cities the chance to gain renown in the Roman empire by age-old Greek means.[67]

Seemingly paradoxically, therefore, agonistic games simultaneously encouraged local distinctiveness and a universal consciousness.[68] Their significance for individual cities can be gauged by the immunity from local liturgies and free meals at public expense home cities granted winners of

---

[63] Merkelbach 1978. For the senate's involvement in neocorate designations, see L. Robert, *RPh* 1967, 49–50.

[64] Quotation from Friesen 1995, 224.

[65] See S. Mitchell 1993, I:218, 210–11. S. Mitchell 1990, 188, construes lines 110–12 of the Demostheneia inscription as implying that provincial governors generally encouraged foundations for competitions.

[66] Wörrle 1988, 229–32.

[67] On inscriptions not only victorious contestants but also agonothetes and others who supervised and judged contests boasted their participation. See the fundamental collection of Moretti 1953.

[68] The competitions' universal aspect is marked by their occasional epithet "oikoumenikos": Robert 1984, 44–45. Ziegler 1985, 10, offers a narrower interpretation of the epithet.

sacred games.[69] A well-sponsored game featured the unique history of the city staging it, even while it united contestants, performers, judges, and spectators, regardless of origin, in a spectacle theoretically open to all.

As the inscription from Oenoanda makes clear, agonistic games validated the distribution of power in the host city. They often reinforced ties between emperor and city, as when Hadrian endorsed the Demostheneia, and they commemorated local euergetism and distinctions of political and religious clout.[70] Imperial approval of new games heightened the status of those mediating the favor. In the Demostheneia document, for example, Hadrian extols Demosthenes and names the ambassadors who relayed the affair to him. In a list of benefactions to Smyrna, which corresponds to a passage in Philostratus, donations from Hadrian and his designation of Smyrna as "twice neocoros" are explicitly attributed to the agency of Polemo (*ISmyrna* II.1 #687, lines 33–39, and Philostr. *VS* 531; see chapter 7).

A different but equally important point is that cities were flooded with visitors during games, especially the sacred crown ones. Contestants and performers, their families and trainers, ritual personnel, spectators, and all who would make money from the crowd flocked to the competitions, thus increasing local revenues (cf. Dio Chrys. 35.15, indicating that more individuals visited cities hosting provincial imperial cult games than cities in which provincial governors held judicial hearings).[71] Rome recognized various economic implications: in the Oenoanda document Hadrian stresses that costs were to be borne by Demosthenes, and the governor specifies that the games' tax-free status and the five-year immunity granted agonothetes depend on the city's maintaining high contributions to Rome.[72] Hadrian's general favor of festivals contrasts with their depreciation by his successor. In A.D. 145 Antoninus Pius praised Vedius Antoninus for embellishing Ephesus's buildings rather than choosing to garner transitory fame by distributions, shows, and competitive games (*IEphesos*

---

[69] Home cities may even have granted heroic processional entry through their walls to the winners of special sacred games (the "iselastic" or "eiselastikoi" games, whose name derives from the right of processional entry): Pliny *Ep*. 10.118–19, with Weiss 1982; Robert 1984, 43–45; S. Mitchell 1990, 189.

[70] Cf., e.g., Rogers 1991, 148. S. Mitchell 1993, I:211, holds that the detailed negotiations for the Demostheneia correspond to the appearance in cities of southern Asia Minor of small committees to screen political matters, indicating the increasingly small numbers of citizens who actually wielded political power.

[71] E.g., an athlete who traveled to competitions in Asia from his Egyptian home, Hermoupolis, with his wife, first pregnant and then with infant son: Robert 1984, 44.

[72] Parts IV and V. See S. Mitchell 1993, I:210. Local taxes may have been suspended during the celebration of sacred games: Petzl 1987, p. 196, ad *ISmyrna* II.1 #697, line 38. We can also compare the emperor's attention to festival business in his letter to Pergamum (this chapter, discussion at n. 30).

V #1491 = *Syll.*[3] 850).[73] Festivals were key to civic life in the Greek East. It should come as no surprise that games in twenty-one cities carried some form of Hadrian's name in their titles.[74]

The cities are found throughout the Eastern Mediterranean. In Egypt Alexandria and Antinoopolis celebrated Hadrianic festivals, as did Gaza (Judaea), Antioch (Syria), Tarsus and Anazarbus (Cilicia), Oenoanda (Lycia), and Ankyra (Galatia). Eight cities are in Asia: Attuda, Cyzicus, Ephesus, Erythrae, Smyrna, Synnada, Thyateira, and Tralles. Two are in Bithynia-Pontus, Bithynion-Claudiopolis and Heraclea Pontica, and three cities, Athens, Mantinea, and Nemea, are located in Achaea.[75] The pre-

---

[73] Translated in Lewis and Reinhold 1990, II:261, #71. See S. Mitchell 1993, I:220.

[74] S. Mitchell 1993, I:221, goes so far as to state that Hadrian "had founded new festivals as part of a programme to foster Hellenic culture and civic life." I refer below to games as "Hadrianic" if they carry some form of Hadrian's name.

[75] Alexandria, Hadrianeia Philadelpheia games, Moretti 1953, #84 = *IGR* IV 1519b, and see n. 80 below. For Antinoopolis, see chapter 8 at nn. 112, 130. Gaza, *panegyris Hadriane* (Hadrianic games), which *Chron. Pasch.* 1.474, with confused dating and motivation, holds were founded in A.D. 119 as a slave market for the sale of Jewish prisoners taken during the Second Revolt: A. Kindler, *Shnaton Museion Ha'aretz, Tel Aviv* (Tel Aviv, 1974–75), 61–67; Glucker 1987; Halfmann 1986, n. 405. At Antioch a Festival of the Springs, later called the Hadrianeion, was dedicated on 23 June 129; it accompanied the dedication of Hadrian's Temple of the Nymphs and water works there: Malal. XI.278.16; E. Bey, "Fouilles de Tralles," *BCH* 28 (1904): 87–88; M. Gough, "Anazarbus," *Anatolian Studies* 2 (1952): 128–29; Downey 1961, 222–23 and n. 104; Halfmann 1986, 206, correcting both Downey 1961 and Weber 1907, 121n. 232, on the date. Tarsus, Hadrianeia Olympia games, *ASAA* n.s. 14–16 (1952–54): 293–95, #67, Mionnet, Supp. VII, p. 283, #516, G. F. Hill, *British Museum Catalogue of the Greek Coins of Lycaonia, Isauria, and Cilicia* (London, 1900), xciii; Anazarbus, Hadrianeia iera games, Moretti 1953, #86, and Hadriana Olympia games, Moretti 1953, #87, *SEG* XXVIII 1253. Oenoanda is discussed above. Ankyra: see n. 81 below. Attuda, Hadrianeia games, *IGR* IV 844, *CIG* 3952, Le Bas and Waddington 1870, 743, with *MAMA* VI 76. Cyzicus, Olympia Hadrianeia games, ?after A.D. 124: *IGR* I 802; *IGR* IV 154, 162 (with *koinon Asias*); *MDAI(A)* 22 (1897): 414, cf. L. Robert, *RPh* 1929, p. 153; Cyzicus's games as simply Olympia: *CIG* 2810, 3672; *IG* II² 3169–70, line 28; *IGR* IV 161; *MDAI(A)* 7 (1882): 255, #26; Cyzicus's games as simply Hadrianeia: *BCH* 28 (1904): 84f, #5, and 86, #7 line 20. Ephesus (where there was also a phyle "Hadriane"), Hadrianeia games, n.d.: *IG* XIV 739 line 13, 1102 line 31, 1113; *CIL* III 296; *IG* III 129, line 25, *CIG* 2937b; *CIG* II 3208, cf. *JÖAI* 16 (1913): 247. Erythae, Megala Hadrianeia Epibateria games, *IErythrai* #60 = *IGR* IV 1542. Smyrna, Hadrianeia Olympia games, ?after A.D. 123: *ISmyrna* II.1 #659 line 6, #668 lines 4–5. Synnada, Hadrianeia games, Mionnet IV, p. 367, #983. Thyateira, Hadrianeia games begun in A.D. 123, *CIG* 3491, Weiss 1995, 218. Tralles, Olympia Pythia Hadriana games, n.d.: *BCH* 28 (1904): 80, 82, #5 line 14; Weber 1907, 222–23. Bithynion-Claudiopolis, Hadrianeia Antinoeia festival, n.d.: *BCH* 9 (1885): 38; Moretti 1953, #80, Robert 1980, 132–38; Moretti 1953, #208 (*Syll.*[3] 841 attests a stoa, dedicated by a member of a Roman senatorial family, to his native city and to the god of the country, Antinoos). Heraclea Pontica, Hadrianeia Heracleia eisaktika games, *BCH* 9 (1885): 68–69, with Weber 1907, 125, and *MAMA* VIII 521. Athens: see below, at n. 77. Mantinea, annual games in honor of Antinoos, and penteteric Antinoeia mysteries, after A.D.

ponderance of cities in Asia and nearby provinces is consonant with the overall history of agonistic games during the principate, when rising numbers of festivals in this area apparently correspond to falling numbers in Greece proper.[76] Various other distinctions can be noted.

Athens received Hadrian's greatest and most varied encouragement of festivals. In 124/125 Hadrian participated in the Eleusinian Mysteries and personally presided over its Dionysiac festival. More lastingly, between his new creations of the Panhellenia, Hadrianeia, and Olympieia, and his promotion of the Panathenaia, Hadrian seems to have accorded this city the unique position of having four sacred, iselastic games.[77] In four other of the twenty-one cities, Ephesus, Smyrna, Cyzicus, and Tarsus, Hadrian's games can be linked with the city's new status as "twice neocoros" (Ephesus and Smyrna) or neocoros (Cyzicus and Tarsus).[78] Further, in Smyrna and Cyzicus Hadrian endowed extraordinarily large temples, which most likely served as temples of the imperial cult, and in Smyrna he also financed a gymnasium, "the finest in all of Asia."[79] Games with which Hadrian is associated in Antinoopolis, Alexandria, Mantinea, and Bithynion-Claudiopolis honored Antinoos, heroized after his death in A.D. 130. Antinoopolis marked the spot of the youth's drowning in the Nile, and Alexandria was the Nile's most famous city. Mantinea boasted of having founded Bithynion-Claudiopolis, the city of Antinoos's birth (see chapters 6 and 7).[80]

---

130 (literary; epigraphic), both held in a racecourse near Mantinea's shrine of Poseidon Hippios: Paus. 8.10.1, 8.9.7–8; J. Keil and A. von Premerstein, *Denkschriften d. kaiserl. Akad. d. Wiss. in Wien* 53.3 (1910): 23; Fougères 1898, 319. Nemea, below at n. 89. Newer evidence disproves some inclusions in earlier lists: see L. Robert, *RPh* 1930, 37–38. For Hadrian's possible encouragement of imperial cult games in Cyrene, see chapter 8 at n. 53.

[76] Robert 1984, 40.

[77] Spawforth and Walker 1985, 90–91; Spawforth 1989, 194; for dates, see Follet 1976, 346–48, 331–33. Athens and Eleusis also celebrated a festival for Antinoos: Geagan 1972, 148–49, and Follet 1976, 109, with references. For Hadrian's participation in the Mysteries in A.D. 124, see Follet 1976, 113–14.

[78] Ephesus, twice neocoros in 131/132: Habicht 1969, #28, cf. *IEphesos* II #428; Smyrna, twice neocoros in 123: *ISmyrna* II.1, #697, with #594; Cyzicus, neocorate in 124 or later: Schulz and Winter 1990, 51; Tarsus as neocorate: Ziegler 1985, 58, and Ziegler 1995.

[79] He may also have dredged Ephesus's harbor in A.D. 129: Smallwood, #494 = *Syll.*³ 839 = *IEphesos* II #274, a dedicatory inscription from Ephesus's boule and demos to Hadrian, "founder and savior," which notes that he made their harbors navigable after turbulent devastation by the Cayster River (cf. Strabo 14.1.24, and *IEphesos* Ia #23). Work on Ephesus's Marnas River may also have been undertaken around this time, according to a reused, fragmentary inscription: *JÖAI* 15 (1912) Beiblatt, p. 176. See Zabehlicky 1995, 204–5. The effect of Hadrian's gifts on the civic rivalry between Ephesus and Smyrna (e.g., Dio Chrys. *Or.* 34.48) is reflected in Philostr. *VS* 531. For Hadrian and Smyrna, see chapter 7.

[80] Megala Antinoeia games in Alexandria: *Bull.Ep.* 1952, 68–70, #180; Follet 1968, 63; for Mysteries concerning Antinoos in Antinoopolis, see chapter 8, n. 112; in Mantinea, Paus.

Hadrian has also been credited with creating a group of *mystikoi agones* (mystic games) in Galatia and Pamphylia, whose programs may have been restricted to dramatic events of a mystical type. Our only sure evidence for his direct involvement comes from Ankyra's games, where Hadrian may have appointed Ankyra's first agonothete, Ulpius Aelius Pompeianus.[81] Such mystic festivals correspond to Hadrian's fascination with mysteries and his personal participation in the Eleusinian Mysteries.[82] They witness again the individualized nature of Hadrian's benefactions, often shaped by the combination of Hadrian's own interests and the recipient city's needs and culture. Games in other cities have been connected with a visit by Hadrian: in Antioch,[83] Gaza,[84] Erythrae,[85] Thyateira,[86] and Tralles,[87] although it is unclear if all these were new foundations or just renamings of earlier games. Little is known about the festivals in Attuda, Anazarbus, Tarsus, Synnada, and Heraclea Pontica, other than that they bore Hadrian's name.[88]

More detailed documentation for other games associated with Hadrian discloses a sensitivity to local and pan-Hellenic traditions, and an antiquarianism encountered elsewhere in his municipal work. For example, Hadrian restored to the winter Nemean games a "horse-course" (double-length) race for boys (Paus. 6.16.4), which had fallen into desuetude after the heyday of this prototypical festival.[89] (Hadrian may also have been di-

---

8.9.7 and Spawforth 1989, 195; for Bithynion-Claudiopolis, L. Robert, *RPh* 17 (1943): 184–85n. 9. Although these examples might suggest Hadrian's personal involvement with other known Antinoeia (e.g., in Athens and Eleusis, Argos, and Hexapolis on the Black Sea: Follet 1976, 109, 322–23; *IG* IV 590, lines 11–13, cf. *IG* V.2 313; *IOlympia* ##450, 452; and *IGR* I 634), these others were probably launched spontaneously by their host cities. See *HA, Hadr.* 14.7, and L. Robert, *REG* 65 (1952): ##191–93; also Origen *C. Cels.* 3.36; Clem. Al. *Protr.* 4.49.

[81] S. Mitchell 1993, I:219–20; see Bosch 1967, ##127–29, esp. #128, lines 8–12; Iconium: Bosch 1967, #130, col. I line 9 (*mystikos* supplied in the reconstructed text); Pessinus, *IGR* III 231 (though lacking explicit mention of an *agon mystikos*); Side, J. Nollé, *Chiron* 16 (1986): 204–6.

[82] Guarducci 1941; Beaujeu 1955, 167–69; Kienast 1959–60.

[83] In A.D. 123 or 131: Halfmann 1986, 206, correcting (e.g.) Downey 1961, 222–23.

[84] The city also revamped its dating system at Hadrian's visit in A.D. 130, establishing a new era: Halfmann 1986, 112n. 405. Gaza long had been Hellenized: Glucker 1987, 38–42; F. Millar, "The Phoenician Cities: A Case-Study of Hellenisation," *PCPS* 209 (1983): 55.

[85] Magie 1950, 615.

[86] Weiss 1995, 218.

[87] Weber 1907, 222–23, considers these Olympia Pythia Hadriana games a renewal of earlier ones.

[88] The concurrent appearance of Hadrianeia Olympia games in Tarsus and Anazarbus indicates the relative equality of the two cities in the new Cilician Assembly: Ziegler 1985, 21, 32; S. Mitchell 1990, 192.

[89] The unusual race was about 710 meters long: Miller 1990, 4.

rectly concerned with the Pythian games, another of the four original pan-Hellenic festivals, if a restoration to a fragmentary letter he wrote to Delphi in A.D. 125 is correct [Oliver, #74bis, line 26].[90] When Hadrian personally presided over Athens's Dionysiac festival, he deliberately donned Athenian native costume (Cass. Dio 69.16.1).[91] When ratifying the Demostheneia, Hadrian even used an archaic epithet for the theatrical festival, implicitly correcting the common but less precise term Demosthenes and others employed.[92]

Beside such displays of tradition stand the innovations Hadrian brought to guilds connected with games. The earliest guild or "synod" of "artists" (i.e., professional theatrical performers) dates to the early third century B.C., when it was centered in Athens under the patronage of the god Dionysos. As games proliferated during that century, regional guilds began to be established in other locales, including Teos (see chapter 6).[93] Actors' guilds, which helped organize the theatrical and musical festivals of the Greek East, became so powerful that they could request and receive corporate privileges from kings, cities, leagues, and Rome itself. By the end of the Republic, a "worldwide" ("oikoumenikos," or ecumenical) synod of Dionysiac artists had been established, and during the Empire this eclipsed the regional synods.

Athletes were the other performers essential to games. In contrast with theatrical performers, however, athletes seem to have been organized into professional guilds only in the first century B.C., when a guild of athletes was distinguished from the guild of "athletes who were sacred victors." The athletes' guild became known as "worldwide" during the Empire, like the synod of Dionysiac artists.[94] Mark Antony (in 41 or 32 B.C.), Claudius (in A.D. 44), and Vespasian granted or restored to athletes in guilds privileges such as exemption from military service.[95]

Hadrian reaffirmed the privileges of the worldwide synod of Dionysiac artists (Oliver, #96A–C).[96] He seems to have personally encouraged the

---

[90] Halfmann 1986, 202–3, notes that it must be simply by chance that we now have no evidence attesting Hadrian's concern for Olympia.

[91] His use of Athenian costume apparently dates to the first time he presided as agonothetes, in 112/113, rather than to 125. Cf. *HA, Hadr.* 13.1; for date, see Halfmann 1986, 202. For the rarity of a Roman emperor appearing in Greek dress, see chapter 8 at n. 56.

[92] Hadrian used *mousikos*, not *thymelikos:* Wörrle 1988, 227–28.

[93] Pickard-Cambridge 1968, 279–321; P. Frisch, *Zehn Agonistische Papyri* (Opladen, 1986), with Poliakoff 1989; Boatwright 1987, 209–12.

[94] Pleket 1973.

[95] Millar 1983, 81–82, and Millar 1977, 456–63; cf. Boatwright 1987, 209n. 87.

[96] Specifically, "inviolability, right to front-row seats, freedom from military service, immunity from public liturgies, to keep without tax whatever they procure for sacred use or the contests and to use it as they see fit(?), the right not to present guarantors of their immunity from taxation, the right to meet together for sacrifice, the right not to be compelled to ac-

Athenian synod of musical artists (Oliver, #97), to or about which he wrote numerous epistles (Oliver, ##98–104). D. J. Geagan has noted that during Hadrian's reign this Athenian group emerges after an obscurity of some two hundred years.[97] The emperor apparently fostered other guilds of festival performers. The synod at Nemausus (Nîmes, France) assumed the unique title of "the Sacred Thymelic Hadriana Synod of Those Who Compete Together for the Sake of Imperator Caesar Traianus Hadrianus Augustus, the New Dionysus" (*IGR* I 17).[98] He may have located in Rome itself the headquarters of the ecumenical guild of Dionysiac artists, hitherto centered in the Greek East,[99] and he allowed the "synod of athletes and sacred victors," as the two athletic guilds were known after conflation in the early second century, to establish their headquarters in the capital city (A.D. 134; Oliver, #86 = *IG* XIV 1054 = *IGUR* I 235 = *IGR* I 149; cf. *IG* XIV 1055 = *IGUR* I 236 = *IGR* I 146).[100] The new establishment made Rome the athletic hub of the world,[101] and in recognition of the benefaction several guilds of athletes throughout the Roman empire added the epithet "Hadriana" to their names.[102]

Overall, Hadrian's involvement with cities' competitive games is characterized by complementary aspects discerned in other municipal benefactions: attention to infrastructure and promotion of local individuals. The privileges Hadrian accorded guilds connected with competitive games are matched by his concern for cities' gymnasia and ephebic training (see chapters 6–8). By publicly approving individual euergetes, he must have encouraged cities' elites to endow or contribute to local festivals. Finally, by locating in Rome itself the guilds of professional performers, he asserted the central importance of festivals in the Roman empire. Although agonistic games were celebrated in merely a handful of cities in the Latin West, Antoninus Pius appropriately recognized Hadrian's abiding interest by establishing in his honor a new festival, the Eusebia, in Puteoli. Only the third "Greek-type" games on Italian soil,

---

commodate strangers with billets, freedom from imprisonment or any other form of detention [———] death penalty": trans. Oliver 1989, ad loc., p. 241.

[97] Geagan 1972, 147–51.

[98] = *CIL* XII 3232 = *IG* XIV 2495. See also Lavagne 1986; Gros 1984, 131–32; Robert 1938, 45–53; Boatwright 1987, 210.

[99] Pleket 1973, 225–27; Geagan 1972, 149; its previous location is unknown.

[100] The headquarters, apparently not built until after Hadrian's reign, went up near Trajan's Baths. See Pleket 1973, 223–27; M. L. Caldelli, "*Curia athletarum, iera xystike synodos* e organizzazione delle terme a Roma," *ZPE* 93 (1992): 75–87.

[101] Forbes 1955, 243–44.

[102] Pleket 1973, 208, with examples.

the Eusebia quickly became popular. Their prestige would be unthinkable without Hadrian's earlier favor of festivals and their infrastructure.[103]

NAMES AND TITLES

Nomenclature figures frequently in the preceding discussion of agonistic games, for festivals could be linked to Hadrian's designation of cities as neocoros or twice neocoros, and they often bore some form of Hadrian's name. Other epithets and official designations attest Hadrian. At least four cities gained the title *metropolis* (mother-city) from Hadrian. Further, some form of Hadrian's name appears in the names of at least twenty-seven cities other than those he founded or whose civic status he changed (discussed in chapters 3 and 8). It is unclear what we can conclude from most appellations during Hadrian's reign, other than that of neocoros.[104] Designation of a city as metropolis required formal sanction by Roman emperor and senate. In contrast, a city apparently could add the honorific "Hadriane" or "Hadrianopolis" to its name without external authorization.[105] Neither type of title, however, marked a change in a city's juridical status.[106] Despite the questions surrounding them, the recurrence of such titles indicates their importance to cities' self-presentation.[107]

Hadrian conferred the title metropolis on Nicaea in Bithynia-Pontus, although neighboring Nicomedia already possessed it;[108] on Pergamum in Asia;[109] on Damascus and perhaps also on Tyre in Syria;[110] on Petra in

---

[103] L. Robert, *CRAI* 1970, 9–11. For possible Greek-type athletic competition in North African gymnasia by the third century A.D., see F. Ghedini, "*Gymnasia . . . in thermis:* Ancora sul testamento di C. Cornelio Egriliano," in *L'Africa romana: Atti del IX Convegno di Studio* (Sassari, 1992), 353–59.

[104] For economic and other effects of the neocorate designation, see Friesen 1995, 236–45.

[105] Robert 1977, 22n. 100; L. Robert, *RPh* 1967, p. 54n. 6; L. Robert, *Hellenica* II, 77–79; Talbert 1984, 414. Le Glay 1976, 358–59, lists thirteen cities with Hadriane added to their titles: see below, n. 114. *ILS* 6092 (= *CIL* II 1423), recording Vespasian's permission to Sabora to assume his name, significantly also records his permission to the town to relocate. Cassius Dio remarks (54.23.8) that under Augustus the emperor and even the senate assigned names to cities as a mark of honor, in contrast with his own day when cities made for themselves long lists of names.

[106] Galsterer-Kröll 1972, 135–36.

[107] Robert 1977; Friesen 1995, 236–45. See also Cass. Dio 52.37.10.

[108] Şahin 1978, #5, line 2, and pp. 24–25, and Robert 1977; Bowersock 1985, 79–80, 86.

[109] Habicht 1969, 160. Ephesus is entitled metropolis early in the reign of Pius: Bowersock 1985, 78n. 7.

[110] Numismatic evidence for Tyre is more convincing than the uncorroborated Suda entry for the city. See Bowersock 1985, 75–76, for references to both.

Arabia;[111] and, G. W. Bowersock holds, on Pontic Amaseia, Neocaesarea, and Nicopolis, and on Lycian Tlos, Patara, Myra, and Telmessus.[112] Even if Hadrian is not responsible for granting all twelve cities the title metropolis, his reign is the earliest documented time in which we find more than one metropolis in a province.[113]

Even more common, and sometimes occurring in conjunction with the title metropolis, is the addition of "Hadriane" to a city's title, or the naming of a city Hadrianopolis. Hadrian himself acknowledged the symbolic value of a city's name when, in a typically antiquarian move, he restored its original name to Mantinea, which had been called Antigoneia for more than three hundred years (Paus. 8.8.12). Coins and inscriptions show "Hadriane" added to the titles of Abdera in Thrace; Nicomedia, Bithynion-Claudiopolis, Parium, and Cius in Bithynia-Pontus; Nicopolis on Lycos, Cyzicus, and Smyrna in Asia; Iconium in Lycaonia; Germanicopolis, Diocaesaria, Tarsus, Adana, and Mopsuestia in Cilicia; Palmyra in Syria; and Petra in Arabia.[114] "Hadrianopolis" is attested for Adaras in Phrygia, Asia; Stratoniceia in Lydia, Asia; Caesareia and an unknown city near modern Viranşehir in Paphlagonia; Neocaesarea and Amaseia in Bithynia-Pontus; Thymbrion in Pisidia; Zephyrion in Cilicia; and Palmyra.[115] Reflecting the perception of such titles as a sign of favor, Hadrian's biography remarks that although the emperor did not like to put his own name on buildings, he named many cities Hadrianopolis, such as Carthage and part of Athens (*HA, Hadr.* 20.4).[116]

It thus seems that many cities spontaneously assumed names evoking Hadrian. In some cities, such as Abdera, Parium, and others discussed earlier in this chapter, the term *Hadriane* evidently commemorates actual benefactions from Hadrian. In others, as with the Hadrianopoleis listed above other than Athens, no other evidence links Hadrian to the city. This latter group of cities, found in cultural backwaters where Roman-style urbanism came later than in Asia or along the coasts, may have called themselves "Hadrianic" or "the City of Hadrian" as a way of asserting their arrival in the Greco-Roman oikumene.

[111] Millar 1990, 51, referring to H. J. Polotsky, *IEJ* 1962, 260.

[112] Bowersock 1985, 78n. 7, 82–86.

[113] Ibid.

[114] Le Glay 1976, 358–59, provides references for the "Hadriane" in the titles of Cyzicus, Smyrna, Nicopolis, Nicomedia, Bithynion-Claudiopolis, Cius, Iconium, Germanicopolis, Diocaesareia, Tarsus, Adana, Mopsuestia. See Weber 1907, 244, for Petra. For Parium, see this chapter, at n. 12.

[115] Le Glay 1976, 358, provides references for Stratoniceia, Adaras, Caesareia and the other Paphlagonian city, Neocaesarea, Amaseia, Thymbrion, and Zephyrion. See Weber 1907, 237–38, for Palmyra.

[116] There is no other evidence for Carthage's new name, and the reference to part of Athens as "Hadrianopolis" appears to derive from the famous extant inscription on the city's Arch of Hadrian (see chapter 7, n. 10). The lack of corroboration for these two "Hadrianopoleis" indicates that the titles were not officially bestowed.

CONCLUSIONS

Despite primitive communications, cities in the Roman empire were neither isolated from one another nor linked only to Rome. They were bound to their neighbors and other cities further afield by numerous ties from mutual borders to shared rituals at regional shrines. As we see in chapters 6 and 7, Hadrian intensified ritual bonds by establishing the Panhellenion for the Greek East, and by reinforcing the imperial cult in Tarraconensis and elsewhere in the Latin West. Yet bettered connections and communalities, paradoxically, seem to have pushed cities to strive ever more vigorously for special prominence.

Civic emulation was an unmistakable factor of Roman life, and many cities, particularly in the Greek East, North Africa, and other highly urbanized areas, were acutely aware of the status and power of their neighbors. One city's splendor, reflected in its remission of taxes or building patronage by an emperor, was not viewed as reflecting glory on the province or region. Rather, it served as a spur to neighboring cities, especially in the Greek East, site of almost all of Hadrian's changes discussed in this chapter. The economic ramifications of such zeal were considerable. Civic munificence by members of the provincial elite, although immediately appreciable in splendid buildings or glorious games, could backfire over time. In many cities, as Pliny and others noted, delapidated and unfinished buildings were dangerous eyesores: funding for maintenance had not been included in the original donation, or the funds had run out (e.g., Pliny *Ep.* 10.70.2). In a slightly later discussion of the terms on which new works at private expense are acceptable, the jurist Macer reports that imperial approval is necessary for a public project *si ad aemulationem alterius civitatis pertineat* (if it relates to emulation of another city; *Dig.* 50.10.3.*pr.,* Lib. 2 *de officio praesidis*).[117]

Given the passions of intercity rivalry, it is probably no fluke that we have only nine boundary settlements credited directly to Hadrian. Such inherently invidious decisions struck at the basis of a city's livelihood. They are relatively infrequent when compared to Hadrian's other activities affecting cities' relations with one another and with Rome, especially his presumable attention to cities' competitive games. Comparably rare, too, are Hadrian's ten or so administrative decisions that affected imperial revenues or expenditures.[118] In contrast, as we see in the following chapters, Hadrian pa-

---

[117] Johnston 1985, 123–24, noting that imperial legislation concerning bequests to towns included, by the second half of the second century, regulations for maintenance funds.

[118] To recapitulate: three or possibly four communities had their freedom and immunity from taxes confirmed, Aphrodisias, Delphi, Astypalaea, and perhaps Samos; three cities, Athens, Ephesus, and Tralles, received grain from imperial stores (although the last two cities did not receive their supplies gratis); only one city, Astypalaea, may be documented as having its crown tax reduced. In three cities, Stratonicea-Hadrianopolis, Pergamum, and Eleusis, Hadrian's judgments benefited citizens' or city revenues while concurrently reducing those of the imperial fiscus.

tronized some hundred buildings or engineering projects in cities from Syrian Antioch, to Trapezus on the Black Sea, to Italica in southern Spain. He preferred lasting demonstrations of his municipal concern to more transient ones, such as tax remissions.

The effect of Hadrian's benefactions was profound. Only a generation later, when Aelius Aristides wrote his panegyric *On Rome* from his perspective as a Roman of Greek origin, he exemplified the full and felicitous development of the Roman world in its many cities, full of beautiful buildings, radiance, charm, and splendid civic festivals (26.97–99; cf. *HA, Hadr.* 19.2, Cass. Dio 69.10.1).

CHAPTER 6

Engineering and Architectural Donations

THE LARGEST CATEGORY of Hadrian's urban benefactions is that of his material changes of the urban structures and territories of cities: engineering projects, such as measures for flood control and aqueducts, and new buildings and reconstructions, completions, architectural enhancement, or decoration of older edifices. Although the ninety endeavors in fifty-four cities I have compiled (see tables 6.1 and 6.2) are provisional totals, this category of Hadrian's urban interactions is almost three times greater than the next most numerous one, his changes of city status (90:34).[1] The high totals necessitate two chapters. In this chapter I discuss engineering projects and other utilitarian buildings; buildings serving spectacle and leisure; and temples, shrines, and tombs. Most of the projects noted here are the only interventions by Hadrian in their cities,[2] and my examples illustrate the widely varying motivations and effects of this type of Hadrianic benefaction, including civic emulation and the encouragement of local euergetism. To Athens, Smyrna, and Italica, however, Hadrian gave so many buildings

---

[1] The numbers in the present chapter build on those in Boatwright 1997a. Subtotals in this chapter's sections will not add up to ninety and fifty-four, since I do not include buildings and restorations attested by inscriptions too lacunose or ambiguous to allow determining what Hadrian donated. Such activity occurred at Aequiculi (restoration in A.D. 128/129, *CIL* IX 4116), Aleria in Corsica (building ?with pool or bath, A.D. 124/125, *AE* 1968, 283 = *AE* 1967, 279; J. Jehasse, "Inscriptions d'Aleria (1965–67)," *Bulletin de la Société nationale des antiquaires de France* [1967]: 144–45, 148–51), Altinum (building, A.D. 137/138, known from the heavily restored *CIL* V 2152; Boatwright 1989, 257), Antium (restoration of unidentified temple, terminus post quem of A.D. 120/121, *CIL* X 6652; Boatwright 1989, 252), Caesena (?restoration, n.d., G. Susini, "La liberalitas di Adriano a Cesena," *Atti e Memorie, Deputazione di Storia Patria per la Romagna* 10 [1958–59]:281–85), Caiatia (?restoration, or embellishment, of a building with Cubulterian marble, ?A.D. 120/121, *CIL* X 4574; Boatwright 1989, 252), Castrimoenium (building restoration, n.d., *CIL* XIV 2460; Boatwright 1989, 266), Fabrateria Vetus (restoration, n.d., *CIL* X 5649; Boatwright 1989, 266), Firmum (endowment of a building later completed by Antoninus Pius, n.d., *CIL* IX 5353; Boatwright 1989, 265), Heba (renovation of a building, perhaps a temple, n.d., *AE* 1946, 222; Boatwright 1989, 265–66), Nomentum (restoration of sacred buildings, A.D. 136, *AE* 1976, 114; C. Pala, *Nomentum. Forma Italiae. Reg. I, vol. XII* [Rome, 1976], 48), and Signia (testamentary donation of money for public works, after 138, *CIL* X 5963; Boatwright 1989, 258).

[2] Although I do include projects in cities such as Megara, where Hadrian's benefactions, though multiple, do not suggest any "program."

TABLE 6.1

Cities with Engineering Projects or Utilitarian Structures from Hadrian
(excluding cities discussed in Chapter 8)

City	Engineering Project	Utilitarian Structure
Aeclanum, Italia	*Roadwork*	
Alba Fucens, Marruvium, and Angitiae, Italia	*Drainage work at Fucine Lake*	
Alexandria Troas, Asia	<u>Aqueduct</u>	
Antioch, Syria	<u>Aqueduct, with nymphaeum</u>	
Argos, Achaea	<u>Aqueduct, with nymphaeum</u>	
Athens, Achaea	<u>Aqueduct, with nymphaeum</u> <u>Bridge</u>	*Roman Agora?*
Caesarea, Judaea	*Aqueduct*	
Cingulum, Italia	Aqueduct	
Corinth, Achaea	<u>Aqueduct</u>	
Coronea, Achaea	*Drainage of Lake Copais* <u>Aqueduct</u>	
Dyrrachium, Macedonia	<u>Aqueduct</u>	
Ephesus, Asia	*Harbor works*	
Gabii, Italia	Aqueduct	
Italica, Baetica	*Aqueduct, roadwork*	
Lupiae, Italia	<u>Harbor works</u>	
Megara, Achaea	<u>*Roadwork*</u>	
Myra, Lycia		<u>Horrea</u>
Nicaea, Bithynia–P.		*City walls, squares, blvds*
Nicomedia, Bithynia–P.		*City walls, squares, blvds*
Patara, Lycia		<u>Horrea</u>
Puteoli, Italia	*Harbor works*	
Quiza, Mauretania (Caes.)		<u>City arch</u>
Sarmizegetusa, Dacia	<u>Aqueduct</u>	
Smyrna, Asia		<u>Grain market</u>
Trapezus, Cappadocia	<u>Harbor works</u>	

Note: <u>Underlined</u> items indicate new construction, and *italicized*, restoration or completion; items in plain text are of indeterminate status. Cities in **bold face** also received other benefactions from Hadrian (see also table 6.2).

TABLE 6.2

Cities with Non-Utilitarian Public Works from Hadrian (excluding cities discussed in Chapter 8)

City	Temple	Tomb	Entertainment & Leisure	Arch. Decor.	Unidentifiable
Abae, Achaea	Apollo				
Aequiculi, Italia					Public works
Aleria, Corsica			?Baths		
Antioch, Syria	Nymphs, w/Zeus		?Baths		
Antium, Italia	Unknown				
Apta Julia, Gall. Narb.		Borysthenes			
Argos, Achaea	Hera			Gilded peacock	
Aricia (Nemi), Italia	Unknown				
Athens, Achaea	?Hera & Zeus Panhell. Pantheon Olympieion (Roman Agora)		Gymnasium Library		
Caiatia, Italia				Marble	
Capua, Italia				Col. & ?stat. to amph.	
Castrimoenium, It.					Unknown
Claros, Asia	Apollo				
Corinth, Achaea			Baths		
Cupra Maritima, It.	Dea Cupra				
Cyzicus, Asia	Zeus				

City	Temple	Tomb	& Leisure	Arch. Decor.	Unidentifiable
Gabii, Italia	*Juno Gabina?*				
Heba, Italia	*Unknown*				
Hyampolis, Achaea			<u>Stoa</u>		
Ilium, Asia		*Hector & Ajax*			
Italica, Baetica	<u>Traianeum</u>		<u>Baths</u>		
Lanuvium, Italia	*Hercules?*			<u>Stat. I.S.M.</u>	
Mantinea, Achaea	*Horse Poseidon*	*Epaminondas*			
Megara, Achaea	*Apollo*				
Melissa, Asia		*Alcibiades*			
Nemausus, Gallia	<u>Basilica Plotinae</u>				
Nomentum, Italia	*Unknown*				
Ostia, Italia			<u>Baths</u>		
Paros, Asia		*Archilochus*			
Pelusium, Egypt		*Pompey*			
Signia, Italia					<u>Unknown</u>
Smyrna, Asia	*Imp. cult (Z. Akraios)*	<u>Gymnasium</u>	Columns		
Tarraco, Tarracon.	*Augustus*				
Teos, Asia	*Dionysus*				
Trapezus, Cappad.				*Stats. Hadrian, Hermes, & Philesios*	

Note: Underlined items indicate new construction, and *italicized*, restoration or completion; items in plain text are of indeterminate status. Cities in **bold** face also received other benefactions from Hadrian (see also table 6.1).

and other marks of favor that these cities deserve individual discussion in a chapter of their own, chapter 7.

ENGINEERING PROJECTS AND OTHER UTILITARIAN BUILDINGS

Engineering Projects

Hadrian's twenty-one engineering projects are found in Achaea (seven), Italy (six), Asia (two), and Dacia, Baetica, Macedonia, Syria, Judaea, and Cappadocia (one each). (See table 6.1 and endpapers.) His involvement in flood control at two of the most troublesome lakes of the ancient world, Lake Copais in Boeotia (Achaea) (*SEG* XXXII 460–63, and below) and the Fucine Lake in Italy (*HA, Hadr.* 22.12),[3] respectively benefited Coronea and its neighbors, and Alba Fucens and nearby Italian cities. His work at the River Cephisus served Athens (see chapter 7). His "countless" aqueducts (*HA, Hadr.* 20.5) are exemplified by eight new constructions:[4] at Alexandria Troas (Philostr. *VS* 548–49), Syrian Antioch (Malal. XI 277.20–278.19), Argos (*BCH* 68–69 [1944–45]: 397–401), Athens (*CIL* III 549 = *ILS* 337, see chapter 7), Corinth (Paus. 2.3.5, 8.22.3), Coronea in Boeotia (*SEG* XXXII 460), Dyrrachium (*CIL* III 709), and Sarmizegetusa (*CIL* III 1446). Additionally, Hadrian apparently restored, extended, or built four other aqueducts, at Caesarea in Judaea (e.g., *AE* 1928, 136), Cingulum and Gabii in Italy (*CIL* IX 5681, XIV 2797), and Italica in Baetica (see chapter 7). Hadrian is responsible for work on the harbors of Ephesus (*IEphesos* #274 = *Syll.*³ 839 = Smallwood, #494, A.D. 129), Lupiae in Bruttium (Italy; Paus. 6.19.9), Puteoli (*CIL* X 1640 = *ILS* 336), and Trapezus (Arr. *Perip. M. Eux.* 16.6). Finally, although Hadrian's provincial roadwork falls outside the scope of this book, I include here Hadrian's involvement with roads around Aeclanum in Italy (*CIL* IX 1414 = *ILS* 5877, *CIL* IX 6075 = *ILS* 5875) and his enlargement of the Scironian Road in Megara (Paus. 1.44.6). Both clearly involved local elites and local traditions.

Engineering projects were often judged the most magnificent of Roman works and the greatest demonstration of Roman might (e.g., Dion. Hal. 3.67.5; Frontin. *Aq.* 1.16; Pliny *HN* 36.104, 36.121–24; Cic. *De Off.* 2.60). Technical prowess was considered to reflect the majesty and

---

[3] The third such problematic area is the Fayum: Leveau 1993, 4.

[4] Hadrian's interest in aqueducts can also be seen in his strict regulations for land near Nicaea's aqueduct: *AE* 1939, 293 = *MuseumIznik* I #1a = Smallwood, #456. Fittingly, the aqueduct seems to have been dedicated to him: *MuseumIznik* I #55. Lacking good evidence, I exclude the twelve-kilometer aqueduct at Sparta tentatively linked to Hadrian by Cartledge and Spawforth 1989, 109. To the enormous bibliography on aqueducts, add Eck 1987.

grandeur of the Roman empire, as well as to validate the emperor's ascendancy over nature. The vast scope of most imperial engineering projects reinforced the emperor's position as the ultimate benefactor. Furthermore, such projects allowed for economic benefits.[5] Besides being generally advantageous, engineering projects immediately affected individual cities and regions. For example, when representatives of cities in the Tiber's watershed addressed the senate about plans to control the river's chronic flooding, they mentioned the project's impact on their hydrology, agriculture, communications, technology, and (less predictably) religion and cult (Tac. *Ann.* 1.79, cf. 1.76.1; A.D. 15). Hadrian's flood control of the Copaic Lake in central Boeotia (Achaea), relatively well documented in a dossier from Coronea although without any identifiable remains on the ground,[6] typifies many benefits of his engineering projects, as well as some unintentional consequences.

Lake Copais, subject to annual winter inundation until successfully drained in the 1880s, actually was a fen in a basin measuring some 180 square kilometers within its natural contours 94.5 meters above sea level. (See fig. 1.) The lake was fed from the northwest by the rivers Melas and Cephesus, and from the south and southwest by a few torrents, notably the Hercynne and Phalerus.[7] In winter two dozen or so *katavothres,* natural drainage holes that discharged water from the eastern side of the lake during summers, could not cope with the season's torrential rains, and the lake habitually rose to its 94.5-meter contour line. But an unusual flood rise, even of only two and a half meters, could almost double the water's extent, to 350 square kilometers. Such flooding occurred fairly frequently, according to ancient literary sources.[8]

Others before Hadrian had attended to flooding and drainage in the rich agricultural area. An elaborate and effective Mycenaean scheme had intercepted the inflowing waters by channeling them to the *katavothres*

[5] Particularly so if the emperor could interest the local elite in participating: Leveau 1993, 7–8, referring to Suet. *Claud.* 20.

[6] To the dossier published by Oliver, ##108–18, pp. 253–73, can be added the fragments published by P. Roesch, "Appendix: Epigraphica 1982/85," *Teiresias* 15 (1985): 7–8 = SEG XXXV 405 B–C. See also Fossey 1991.

[7] Kenny 1935; N. Rolland, "Observations on the Pre-Neolithic Human Occupation in the Kopais Basin," in *Boeotia Antiqua* I, ed. J. M. Fossey (Amsterdam, 1989), 24–27. Since Hadrian's letters to Coronea give instructions about the Cephesus, Hercynne, and Phalerus, apparently in his day these three torrents ran through Coronea's territory, and the Melas was Orchomenian. J. M. Fossey, "Appendix 3: Boundaries in the South West Kopaïs," in *Topography and Population of Ancient Boiotia* (Chicago, 1988), 496–500, assigns to Coronea only the Phalerus, and considers the Hercynne as the border of Coronea and Orchomenos.

[8] See Kalcyk and Heinrich 1989, 56, 69; J. Knauss, "Purpose and Function of the Ancient Hydraulic Structures at Thisbe," in *Boeotia Antiqua* II, ed. J. M. Fossey (Amsterdam, 1992), 35; Kenny 1935, 190; cf. Fossey 1991, 16n. 15.

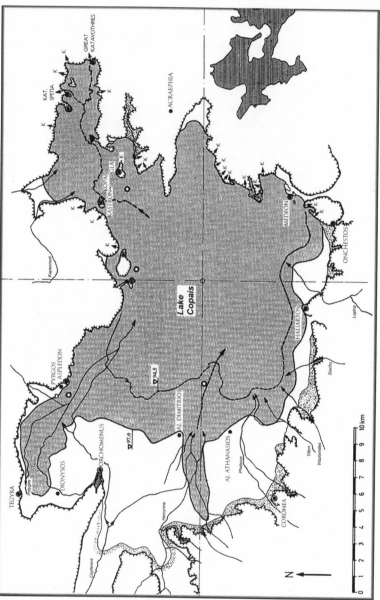

Fig. 1. Lake Copais, in Boeotia (Achaea), showing the extent of the lake before the modern drainage in the nineteenth century. The dashed line at 94.5 (m above sea level) indicates the natural contours of the basin, whose surface area (ca. 180 square km) was the usual extent of the lake in winter. Arrows show the probable courses of the torrents and rivers from the west, the Melas, Cephesus, Hercynne, and Phalerus (from north to south). K and Kat. signify *katavothres*, the natural drainage holes on the eastern side of the lake. Thisbe, Coronea's southern neighbor, is south of the area depicted in this map.

through embanked canals on the lake's north and south, facilitating reclamation of land in the lake's bays by polder dams and dikes.[9] Such projects, attributed to Heracles by locals (Paus. 9.38.7), had silted up by the third century B.C., when the engineer Crates unsuccessfully began a canal to drain the lake.[10] Around A.D. 40 one Epaminondas contributed six thousand denarii to repair the Mycenaean dike near his city Acraephia, east of the lake (*IG* VII 2712).[11] Although the extant letters do not mention this, Hadrian's interest in the region may have had an antiquarian cast, as was certainly true for the completion of Athens's Olympieion and other building endeavors he patronized (see chapter 7).

Hadrian's earliest missive (Oliver, #108, A.D. 124/125), however, declares his awareness of the project's agricultural benefits, expense, and (perhaps) potential ramifications, and his care to involve the Coroneans in the enterprise. The letter proclaims to the Coroneans Hadrian's intention to have dikes made for the Cephesus, Hercynne, and other waterways where they flowed together before emptying into the Copaic Lake, so as to keep the rivers in their banks and to prevent them from, "as now happened, flood[ing] the cultivable land." Committing sufficient funds of 65,000 denarii, Hadrian instructed the Coroneans to choose men to oversee the work. He vowed also to construct an aqueduct, perhaps suspecting that the new embankments might divert water from Coronea. The sum Hadrian promised for embankments is about eleven times greater than what Epaminondas of Acraephia had spent for repairs a century earlier,[12] indicating both the scope of the emperor's project and his not surprisingly greater resources.

In an undated letter from the dossier (Oliver, #110), Hadrian recognized the project as useful and attractive, and he reiterated the necessity of local involvement: complimenting the Coroneans for work on the Phalerus River, he charged them to maintain the dikes assiduously. Further, he ordered persons who had acquired land in the area[13] not to harm the constructions or the river, on pain of paying both for repairs and an additional fine of fifteen hundred denarii. The letter implies that individuals had already bought up newly available land near the dikes in the southwestern

---

[9] Kalcyk and Heinrich 1989, 55–71; Fossey 1991, 14–15.

[10] This scheme, abandoned because of Boeotian quarreling, has been tentatively linked with a canal leading flood water from the Hercynne to the center of the Copais, and another leading from the northern river Melas to a northeast drainage hole: Kenny 1935, 204–5, 199–201; cf. Strabo 9.2.18 (407).

[11] J. H. Oliver, "Epaminondas of Acraephia," *GRBS* 12 (1971): 221–37.

[12] Fossey 1991, 15 = *Euphrosyne* n.s. 11 (1981–82): 54.

[13] For this, a more plausible conjecture for the lacuna of this section of the letter than what Oliver offers, see C. P. Jones, in *AJP* 113 (1992): 146.

area of the lake, and that the land belonged to Coronea, to whom fines would go.[14]

But two other letters indicate that the project kindled problems requiring imperial intervention. A fragmentary missive, apparently written by Hadrian to Coronea (Oliver, #111), concerns construction and taxes disputed by the Coroneans and the neighboring Orchomenians. It directs the Coroneans to defer further unresolved questions to the proconsul M. Calpurnius Longus (governor of Achaea sometime between 125/127 and 135).[15] This letter, engraved in Coronea's archive between Hadrian's other letters about construction and the Phalerus River, suggests that the Coroneans' dispute with the Orchomenians concerned taxes on land reclaimed from the northwestern flood plain of the Copaic Lake. In Hadrian's letter of A.D. 135 (Oliver, #112), the emperor additionally informed the Coroneans that he had instructed his "friend" Aemilius Iuncus "to go to the River Phalerus and do what he considers suitable." In 135 L. Aemilius Iuncus was "corrector of the free cities of Achaea," an extraordinary imperial post overseeing allegedly autonomous cities.[16] The imperial project seems to have incited smoldering local rivalries, inadvertently causing greater outside interference in the region rather than a more stable autonomy.[17]

Similar aspects of imperial building patronage attend the aqueduct at Alexandria Troas, an example that also illuminates one means by which Hadrian's attention was drawn to various projects. The relatively full literary information for the aqueduct near fabled Troy has been tentatively linked to archaeological finds. Nineteenth-century reports note regularly spaced piers running about one kilometer from Alexandria Troas east toward Mt. Ida, and a raised mortar channel, ca. seventy centimeters wide, within the city walls.[18] The aqueduct figures prominently in Philostratus's depiction of the sophist Herodes Atticus (*VS* 548–49): while "corrector

[14] Similarly, one piece of evidence for Hadrian's successful drainage of part of the Fucine Lake is a boundary stone of A.D. 149 found dividing the land his work reclaimed between Alba Fucens, the city of the Marsi Marruvium, and Lucus Angitiae: G. Chouquer, M. Clavel-Lévêque, F. Favory, and J.-P. Vallat, *Structures agraires en Italie centro-méridionale. Cadastres et paysages ruraux,* CollEFR 100 (Paris-Rome, 1987), 130–33, cf. *HA, Hadr.* 22.12.

[15] W. Eck, "L. Marcius Celer M. Calpurnius Longus, Prokonsul von Achaia und Suffektkonsul unter Hadrian," *ZPE* 86 (1991): 97–101.

[16] For L. Aemilius Iuncus, cos. 127, see Follet 1976, 32–34. See n. 19 for Herodes Atticus, "corrector of the free cities of Asia."

[17] Here we should recall Plutarch's advice to conduct municipal affairs so as to minimize imperial interference: *Mor.* 814e–815c. Other letters from the Coronea archive, concerning land disputes with neighboring Thisbe that began in Hadrian's reign and continued into that of Antoninus Pius (Oliver, ##113 and 114), may similarly result from civic emulation: see the end of chapter 5.

[18] Cook 1973, 325; Tobin 1997, 327–30, reports tracing the final fifty meters of the aqueduct's channel (now two meters above ground level), to where it terminates at a fountain, presumably donated by Herodes Atticus.

of the free cities of Asia" (in A.D. 135),[19] he pitied the wretched condition of Alexandria Troas, for it lacked abundant, free-flowing water, its citizens had no baths, and they were constrained to drink muddy well-water and rainwater from cisterns. Herodes Atticus successfully appealed to Hadrian for three million denarii for an aqueduct,[20] pleading the antiquity and location of this maritime city and belittling the sum by contrasting it with Hadrian's liberality to "mere villages." When the costs had run to seven million, the administrators of Asia contentiously protested that the tribute of five hundred cities was being commandeered for the water supply of one city alone. Hadrian's rebuke to Herodes' father, Atticus, was met with a haughty retort, that the wealthy man would give the "trifling" cost overrun to his son to present to the city.

Although the anecdote is told to underline the wealth, power, and insolence of the family, it provides five important insights into imperial civic munificence. First, it vividly illustrates the consequence of imperial agents for the conferral of patronage.[21] This is all the more remarkable at Alexandria Troas, because the mandate of this "corrector of the free cities of Asia" did not include the city, which was a Roman colony.[22] Second, although Herodes' successful plea to Hadrian emphasizes the importance of aqueducts for baths, the quintessential Roman urban amenity,[23] and for clean drinking water, it also urges Alexandria Troas's antiquity and lovely location on the sea, denoting the influence of history and of aesthetics during Hadrian's reign. Third, Philostratus incidentally underscores the significance of private patrons' contributing to imperial projects or buildings advanced by the emperor.[24] Although most had neither the wealth of Atticus nor, presumably, his arrogance, the impressive opportunity to "col-

---

[19] Graindor 1930, 32, noting that the only title in use at this time for the position was *legatus Augusti ad corrigendum statum civitatium liberarum* ("legate of Augustus for the purpose of regulating free city states").

[20] Drachmae and denarii were equivalent at the time. See Graindor 1930, 32n. 2.

[21] Analogously, Cn. Papirius Aelianus, the governor of Dacia, supervised the construction of Hadrian's aqueduct at Sarmizegetusa in A.D. 132/133 (*CIL* III 1446). See n. 29 below.

[22] Alexandria Troas as a colony: Hirschfeld, *RE* 1.1 (1893): 1396, s.v. Alexandria Troas; W. Ruge, *RE* 7.A.1 (1939): 583–84, s.v. Troas #2; and (e.g.) *CIL* III 7282 = *ILS* 315 (n. 26 below).

[23] Pliny, *Ep.* 10.23.1, records a similar plea. The "Baths of Herodes Atticus" at Alexandria Troas, so identified only because of the passage of Philostratus (which does not mention baths), are discussed (with plan) by Yegül 1992, 282, and A. C. G. Smith, "The Gymnasium at Alexandria Troas: Evidence for an Outline Reconstruction," *AnatSt* 29 (1979): 23–50. See also Tobin 1997, 328–29. The connection of aqueducts and baths seems key also for Hadrian's aqueducts at Corinth (Paus. 2.3.5, with Lolos 1997, 297–98, 300–302), Antioch (below, n. 113), and Italica (see chapter 7).

[24] The reverse situation was more notorious, to judge from (e.g.) Pliny to Trajan about Nicomedia's aqueducts (*Ep.* 10.37; below, n. 27) and *CIL* III 2909 (= Smallwood, #392), recording Iader's aqueduct finished by Trajan when the town ran out of money.

laborate" with the emperor apparently encouraged private patronage.[25] Philostratus's story also highlights the ill will imperial liberality could arouse among a city's neighbors and rivals, a phenomenon discerned in Hadrian's flood control measures at Coronea (and see chapter 5).[26] Fifth, Philostratus alludes to the duration and expense of aqueduct projects.[27]

Neither project discussed so far provides explicit information about its work force.[28] In both cases local, unskilled laborers may have been employed, paid or not, to infer from Hadrian's stipulation that Coroneans voluntarily supervise the work. Scanty evidence for two of Hadrian's other aqueducts shows that the Roman military also provided labor for some utilitarian projects financed by the emperor. At Sarmizegetusa, one of the most important cities of Rome's new province Dacia, Hadrian had an aqueduct built in 131/132 under the management of the governor, Cn. Papirius Aelianus (*CIL* III 1446).[29] We may infer that the military legate used soldiers for the work.[30] Such certainly was the case at Caesarea, where Hadrian's restorations of the seventeen-kilometer (Herodian?) high-level aqueduct in 132–34 were realized by *vexillationes* (units) of at least three different legions stationed there during the Bar Kokhba Revolt: the Second Traiana, the Sixth Ferrata, and the Tenth Fretensis.[31]

---

[25] Cf. *CIL* X 6090 = *ILS* 6295, discussed in chapter 4, and Smyrna's gymnasium, discussed in chapter 7 following n. 58.

[26] For a classic study, see Robert 1977; see also n. 17 above. Alexandria Troas vaunted Hadrian's favor, e.g., in a dedication raised in Athens to Hadrian by the citizens of Troas, *colonia sua* (his own colony), "because of his many benefits both to individuals and to the city at large" (*CIL* III 7282 = *ILS* 315, A.D. 131/132 in Athens's Olympieion), and in a newly published statue base found in the territorium of Troas, which a C. Nymphidius Sabinus dedicated to Hadrian *conservator* (the preserver): Mühlenbrock 1994.

[27] When Pliny stepped in, Nicomedia had already spent 3,329,000 HS on one failed aqueduct, and 200,000 on another (882,250 denarii in all), sums Trajan considers wasteful (Pliny *Ep.* 10.37 and 38). The length such projects took to complete is suggested by the presumable duration of Hadrian's aqueduct at Athens. Although it was only some twenty kilometers, construction took perhaps ten years. See chapter 7, appendix 7.1.

[28] Cf. Brunt 1980.

[29] Piso 1993, 51–53; cf. Eck 1987, 72. The inscription's unusual ablative for Hadrian's name, apparently for dating purposes (though no co-consul is listed), is paralleled in one of the inscriptions attesting Lepcis Magna's aqueduct, *IRT* 357, cf. *IRT* 358 and 359. Sarmizegetusa's aqueduct is not mentioned in H. Daicoviciu and D. Alicu, *Colonia Ulpia Traiana Augusta Dacica Sarmizegetusa* (Bucharest, 1984); there may be no remains.

[30] Février 1983; MacMullen 1959, 214–17.

[31] B. Isaac and I. Roll, "Judea in the Early Years of Hadrian's Reign," *Latomus* 38 (1979): 59–61, list eight inscriptions witnessing the restoration (including *AE* 1928, 136; cf. *AE* 1928, 137) and suggest that the XXII Deiotariana also participated in the repairs before its disgrace for events in the Third Jewish Revolt. The reason for the restoration is unclear: there is no evidence of damage from the local earthquake of A.D. 130 or from the tsunami of A.D. 115. The repair may have been due to the overly soft local stone used in the aqueduct's original construction (Nir 1985) or to the need to provide fresh water to the many Roman soldiers stationed at Caesarea during the Revolt (Negev 1964 and 1972). See also Ringel 1975, 59–71.

Hadrian's harbor works at Lupiae, Ephesus, Trapezus, and Puteoli are not well known: nothing remains of the first two, and his breakwaters at Trapezus and Puteoli have been repeatedly rebuilt.[32] Nevertheless, the scanty information corroborates Hadrian's attraction to Greek antiquity and demonstrates his attention to the empire's strategic and economic needs. The first theme is key at Lupiae. The location of Hadrian's harbor at either spot now identified as Roman Lupiae, Parco del Cavallo on the Gulf of Taranto and Lecce on the Adriatic Sea, is puzzling in light of the inhospitable coastlines and minor standing of these regions during the empire.[33] But Pausanias puts Hadrian's harbor in a different context. Saying, "Those who have studied the history of Italy and of the Italian cities say that . . . Lupiae . . . was Sybaris in ancient times" (6.19.9), Pausanias conflates Lupiae with Copia. The Romans had established Copia as a colony in 193 B.C. at the site of Sybaris, an early and proverbial colony of Magna Graecia. Lupiae may have promoted the ancient Greek connection to sway Hadrian:[34] as we saw, the antiquity of Alexandria Troas was prominent in Herodes Atticus's successful plea to Hadrian to sponsor an aqueduct there.

In contrast, although the cities' Greek ancestry may have been influential, Hadrian's harbors at Trapezus and Puteoli have obvious strategic and economic ramifications. At Trapezus Hadrian replaced, sometime before the 130s, a natural harbor navigable only in summer (Arr. *Perip. M. Eux.* 16.6).[35] The project reflects the port's increased importance in imperial Rome's relations with Armenia. Hadrian himself apparently stopped in Trapezus in 131 (or earlier) while inspecting Cappadocia's borders, which he extended eastward as far as the Caucasus. Slightly later Arrian, as governor, used the Hadrianic port as a base when checking newly critical an-

---

[32] All are discussed in the text below except Ephesus, for which see chapter 5, n. 79. Lacking good evidence, I exclude the harbor of Pompeiopolis (Cilicia), credited to Hadrian by A. A. Boyce, "The Harbor of Pompeiopolis," *AJA* 62 (1958): 69, 71. Rickman 1985, 111, suggests that Rome's "central government, or emperor," had at most limited interest in encouraging "for the sake of commerce . . . port building, and efficiency in their administration."

[33] Birley 1997, 340n. 4, tentatively suggests that Hadrian may have given the boon as a favor to the family of the future Marcus Aurelius, who claimed descent from the lengendary founder of the place (*HA, M.Aur.* 1.6).

[34] For the revived importance of Greek ancestry in Magna Graecia during the Empire and particularly in this period, see Lomas 1995. As Birley has pointed out to me, Pausanias may simply have misread "Copia" as "Lupiae" in his source: C and L are easily confused in Latin cursive.

[35] Roman remains under Byzantine and later structures show that the Roman moles began at the seaward end of the walls of the ancient city, to form a half-round basin (ca. 150 meters diam.). The harbor's entrance (seventy meters wide) faces northeast so as to provide protection against the prevailing winter storms: Lehmann-Hartleben 1923, 199; Mitford 1974, 163.

chorages along the southern shore of the Black Sea.[36] Some ancient remains and art-historical evidence help flesh out our knowledge of Hadrian's harbor work at Puteoli, completed by Antoninus Pius (*CIL* X 1640 and 1641).[37] Hadrian's undertaking here, the restoration of an Augustan mole, must relate to Puteoli's critical role in Rome's provisionment.[38]

One of the two instances of Hadrian's roadwork I discuss corroborates again the power of the Greek past, since his widening at Megara of the Athens-Corinth road into two lanes evoked Megara's storied brigand Sciron for Pausanias (1.44.6–8).[39] The other, a two-mile stretch from Aeclanum to the new Via Traiana (leading to Apulia), underscores imperial co-option of local elites for municipal benefactions. Hadrian authorized a certain Ti. Claudius Bithynicus, a prominent local from Aeclanum, to [pave] the road (*CIL* IX 1414 = *ILS* 5877). The road was part of a larger-scale joint effort between emperor and locals to improve communications in this region of Samnium. Other road inscriptions attribute renovations of the Via Appia between Beneventum and Aeclanum to Hadrian's cooperation with rural landowners (*possessores agrorum,* with no city nor landowner named: *ILS* 5875 = *CIL* 6075, *CIL* IX 6072; *NSc* 1897, 160; *AE* 1930, 122).[40] These last two engineering projects, at Megara and in Samnium, underscore the diverse motivations for Hadrian's interaction with cities, the variety of the means used to achieve them, and their multiple effects.

---

[36] Commanding the seaward approaches to this volatile region from the Black Sea as well as the short land route to Iberia farther east, Trapezus had been garrisoned and designated by Vespasian as the headquarters of the *classis Pontica*, reinforced during the second century by extra troops: Mitford 1980, esp. 1187, 1201; Mitford 1974, 160–63.

[37] The series of Roman decorated glass flasks representing Puteoli viewed from the sea (third century A.D. or later) show on its quay two grandiose arches and other monuments, including two columns with standing figures: S. E. Ostrow, "The topography of Puteoli and Baiae on the eight glass flasks," *Puteoli* 3 (1979) [1980]: 113–19. Hadrian's interest in the attractiveness of his engineering projects, as seen in Coronea, suggests that he is responsible for the decoration, although the lacunose inscriptions and archaeological evidence are inconclusive.

[38] P. Sommella, *Forma e urbanistica di Pozzuoli romana* = Puteoli 2 (1978) [1980]: 74; Boatwright 1989, 260. Hadrian's dredging of Ephesus's harbor similarly seems motivated by concern for provisioning.

[39] The difficult feat of engineering greatly facilitated traffic between the Corinthian and Eleusinian Gulfs, and between Athens and Corinth (as did Hadrian's bridge over the Cephisus, which bettered the road leading west from Athens): Wiseman 1978, 17; A. Muller, "Megarika," *BCH* 107 (1983): 166 and fig. 42, p. 159. The modern highway passes below the ancient road Hadrian enlarged on the cliffs, now the general route of the railroad tracks. Alcock 1993, 121, discusses Roman roadwork in Achaea.

[40] See Siculus Flaccus in Thulin 1923, 110; Boatwright 1989, 239–40.

Other Utilitarian Building

Hadrian is credited with some ten other utilitarian buildings: the reconstruction or construction of city walls, markets, and crossings of city thoroughfares in Bithynian Nicaea and Nicomedia (evidence footnoted below); a city gate in Quiza, Mauretania (*CIL* VIII 9697 = 21514);[41] grain storehouses and markets in Lycian Myra and Patara (*CIL* III 232 = 6738, 12129) and in Smyrna (Philostr. *VS* 531; discussed in chapter 7); and a stoa in Hyampolis, Achaea (Paus. 10.35.6).[42] Hadrian's presumed renovation of Athens's "Roman Agora" figures in chapter 7.

In comparison to Augustus,[43] Hadrian was responsible for very few walls and city gates. By Hadrian's day the *pax Augusta* (the imperial peace) prevailed in most of the empire, and the heyday of military colonies had passed (see chapter 8).[44] None of Hadrian's new city foundations originally included city walls (see chapter 8).[45] In Bithynian Nicaea and Nicomedia the walls credited to Hadrian, along with markets and crossings of city thoroughfares (*tetraplateia* or *quadrivia*), were reconstruction efforts after a terrible earthquake in A.D. 120.[46] The benefaction demonstrated imperial

[41] I omit the "Arch of Hadrian" in Athens, as well as the arches at Phaselis, Attaleia (modern Antalya), and elsewhere that scholars deceptively call "Hadrianic" only because of dedications to him (e.g., *TAM* II 1187, for Phaselis) or general date.

[42] And perhaps in Apollonia on the Rhyndacus, Asia, after A.D. 120. The evidence is a fragmentary inscribed frieze (*IGR* IV 121 = Le Bas and Waddington 1870, #1068), reconstructed as acclaiming Hadrian's donation of a stoa (*stoan*) to the city. Since the original inscription was on only one line, any feminine noun could be restored. From Apollonia also come twin anonymous dedications to Hadrian as "savior and founder" (*IGR* IV 122, 123); Abmeier suggests that their occasion was Hadrian's work on the stoa while responding to the earthquake of 120 (see below, at n. 46). To my knowledge no archaeological finds support attributing to Hadrian any public building at Apollonia. See Abmeier 1990; F. K. Dörner, "Ausserbithynische Inschriften im Museum von Bursa und neue Funde aus Eskişehir (Dorylaion)," *Wiener Jahreshefte* 32 (1940), Beiblatt 125–28, on *IGR* IV 121, 122, 123; Halfmann 1986, 191, 199; cf. Schwertheim 1983, 127, and Hirschfeld, *RE* II 1 (1895): 115, s.v. Apollonia, #15.

[43] Walls and city gates were frequent at cities rebuilt or refurbished by Augustus, often linked to his veteran settlements in Italy: Keppie 1983, 114–16, 118–20.

[44] After Augustus's city walls (see n. 43 above), most urban defense systems in the Latin West date to or after the later second century A.D.: Maloney and Hobley 1983; Frere 1984, with a good discussion of the legal texts (e.g., *Dig.* 1.10.6, 1.16.7, 1.8.9.4), which date from the reign of Marcus Aurelius or later. As Frere points out (p. 65), "In Greece and early Italy self-governing cities tended to have walls . . . but there were strong reasons to discourage the erection of defences round new towns by communities only recently pacified."

[45] Although Jouffroy 1986, 220, attributes to Hadrian Quiza's defensive walls, the datable defense systems of Roman North African cities were constructed when new colonies were founded, when cities experienced a change of civic status, or during unsettled conditions postdating Hadrian: Rebuffat 1986, and Daniels 1983.

[46] *Chron. Pasch.* 1.475; cf. Eusebius, ad 120, and Hieron. *Chron.* 198.10 = Prosper Tiro

concern for cities struck by disaster.[47] Hadrian's even-handedness when assisting Nicaea and Nicomedia is particularly noteworthy in light of their long-standing, bitter rivalry. The two neighboring cities had vied for centuries for greater prestige in the region,[48] and Hadrian's simultaneous and parallel donations to both indicate his sensitivity to the divisive effects imperial munificence could have.

Two of the city gates of Nicaea, the East Gate ("Lefke Kapi") and the North Gate ("Gate of Istanbul"), had been dedicated to the imperial house and to Nicaea when built as part of the Roman walls supplanting shorter Hellenistic ones.[49] Their donor was M. Plancius Varus, proconsul of Bithynia and Pontus in the middle or end of Vespasian's reign.[50] Since the two gates carry a long dedication to Hadrian in addition to Varus's original inscription, Hadrian is thought to have rebuilt these city gates as well as the city walls the *Chronicon Paschale* mentions.[51] The frequent rebuilding of

---

598, in *Chron. Min.* I 422. The force of "and [Nicaea's] city walls toward Bithynia" in the *Chronicon Paschale* is unclear, since it suggests that the city walls were rebuilt only in the section toward the peaceful east. The *tetraplateia* of the same text (the Latin texts use *quadrivia*) is not found in Liddell-Scott-Jones or its supplement. Robert 1978, 397–98nn. 15–16, interprets *tetraplateia* as the crossroads of large porticoed avenues, ornamented by tetrapyla. I follow Robert for the earthquake's date, given variously by modern sources. In Nicomedia, part of a highly decorated frieze (found in the ruins of a nymphaeum) cites Hadrian in the nominative (*TAM* IV 10, and N. Firatli, *Izmit Sehri ve Eski Eserleri Rehberi* [Istanbul, 1971], pl. 20, 30), indicating his responsibility for erecting or re-erecting the now-lost building. An inscription, fragmentary and now lost (Oliver, #93 = *TAM* IV 5), recorded a letter of Hadrian to the city (after A.D. 129) that seems to have discussed an increase in Nicomedia's population (cf. W. Eck, *BonnJbb* 181 [1981]: 663). This may be corroborated by *TAM* IV 40, recording a tribe named for Hadrian, and *TAM* IV 238, citing a tribe named for Plotina. Hadrian is hailed as *Restitutor Nicomediae* on a Roman coin, one of only two issues in the "restitutor" series that commemorate a city rather than a province or region (*BMC, Emp.* III, p. 524, #1827 and plate 97.1, and Strack 1933, 164–65). Oliver tentatively assigns to Hadrian the fragmentary imperial epistles to Nicomedia he publishes as ##94, 95, pp. 239–40.

[47] See chapter 2 at n. 6. Hadrian's rebuilding of the Temple of Zeus at nearby Cyzicus was similarly impelled by the earthquake of A.D. 120: see Boatwright 1997a, 127–30; Schultz and Winter 1990.

[48] Robert 1977, 19n. 87.

[49] Schneider and Karnapp 1938, 1–2; cf. Merkelbach 1987, 9–10. Nicaea's Roman walls, 4,970 meters long, were longer than most, to judge from the comparative figures of Rebuffat 1986, 361.

[50] *MuseumIznik* I #1; S. Mitchell, "The Plancii in Asia Minor," *JRS* 64 (1974): 28–29. In contrast to Plancius Varus, an imperial representative not from the region he was supervising, the local citizen Patrocles was chosen to oversee Hadrian's construction in Nicaea: *MuseumIznik* I #56 = *ILS* 8867; T. Corsten, "Ein Baubeauftragter Hadrians in Nikaia," *EpigAnat* 10 (1987): 111–14, with corrections suggested by S. Mitchell 1993, I:213n. 87. See also chapter 4, on Hadrianic curatores.

[51] S. Mitchell 1993, I:213; for texts of the inscriptions, see Robert 1977, 6–9, modified slightly by Şahin 1978, 12 f (*SEG* XXVII 819–21); *MuseumIznik* I ##25–28. Though the surviving decoration of the gates has not been claimed as Hadrianic, the walls around the North Gate belong to this period: Schneider and Karnapp 1938, 42. It could also be that lit-

Nicaea's walls has obscured their Hadrianic phase, and Hadrian's work on the city gates has a comparandum only at Quiza in Mauretania Caesarensis, if the interpretation of a lacunose and problematic inscription is correct.[52] At the least, Hadrian's reconstruction in Nicaea reiterated the city's ties with the Roman emperors.

Hadrian's *horrea* (grain storehouses) in Myra and Patara, Lycia, seem to have been aimed primarily at facilitating imperial needs: the similar buildings are unusually designed, and their duplicate inscriptions are in Latin rather than the Greek common in the region. Some eighty-five kilometers apart on Turkey's southwestern shore, the horrea seem to have been built simultaneously around A.D. 130.[53] The rooms of both structures, on one story, open only to the front and can be easily guarded.[54] (See fig. 2.) Their inscriptions, originally spanning the facades, proclaimed simply, "Granaries [*horrea*] of Imperator Caesar Trajan Hadrian Augustus, son of the deified Trajan Parthicus and grandson of the deified Nerva, consul for the third time" (*CIL* III 232, Myra; *CIL* III 12129, at Patara, now breaks off after Hadrian's filiation). As embellishment or perhaps additional identification, busts of Hadrian and Sabina, now weathered but once protected by a bronze frame, are placed above the center of Myra's intact inscription (presumably similar at Patara).[55] The term *horrea* is commonly used for official imperial granaries.[56] Patara was the principle port of Lycia, and it and neighboring ports may have been regular stops for the freighters carrying grain from Alexandria to Rome.[57] Further, at Myra a small but prominent

tle actual reconstruction was needed, but Hadrian simply appropriated the glory of rebuilding the gates by the inscriptions.

[52] Little attests Quiza, the site of Pont du Chélif: H. Treidler, *RE* 24 (1963): 1333, s.v. Quiza; Gsell 1911, folio 11, no. 2, and "Additions et corrections," p. 6; *CIL* VIII 9697–9703, 21514–15. The Hadrianic inscription begins with Hadrian's name and titulature in the nominative, and commemorates his installation or reconstruction of an *arcus portaru*[*m*] perhaps in A.D. 128 or thereafter (*CIL* VIII 9697 = 21514): Halfmann 1986, 192, 132, tentatively relates the arch to Hadrian's visit to Africa in 128. The unusual phrase seems to mean, redundantly, "the arch of the city gates." Though *arcus* can designate a monumental arch, *porta* (or plural *portae*) also appears epigraphically: see *arcus* and *porta* in *OLD*, and *DizEpig* I, A–B, 647–48, s.v. "arcus"; cf. Wallace-Hadrill 1990, 144–46. Gsell 1901, I:185n. 1, suggests that the construction was single arches above individual city gates; Jouffroy 1986, 446, simply the gates of the walled city.

[53] Only Myra has received thorough publication: M. Wörrle, in Borchhardt et al. 1975, 64–71. Wörrle dates the horrea (pp. 67–68) on the basis of Hadrian's titulature, Sabina's hairstyle, and Hadrian's Lycian visit of 129.

[54] At Myra single guardrooms project from either end of the horrea to face one another. Further, the ashlar building technique at either site is alike, although the exterior blocks at Myra are slightly rusticated whereas those at Patara are smooth. Rickman 1971, 137–40, likens the unusual plan to that of North African granaries.

[55] Wörrle in Borchhardt et al. 1975, 68, and his pl. 38, A.

[56] Ibid., 67.

[57] Bean 1978, 84–85, 120–21; Rickman 1971, 140, noting that at Myra Paul encountered an Alexandrian grain ship bound for Italy (*Acts of the Apostles* 27).

Fig. 2. The front of the *horrea* (granaries) of Hadrian in Myra, built around A.D. 130. The heads of Hadrian and Sabina, placed in the middle of the inscription on the architrave, are just visible above the central entranceway.

relief, a round shield and two crossed spears, has led M. Wörrle to conclude that grain stored here was destined for the army in the East.[58]

In Myra and Patara, then, Hadrian's large-scale concerns profited individual cities, as at Trapezus and Puteoli. No such extensive benefits can be discerned for the stoas attributed to Hadrian, although this building type is often associated with trade.[59] For instance, Pausanias provides no clue for why Hadrian built the stoa at impoverished Hyampolis, which he alone attests, other than by implying an interest in cities destroyed by Xerxes and Philip (Paus. 10.35; see below on the Temple of Apollo at nearby Abae).[60] The building scholars associate with Pausanias's note has never been fully excavated.[61]

Hadrian's stoa at Hyampolis underscores the diversity and frequent puzzle of his municipal benefactions: nothing indicates that he visited Hyampolis, or that local landowners or notables caught his attention. It is equally

[58] Wörrle in Borchhardt et al. 1975, 68, and pl. 41, D: the relief decorates the pier between the two windows above the granary's fifth door.

[59] Cf. J. J. Coulton, *The Architectural Development of the Greek Stoa* (Oxford, 1976), who notes (pp. 168–69) the relative anachronism of new freestanding stoas in the second century A.D. (naming neither this stoa nor the purported one at Apollonia).

[60] Yorke 1896, with Fossey 1986, 72–76. The two cities overlook eastern Phocis's major road from Opous on the Euboean Gulf to Copaic Orchomenos.

[61] Yorke 1896, 303–4; Fossey 1986, 72, identifies the stoa as Hadrian's.

obscure why he gave the Hyampolitans a stoa rather than some other structure: Pausanias's narrative suggests that an aqueduct would have been
more useful. Despite the famed practicality of the Romans, considerations
of economic rationality cannot fully explain each of Hadrian's engineering
and building projects outside Rome. We see this especially clearly when assessing the next two groups of Hadrian's projects, his donations serving
spectacle and leisure, and those relating to temples, shrines, and tombs.

BUILDINGS SERVING SPECTACLES AND LEISURE ACTIVITIES

Despite Cassius Dio's claim that Hadrian constructed theaters and produced games as he traveled from city to city (69.10.1), relatively few buildings serving these purposes can be attributed to Hadrian.[62] (See table 6.2.)
He embellished the amphitheater at Capua (*CIL* X 3832), provided for
gymnasia in Athens (Paus. 1.18.9, cf. Oliver, #85; see chapter 7, appendix
7.3) and in Smyrna (Philostr. *VS* 531, cf. *IGR* IV 1431; see chapter 7),[63]
and built baths at Ostia (*CIL* XIV 98 = *ILS* 334 = Smallwood, #386),
Corinth (Paus. 2.3.5), Antioch (Malal. XI 277.20–278.19), and Italica

[62] Hadrian has been credited with restoring the theater at Argos after its devastation by
fire (e.g., Spawforth and Walker 1986, 102) on the basis of a fragmentary inscription published by W. Vollgraff, "Inscriptions d'Argos," *BCH* 68–69 (1944–45): 400–401, #9 and
fig. 3. Although the inscription was found in Argos's theater, the word *theatron* is restored in
the inscription. I exclude Hadrian's alleged restoration of the theater in Augusta Emerita
(Mérida, Spain). The theater, heavily restored in the early twentieth century, was originally
built by Agrippa (*CIL* II 474 = *ILS* 130), and in A.D. 105 its *ima cavea* (lowest part of the
seating) was modified to include a *sacrarium* (shrine) specifically for imperial cult (J. M.
Álvarez Martínez, "Roman Towns in Extremadura," in Bendala Galán 1993, 131–36, 141,
with ##38, 50, 52, on pp. 287, 292, 294; W. Trillmich, "Un *sacrarium* del culto imperial
en el Teatro de Mérida," *Anas* 2–3 [1990]: 87–102). Three capitals found at the theater have
been attributed to Hadrian (e.g., by Fuchs 1987, 160, 167–69, 186–89) on the basis of a
fragmentary inscription Hübner restored to read that in 135 Hadrian rebuilt the theater's
seating and *scaenae frons* after fire, dedicating the reconstruction with circus and scenic(?)
games (*CIL* II 478). But García Iglesias 1975 has convincingly rejected the inscription as a
hodgepodge of different materials with incompatible orthography. The capitals are now
likened to Trajanic capitals in Mérida (Diaz Martos 1985, 81–82, E 1–3), or even claimed
as late Flavian (J. Alvarez Sáenz de Buruaga, "Observaciónes sobre el teatro romano de
Mérida," in *Actas del simposio "El teatro en la Hispania romana"* [Badajoz, 1982], 308–10).
No statuary has been dated to the Hadrianic period. If Hadrian did restore the *scaenae frons*
of the theater at Augusta Emerita, this is his only building donation in Lusitania, and one of
only two possible interventions at theaters. I classify the Library of Hadrian in Athens (see
chapter 7) among temples and shrines.

[63] Hadrian's promised gymnasium in Cyrene (Oliver, #122) is discussed in chapter 8, at
n. 51 and following; a possible gymnasium in Italica tentatively associated with him is discussed in chapter 7, at n. 86.

(see chapter 7).[64] Although Smyrna's gymnasium simultaneously demonstrates Hadrian's collaboration with locals and elucidates the logistics of his building projects (see chapter 7), the six other buildings in this group, less well documented and scattered from east to west, more simply confirm aspects of Hadrian's building activity delineated above.

The extraordinarily large and splendid amphitheater at Capua was a joint project: its lacunose inscription seems once to have recorded that the city constructed the edifice, *divus Hadrianus* embellished it with columns and something else now unidentifiable (statues?), and Antoninus Pius dedicated it (*CIL* X 3832). The archaeological material supports a late Hadrianic date.[65] The brick-faced concrete and stone structure, its axes about 170 × 140 meters long, is second in size in Italy only to Rome's Colosseum, and it was lavishly decorated.[66] It must have conspicuously exemplified the benefits of local and imperial cooperation.[67] Of Hadrian's other donations mentioned above, his baths in Corinth and Antioch are witnessed but poorly.[68] Baths at Ostia, which he began and Antoninus Pius completed (*CIL* XIV 98 = *ILS* 334 = Smallwood, #386), have been identified with the considerable archaeological remains of the Baths of Neptune.[69] They are remarkable here for the large sum of two million sester-

---

[64] Yegül 1992, 1–5 and passim, notes the lack of real distinction between gymnasia and baths at this period. Hadrian may also have patronized baths in Aleria, Corsica, if a fragmentary inscription has been correctly interpreted. See n. 1 in this chapter.

[65] For the difficulties besetting Mommsen's restoration in *CIL,* see Boatwright 1989, 258–59. For the Hadrianic amphitheater, which supplanted a Republican one, see Blake, Bishop, and Bishop 1973, 261; Pesce 1941; De Caro and Greco 1981, 215–18; J. Heurgon, "Note sur Capoue et les villes campaniennes au IIe siècle de notre ère," in *Studies Presented to D. M. Robinson on His 70th Birthday,* ed. G. E. Mylonas and D. Raymond (St. Louis, 1953), II:931–37, cf. Golvin and Landes 1990, 25, 33–42. A similar decorative donation is Hadrian's gift to neighboring Caiatia of high-quality marble elements from quarries nearby at Cubulteria (*CIL* X 4574; perhaps in 120/121): Boatwright 1989, 252.

[66] The arcaded lower three stories had 240 sculpted protomes on their keystones, with gods and deities (from Jupiter and Juno to Voltunus, Mithras, and Isis) on the lower two; satyrs, tragic masks, Pan, and the like on the third. The vaulted entrance and exit passages (*vomitoria*) displayed reliefs of animals, mythological scenes with Marsyas, Hercules, and others, and generic and historical scenes. Sculptures in the round, such as the ones of Venus, Eros, and Psyche found at the amphitheater, may have decorated the fourth story. Grey granite columns also formed part of the embellishment. De Caro and Greco 1981, 215–17; Pesce 1941.

[67] Capua was one of the most important stops south from Rome on the road system that included the roads around Aeclanum mentioned above (at n. 40).

[68] To my knowledge none of the many existing baths of Corinth has been linked to Hadrian on archaeological evidence: cf. D. Engels, *Roman Corinth* (Chicago, 1990), 46. For Malalas's statement that in Antioch Hadrian built a public bath (XI 278.14), see n. 113 below.

[69] I have discussed these, in 1997a. A lovely, more than life-size statue of Sabina as Ceres was found in a shallow room opening to the palestra. On analogy with "Kaisersäle" of bath-gymnasia, Yegül 1992, 68, suggests that this was a "cult room."

ces (= 500,000 denarii) Hadrian promised when beginning the project; that this proved insufficient for the construction emphasizes yet again the costs associated with imperial buildings.

The relatively small number, possibly as few as seven, of spectacle and leisure buildings attended to by Hadrian in cities outside Rome is surprising: such structures were very popular and were often patronized by Augustus and other emperors.[70] In theaters, amphitheaters, circuses, and analogous spectacle buildings, religion coincided with other aspects of city life in the Roman world. Cult processions often ended at, or wound their way through, such edifices, and every public performance began and concluded with religious ceremonies.[71] Similarly, in the Greek East and in "Greek" cities of the Latin West such as Neapolis, gymnasia were used for training for the athletic competitions so essential to cities' festivals (see chapter 5), and they probably even staged the games. The more striking number of temples, shrines, and tombs Hadrian worked on in various cities (discussed in the next section) indicates that, when donating permanent structures, he preferred to shape religious life more directly than through constructions ostensibly aimed at spectacle and leisure. On the other hand, the relatively vast number of civic games associated with Hadrian (discussed in the preceding chapter) shows that Hadrian was quite aware of the roles public spectacle played in the Roman world. The discordant totals of Hadrian's games and his buildings for games seem to reflect the realization that it is not enough simply to build structures; one must integrate them with the patterns of daily life. Key to this last achievement were Hadrian's voracious desire to know the Roman world and his attentiveness to local differences.

TEMPLES, SHRINES, AND TOMBS

Hadrian was involved in building, restoring, or completing twenty temples and shrines in eighteen cities, adding sculpture and architectural decoration to four other shrines in four cities, and working on seven tombs in six different locales.[72] (See table 6.2.) His thirty-one physical contributions to

[70] E.g., after the earthquake of 62, by A.D. 79 Pompeii had rebuilt its baths, theater, amphitheater, and odeon, but most temples and governmental buildings were still under reconstruction. See also the lists of buildings in Jouffroy 1986, and S. L. Dyson, *Community and Society in Roman Italy* (Baltimore, 1992), 108–111.

[71] See Price 1984b, 110–12; Clavel-Lévêque 1986, 2439–46. Rogers 1991, 81–126, investigates the procession known from the Salutaris inscription of Ephesus (chapter 5, at n. 57 and following).

[72] Hadrian's infrequent patronage to "extra-urban" sanctuaries went to ones close to the settlement on which they depended (e.g., to Argive Hera): of the twenty-nine extra-urban sanctuaries named in Pausanias (listed in Alcock 1993, 204), Hadrian affected solely the sanctuary of Poseidon Hippios in Mantinea.

religious structures are about a third of all his known architectural and engineering donations, and his most frequent single type.[73] Ancient sources furnish few clues for this activity. The biography holds that Hadrian cared for Roman sacred things most assiduously, but scorned foreign ones (*sacra Romana diligentissime curavit, peregrina contempsit, HA, Hadr.* 22.10). Although the first assertion is justified by Hadrian's attention to archaic shrines in Italy, the second is belied by his care for Greek cult buildings, his introduction into Rome of the Eleusinian Mysteries (Aur. Vict. *Caes.* 14.4), and his divinization of Antinoos.[74] The statement is generally valid only if we distinguish "Roman" and "foreign" as Hadrian apparently did, with "Roman" embracing *Greco*-Roman culture, and "foreign" referring to cultures falling outside or rejecting the Greco-Roman one. (See chapter 8.) The biography reports, misleadingly, that Hadrian consecrated temples "to his own name" during his (129–30) trip through Asia (*HA, Hadr.* 13.6; cf. *HA, AlexSev.* 43.6).[75] Although the statement must refer generally to temples of the imperial cult,[76] the frequency of Hadrianic donor inscriptions on restored and completed temples and shrines in Asia, eight in all, indicates one possible source of the invention.

Hadrian's work at temples and shrines must have helped impress upon polytheistic city dwellers a belief in the emperor's beneficent ubiquity. Religion and religious rituals pervaded city life in the Roman world.[77] Although the actual deities and divinized individuals advanced by Hadrian's donations are a miscellany, including Olympian gods, members of the imperial family, and Homeric and other heroes, more important was the identification of religious life, of whatever sort, with the emperor himself. This was furthered by building inscriptions displaying Hadrian's name,[78] statues of Hadrian erected in a temple's temenos or cella,[79] and festivals asso-

---

[73] I exclude consideration of his work in Rome itself. According to Pausanias (1.5.5), to honor Hadrian all the temples and shrines he had built, decorated, or repaired, as well as the boons he gave to Greek cities, sometimes even to foreigners who asked him, were listed on the sanctuary at Athens "common to all the gods" (the "Pantheon" raised by Hadrian himself; see chapter 7, appendix 7.4). Temples and shrines are listed first in this summarized inventory, perhaps reflecting the actual inscription.

[74] Beaujeu 1955, 114–64, 274–78; Callu 1992, 128–29n. 230.

[75] The line in Hadrian's biography *per Asiam iter faciens templa sui nominis consecravit* implies both that Hadrian consecrated temples involving worship of himself even while he was alive, and that he did so in Asia but not in other provinces.

[76] W. Schmid, "Bilderloser Kult und christliche Intoleranz. Wesen und Herkunft zweier Nachrichten bei Aelius Lampridius (*Alex,* 43.6f)," in *Festschrift Th. Klauser,* ed. A. Stuiber and A. Hermann (Munich, 1964), 298–315.

[77] E.g., North 1992, 177–79.

[78] A temple's dedicatory inscription could omit the name of the deity honored while commemorating the patron: cf. the inscription of the Pantheon in Rome.

[79] Nock 1930; Le Glay 1976, 354.

ciated with a new or restored temple or shrine (chapters 5, 7). For example, in Megara Hadrian was honored with the epithet "Pythios" (like Pythian Apollo, *IG* VII 70–72, 3491): here, among other benefactions, he rebuilt completely in white marble an archaic Temple of Apollo associated with the Lesser Pytheia games.[80]

Besides integrating emperor and gods generally, more direct consequences can be inferred for how Hadrian's building donations affected cities' religious life. These emerge most clearly when we divide the donations into four main groups:[81] the famous Hellenistic temples he finished; the archaic sanctuaries he renovated in Italy and the Greek East; the temples and shrines more immediately connected with imperial cult he built or restored throughout the empire; and his work at tombs in Achaea, Asia, and Egypt.

Work on Prominent Hellenistic Temples

Donations in this group relate both to the Roman proclivity for large-scale projects, a trait discussed with Hadrian's engineering undertakings, and to Hadrian's own architectural interests, which helped shape his Temple of Venus and Roma in Rome (Cass. Dio 69.4.2–6; cf. *HA, Hadr.* 16.10, *Epit. de Caes.* 14.2).[82] We cannot know if this huge temple in the capital city (built ca. 121–41) was planned by Hadrian himself, but its design plainly recalls temples planned by Hermogenes and other Hellenistic architects.[83] Moreover, Hermogenes had designed the renowned Temple of Dionysus at Teos around the turn of the second century B.C., a temple Hadrian restored in A.D. 132 or thereafter, and

[80] Paus. 1.42.5, on the temple; see n. 97 below. Citing no evidence, Weber 1907, 181 (followed by many), holds that the temple was begun in 124 and finished in 135 or 136. Megara's Lesser Pytheia games, celebrated in the Hadrianic period, were associated with this temple: Rigsby 1987, with Philostr. *VS* 529 and *IG* VII 106. See E. Meyer, *RE* 15.1 (1931): 201–2, s.v. Megara, and A. Muller, "Megarika," *BCH* 108 (1984): 263–66. Hadrian was also called Pythios (and Panhellenios and Olympios) at Delphi in 132 (Flacelière 1971, 175, #16 = A. Plassart, *F.Delphes* III.4.308), where he accepted the position of archon twice (probably in 118–120 and 125), and undertook restorations, perhaps of the area Pylaia (*Syll.*[3] 830, 836; see chapter 4, n. 55). Similarly, Hadrian is identified as the "New Dionysus" by the Dionysiac artists, to whom he gave signal benefits: see chapter 5, at n. 98, and Le Glay 1976, 355n. 37; Beaujeu 1955, 172–73, 187, 194–97.

[81] These categories are not exclusive: some donations fit into two or more, such as Hadrian's restorations at Juno Gabina and at Nemi. In the third group I include buildings whose primary purpose was imperial cult, but not multifunctional ones that could be used occasionally for imperial cult, as seems to have happened at Athens's "Roman Agora."

[82] Boatwright 1987, 30–31.

[83] Ibid., 128–29, 30–31.

Hermogenes's plans and canons were influential in the second-century (B.C.) rebuilding of the Temple of Juno Gabina at Gabii,[84] an archaic sanctuary Hadrian patronized after A.D. 123 (*AE* 1982, 142).[85] The second-century (B.C.) temple at Nemi, at another archaic shrine also restored in some way by Hadrian (*CIL* XIV 2216 = *ILS* 843, 121/122), is discussed by Vitruvius as an example of beautiful Hellenistic architecture (*De Arch.* 4.8.4).[86] A fourth restoration by Hadrian I include here is that at the Temple of Apollo at Claros (third century B.C.).[87] Although the extent of Hadrian's undated restoration is still unclear, this shrine exemplifies the grand Hellenistic design characterizing Hadrianic restorations such as the Temple of Venus and Roma and the Olympieion, which Hadrian completed in Athens by A.D. 131 (see chapter 7). Discussion of the Temple of Dionysus at Teos illuminates this category. (See fig. 3.)

The Temple of Dionysus at Teos is an architectural masterpiece, described by Hermogenes himself (Vitr. *De Arch.* 7.praef.12). It was associated with the celebrated synod of the Artists of Dionysus when the group

---

[84] M. Almagro-Gorbea and J. L. Jiménez, "Metrologia, Modulación, Trazado y Reconstrucción del Templo," in Almagro-Gorbea 1982, 123, 614, referring to both Hermogenes and his follower Hermodoros of Salamis, active in Rome after 146 B.C.

[85] Date from corroborating brick stamps of A.D. 123, found in restorations of the western portico: C. Basas-Faure, in Almagro-Gorbea 1982, 226–27, #16; J. Arxé in Almagro-Gorbea 1982, 219–20, and ibid., 619, 623. See also E. Rodriguez Almeida, "Epigrafía Gabina Novísima. Hallazgos epigráficos de las excavaciónes españolas en las campañas de 1956 a 1965," *Cuadernos de trabajos de la Escuela Española de Historia y Arquelogía en Roma* 12 (1969): 39–41.

[86] I have treated this restoration in other contexts, particularly that of Hadrian's interest both in Italian archaic cults and in linking such tokens of the past to more recent and "foreign" events: see Boatwright 1989, 252–54.

[87] On epigraphic evidence, Hadrian has been associated with restorations in the sanctuary of Apollo at Claros (*RA* 1963, 109–11; I saw two additional fragments in Claros, 10 June 1995). Excavations confirm the first half of the second century A.D. as a time of great changes for the shrine. A colossal Roman statuary group (at least 7–8 meters high; Apollo seated between standing figures of Artemis and Leto), was installed in the cella of the temple of Apollo, a third-century (B.C.) 6 × 11 Doric peripteros of local marble (26 × 46 meters on a five-stepped crepidoma) with interior subterranean chamber from which the priest prophesized. The statues necessitated modification of the temple. C. Picard, *RA* 1963, 109–111, holds that Hadrian completely rebuilt the temple; Robert 1954, that Hadrian was responsible only for completing a restoration of the peripteros begun in the early Empire (cf. Paus. 7.5.4: the sanctuary was unfinished but imposing). Adjacent, and around the same time, a new Ionic temple and altar were built above earlier ones dedicated to Artemis; the ground level around the 9 × 18.45-meter altar of Apollo was raised ca. 0.3 meters; and new honorific monuments went up on the higher level. See La Genière 1990; J. de La Genière, "Les Nouvelles fouilles de Claros," *Türk Arkeoloji Dergisi* 28 (1989): 287–92; Akurgal 1983, 136–39; J. de La Genière, *Cahiers de Claros,* vol. I (Paris, 1992), and J. de La Genière, "Le Sanctuaire d'Apollon à Claros," *CRAI* 1992, 195–210.

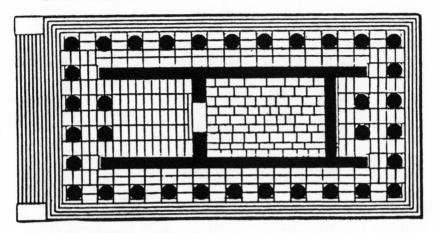

Fig. 3. Plan of the Temple of Dionysus at Teos, famous for its design by Hermogenes on the "eustyle" (beautiful-columned) principle, with intercolumniation two-and-a-quarter times the lower columnar diameter.

established a headquarters in Teos sometime after 200 B.C.; it was represented on Teos's coinage; and its excavations have resulted in a partial anastylosis.[88] Excavations reveal Hadrian's responsibility for some restoration here toward the end of his life. A fragmentary inscription on an architrave begins with Hadrian's name and titles in the nominative; among his epithets is the unusual but not unparalleled "Panionios," used for Hadrian only after A.D. 131.[89] Just as Hadrian's epithet on Teos's donor inscription referred to the region's glorious "Pan-Ionic" past, his restorations carefully respected the earlier architecture.

The large Ionic temple, a 6 × 11 peripteros on a stylobate approximately 19 × 35 meters, has an unusually deep two-columned pronaos and a narrower two-columned opisthodomos. Its intercolumniation, two-and-a-quarter times the lower columnar diameter, represents the "eustyle" (beautiful-columned) principle Vitruvius attributes to Hermogenes (Vitr. *De Arch.* 3.8). Also consonant with known features of Hermogenes's work are the temple's Attic column bases and finely sculpted frieze. The frieze de-

[88] Akurgal 1983, 139–42; A. Davesne, "Numismatique et archéologie: Le Temple de Dionysos à Téos," *Revue Numismatique* 29 (1987): 15–20; Hahland 1950. For Hadrian and the synod of the Artists of Dionysus, see chapter 5.

[89] L. Robert, "La dédicace du Temple de Dionysos à Teos," *Hellenica* III (Paris, 1946), 86–89. Some fragments were published earlier in *BCH* 46 (1922): 330 no. 10 = *SEG* II 588: the letters of the (at least) three-line inscription measure 11–16 cm high. Kienast 1990, 130, discusses "Panionios."

picts scenes of Dionysus's life and myth, and has been dated to the end of the third and the beginning of the second centuries B.C., Hermogenes's heyday. Most of the Ionic capitals, however, are Roman, deliberate copies of the few Hellenistic capitals either left in place or reinstalled in Hadrian's rebuilding. Some acroteria also are Hadrianic, again mimicking reused Hellenistic ones.[90] The Hadrianic rebuilding carefully reused the original frieze with minimal changes,[91] thus intermingling the glorious past and its restoration by Hadrian.

Renovations at Archaic Sanctuaries

Both the shrine of Diana at Nemi and that of Juno Gabina at Gabii were famous for the antiquity of their cults as well as for the Hellenistic architecture of their Republican rebuildings; they serve as a bridge to the second category of Hadrian's religious work I discuss, his renovations at archaic sanctuaries. In Italy Hadrian undertook restorations or embellishments at the famous archaic sanctuary at Cupra Maritima (*CIL* IX 5294 = *ILS* 313, 126/127) and at two ancient temples in Lanuvium (*CIL* XIV 2088 = *ILS* 316, 135/136; *EE* IX 610, undated), besides those at Nemi and Gabii.[92] Although Cupra Maritima was not one of the original Latin cities, the other shrines were within Latium Vetus (the site of the original Latin cities, close to Rome; see fig. 4). Hadrian's attention to them may have been spurred by his early position as *praefectus urbi feriarum Latinarum causa* (supervisor of the city of Rome, so that the Latin festival can be carried out, *ILS* 308 = Smallwood, #109). Although his duties would have been at Rome (if any duties were still performed in this symbolic position),[93] Hadrian's tenure in this outdated post may have impressed him with the continuing symbolism of archaic Italic religion, especially that tied to Latium.[94]

[90] Pülz 1989, 77–78, with illustrations and referring to R. P. Pullan, *Antiquities of Ionia* 4 (1882): 35ff, plates 22–25 (non vidi); Y. Bequignon and L. Laumonier, "Fouilles de Téos (1924)," *BCH* 49 (1925): 281–98; H. Weber, "Zum Apollo Smintheus-Tempel in der Troas," *IstMitt* 16 (1966): 114n. 12. M. Uz has been excavating in Teos since 1982, but I am unaware of any published results.

[91] Hahland 1950, 74, 105.

[92] See Boatwright 1989, 255–57.

[93] For the *feriae Latinae,* see G. Wissowa, *Religion und Kultus der Römer,* 2nd ed. (Munich, 1912), 123–25; H. H. Scullard, *Festivals and Ceremonies of the Roman Republic* (Ithaca, NY, 1981), 111–15; G. Vitucci, *Ricerche sulla praefectura urbi in età imperiale (sec. I–III)* (Rome, 1956), 10–11.

[94] Although the antiquity of the sacred buildings Hadrian renovated at Antium and Nomentum is stressed in the deficient documentation for them (*CIL* X 6652, 120/121 or thereafter; *AE* 1976, 114, A.D. 136), we cannot identify the buildings, and such language was conventional. See chapter 2.

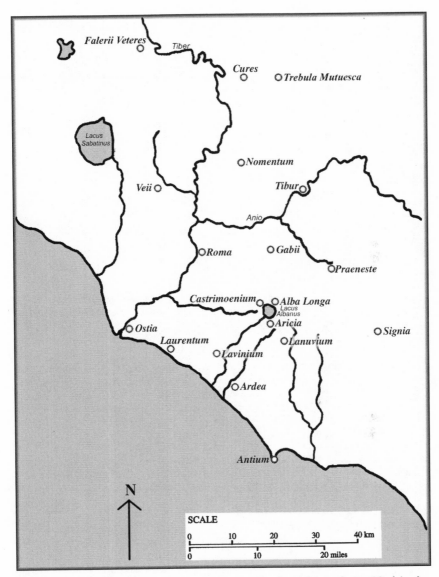

Fig. 4. Map of central Italy, including cities benefiting from Hadrian's largesse.

Hadrian's restorations of archaic shrines in the Greek East are better known. Pausanias carefully describes Hadrian's restorations and embellishments of archaic temples or sanctuaries, at Abae (Paus. 10.35.4), Argos (Paus. 2.17.6), Mantinea (Paus. 8.10.2), and Megara (Paus. 1.42.5).[95] The Argive Heraion, still internationally famous, had long been associated with Roman emperors.[96] The oracular Temple of Apollo at Abae apparently attracted Hadrian because of its remarkable history (Paus. 10.35.1–5; see below). Mantinea's archaic sanctuary of Poseidon Hippios seems to have profited from Hadrian probably because the city was the metropolis of Bithynion-Claudiopolis, the birthplace of his beloved Antinoos (Paus. 8.9.7–8, 8.10.2). Megara's Temple of Apollo may have been restored by Hadrian simply because he noticed that it was old and ugly.[97] I discuss the renovation of the Temple of Apollo at Phocian Abae, to elucidate some aims and effects of Hadrian's archaistic activity.

Before Hadrian, the history of Abae's oracular Temple of Apollo was as illustrious as its structure was precarious. Croesus had consulted this oracle, which grew to remarkable wealth before Xerxes destroyed it in 480 (Hdt. 1.46, 8.33).[98] Abae survived, however, to become one of the few Greek cities to which the Romans granted the special status of a "free city."[99] But the oracle was out of use, and the old sanctuary, burnt first by Xerxes and then by the Thebans (in 347 B.C.), barely stood during Pausa-

---

[95] Hadrian was responsible for other donations in Argos (see next note; also, the construction of an aqueduct, with perhaps a nymphaeum at its termination, perhaps before 124: W. Vollgraff, "Inscriptions d'Argos," *BCH* 68–69 [1944–45]: 397–401, ##8 and 7, "Fouilles d'Argos (1912)," *BCH* 44 [1920]: 224–25, and "Fouilles et sondages sur le flanc oriental de la Larissa à Argos," *BCH* 82 [1958]: 539–58; Aupert 1989 and 1994; R. Ginouvès, *Le Théâtron à gradins droits et l'odéon d'Argos* [Paris, 1972], 234–35; S. Walker, "Roman Nymphaea in the Greek World," in Macready and Thompson 1987, 64); in Mantinea (annual and penteteric games honoring Antinoos, and an epigram for the tomb of Epaminondas: see chapter 8, at n. 22, and below, at n. 137); and Megara (including broadening the Scironian Road into two lanes: Paus. 1.44.6–8; see above).

[96] Hadrian dedicated a gold and bejewelled statue of a peacock at the Argive Heraion (Paus. 2.17.6), which was represented on the city's coins: J. G. Frazer, *Pausanias's Description of Greece* (London, 1898), III:185–86, citing the coins. Before the temple's entrance stood a statue of Orestes, identified as Augustus by an inscription; Nero offered a golden crown and purple robe to Hera (Paus. 2.17.3, 6).

[97] In contrast to his careful preservation of the earlier sanctuaries at Abae and Mantinea, at Megara Hadrian replaced the archaic temple of Apollo, made of mud-brick, with a temple made of white marble. It was on the western acropolis of Megara: see n. 80 above.

[98] Fossey 1986, 78–81, 142–43. Sophocles ranks Abae with Delphi and Olympia (*OT* 897–900), and its walls seem to indicate rebuilding almost immediately after its destruction by the Persians: Fossey 1986, 127.

[99] Cf. Bernhardt 1971, 93–96, on this and other centers of Greek cult and festival thus distinguished by the Romans.

nias's visit (10.35.1–5). Pausanias calls the older temple "the frailest of buildings ever damaged by fire," saying that Hadrian left it undisturbed as a "memorial to barbarian hatred" when juxtaposing with it a deliberately modest temple (Paus. 10.35.2–4). Excavations a century ago in a small outlying temenos of Abae apparently confirm Pausanias's account, for two neighboring and parallel temples were discovered, the northern about half the size of the southern one.[100]

The careful juxtaposition of new and old temples at Abae corresponds to other manifestations of Hadrian's respect for archaic cults. At Poseidon Hippios in Mantinea, for example, the emperor charged his overseers to prevent workmen from looking into the old sanctuary or removing its remains, and his new construction purposefully surrounded the old so completely as to obscure the archaic shrine (Paus. 8.10.2).[101] Additionally, Pausanias's words indicate that at Abae Hadrian emphasized a distinction between barbarian and Greek. The ruinous temple, left standing as "a memorial to barbarian hatred" (a reference to the legendary Oath of Plataea), implicitly identified as Greek the new temple Hadrian raised alongside it.[102]

Yet cultivating a glorious past by renovating a famous archaic shrine did not necessarily revitalize a city. Pausanias implies that Abae remained impoverished, as did its neighbor Hyampolis, notwithstanding Hadrian's gift to it of a stoa (Paus. 10.35.6; see above). Megara, Gabii, and Lanuvium, all of which benefited from Hadrian's building largesse, were proverbial for their desolation.[103] Despite his acclaim as "the enricher of the town" at Gabii (together with his wife Sabina: *CIL* XIV 2799), and as "like Pythian Apollo" at Megara (*IG* VII 70–72, 3491), Hadrian could not make cities prosper simply by renovating their archaic shrines.

---

[100] The northern temple, whose west wall measured in entirety only fifteen feet (about 4.6 meters), is identified as Hadrian's temple, the southern one as the original Temple of Apollo. Behind the two temples a large stoa echoed their eastern orientation. Dated to the fourth century B.C. by architectural terracottas, it may have been in disrepair when Pausanias visited, and therefore was overlooked. An inscription from the precinct indicates imperial restoration of a temple to Apollo: Yorke 1896, 291–305.

[101] J. G. Frazer, *Pausanias's Description of Greece* (London, 1898), IV:217; G. Fougères, "Fouilles de Mantinée," *BCH* 14 (1890): 80–81, and Beaujeu 1955, 242–57.

[102] Oath of Plataea: Lycurg. *Leoc.* 81; Diod. Sic. 11.29.2–4; in brief, R. Meiggs, *The Athenian Empire* (Oxford, 1972), 504–7. The Panhellenion similarly stressed the distinction between Greek and "barbarian" (see chapter 7 at n. 14 and following).

[103] On this topos, see Alcock 1993, 26–32. Megara: Paus. 1.36.3, cf. Cic. *Ad fam.* 4.5.4; Gabii: Cic. *Planc.* 23, Hor. *Ep.* 1.11.7, Prop. 4.1.34, Luc. 7.392, Juv. 3.192, 6.56, 7.4 and 10.100; Lanuvium: Pliny *NH* 35.6.17, cf. *HA, Pii* 8.3. At Gabii archaeological material diminishes after Hadrian, and the temple fell out of use after 266: Almagro-Gorbea 1982, 623–24, and P. P. Ripollés, "Hallazgos Numismaticos," in Almagro-Gorbea 1982, 231–50.

Temples of Imperial Cult

Designation as the provincial seat of imperial cult promised more economic benefits, as we saw in chapter 5. But this is not the only significance of imperial cult, as S. R. F. Price, D. Fishwick, and others have shown, nor was this the sole means of encouraging the fealty of communities and individuals to the Roman emperor.[104] Hadrian increased the presence of imperial cult in Italy and the provinces. In addition to sponsoring festivals and designating individual cities as neocoros (see chapters 5 and 7), Hadrian built, restored, or embellished at least eleven temples and shrines that are more or less obviously connected with imperial cult.[105] (See table 6.2.)

Four of these eleven buildings exalted individual emperors or the imperial family: the "Traianeum" of Italica and the Library of Hadrian of Athens, both apparently dating to the middle of Hadrian's reign (see chapter 7 for both), the "Basilica of Plotina" in Nemausus (Nîmes) of the early 120s (*HA, Hadr.* 12.2, cf. Cass. Dio 69.10.3[1]), which should be connected to imperial cult,[106] and the restoration of the Temple of Augustus in Tarraco in 122/123 (*HA, Hadr.* 12.3).[107] These have more problematic evidence than do the seven imperial cult temples and shrines Hadrian built or restored in Rome itself.[108] Yet both Italica's "Traianeum" and Ne-

[104] E.g., Price 1984b; Fishwick 1987–92; Le Glay 1976; K. Hopkins, *Conquerors and Slaves* (Cambridge, Eng., 1978), 197–242.

[105] In this chapter or the next I discuss the "Traianeum" of Italica; the Library of Hadrian, the Olympieion, the Temple of Zeus Panhellenius, and the "Pantheon" of Athens; the imperial cult temple at Smyrna; the Temple of the Nymphs at Antioch; and the sanctuary of Hermes at Trapezus. Information on the "Basilica of Plotina" in Nemausus, the Temple of Augustus in Tarraco, and the Temple of Zeus in Cyzicus is in the following notes.

[106] These passages, the only direct evidence for the Basilica, have been linked with *ILS* 4844 = Smallwood, #142, an undated dedication to Jupiter and Nemausus from a T. Flavius Herm., *exactor oper(i) basilicae marmorari et lapidari* (the supervisor of the marble and stone work for the Basilica). An inscription found in 1970s salvage excavations in Nîmes records that as thanks for her position, a *flaminica perpetua* (priestess for life of the imperial cult) installed a silver statue of herself in a basilica: inscription photographed and erroneously transcribed in B. Dedet, P. Garmy, and J. Pey, "Découverte d'une enceinte de l'Antiquité tardive ou du Haut Moyen Age à Nîmes (Gard)," *Bulletin d'Ecole Antique de Nîmes*, n.s. 16 (1981): 158 and fig. 33. P. Gros identifies the Basilica of Plotina with the South Building of the Sanctuary of Nemausus (and of the imperial cult, often called the Temple of Diana), arguing on stylistic and architectural grounds (its remaining Corinthian capitals; and that the structure was a propylon set axially within a deep porticus rather than a closed building); he argues, too (referring to Malalas's vocabulary and usage), that the *Historia Augusta*'s *basilica* is synonymous with *porticus:* Gros 1984; P. Gros, "Théâtre et culte impérial en Gaule Narbonnaise et dans la péninsule ibérique," in Trillmich and Zanker 1990, 383–85; P. Gros, "Le Sanctuaire des eaux à Nîmes, 2ème partie: l'édifice sud," *RAC* 22 (1983): 163–72. Fishwick 1987, I.2.315, is more dubious about this identification.

[107] G. Alföldy, "Tarraco," *Forum* 8 (1991): 43–62.

[108] The Pantheon, Divorum, Temple of the Deified Matidia, Basilicas of Matidia and of

mausus's Basilica of Plotina can be said to demonstrate Hadrian's honor for his adoptive parents in their native cities and to reinforce the personal ties between the imperial family and provincial communities.[109]

As we see in the following chapter, the Library of Hadrian featured a design borrowed from Hellenistic gymnasia and associated with ruler cult as it united public recognition of Hadrian as benefactor with Athens's traditional erudition and education. Although the extent of Hadrian's restoration in 122/123 is not yet clear, his work at the Temple of Augustus in Tarraco, the earliest imperial cult shrine officially sanctioned in the Latin West, signified his position as the successor of the prototypical princeps, the head of the state and of state religion. Moreover, Tiberian coins show that the cult statue in Tarraco depicted Augustus in the guise of Jupiter, seated on a throne and holding an upraised spear(?) in his left hand, and a globe with a small winged Victory in his right.[110] The statue is like the icon of Zeus Hadrian gave to his new Temple of the Nymphs at Antioch, denoting a context of imperial cult for this later and more enigmatic building donation.

Two of the other seven imperial cult shrines Hadrian patronized, the Temple of the Nymphs at Antioch and Trapezus's sanctuary of Hermes, well illustrate some ways imperial cult could be advanced at sanctuaries nominally dedicated to other gods.[111] At first sight the Temple of the Nymphs appears unique, since Hadrian is not otherwise linked to these deities.[112] But consideration of all the testimony, most of which comes from the sixth-century chronicler Malalas, reveals the close connection of the temple with imperial cult. While describing Hadrian's wondrous waterworks at the springs of Antioch's suburb Daphne,[113] Malalas reports

---

Marciana, Temple of the Deified Trajan and Plotina, and Forum Augustum: Boatwright 1987, passim.

[109] Nîmes seems to have been the *origo* of Plotina's family: M. T. Boatwright, "The Imperial Women of the Early Second Century A.C.," *AJP* 112 (1991): 515; Syme 1958, II:604.

[110] Fishwick 1987, I.1.153, and Taller Escola d'Arqueologia de Tarragona, "El Foro provincial de Tarraco, un complejo arquetectónico de época flavia," *ArchEspArq* 62 (1989): 151–57, illustrate the coins struck during the reign of Tiberius. Date and identification of temple and precinct are controversial: coins and Tacitus (*Ann.* 1.78) date the temple, a "Temple of Augustus," to the beginning of Tiberius's reign, but archaeological evidence dates the completion of the uppermost terraco of Tarraco, in which the temple rose, only to the Vespasianic period: Hauschild 1972/1974, 3–44.

[111] I do not discuss here Hadrian's reconstruction of the Temple of Zeus at Cyzicus, which I have treated elsewhere: Boatwright 1997a, 127–30. See also Schulz and Winter 1990, and A. Schulz, "Bonsignore Bonsignori in Kyzikos," in *Studien zum antiken Kleinasien III* (Bonn, 1995), 113–25.

[112] Beaujeu 1955, 187, interprets Hadrian's Temple to the Nymphs as part of a general extension of water cults in the second century.

[113] Malalas reports that before 129 Hadrian gave Antioch an aqueduct with "theatron" and baths named after himself (XI 278.14), but the notice is so similar to his earlier account of the baths and aqueduct Trajan built and named after himself (XI 276.1–2) as to make it

that Hadrian built there a Temple of the Springs, or "Nymphs." Adding that Hadrian had installed a large seated statue of Zeus holding the celestial sphere,[114] Malalas specifies that "in honor of the Naiads [Nymphs], this was a thank-offering for having completed such a tremendous task" (XI 278.14).[115]

Roman shrines at springs and the sources of aqueducts usually honored major and minor deities of water and other liquids, or of health:[116] Zeus's statue at this Temple of the Nymphs appears anomalous.[117] Throughout Hadrian's reign, however, and even before his restoration of the Olympieion in Athens cemented his identification with Zeus Olympios (see chapter 7), Hadrian was associated with Zeus and Jupiter.[118] At Smyrna, Cyzicus, and elsewhere, he contributed to huge temples to Zeus, and festivals at these and other Zeus temples in the Greek East linked Hadrian, Zeus, and the imperial cult (see chapters 5, 7).[119] It was natural that the emperor,

---

almost certain that Hadrian was simply completing or restoring Trajan's earlier structures after Antioch's devastating earthquake of 115. Some remains reported earlier in this century seem to be from an aqueduct six kilometers long between Antioch and springs at Antioch's southern suburb, Daphne. See Jeffreys et al. 1986, 147; Downey 1961, 221–23; G. Downey, "The Water Supply of Antioch on the Orontes in Antiquity," *Annales archéologiques de Syrie* 1 (1951): 174–75, 179–83; Wilber 1938; cf. Syme 1983 (discounting *HA, Hadr.* 14.1). According to Malalas and archaeological comparanda, Hadrian's project collected the water from Daphne's many springs into a cistern, which then provided water to Antioch's aqueduct and to a "theatron," or nymphaeum. From the nymphaeum's catch basin, perhaps after diversion to a smaller catch basin (Malalas's "theatridion"), the water was divided into five streams of different capacities by means of discharge pipes or channels. See R. H. Chowen, "The Nature of Hadrian's *Theatron* at Daphne," *AJA* 60 (1956): 275; cf. Ginouvès 1969, 162–64; Glaser 1987.

[114] *Polos*, celestial sphere, is the result of a sound textual emandation: see Jeffreys et al. 1986, ad loc. p. 147, and Downey 1961, 222n. 102.

[115] Malalas seems to be repeating part of the inscription on the statue's base: Moffatt 1990, 103; E. Jeffreys, "Malalas' Sources," in Jeffreys et al. 1990, 201.

[116] Glaser 1987, 126–28; J. Scheid, "Sanctuaires et thermes sous l'empire," in *Les Thermes romains* (Rome, 1991), 207–9. For the scant evidence for worship of the Nymphs at Antioch, see F. W. Norris, "Antioch-on-the-Orontes as a Religious Center, 1. Paganism before Constantine," *ANRW* 2.18.4 (1990): 2347–48.

[117] F. W. Norris, "Antioch-on-the-Orontes as a Religious Center, 1," 2333, 2347, first groups it with other demonstrations of Zeus's prominence in Antioch, then suggests that it resembled Hadrian himself and not Zeus at all. Norris follows C. Müller, *Antiquitates Antiochenae* (Göttingen, 1839), 89, and Downey 1961, 222. Beaujeu 1955, 187, simply overlooks the statue to Zeus.

[118] As early as A.D. 129 he is termed "Olympios" on coins from Ephesus, and he is honored as Olympios in Cyzicus in 124: *IKyzikos* II #27 b–d; Metcalf 1974.

[119] For Cyzicus and Colonia Aelia Capitolina, see above, n. 111, and chapter 8, at n. 135 and following; for Hadrian and Olympieia in Alexandria Troas, see Weber 1907, 133, Le Glay 1976, 354n. 31; in Anemurium, see Weber 1907, 229, and Le Glay 1976, 354n. 31; Hadrian and Zeus together in a temple in Lydia, *IGR* IV 1607 and Le Glay 1976, 354n. 31. Cf. Willers 1990, 59–60.

the savior, benefactor, and lord of the world, be assimilated to Jupiter/ Zeus, the most powerful god, the head of the Roman state religion (cf. Pliny *Pan.* 80.4 and 88.8).[120]

This assimilation was fostered at Antioch by the celestial globe that Hadrian's statue of Zeus held in the Temple of the Nymphs.[121] After Augustus had assumed power, an essential part of imperial image was control of the *oikoumene* (the inhabited world),[122] as symbolized in Tarraco's statue of Augustus as Jupiter, for example. Malalas's words imply that the seated statue of Zeus was the most prominent sculpture in the new temple at Antioch. Hadrian's constructions at Daphne were dedicated with the institution of a festival, named Hadrianeion after the emperor and first held on 23 June (see chapter 5, nn. 75 and 83).[123] The Temple of the Nymphs here must have evoked Hadrian and imperial cult just as much as it did veneration of the Nymphs.[124]

At Antioch large-scale building activities, together with the introduction of a festival, tied the cult of the emperor to local cults. In contrast, in Trapezus imperial cult was advanced with relatively little cost or effort. Arrian's *Periplus Maris Euxini* opens with an invocation to Hadrian as Arrian describes disembarking in Trapezus at a sanctuary to Hermes (in the 130s). Arrian, then governor of Cappadocia, reports his decision to renovate the sanctuary, which had two engraved stone altars, a statue of Hadrian pointing toward the sea, and a stone temple with a statue of Hermes within. Promising to rebuild the altars in marble and to recut their inscriptions, Arrian requests that Hadrian send three statues, one to replace a substandard image of Hadrian already there, a five-foot one to supersede the temple's disproportionately small icon of Hermes, and a four-foot one of Philesios, Hermes' "descendant."[125] Arrian concludes the preamble by recounting his sacrifice of an ox and the prayers he made "deservedly" on Hadrian's behalf (*Perip. M. Eux.,* 1–2). Although no trace of statues or al-

---

[120] See, e.g., Beaujeu 1955, 71–80. Whittaker 1997, 151–52, sees a "conscious propagation in the 2nd c. of a new imperial ideology of Jupiter-Zeus as protector of cities."

[121] P. Arnaud, "L'image du globe dans le monde romain," *MEFRA* 96.1 (1984): 53–116, esp. 105–6n. 136.

[122] Cf. C. Nicolet, *Space, Geography, and Politics in the Early Roman Empire* (Ann Arbor, MI, 1991), 36–47.

[123] Downey 1961, 223n. 104. Halfmann 1986, 206, notes that Hadrian could not have been at the inauguration of the festival on 23 June 129, since he was still in Phrygia in July 129.

[124] An analagous process of assimilation is suggested by two votive altars dedicated to the Nymphae Augustae (*CIL* XII 3108 and 3109) in the imperial cult sanctuary at Nemausus (Nîmes). This had evolved from a sanctuary to Nemausus, the eponymous god of the city and the god of the spring there, and it seems to have been where the Basilica of Plotina was built (see above, n. 106).

[125] Arrian's discursive aside implies that this last statue was new.

tars remains,[126] the passage depicts the appropriation of a provincial sanctuary by imperial cult. Hadrian's statue must have been larger than the others; overlooking the sea, it may have been conspicuous from afar, and it is the only statue whose height Arrian does not specify. Its juxtaposition with altars and temple blurred the distinction between emperor and deity. Arrian, and probably others, used the shrine for ritual homage to Hadrian. The restorations in Trapezus integrated emperor and local cult, even while enhancing the image of Hadrian himself.

Tombs

Hadrian restored, embellished, or composed epigrams for six tombs of heroes, poets, or great leaders in five cities in Asia, Achaea, and Egypt, displaying his appreciation of the past and his averred authority as a true interpreter and reviver of literature and history.[127] (See table 6.2.) The concern for heroes evinced in Hadrian's datable activity of this type precedes Antinoos's death and heroization in A.D. 130 (see chapter 8), thus casting his honors for the youth in a less anomalous light. Most significantly, however, Hadrian's work with tombs in various cities associated him with local cult and tradition.[128]

At Ilium, considered the site of ancient Troy, Hadrian rebuilt the tomb of Ajax (Philostr. *Heroic.* 8.1 [137]),[129] and an epigram from Hector's tomb there is credited to Hadrian (*Anth. Pal.* 9.387; cf. *Anth. Lat.* 708). Although Hadrian's attitude toward Homer was reportedly one of jealousy

---

[126] For possible fragments of the sanctuary, see Mitford 1974, 160–64, referring to F. Cumont, *Studia Pontica* II (1906): 366, and W. J. Hamilton, *Researches in Asia Minor, Pontus and Armenia* (London, 1852), I:162 (I could not check either).

[127] This claim was inherent in his notorious intellectual one-upmanship: e.g., *HA, Hadr.* 14.8–9, 15.10–13, 16.2–11; Cass. Dio 69.3.4; Syme 1965, 242–44. See also André 1993; Fein 1994, 26–64; and Birley 1994. In Apta Julia (southern France), Hadrian more idiosyncratically constructed a tomb for his horse Borysthenes (n.d.), according to a marble inscription now lost (*CIL* XII 1122 = Smallwood, #520 = *Poet. Lat. Min.*, ed. Bahrens, 4, 126 = *Anth. Lat.* #903 = Buecheler, *Carm. Epig.* II.2 #1522; cf. Cass. Dio 69.10.2, and *HA, Hadr.* 20.12). Mommsen and others doubt the authenticity of this inscription, no longer extant but whose copy reportedly dates to the sixteenth century; Bardon 1968, 419–20, holds that nothing in its history precludes its authenticity. See at *CIL* XII 1122; Buecheler, *Carm. Epig.*, pp. 718–19, ad #1522.

[128] None of the eight tombs Hadrian is known to have built, restored, or somehow embellished has survived, and their effects on land use and cultic practices cannot be determined; cf. S. E. Alcock, "Tomb Cult and the Post-classical Polis," *AJA* 95 (1991): 449–51. I omit as unlocatable the tomb of Hadrian's friend Voconius, for whom Hadrian wrote the epigram, *lascivus versu, mente pudicus eras* (You were wanton in your verse, chaste in your mind: Apul. *Apol.* 11.3). See chapter 2, at n. 41 and following for Fronto's disparagement of Hadrian's work with tombs (*Princ. Hist.* 11, p. 209 VDH).

[129] Teubner text in *Flavii Philostrati Heroicus,* ed. L. de Lannoy (Leipzig, 1977).

(Cass. Dio 69.4.6, cf. *HA, Hadr.* 16.6), like others of his era he was swayed by the Homeric epics and heroes,[130] and like Caesar, Augustus, and other emperors he favored Ilium, the ancestral home of the Romans.[131] Hadrian's attention to both heroes might strike us as perverse in light of their legendary fierce conflict (*Il.* 7 and 14), but Hadrian was similarly evenhanded in his benefactions to the vying Nicaea and Nicomedia (see above). He visited Ilium in 124,[132] and Philostratus depicts him participating personally in the rebuilding of Ajax's grave. The ritual act reaffirmed the importance of burial, the Greek hero within the tomb, and local traditions.[133] Balancing his show of respect for Ajax, Hadrian wrote the epigram for the tomb of Hector.[134] The elegy consoles Hector that Ilium is inhabited and famous once again, with inhabitants still warlike (though inferior to Hector himself); it commands the Trojan hero to tell Achilles that the Myrmidons have perished, and that all Thessaly is subject to the sons of Aeneas.[135] Hadrian's work at Ajax's and Hector's tombs conflated local cult and Greek epic into the living history of the Roman empire.

Hadrian wrote an epigram for the tomb of Archilochus at Paros (*Anth. Graec.* 7.674, Beckby), parading his veneration for archaic Greek poetry, his awareness of his own position within the poetical tradition, and his broad interpretation of hero cults.[136] Perhaps in person at Mantinea in 124, Hadrian composed a epigram for Epaminondas, setting up his inscribed stele on the leader's tomb next to the older epigram (in Boeotian)

---

[130] W. Leaf, *Strabo on the Troad* (Cambridge, Eng., 1923).

[131] Ibid., 144–48; C. B. Rose, "The 1993 Post–Bronze Age Excavations at Troia," *Studia Troica* 4 (1994): 80–82, 88–93, suggesting that a costly rebuilding of Ilium's Odeon, whose splendid cuirassed statue of Hadrian perhaps dominated the stage, was dedicated to Hadrian.

[132] Halfmann 1986, 43, 191; (fragmentary) inscriptions from Ilium concerning Hadrian: P. Frisch, *Die Inschriften von Ilion*, IK 3 (Bonn, 1975), 197–99, ##93, 94, 94a. See also *CIL* III 466 (non vidi), a milestone from 124 found near Alexandria Troas. For Hadrian's work in Alexandria Troas, see above, at n. 18 and following.

[133] Cf. J. Whitley, "Early States and Hero Cults: A Reappraisal," *JHS* 108 (1988): 173–82; I. Morris, "Tomb Cult and the 'Greek Renaissance': The Past in the Present in the 8th Century B.C.," *Antiquity* 62 (1988): 750–61; C. Antonaccio, "Contesting the Past: Hero Cult, Tomb Cult, and Epic in Early Greece," *AJA* 98 (1994): 389–410, esp. 398. For the rite of inhumation, common in the Greek East but just beginning to be practiced in the Latin West in the second century, see Morris 1992, 43, 53, 59–61.

[134] Bardon 1968, 422.

[135] The longer Latin version (*Anth. Lat.* 708) adds the parenthetical filler line 2: (*Fas audire tamen si mea verba tibi*) ([if only it were right for you to hear my words]), and line 3, that Hector's avenger has come to the tomb.

[136] There is no evidence that Hadrian ever visited Paros, and the epigram cannot be dated. L. R. Farnell, *Hero Cults and Ideas of Immortality* (Oxford, 1921), omits Archilochus, Epaminondas, and Pompey. The shrine at Paros, to be published by Diskin Clay, originally dates perhaps to the archaic period, and certainly to the fourth century B.C.

(Paus. 8.11.8).[137] Here Hadrian juxtaposed his reworking of the past with the original monument, as at Abae and Teos. His activity publicly expressed admiration for a great military predecessor, and the compatibility of military and literary interests (cf. Cass. Dio 69.3.2).

Military considerations may have played a part in Hadrian's renovation of Pompey's ruined tomb at Mons Casius, near Pelusium, Egypt, where he stopped while en route to Egypt in 130. There Hadrian offered sacrifice to Pompey's *manes* (deified spirit), and perhaps composed a hexameter epigram for the tomb (App. *BCiv.* 2.86; Cass. Dio 69.11.1; *HA, Hadr.* 14.4).[138] The tomb lay on the land route from Palestine and Arabia to Egypt, and Pelusium was the eastern entry to the Nile delta.[139] Hadrian's sacrifice reaffirmed the hero status of Pompey,[140] who was revered for settling the eastern Mediterranean. The act seems aimed at restoring the image of Roman supremacy, for this region had been convulsed by the Jewish revolt at the end of Trajan's reign (see chapter 8).[141]

According to Athenaeus, Hadrian greatly honored the monument (*mnema*) of Alcibiades in Phrygian Melissa, where he ordered an annual ox sacrifice and a new statue of the Athenian statesman made from Parian marble (13.574f). He may have personally visited the tomb while traveling from Laodicea to Syria in 129.[142] Alcibiades was, at best, a problematic hero, whose greatest notoriety came from his infamous fickleness and individualism: it seems fitting that Hadrian, *semper varius,* honored him.[143] Less idiosyncratically, Hadrian's renovation of Alcibiades's tomb in Melissa, like his activity with tombs elsewhere, reaffirmed the importance of local cults and their cities while amalgamating local religious life and monuments with the Roman emperor.

---

[137] If he did or ordered this in situ, it dates to his visit to the Peloponnese in 124: see Halfmann 1986, 191.

[138] Although P. Chuvin and J. Yoyotte, "Documents relatifs au culte pélusien de Zeus Casios," *RA* n.s. 1 (1986): 43, hold that Hadrian restored the Temple of Zeus Casius at Pelusium, the mutilated inscription they cite cannot be so construed: see A. Salač "[Zeus Casios]," *BHC* 46 (1922): 167–68, with references. See also T. Pekáry, "Das Grab des Pompeius," *Bonner HAC* 1970 (Bonn, 1972), 195–98.

[139] Florus 2.21; H. Kees, *RE* 19.1 (1937): 409–12, s.v. Pelusion.

[140] The word Cassius Dio uses, *enagizo*, is a technical term strictly meaning "to offer sacrifice to the dead" (= *parentare*).

[141] A more personal reason might also be conjectured from the hexameter and grave: the self-contradictory, ever-changing Hadrian may have been drawn naturally to the paradoxical memorial of Pompey the Great.

[142] Halfmann 1986, 208, 193.

[143] The wealth of detail Plutarch offers in his *Life of Alcibiades* reveals the fascination exerted by this mixed character up to Hadrian's day: C. B. R. Pelling, "Plutarch and Thucydides," in *Plutarch and the Historical Tradition,* ed. P. A. Stadter (London, 1992), 18–19, 23–24. On Hadrian's personality, see chapter 1.

CONCLUSIONS

Scholars rightly note that municipal building patronage by an emperor provided employment for local contractors and workers even while leaving a permanent mark on the city thus favored. The emperor thus simultaneously garnered contemporary acclaim and built up his future reputation.[144] Although Hadrian's building donations have long been admired (see chapter 1), only with this compilation of the scattered evidence can we begin to discern his choices. (See tables 6.1 and 6.2.) The two largest categories, utilitarian constructions and religious edifices, reveal both Hadrian's adherence to the principle that Roman emperors build for the welfare of their subjects, and his particular understanding of his duty. His drainage schemes, aqueducts, roadwork, harbors, and similar work extended the practical benefits of Roman rule while providing an infrastructure that united the far-flung Roman empire relatively well for a preindustrial economy. Hadrian's temple and tomb restorations, completions, and embellishments impressed cities' sacred landscapes with the image of an allpowerful emperor, even as they more simply substantiated the imperial presence, particularly in the Greek East. In Hadrian's day religion was inseparable from Roman politics, culture, society, even economy, as we have seen. More than other emperors of the first two centuries, Hadrian seems to have viewed religion as a unifying force. The material collected here discloses his promotion of the emperor's role as religious leader of the Roman empire. Hadrian's building donations pertain to a wide spectrum of religious structures, appealing to many different people; Hadrian's benefactions to Athens, Smyrna, and Italica, the subject of chapter 7, emphasized religious structures. We see in chapter 8, however, the fatal limitations of this understanding as we discuss Hadrian's interactions with the Jews.

---

[144] See chapter 1, and *IEphesos* V #1491 = *Syll.*[3] 850, discussed in chapter 5 at n. 73.

Athens, Smyrna, and Italica

IN THIS CHAPTER and the next I evaluate Hadrian's municipal benefactions not by type, as previously, but as they affected select cities: Athens, Smyrna, and Italica. The abundant and detailed evidence for their buildings from Hadrian, seen in conjunction with other marks of favor from him to these three cities (introduced in previous chapters), allows us to perceive the thoroughness with which Hadrian could act, the consequence of personal biases for imperial largesse to cities, the more impersonal infrastructure behind imperial building, and the audacious reach of Hadrian's city-based vision of the Roman world. Despite apparent transformation, however, these cities were not among Hadrian's new or renewed city foundations, the group I explore in the following chapter.[1] No earthquake or other disaster drew Hadrian to any of the cities of this chapter, but rather particular circumstances and individuals. Hadrian's work in all three is characterized by the integration of the city's past with the Roman present, by focus on the person of the emperor, and by cooperation with, and elevation of, members of the local elite.

ATHENS

The evidence is best for Athens, which the emperor's munificence established as the center of a Greco-Roman world closely associated with Hadrian himself (cf. Paus. 1.18.6). Hadrian was so enamored of Greek culture from an early age that he was nicknamed "Graeculus" (the little Greek, *HA, Hadr.* 1.5, *Epit. de Caes.* 14.2) and he held the archonship of Athens in 111/112 or 112/113 (most likely in absentia), even before he became emperor (see chapter 4). After assuming imperial power in 117, he visited Athens in 124/125, 128/129, and 131/132, spending more time there than in any other city save Rome.[2] His benefactions to Athens were many, and of many different types, as we see below. The city reciprocated by beginning a new era with Hadrian's first visit in 124/125, by adding the tribe

---

[1] For the professed "City of Hadrian" at Athens, see below, at n. 10. Italica's "Hadrianic" "Nova Urbs" is a modern concept: below, n. 82.

[2] Halfmann 1986, 41–42, 191–94, 202–4, 208–9; Follet 1976, 107–25; Graindor 1934, 1–58; Day 1942, 183–96; Kienast 1993, 206–22.

"Hadrianis" as an unprecedented thirteenth division of the citizen body, and by erecting to Hadrian numerous dedications and statues, including one on the Altar of the Eponymous Heroes in the Athenian Agora.[3]

Many of Hadrian's benefactions to Athens have been dated to his third visit in 131/132. This is when he formally established the Panhellenion, a league of Greek cities with headquarters in Athens, and when he personally supervised the (re)dedication of the Olympieion, the enormous sanctuary to Olympian Zeus whose construction he brought to completion after more than six centuries (Paus. 1.18.6–7, Cass. Dio 69.16.1–2; *HA, Hadr.* 13.6; Philostr. *VS* 533). (See fig. 5.) Hadrian's creation of the penteteric Panhellenia games for Athens is associated with the Panhellenion (Cass. Dio 69.16.2). New buildings that he gave to the Athenians, the Temple of Hera and Zeus Panhellenios (Paus. 1.18.9; Cass. Dio 69.16.2),[4] the "Pantheon" (Paus. 1.18.9, 1.5.5), and the "Library of Hadrian" (Paus. 1.18.9, and see below), have also been dated to this time, though by inference only.[5] Perhaps to provide for the annual influx of Panhellenes and other visitors, as Spawforth and Walker have attractively suggested, Hadrian perpetually endowed the city's grain supply (Cass. Dio 69.16.1; see chapter 5) and donated an aqueduct and its terminating ornate reservoir (finished in 140 by Antoninus Pius, *CIL* III 549 = *ILS* 337 = Smallwood, #396).[6]

Other benefactions came earlier or later, or cannot be dated. As we saw in chapter 5 (at n. 6), Hadrian "gave" Athens the island of Cephallenia and large sums of money (Cass. Dio 69.16.2), he wrote the Athenian Oil Decree sometime after 126/127, and he is sometimes credited with revising Athens's civic constitution.[7] Probably while celebrating the Eleusinian Mysteries during the winter of 124/125, he had a bridge built over the Cephisus River between Athens and Eleusis. He may have undertaken a new gymnasium as well as renovations at the "Roman Agora." (See this chapter's appendix for all three structures.) He also raised the Panathenaic festival to the highest status, and by the end of his reign Athens had a four-

---

[3] Zahrnt 1979; Follet 1976, 117, with references. This was the first new tribe in more than three hundred years. Benjamin 1963, 61–71, counts ninety-five dedications to Hadrian found in Athens.

[4] It may be that the temple of Hera and Zeus Panhellenios Pausanias mentions included a shrine or at least a statue of Hadrian Panhellenius, and that the temple itself was called the Panhellenion. Zeus Panhellenios alone is attested otherwise only in *IG* II² 1088, line 10, a (partially restored) decree of the Panhellenion. See appendix 7.6, below.

[5] E.g., the Library of Hadrian: Travlos 1971, 224. See comments of Willers 1990, 20–21 (favoring an earlier date).

[6] Spawforth and Walker 1985, 90. I discuss the aqueduct in appendix 7.1.

[7] The alleged revision of Athens's constitution is discussed in chapter 5, n. 39. See also Calandra 1996, 100–102, although she goes too far in proposing and attributing changes to Hadrian.

Fig. 5. Plan of Roman Athens in relation to the modern city, showing location of the Olympieion, with the Arch of Hadrian above its northwest corner (lower right); the Acropolis and the Agora; the Library of Hadrian above the "Roman Agora" (center); and the east-west road that passes between the Library and the "Roman Agora" in its course between the Dipylon and the Diochares Gate.

year cycle of sacred games unique in Greece (see chapter 5).[8] Inscriptions on Athens's Arch of Hadrian underscore the emperor's role as the city's reviver: the western face of this thin and elegant arch proclaims, "This is Athens, the former city of Theseus," and the eastern, "This is the city of Hadrian, not of Theseus" (*IG* II[2] 5185).[9] But east of the arch no new Hadrianic "city" or city quarter has been discerned, and west of the arch the "ancient" city bore Hadrian's imprint. The inscriptions make a fallacious distinction: Hadrian's Athens is inseparable from what came before.[10]

Hadrian's transformation of Athens transcends merely physical changes, and it has engrossed many scholars. The topic is worthy of a book in itself, but here I aim merely to set his interactions in Athens within the wider context of his municipal work throughout the empire.[11] Some benefactions have already been discussed in this framework, such as his Athenian Oil Decree and Panhellenia games (chapter 5); others are so obscure or routine that I relegate their details to the appendix to this chapter (gymnasium, "Pantheon," possible renovation of the "Roman Agora," and Temple of Hera and Zeus Panhellenios; and aqueduct and bridge, respectively). In this chapter I examine Hadrian's establishment of the Panhellenion League in Athens, which is unparalleled,[12] and two of his buildings, the completion of the Olympieion and the Library. These epitomize much of his municipal work. Recent reassessments of the Panhellenion provide the starting point for my discussion.[13]

The Panhellenion, a league of Greek cities with intertwined religious, cultural, and political purposes, had as members at least eleven cities in Achaea, ten in Asia, five in Crete-and-Cyrene, one in Thrace, and one in Macedonia (at least twenty-eight in all; see fig. 6).[14] Some cities, such as

[8] The Panhellenia, Hadrianeia, Olympieia, and (upgraded) Panathenaea: Spawforth and Walker 1985, 90–91. See also Spawforth 1989, 194, and chapter 5, at n. 77.

[9] Travlos 1971, 253; Schol. Aristides *Panathenaicus* III, p. 201.32, ed. Dindorf; Willers 1990, 68–92; Adams 1989; Spawforth and Walker 1985, 93.

[10] Willers 1990, 70–72, Adams 1989, 10–12. It is doubtful that a "new city" was built.

[11] Calandra 1996, 91–115, discusses Hadrian's dealings with Athens within her overall thesis that Hadrian used an ecumenical vision of the past as a way to bind together the empire and center it on himself.

[12] Although he had envisioned making Delphi the center of a new panhellenic league sometime before A.D. 125: Oliver, ##75–76 (A.D. 125); Flacelière 1971, 168–72; Willers 1990, 99–100; Beaujeu 1955, 180–81; Weber 1907, 195.

[13] Spawforth and Walker 1985, and 1986, 88–105, who draw attention to the work of their predecessors, Oliver 1970b, M. N. Tod, "Greek Inscriptions from Macedonia," *JHS* 42 (1922): 167–80, and Graindor 1934, 102–11. C. P. Jones 1996, 29–56, is valuable, although he de-emphasizes political aspects too much in favor of religious ones.

[14] Since its membership is known only through inscriptions, new finds may add other members. Spawforth and Walker 1985, 79–81: Athens, Megara, Sparta, Chalcis, Argos, Acraephiae, Epidaurus, Amphicleia?, Methana and Corinth, and Hypata and Demetrias

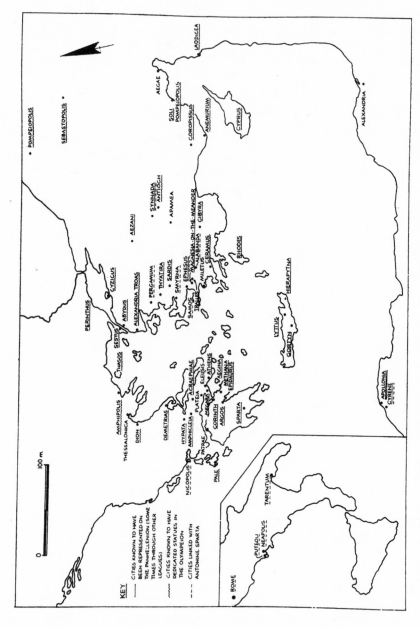

Fig. 6. Map showing the known member-cities of the Panhellenion, and cities that made dedications to Hadrian in the Olympieion at Athens.

Cyrene and Sparta, sent to Athens more than one Panhellene (delegate to the league), but many must have sent only one. The senior executive (*archon*), in a four-year appointment (probably approved by the emperor himself) and assisted by a deputy archon (*antarchon*), oversaw the council (*synedrion*) of Panhellenes in Athens. Subordinate officials may have included a treasurer and secretary. Most of the few identified officers of the league are from the highest provincial echelons, Roman citizens and of at least equestrian standing; they represent many cities in the league rather than Athens or any other single city. The delegates were elected by their home cities according to rules Hadrian had made about eligibility, which included a minimum age-limit and the requirement to have already held local office. The delegates thus were already notables in their cities (see chapter 3), although the majority of identifiable Panhellenes (and Panhellenes-elect) were not Roman citizens.[15] The league brought together men and cities otherwise largely isolated from one another, and may even have encouraged local office holding. Meetings and management of the Panhellenion ensured for Athens a steady stream of well-cultivated and wealthy visitors.

Spawforth and Walker maintain that applications for admission to the league were jointly decided upon by emperor, archon, and Panhellenes. This would make the Panhellenion's procedures unusually cooperative in a vertical sense. Some cities, such as Magnesia-on-the-Maeander, apparently applied for membership on their own, and the emperor may have encouraged others.[16] The most important criteria for admission were, first, a city's Greek ancestry, then its history of good relations with Rome, and finally the benefactions it had received from Hadrian. Member cities were either on mainland Greece or overseas Greek colonies. But Cibyra in Asia, a member-city although a non-Greek foundation, successfully paraded a fictitious Greek heritage, and others may have done the same.[17] Heroic

---

(these two probably represented by the Thessalian koinon); Aezani, Thyateira, Tralles, Sardis, Miletus, Magnesia-on-the-Maeander, Apamea, Rhodes, Cibyra, and Synnada; Cyrene, Apollonia, and Lyttos, Gortyn, and Hierapytna (the latter three represented through the Cretan koinon); Thessalonica; and Perinthus. The cities represented through the Cretan koinon, as probably those represented through the Thessalian one, were called *ethne* ("peoples"). C. P. Jones 1996, 34n. 22, 39–41, 47–53, would remove Synnada and add Ptolemais-Barca, but see below, chapter 8, n. 55.

[15] Spawforth and Walker 1985, 79, 85–89. Cyrene sent two Panhellenes; Sparta two or more. Archons seem usually not to have been members of the Roman senate. The position of Panhellenes, further down the hierarchy, seems to have been held relatively early in a man's career. There also must have been "more humble employees" for building maintenance.

[16] Ibid., 81–82. C. P. Jones 1996, 30–31, 41, argues from Cassius Dio's vocabulary (in 69.16.1–2) that the initiative for the Panhellenion came from the "Greeks," probably "charter members" such as Athens, Sparta, and Argos, and that Hadrian subsequently modified the league. See Birley 1997, 344n. 10, for a different view.

[17] Spawforth and Walker 1985, 82: Strabo had classified the city as a non-Greek foundation (13.4.17), but the inscription establishing Cibyra as a member of the Panhellenion ac-

Greek backgrounds were increasingly fabricated by cities in the Greek East during the imperial period, and the Panhellenion could only have increased the tendency.[18] The league fostered by Hadrian elevated and rewarded "Greekness" and looked to the past for self-definition. The past, however, embraced legendary history and more recent interactions with Rome and the emperor, and "Greekness" seems to have been as much cultural as strictly ancestral.

Although its main activities focused on honoring the imperial house and regulating itself,[19] the Panhellenion was also involved in Athens's daily life. The Panhellenion was concerned with religion at Eleusis and in Athens itself, where it administered the cult of Hadrian Panhellenius and generally supervised the Panhellenia games.[20] The first known archon of the league, Cn. Cornelius Pulcher (from Corinth), was also priest of Hadrian Panhellenius sometime between A.D. 132 and 138; subsequent archons often served as agonothetes of the Panhellenia and/or as priests of Hadrian Panhellenius.[21] The league dealt with financial matters such as distributions to athletes, building costs, and, presumably, the maintenance of the shrine of the Panhellenion and other associated buildings. It may also have functioned as a court, if Spawforth and Walker have rightly interpreted a document Eusebius cites to attest an imperial policy of tolerance for the Christians.[22] By establishing the Panhellenion in Athens, Hadrian promoted visits to the city, multiplied religious and social activities there, and reaffirmed Athens as the center of the Greek East.

These effects are reflected in Hadrian's completion of the Olympieion, the Temple of Olympian Zeus near the Ilissos in southeast Athens (see fig. 7), whose rededication apparently marked the formal beginning of the Panhellenion and the establishment of the Panhellenia games.[23] The comple-

---

claims Cibyra as a "colony of the Spartans and kin to the Athenians, friendly to [Rome?], being like others among the most celebrated and greatest cities of the commonwealth of Hellas because of its descent, which is Hellenic, and of its ancient friendship and goodwill in relation to the Romans, and because it has been favored with great honors by the God Hadrian" (*OGIS* II 497, early third century, from Oenoanda, translated by C. P. Jones 1996, 39).

[18] Spawforth and Walker 1985, 82, with references to various works of L. Robert. See too Curty 1995, 254–63, and Scheer 1993.

[19] Spawforth and Walker 1985, 82–84. Willers 1990, 103, attributes the league's relatively short history to its close association with Hadrian himself.

[20] Spawforth and Walker 1985, 82.

[21] Ibid., 84–86; Willers 1990, 60; Benjamin 1963, 59; Oliver 1970b, #35–36, for Pulcher.

[22] Spawforth and Walker 1985, 82–84, referring to Euseb. *Hist. Eccl.* 4.26.10; rejected by C. P. Jones 1996, 36–37, who also denies other judicial activities they suggest.

[23] Spawforth and Walker 1985, 79, are more cautious than Willers in linking the Panhellenion League to the Olympieion. The Panhellenia games were first held only in late summer 137: C. P. Jones 1996, 33, with M. Wörrle, "Neue Inscriftenfunde aus Aizanoi I," *Chiron* 22 (1992): 342–45. See also Boatwright 1997a, 121–27.

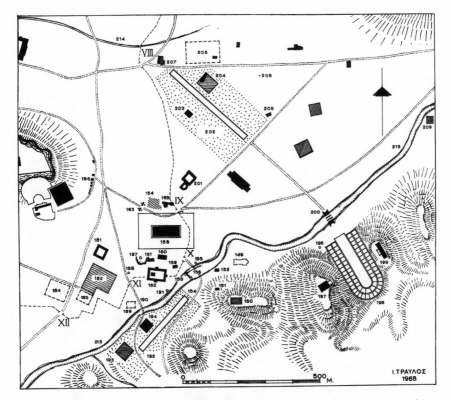

Fig. 7. Prominent in this plan of southeast Athens is the Olympieion and its terrace (#158), as completed and rededicated by Hadrian in A.D. 131/132. The Arch of Hadrian is #163, and #162, a building but poorly documented, has been associated with Hadrian's "Temple of Zeus Panhellenios." East of the Arch of Hadrian are mostly baths or gardens, such as #202, the Lyceum. The Ilissos River runs south of the Olympieion and #162.

tion of the sanctuary exemplifies one means by which Hadrian's municipal benefactions identified him with local history even while asserting his transcendence. Although not the most renowned Athenian sanctuary, the Temple of Olympian Zeus had a singular past. It was first monumentalized by the Peisistratids around 515 B.C.[24] Incomplete at the fall of the tyrants, its huge foundations supplied the plan and dimensions for the subsequent Hellenistic-Roman temple (ca. 44 × 110 meters for the stylobate).[25] Cul-

[24] See Travlos 1971, 102. References include Thuc. 2.15.4 and Paus. 1.18.8.

[25] The aedes measures 43.68 × 110.35 meters on its stylobate (cella ca. 19 × 75 meters). The final design was dipteral, with eight by twenty Corinthian columns and an added row of four columns on each short side, 104 columns in all.

tural activities must have continued at the site after the sixth century,[26] but construction of the temple itself resumed only in 174 B.C. when Antiochus Epiphanes of Syria, employing the Roman architect Cossutius, set out to finish the building. After Antiochus's death in 165 B.C., the gigantic, still-unfinished temple remained a source of wonder, interest, and, perhaps, building material.[27] During Augustus's reign the Eastern client kings planned together to complete the temple and dedicate it to the Genius Augusti (Suet. *Aug.* 60), but how much work was actually accomplished is unclear.[28] The history of this huge and conspicuous temple included great rulers of Athens and a Hellenistic king; an early and signal example of Greek and Roman cooperation in Antiochus's employment of Cossutius; Augustus, the paradigmatic emperor; and a widespread group of Roman allies.

D. Willers has recently illuminated Hadrian's Olympieion by combining the evidence of Pausanias with archaeological and excavation reports of the area.[29] Hadrian used massive terracing to build up the low ridge on which the temple sits, employing an architectural technique characteristic of Roman architecture.[30] A new wall of rusticated blocks demarcated the temenos, like the "fire walls" and other precinct walls of the great imperial fora at Rome. Typically Roman in its inward focus, the Olympieion's temenos wall had only one off-centered opening, the entrance in the northeast.[31] Inside the Olympieion, columns on pedestals were set very close to the polished temenos wall.[32] The entire area was paved, though with careful preservation of earlier shrines and monuments like that of Cronos and Rhea, or a bronze statue of Zeus (cf. Paus. 1.18.7). Hadrian also put on display a large snake from India (Cass. Dio 69.16.1), a reminder of Rome's far reach. The extent of Hadrian's work on the centrally located aedes is controversial since his renovations corresponded to the original plan and architectural elements (as in Teos and Claros). Most of the surviving decoration dates to the second century B.C., and the Olympieion's newer elements are consciously modeled on them.[33]

---

[26] Willers 1990, 32.

[27] Travlos 1971, 102; Willers 1990, 32–35, arguing that the aedes was more complete under Antiochus than generally assumed, perhaps missing mainly a roof.

[28] Willers 1990, 34–35.

[29] Ibid., 26–53.

[30] Cp. Smyrna, Cyzicus, the archaic Latin shrines, and the Traianeum of Italica.

[31] Willers 1990, 37–38; see Spawforth and Walker 1985, plate II, fig. 3, for similar rustication in the "Pantheon," the building east of the "Roman Agora." The temenos wall's incongruity in Athens is heightened by the anomalous Arch of Hadrian asymmetrically set just northwest of the temenos (nn. 9 and 10 above).

[32] Quite different from the quadriporticus one might expect, although (pace Willers 1990, 36–38) not every temenos had a quadriporticus. The decorative scheme resembles that of the west facade of the Library of Hadrian.

[33] Willers 1990, 39–41, argues that Hadrian merely installed in the aedes the chryselephantine statue that Pausanias says is "worth seeing," which exceeded in size all other statues

When Hadrian rededicated the Olympieion in 131/132, the aedes basically retained both the archaic plan begun by the Peisistratids and the Hellenistic decoration of Antiochus and Cossutius. Yet the venerable Athenian structure was now centrally located in a decidedly Roman temenos.

Analogously, Olympian Zeus and Hadrian were assimilated by the shrine's architectural sculpture. Although Hadrian dedicated a colossal chryselephantine statue of Zeus in the aedes, four more-than-life-size statues of Hadrian himself stood before its entrance (two of Thasian marble, two of porphyry). Throughout the temenos stood numerous bronze statues, "which the Athenians call 'colonies,'" and many statues of Hadrian, most of which were dedicated by the Greek cities of the Panhellenion (Paus. 1.18.6).[34] Athens's Olympieion was plainly associated with Hadrian and imperial cult,[35] although the emperor himself was not worshiped there as "sunnaos" (sharing the temple) with Zeus Olympios.[36] Hadrian's transcendence is reflected in his personal supervision of its rededication ceremony during his visit to Athens in 131/132.[37] The famous sophist Polemo, instrumental in Hadrian's benefactions to Smyrna (see below), presented an oration marking the celebration as the culmination of history, divine inspiration, and erudition (Philostr. *VS* 533).[38] The completion of the Olympieion, like its innumerable statues to Hadrian, wove the Athenian past together with the present of other Greek cities under Roman rule and with the emperor Hadrian.

A similar assertion of Hadrian's pre-eminence in Athens's life, but one more geared to Athens's cultural hegemony and the Athenians themselves, can be seen in Athens's "Library of Hadrian."[39] Pausanias's description of Hadrian's "most famous" structure, which had a hundred columns of Phrygian marble (pavonazzetto), ornate rooms with gilded ceilings, alabaster, paintings, statues, and facilities for storing books (1.18.9), has been identified with the structure east of the Athenian Agora and north of

---

save the colossi at Rhodes and Rome (1.18.6). Walker 1979, 107–9, 128–29, discerns Hadrianic style in at least one of the homogeneous architectural fragments linked to the temple. She adduces the incomplete state of the temple after Antiochus's death (Vitr. *De Arch.* 7.praef.15, Strabo 9.1.17), and the resemblance of architectural decoration in later second-century Athens to that presumably carved by Hadrian's craftsmen for the Olympieion.

[34] Benjamin 1963; Willers 1990, 48–53. No trace of the "colony" statues survives: see especially Benjamin 1963, 58–59, and Willers 1990, 51–53.

[35] E.g., Le Glay 1976, 357; Calandra 1996, 85–89.

[36] Cf. Jones's distinction of worhip of Hadrian Panhellenius from that of Zeus Panhellenios in the shrine(s) of the latter and of the Panhellenion: C. P. Jones 1996, 32–33, 35.

[37] Cass. Dio 69.16.1; Follet 1976, 114–15; Travlos 1971, 102. Most scholars date Hadrian's decision to complete the Olympieion to his first imperial visit.

[38] See Gleason 1995, 52–53.

[39] Spawforth and Walker 1985, 96, 98; Shear 1981, 374–76; Willers 1990, 18–21; Calandra 1996, 91–94; Kariviери 1994; and Boatwright 1997b.

the "Roman Agora."[40] (See figs. 5, 8.) The edifice is fully integrated into the street network of Athens, with a location placing it in a continuum from the glory of classical Athens through the revitalization of the city under the Roman emperors.[41] On fairly level ground, it faces the Athenian Agora to its west as does its neighbor, the aligned and similarly-sized "Roman Agora" closely associated with Julius Caesar and Augustus. A major road of ancient Athens, the street leading west from the Dipylon Gate along the northern edge of the Athenian Agora to the Diochares Gate, separates the two Roman precincts.[42]

One of the larger monuments of Athens, the Library measures some 87 × 125 meters within its temenos wall.[43] Its design, which combines Roman and Hellenistic Greek elements (fig. 8), is very unusual in the city. Like Hadrian's Olympieion in Athens and many imperial fora in Rome, the Library's buildings and precinct were enclosed by a high wall. Here it is made of rusticated poros ashlars, except for the Pentelic ornamental entry side. The three roofed exedrae (two semicircular ones flanking a rectangular one) that punctuate each long wall resemble exedrae in the Flavian Templum Pacis in Rome and in Italica's Traianeum and newly discovered "gymnasium" (see below).[44] Further similarities to imperial Roman monuments are found in the treatment of the front (western) wall of the Library. On either side of the tetrastyle propylon with its fluted columns of Phrygian marble, seven Carystian (cipollino) columns rose on cipollino pedestals (fourteen in all), freestanding from the wall behind except for their engaged entablature and cornice. The wall behind them, of Pentelic ashlars drafted on three edges, ended in *pteromata,* protruding wings.[45] This facade resembles the internal one of Rome's Forum Transitorium.[46] The ex-

[40] Travlos 1971, 244–52, Kokkou 1970, 162–65, Willers 1990, 14–20, Sisson 1929, Karivieri 1994, 89–93. The extant structure was first identified as the Stoa of Hadrian by W. Leake in the early 1800s. Pausanias's passage never uses the term *library* or its equivalent, but Jerome states that Hadrian built in Athens "a library of amazing workmanship" (Hieron. *Chron.*, ed. Helm, a.127).

[41] Underscored by Hadrian's assimilation with Theseus on the Arch of Hadrian.

[42] Travlos 1971, 244. For Hadrian's possible restoration of the "Roman Agora," see appendix 7.5.

[43] Without projections, the Library measures some 76 × 115 meters (cf. Willers 1990, 18–20). Sisson used English feet to measure the remains, not Roman feet, as mistakenly assumed by Martini 1985, 191n. 11. The Library's recent cleaning and survey will furnish more exact measurements.

[44] Athens's semicircular exedrae are ca. 9.8 meters internal diameter; rectangular, ca. 10 meters internal diameter.

[45] Sisson 1929, 54–55.

[46] J. B. Ward-Perkins *Roman Imperial Architecture* (Harmondsworth, 1981), 269–71; Boatwright 1997b, 197–98. To my knowledge the other three walls of rusticated poros have Athenian parallels only in Hadrian's Olympieion and other buildings attributed to him (see n. 31 above), although the elaborate treatment of the Pentelic wall is squarely within Greek

Fig. 8. The Library of Hadrian in Athens, as reconstructed in a plaster model in the Museo della Civiltà Romana, Rome.

ternal aspect of the structure must have unmistakably identified the building as imperial Roman,[47] a fitting culmination to the historical progression implied by its location.

The layout of the library's interior, however, is more congruous with architectural traditions of the Greek East. About two-thirds of the area was taken up by the central court, whose perimeter accommodated a quadriporticus of a hundred columns (Pausanias's "hundred columns of Phrygian marble"). An ornamental pool allowed an unencumbered view from the propylon to a series of rooms on the eastern side, which centered around a large hall screened by a colonnade.[48] The height of the three-story hall, which M. A. Sisson calculates as 15.2 meters with a gabled roof perpendicular to the entrance, surpassed that of the four rooms symmetrically arranged to either side. Within, the central room had on back and side walls a columnar screen before rectangular niches, which were arranged in three stories and, on the back wall, around larger round-headed niches. The rectangular niches seem to have been used for storing scrolls in wooden cases.[49] The two larger, outermost rooms of the eastern block

tradition (cf. Waelkens 1989, 77–78). Calandra 1996, 92, suggests that the rustication was to evoke the walls left unfinished at the Peloponnesian war.

[47] E.g., Boatwright 1997b, 195–98; Shear 1981, 374–76; Martini 1985.

[48] Sisson 1929, 58, who presumes ornamental plantings. The courtyard measures 81.75 × 59.88: Kokkou 1970, 162.

[49] Sisson 1929, 58–59, 63–66 (all measurements now converted to meters): central room

originally had floors ramped for banks of seats, allowing them to be used as auditoria.[50] Pausanias must be referring to this set of rooms in describing Hadrian's "most famous" building (1.18.9; see above).

The expansiveness of the courtyard and the internal elaboration of the central eastern room liken the Library to the "Marble Hall" (or "Kaisersaal"), a decorative and architectural scheme recurrent in the Greek East. Such Marble Halls, rich with columnar screens and statuary and opening off a quadriporticus, are often found in bath structures,[51] and their derivation seems to be the gymnasium as it had developed in Hellenistic Greece and Asia Minor. Adding to the original purpose of the Greek gymnasium as the center of civic education, the Hellenistic gymnasium functioned also as a cultural and social center, and in some instances as the seat of ruler worship.[52] By the second half of the fourth century B.C. gymnasia included a palestra, often arranged as a quadriporticus with several rooms opening off of it. One side of the quadriporticus was frequently emphasized architecturally by means of axiality and/or distinctive architectural elements, as in the "Hellenistic gymnasium" in Miletus.[53] This building, perhaps constructed mid second century B.C.,[54] evokes the much later Library of Hadrian in its plan.

Differing strikingly from other known libraries,[55] the interior design of Athens's Library of Hadrian must have reminded its viewers of bath-gymnasia. Such establishments were popular in Achaea and Asia Minor, and closely connected with religious festivals and imperial cult. The familiar plan of the Library of Hadrian in Athens may have had similar signification.[56] The duplicate plan in Italica's Traianeum, the imperial cult sanctuary discussed below, supports my inference.

---

ca. 23.3 long × 15.8 wide; central niches 2.3 long, rectangular ones 1.2 × 0.5 × 2.8; (in the southern half of central room) brick-faced base, once supporting the columnar screen, 2.5 wide, 1.6 high; Ionic columns of screen's lower order, 4 high. Six external buttresses counteracted the weakening effect of the recesses on the eastern (back) wall. Strocka 1981, 318, calculates that twenty thousand bookrolls could be stored; cf. Willers 1990, 16. Karivieri 1994, 92–93, recapitulates and endorses suggestions that the central room, evidently open to the court and thus to humidity, could not have been used to store books; instead, they would have been stored in the side rooms. This ignores the archaeological evidence of the niches, the auditoria, and the use of brick-faced concrete (see preceding and following notes).

[50] Each auditorium measured ca. 15.7 × 14.6 meters. These seem to be part of the original structure: Willers 1990, 16–17.

[51] Yegül 1992, 422–23. See also Martini 1985.

[52] Greco and Torelli 1983, 358; Yegül 1992, 7–8, 422–23.

[53] Yegül 1992, 9–14.

[54] Delorme 1960, 132.

[55] In general these were much smaller establishments, with more articulated rooms and spaces: cf. Strocka 1981, and Karivieri 1994, 92–93.

[56] Calandra 1996, 93, holds that the Olympieion was the site of imperial cult, but the Library was an honorary hall for the emperor and his family. See also Karivieri 1994, 93–102, whose work I did not have while writing this chapter.

Yet the Library of Hadrian is not just another monument of imperial self-glorification. Little remains of its architectural sculpture, but if the two bearded male heads (Severan period?) found in the precinct are indeed Athenian *kosmetai* (directors of ephebic training),[57] I suspect that from its beginning Hadrian intended the Library for education at Athens. One message of the structure may have been that Hadrian preserved and over-saw intellectual life and learning, an impression he aimed repeatedly to strike (see chapter 6, on tombs, and Aur. Vict. *Caes.* 14.2). But another, equally important one, seems to have been that the Athenians themselves, as scholars, sophists, teachers, and students, were essential to the preservation and transmission of the glorious Hellenic past. Hadrian encouraged Athenian endeavors by his Library, which served as a repository for Athens's cultural heritage, a place for rising and established sophists to declaim, and a locale for the privileged leisure made possible by the *pax Augusta*.

SMYRNA

Philostratus reports various benefactions from Hadrian to Smyrna as a way to illustrate the power wielded by the sophist M. Antonius Polemo,[58] stating that by his embassies "Polemo so entirely converted Hadrian to the cause of Smyrna [from that of Ephesus] that in one day the emperor lavished on Smyrna ten million [drachmae = denarii], with which were built a corn-market, a gymnasium—the most magnificent of all those in Asia—and a temple that can be seen from afar, the one on the promontory that seems to challenge Mimas" (*VS* 531; Mimas is the headland of the Erythraean peninsula forming the lower western arm of Smyrna's bay).[59] A forty-five-line inscription from Smyrna lists promised and realized donations to the city from Hadrian, twenty-five other men and women, and the Jews (collectively). Only in lines 33–42 do Hadrian's benefactions appear. Beginning "through the influence of Antonius Polemo," the passage reports that Hadrian proposed, and the senate ratified, Smyrna's neocorate status for the second time (that is, the city received permission to erect a second imperial cult temple). Hadrian also conferred sacred games, im-

---

[57] Boatwright 1997b, 208–10. Other sculpture may have depicted Hadrian, notable authors, deities, and personifications, e.g., inspiration. A colossal white marble Nike on a globe has been found at the Library, and very doubtfully dated to the Augustan or Hadrianic period: Calandra 1996, 93n. 53. In private conversation, Mary Sturgeon has tentatively dated the heads to the Severan period.

[58] Bowie 1982, esp. 52, 55; in general on Polemo, see Gleason 1995, esp. 20–54.

[59] Translation based on the Loeb one of W. C. Wright, *Philostratus and Eunapius: The Lives of the Sophists* (London, 1921), 108 (with sum corrected).

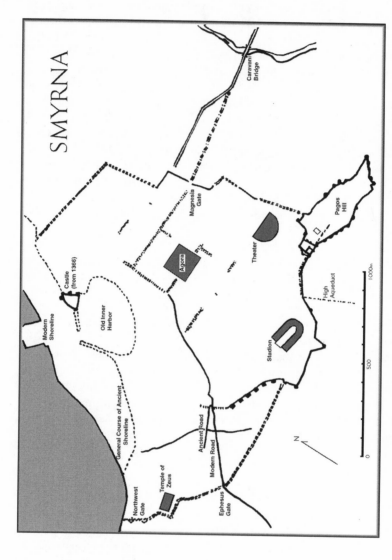

Fig. 9. Plan of Roman Smyrna. The temple oriented east-west on a hill in the southwestern part of the city has been identified as the Temple of Zeus Akraios, or "Zeus on High."

munity from tribute, *theologoi* (imperial encomiasts), hymnodists (who produced hymns for the imperial cult), 1,500,000 drachmae, and certain columns for an *aleipterion* (see below; *ISmyrna* II.1 #697 = *IGR* IV 1431).[60] Archaeology adds some information for the temple, although the port city's turbulent history allows only sketchy knowledge of second-century Smyrna (fig. 9).

The evidence for Hadrian's beneficence to Smyrna is important for three main reasons. First, the dominance of religious buildings and personnel in the lists of Hadrian's donations underscores the importance of religion for Hadrian, even while the corn market he reportedly helped fund is a reminder that he did not neglect cities' infrastructure.[61] Second, the inscription furnishes valuable details about the logistics of imperial building programs. Third, the evidence overall substantiates and illuminates the emperor's interaction with a city's notables, a key element in the nexus of power and obligation holding the Roman world together.

Philostratus does not name the deity of the temple Hadrian sponsored, but his topographical remarks help to locate and identify the shrine. An enormous Corinthian temple, documented in the 1820s and again a century later, once stood at the northwestern edge of the ancient city on a hill (modern Dierman-Tepé).[62] The peripteros was oriented east-west, with its opisthodomos facing the Mimas headland across the bay. The placement fits Philostratus's information. Moreover, the nineteenth-century investigator A. Prokesch found lower column drums measuring about 1.8 meters in diameter, about the same size as those of the Temple of Olympieion Zeus that Hadrian completed in Athens.[63] He inferred that the temple originally had ten columns on its short sides and twenty-three on its long ones. Size and dimensions match what we might expect of a building project involving Hadrian. (See fig. 9.)

[60] See Petzl 1987, 191–97. That the epigraphic record differs from Philostratus about the sums promised or furnished by Hadrian, noting 1,500,000 rather than the 10,000,000 denarii of Philostratus, does not disprove the supposition that both documents refer to a gymnasium. The amount recorded in the inscription may be a separate donation to the city, or part of the sum totaled in Philostratus: Petzl 1987, 196, on lines 39–40; Weber 1907, 141.

[61] A "site of a silo, built by Hadrian" was once reported near Smyrna's harbor, suggesting that Hadrian's grain market was here: Akurgal 1983, 122 (I am unable to locate the original site report). See chapters 5 and 6 for other benefits affecting infrastructure. S. Mitchell 1993, I:244, ranks Smyrna, Ephesus, and Pergamum as the largest cities in Roman Anatolia, suggesting populations of 180,000–200,000. In the fifth century B.C. Smyrna was a prolific grain producer, but by Hadrian's day the Ionian coast suffered repeated famines or food shortages: S. Mitchell 1993, I:244–45; Cadoux 1938, 69, 351, citing (e.g.) Pionios *Vit. Polyc.* 29–32.

[62] A. Prokesch, *Jahrb. der Literatur* 38 (Vienna, 1834), Anz. Bl. 62f, summarized in Bürchner 1927, 755.

[63] The ruins were subsequently robbed, but the one column fragment extant in 1922–24 matches measurements made a century earlier: Walter 1922–24.

Smyrna's Dierman-Tepé temple is probably the neocoros temple that Hadrian proposed and the senate ratified for Smyrna, whose designation as neocoros was accompanied by Hadrian's conferral of sacred games and personnel (*ISmyrna* II.1 #697 = *IGR* IV 1431, cf. *ISmyrna* II.1 #594 = *IGR* IV 1398).[64] The temple was apparently dedicated originally to Zeus Akraios, "Zeus dwelling on High," a deity depicted on coins of Smyrna from the late first through most of the second century A.D. The epithet suits Philostratus's description of the towering temple built or rebuilt with Hadrian's funds.[65] In Smyrna Hadrian was identified with Zeus (e.g., *IGR* IV 1410; *IGR* IV 1394).[66] If Hadrian's benefactions to Smyrna date to 123, when he visited the city,[67] the neocoros temple is an early instance of his assimilation to Zeus. Its stunning architectural expression is repeated in Hadrian's work at Athens's Olympieion and at Cyzicus's Temple of Zeus: in all three grandiose temples Hadrian conflated imperial worship and pre-existing local cults of Zeus.[68]

The Smyrnaean inscription furnishes precious clues about the achievement of such architectural feats when it reports that Hadrian donated "columns for the *aleipterion:* 72 made from Phrygian marble [pavonaz-zetto], 20 from Numidian marble [giallo antico], and six of porphyry" (*ISmyrna* II.1 #697, lines 40–42).[69] The *aleipterion* in Smyrna to which Hadrian gave ninety-eight columns seems to be the gymnasium Philostratus notes (*VS* 531). Athough the term *aleipterion* originally designated a room in a bathing establishment that could be heated for warm oil massage, its meaning changed over time. During the Roman empire it often meant a larger part or even the whole of the bathing establishment itself.[70] This is appropriate here, for elsewhere the inscription seems to record donations to the same bath building.[71] The large number of Hadrian's columns, ninety-eight, suggests that they were clustered around a palestra or a central court, perhaps even a "Marble Hall" (see above on Athens's

---

[64] Ibid. See chapter 5, at n. 62.

[65] G. F. Hill, *British Museum Catalogue of the Greek Coins of Ionia* (London, 1892), 250, #133, 253ff, ##152ff, 258, ##190–92; Head, *Hist. Num.* 594 (cited by Cadoux 1938, 202n. 3). Pausanias's testimony about Smyrna's Temple of Asclepios (2.26.9, 7.5.9) does not suit the Dierman-Tepé location: Bürchner 1927, 755–56; Cadoux 1938, 202–4, 248 (who holds that the Temple of Zeus Akraios was built in 79/80 on the model of the rebuilt Capitolium in Rome).

[66] Cf. Cadoux 1938, 258n. 1.

[67] See Petzl 1987, 74–77, on #594; Price 1984b, 258, #46; Halfmann 1986, 200; Magie 1950, 615, 1474n. 15; Walter 1922–24.

[68] For Cyzicus, see chapter 6, n. 111.

[69] The number seventy-two is an emendation universally accepted: Petzl 1987, 196 ad loc.

[70] Foss 1975; Yegül 1992, 21, 427n. 45, 487.

[71] Lines 16–18, 43–45. Donations to the "Garden of the Palm Grove" similarly recur in the inscription, in lines 8, 9–10, 14–16, 27–29, 32.

Library). None of Smyrna's baths and gymnasia has been located,[72] however, so this must remain speculative.

The total number of columns Hadrian donated to Smyrna's *aleipterion,* ninety-eight, is just two shy of the hundred Libyan columns he gave to Athens's gymnasium, and the hundred Phrygian ones he gave to the Library of Hadrian (Paus. 1.18.9).[73] Such lavish gifts are inconceivable without imperial control of marble quarries, which by Hadrian's day included those furnishing Numidian or Libyan marble (giallo antico), Phrygian (or pavonazzetto or Dokeimion), and porphyry.[74] The great variation of marble Hadrian gave Smyrna's *aleipterion* may account for Philostratus's classifying his gymnasium as the most beautiful in Asia, for the cool violet-veined pavonazzetto, sunny yellow-veined giallo antico, and somber dark purple porphyry must have contrasted with each other splendidly.[75]

Despite the magnificence of Hadrian's benefactions to Smyrna, the inscription simply lists them among others from local citizens. Neither placement nor letter size highlights Hadrian's name or contributions; Hadrian is presented merely as one among many donors. Although this apparent modesty is part of the image of imperial accessibility (*civilitas*), one of the cardinal imperial virtues of the time,[76] more important for my purposes is the inscription's implication for the phenomenon of euergetism. We have seen elsewhere how Hadrian's munificence helped spur local emulation (cf. *CIL* X 6090 = *ILS* 6295, discussed in chapter 4 at nn. 76–77). Smyrna is a particularly illuminating example of this process.

At the same time, however, the Smyraean evidence underlines the vital function of individuals in the conferral of imperial largesse. Both Philostratus and the inscription single out Polemo as the mediator of Smyrna's windfall. His agency is all the more striking in that Smyrna was not his native city, but rather the city he adopted as most suitable to his

[72] The city had many baths: Ael. Arist. *Or.* 17.11, 18.6; cf. Yegül 1992, 306, 455n. 40. Petzl 1987, 196–97, notes giallo antico marble columns found in Smyrna's agora.

[73] Building and donation inscriptions precisely enumerate columns given by individuals, but literary works tend toward round figures: see Petzl 1987, 190, on lines 16–20 of the inscription, and L. Robert, "Les Kordakia de Nicée, le combustible de Synnada et les poissonsscies, II," *Journal des Savants* (1962): 14–15. Cf., e.g., *HA, Gord.* 32 (two hundred columns in the Gordians' palace: fifty Carystian, fifty porphyry, fifty Phrygian, and fifty Numidian), and *HA, Tac.* 10.5 (one hundred columns of Numidian marble given to Ostia by the emperor Tacitus).

[74] See Petzl 1987, 196–97; Robert, "Kordakia" (see n. 73, above), 14; Fant 1993, 155–57; Dodge 1991. Most marbles, though their quarries were controlled by the imperial *ratio marmorum,* could also be used in buildings not imperially sponsored. In contrast, the grey granite from Mons Claudianus (in Egypt) appears to have been restricted to the emperor himself: Peacock and Maxfield 1997, I:334; Fant 1992.

[75] Strabo, 9.5.16, notes the Romans' high estimation of colored marbles.

[76] E.g., A. Wallace-Hadrill, "The Emperor and His Virtues," *Historia* 30 (1981): 311–14; see also chapter 1.

talents and aspirations.[77] Smyrna expressed its appreciation of the benefits he helped obtain by electing him a city magistrate, turning to him to arbitrate factional strife, erecting a statue to him, and, probably, awarding him the new imperial priesthood associated with Smyrna's designation as "twice neocoros."[78] The rich information from Smyrna, therefore, provides valuable detail for Hadrian's municipal benefactions, allowing us to gauge their effects on individuals' prestige and power and on donations by the local elite, their ramifications for trade and the economy, and the many ways in which they could affect the religious life of a city.

ITALICA

Hadrian's benefactions to Italica merit examination as a group both because this is the westernmost city to have received buildings and other marks of his favor, and because the evidence is predominantly archaeological. The *patria* (ancestral city) of Hadrian and his relative Trajan, Italica was transformed in the first half of the second century by an urban form and buildings usually associated with a metropolis of the Greek East (fig. 10).[79] These substantial changes have often been attributed to Hadrian,[80] although there is little unequivocal evidence. Scholars turn, instead, to arguments from iconography, building techniques and types, and the extensiveness of Italica's alterations in the second century.[81]

Cassius Dio remarks that Hadrian showed his native city great honor and bestowed many splendid gifts on it, although he never visited there as emperor (69.10.1). As we saw in chapters 3 and 4, part of Hadrian's honors to Italica were his conferral of colonial status on the city and his assumption, in absentia, of its chief magistracy, the quinquennial duumvirate. Archaeology, inscriptions, and a few coins suggest other, more tangible, imperial benefactions. Construction techniques and archaeological evidence date to the first half of the second century the new quarter commonly called "Nova Urbs," in Italica's northwest sector. This "New City" boasts an orthogonal layout with spacious porticoed streets, wealthy residences, and monumental public buildings,[82] including an enormous amphitheater for

[77] Gleason 1995, 21–25. Polemo was native to Laodicea of Caria.

[78] Ibid., 21–24, with the ancient evidence.

[79] See Caballos and León 1997; Caballos Rufino 1994, esp. 103–21; García y Bellido 1985; Blázquez 1980–81, 233–41, 251–56; Syme 1964.

[80] E.g., Luzón Nogué 1989; Blanco Freijeiro 1982.

[81] Most recently synthesized and argued by León 1992.

[82] J. M. Rodríguez Hidalgo, "Reflexiones en torno a la Itálica de Adriano," *Habis* 18–19 (1987–88): 584, points out that the term *Nova Urbs* and its counterpart *Vetus Urbs* (used to indicate the eastern part of Italica, now under the village of Santiponce) were coined by García y Bellido in his 1960 work. Size of streets: largest sixteen meters, eight for roadway and four each for the porticoed sidewalks; others fourteen meters, with six for roadway: García y

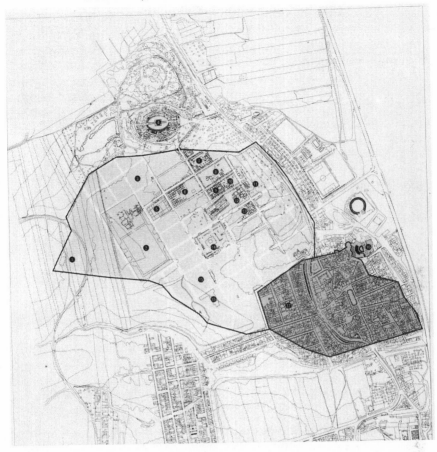

Fig. 10. Plan of Italica in the middle of the second century A.D., in relation to the modern city: the lightly shaded area is the "Nova Urbs" (created in the first half of the second century A.D.), the more darkly shaded
one, "Vetus Urbs." The Hadrianic baths, also called the Baños Mejores,
are north of #2 (the vast gymnasium that has recently been detected); the
amphitheater is #4; and the Traianeum is #14. The city walls probably
postdate Hadrian.

twenty-five thousand spectators in the northernmost part of the town.[83]
The "Baños de la Reina Mora," a vast set of "imperial-type" baths, display

Bellido 1965, 16. The porticoed walkways of Ostia are of similar size, but they also cannot
be surely credited to Hadrian: Boatwright 1997a, 132. The public buildings of Nova Urbs
(baths, amphitheater, and Traianeum), and some other structures, use high-quality cement,
and modules and bricks similar to Hadrianic building in Rome but rare elsewhere in Italica:
León 1988, 38, 49; Roldán Gómez 1987; Rodá 1997.

[83] See García y Bellido 1960, 120–22, and Roldán Gómez 1987, 116. At 160 × 137 me-

Hadrianic construction techniques and lead pipes that bear stamps of the municipality and of Hadrian himself, indicating cooperation between the emperor and city in their construction.[84] The baths seem to have been connected by Hadrian to Italica's aqueduct.[85] Also connected with the new baths, according to a recent archaeological survey, was an immense gymnasium with an exterior plan resembling those of the precincts of Athens's Library of Hadrian and of Italica's "Traianeum" (see below).[86] City walls, possibly Hadrianic but probably later, enclosed Nova Urbs and the rest of Italica's urban area, thirty hectares in all.[87] A new road from the city north to Mons Marmorius (which furnished good local marble) is documented by three well-cut milestones of Hadrian's.[88] Finally, much of the decoration and sculpture from second-century Italica stylistically resembles work found in the Greek East and Rome, and lacks "provincialisms" and indigenous influences.[89]

For my purposes, however, Italica's most interesting monument is that now called the Traianeum, a structure known only from its excavation in the early 1980s by P. León.[90] Evidently associated with the imperial cult, this was an enormous templar precinct, ca. 93 × 120 meters or about one hectare, equivalent to two city blocks in Nova Urbs. It rose at Italica's summit. The Traianeum exhibits unusual materials, architectural decoration,

---

ters, it is one of the largest amphitheaters in the Roman world (the longer axis of Rome's Flavian Amphitheater measures 188 meters).

[84] *CILA* 366 and 579: *IMP C[aesar] H[adrianus] A[ugustus]* and *C[olonia] A[elia] A[ugusta] I[talica]*. The baths, excavated unscientifically in the Nova Urbs in the nineteenth century, have large spacious halls, each about 10–15 meters wide. The statuary found at the baths, including the famous heroizing statue of Trajan, is of excellent quality and materials, although originally the statues may have been associated with the neighboring Traianeum. See P. León, *Esculturas de Itálica* (Seville, 1995), 22–24; León 1988, 38, 49; Roldán Gómez 1987; and García y Bellido 1985, 115–18.

[85] Well-preserved remains of a brick-faced concrete extension lead from the aqueduct to the Hadrianic baths in Italica: Canto 1979, 319–20.

[86] J. M. Rodríguez Hidalgo, "La nueva imagen de la Itálica de Adriano," in Caballos and León 1997, 106.

[87] García y Bellido 1960, 123–26, dates these as Hadrianic by their relation to other buildings of this era as well as to earlier and later city walls, but their patronage by Hadrian would be most unusual: see chapter 6, on Quiza. The city walls are currently under investigation. Italica's city size was surpassed in Spain only by provincial capitals and commercial centers such as Augusta Emerita (50 ha.), Tarraco (36 ha.), and Corduba (70–75 ha.): García y Bellido 1965, 11.

[88] *CILA* 367: [mileage] *HADRIANUS AUG[ustus] FECIT;* cf. Sillières 1990, 137ff, ##78, 79; *Las vías romanas de Andalucía* (Seville, 1992), 172, #93, and 210, #47. Rodá (1997, 174) suggests that the quarries were imperial property.

[89] E.g., León 1989, discussing a statue of Parian marble, not local stone.

[90] León 1988; León 1992; León Alonso 1982. The convenient name "Traianeum" was coined by León.

and design, combining elements from imperial shrines in the Latin West with ones apparently borrowed from structures in the Greek East, particularly the Library of Hadrian in Athens.[91] Yet much of its architectural decoration celebrates Italica's own history. The Traianeum appears to be a signal example of cooperation between Hadrian and a municipal elite, and it embodies the delicate balance in Hadrian's era between imperial commonalities and local pride.

The evidence for the Traianeum can be summarized as follows. The overall layout of the precinct (fig. 11), with a quadriporticus around an octastyle Corinthian podium temple and altar, resembles city fora in imperial Spain, the "Provincial Forum" of Tarraco, and the model from which they derived, the Forum of Augustus in Rome. Yet the external design and general dimensions of the precinct itself echo those of the Library of Hadrian in Athens (see figs. 5, 8).[92] The Traianeum's foundations are of the high-quality cement that appears in Italica only from the first half of the second century A.D., when it was used for many buildings in the Nova Urbs.[93] Luna marble, rare in Spain, is the predominant elaborated material of the Traianeum, and other imported marble appears in conspicuous places: the columns of the entrance porch are unfluted red-veined Chian marble, and the columns of the courtyard are unfluted green-veined cipollino (Carystian).[94] The stylistic comparanda for the Traianeum's architectural elements are all associated with imperial building projects of the Hadrianic period, including two Corinthian capitals from Tarraco and the material from the Library of Hadrian in Athens.[95] Thus in design, materials, and decoration, the Traianeum corresponds closely to other buildings Hadrian sponsored. A Hadrianic date is corroborated by the structure's numismatic material, which indicates a terminus post quem in Trajan's reign.[96]

The building's function is indicated by the inscriptions and sparse fragments of sculpture from the site. The four inscriptions discovered here all relate to priests of the imperial cult, are dedicated to some "August" deity, and/or refer in some way to the "Genius" (tutelary and procreative deity)

---

[91] León 1988, esp. 55–101; Boatwright 1997b.

[92] Boatwright 1997b, 194–204, provides a detailed comparison. With propylaea and exedrae, the Traianeum measures about 93 × 120 meters; the Library, 87 × 125 meters.

[93] León 1988, 38, 49; Roldán Gómez (1987) notes that she could not examine firsthand the concrete of the Traianeum.

[94] Rodá 1997, 169.

[95] León 1988, 64–69; Freyberger 1990, 131; Heilmeyer 1970, 75; cf. Strong 1953, 131–32, 136, 138–39, referring to Pergamum's Traianeum and the Ionic West Colonnade of its Asklepieion (ca. A.D. 150). Ostia's capitals are of Proconnesian marble: Pensabene 1973, 64, ##247–48.

[96] The numismatic evidence begins with a bronze coin of Trajan, found in the drain bordering the northeast corner of the temple, and an *as* of Hadrian, found over virgin earth at the exterior face of the temple: León 1988, 39, 121–27.

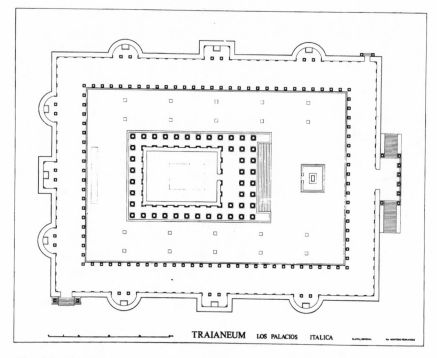

Fig. 11. Plan of the Traianeum in Italica, as reconstructed by P. León and F. Montero Fernández. Plan is slightly off-axis: north is a bit toward the upper right.

of the Colonia Aelia Augusta Italica.[97] Hadrian had conferred on Italica the honorary title and status of colony (see chapter 3). Moreover, the statues recorded by the inscriptions, together with fragments found here, substantiate abundant decoration that included oversized heroic statues and images of Italica's notables.[98] The assembled evidence is most appropriate for a center of imperial cult. The precinct apparently monumentalized Italica's contribution to the imperial rule of Rome, sanctioned by the gods, even as it symbolized Italica's participation in the larger Greco-Roman oikoumene, fostered and controlled by the emperor.

[97] *AE* 1982, 520, cf. Blanco in León 1988, 105–8; *AE* 1983, 520, cf. Blanco, in León 1988, 110; *AE* 1983, 521, cf. Blanco, in León 1988, 110–13; Blanco, in León 1988, 113–16. For a similar but fuller epigraphic dossier from the imperial cult sanctuary at Nîmes, see Gros 1984, 129–32.

[98] León 1988, 82: oversized finger joint with part of the nail and knuckle (0.30 meter long), hand between wrist and fingers (0.26 meter max. height, 0.31 width). Also found were a life-sized marble knee (0.26 meter long) and some marble female drapery; for statues of local notables of the later second and third century, see inscriptions cited in n. 97.

In sum, the vast extent, location, design, and materials of the Traianeum, together with its epigraphic, numismatic, and sculptural evidence, argue that the whole was a center for imperial cult built in Hadrian's period. In the absence of a dedicatory inscription, it seems safe to posit that the magnificent structure was jointly funded by Hadrian and locals in this prosperous city.[99] In the precinct Italica's citizens participated in the empire's shared rituals of imperial cult even as they celebrated their own identity, the city's Genius. Although the Traianeum was only one of many buildings contributing to Italica's splendor in the mid second century, the city's brilliance was relatively short-lived. Moorish and other incursions troubled Italica from the 170s on (*CIL* II 1120, cf. *CIL* II 2015),[100] and the location of the provincial capital at neighboring Hispalis (Seville, only ten kilometers away) had always undermined Italica's standing. Yet the physical transformation of Italica from a provincial town like many others into a glorious city showcasing Greco-Roman art and architecture reveals the confidence of Rome's cities at this period. Hadrian's imperial munificence stimulated and encouraged their expectations for both the present and the future.

APPENDIX

Other Structures in Athens Associated with Hadrian (arranged alphabetically)

1. CONSTRUCTION OF *AQUEDUCT* AND ITS ELABORATE TERMINATION IN ATHENS IN A NYMPHAEUM/RESERVOIR, COMPLETED IN A.D. 140

The "reservoir" on Mt. Lycabettus's southeast slope (27 meters long × 14.55 wide, without protuding apse in back and fronting Ionic propylon) was faced by an Ionic propylon with arcuated lintel. The aqueduct, originally twenty kilometers from Mt. Parnes to Mt. Lycabettus, primarily was a water channel (0.70 × 1.60 m), partly carved in the rock, partly formed by mortar and rubble or brick, with service holes at intervals of 33–37 meters and in places as much as 45 meters below ground level. Like the Argive aqueduct (see chapter 6, n. 95), the Athenian aqueduct was fronted by an Ionic portico at its termination. In Athens the Latin building inscription (*ILS* 337 = *CIL* III 549 = Smallwood, #396) was on the straight entablatures flanking an arcuated central intercolumniation. The aqueduct also supplied a nymphaeum and fountain, usually credited to Antoninus Pius, near the southeast corner of the Agora and west of the Library of Pantainos and the Panathenaic Way. See S. Leigh, "The 'Reservoir' of Hadrian in Athens," *JRA* 10 (1997): 279–90; J. Stuart and N. Revett, *The Antiq-*

[99] For the general prosperity of the region, see Nierhaus 1965, 188–89; Nierhaus 1966, 163–68; Caballos Rufino 1994.
[100] García y Bellido 1960, 23–24.

uities of Athens (London, 1794), vol. III, chapter 4; Travlos 1971, 242–43, with fig. 313 (from Stuart and Revett); Graindor 1934, 252; Kokkou 1970, 169–71; S. Walker, "Roman Nymphaea in the Greek World," in *Roman Architecture in the Greek World,* ed. S. Macready and F. H. Thompson (London, 1987), 62; Spawforth and Walker 1985, 98–99; Willers 1990, 13; Lolos 1997, 304–5. For the nymphaeum and fountain in the Agora, see J. M. Camp, *The Athenian Agora* (London, 1986), fig. 153; H. A. Thompson, "Activities in the Athenian Agora: 1958," *Hesperia* 28 (1959): 97; H. A. Thompson, "Activities in the Athenian Agora: 1959," *Hesperia* 29 (1960): 348; H. A. Thompson and R. E. Wycherley, *The Agora of Athens* (Princeton, NJ, 1972), XIV:202.

2. *BRIDGE* OVER THE RIVER CEPHISUS, 124/125

Carrying the Sacred Road from Athens to Eleusis, Hadrian's bridge was incorporated in the new Athens-Corinth road in 1961. It measured 5.3 meters wide and 50 meters long (overall), spanning the 30-meter-wide riverbed; its three piers were each 1.75 meters wide. The chronicles (Hieron. *Ab Abr.* 2139 = 123; Euseb., ed. Helm, p. 198; cf. Cassiod., a. 127; Vers. Arm. (5th year of Hadrian); Dion. Telm., 63, cf. Hieron. *Chron.,* ed. Helm, p. 592, a. 2138 = 122; Sync., 659.9, Helm, ibid.) link this bridge to an inundation of the Cephisus and a winter visit by Hadrian to Athens, with dates coinciding with Hadrian's first visit to Athens as emperor (winter 124/125) and personal participation in that September's Great Eleusinian Mysteries. See Graindor 1934, 35–36, 6–8; Follet 1976, 113–14; Kokkou 1970, 171–73; I. Travlos, *Prakta* (1950): 122–27; Travlos 1971, 439; Willers 1990, 13.

3. *GYMNASIUM,* ?AFTER 132

This building, considered documented by Paus. 1.18.9 and Oliver, #85 = *IG* II² 1102 (= *SEG* III 111, a partially preserved letter from Hadrian to the Athenians, discovered south of the Ilissos River across from the Olympieion), has been tentatively associated with remains of a large building south of the Ilissos, near the earlier Kynosarges Gymnasium. The structure, not yet fully excavated but measuring 64.50 meters wide × 80 meters long, is of "Hadrianic construction technique" and has "colonnades [on] three sides of the building, with the west side closed by a large room and a wall." Pausanias says that Hadrian's gymnasium had a hundred columns of "Libyan marble" (i.e., giallo antico), in a report corresponding to his record of one hundred columns of Phrygian marble (i.e., pavonezzato) in the Library of Hadrian. After the inscription's heading, Hadrian proclaims his desire to do well for the Athenians both publicly and individually; as he then declares that he is giving to their sons "the . . . ," the break in the stone occurs. In light of Pausanias's passage, the findspot of the inscription in an area known for gymnasia, and the reference to "sons" or "boys," the first publisher of the inscription, T. Sauciuc ("Ein Hadriansbrief und das Hadriansgymnasium in Athen," *AthMitt* 37 [1912]: 183–89), conjectured that "gymnasium" should be restored in the lacuna. The lacuna is followed by a few other words indicating Hadrian's stipulation about the embellishment of the building (or of the city in general) and the costs. Kent J. Rigsby, who kindly discussed this inscription with me, has remarked that "gymnasium" is a reasonable guess but not, strictly speaking, the right word for a boys' school. See Follet 1976, 122n. 11 (noting that Hadrian's tribunician power should perhaps be read as thirteenth, which would date the letter to A.D. 129 rather than 132); M.-F. Billot, "Le Cynosarges, Antiochos et les tanneurs. Questions de topographie," *BCH* 116 (1992): 119–56, esp. 134–35, 142; Travlos 1971, 340, 498–504, 579; Willers 1990, 13–14; Spawforth and Walker 1985, 95; H. A. Thompson, *Hesperia* 19 (1950): 321, fig. 1, 326, plate 102, proposing a location east of the Stoa of Attalus; R. E. Wycherley, *The Stones of Athens* (Princeton, NJ, 1987), 229; Kokkou 1970, 165–67.

4. "*PANTHEON*," OR TEMPLE OR SHRINE "SACRED TO ALL GODS," N.D.

Because its rusticated heavy poros exterior wall resembles the temenos walls of Hadrian's Library and Olympieion, the remains of a triple-naved building ca. fifty meters east of the Roman Agora and Library of Hadrian have been tentatively identified as the Pantheon. This name is modern, used to designate a building noted by Pausanias (1.18.9, 1.5.5) and perhaps referred to by three dedications to other gods that contain the added phrase "to all the gods" (*IG* II^2 2802, 2934; *Agora* I 4348, *Hesperia* 10 [1941], p. 255, #60). Aligned along an ancient east-west road, the rectangular building with slightly wider ends originally measured more than eighty meters; its long main hall (ca. 64 × 40 meters) was divided internally by two rows of cruciform piers. The east end, wider than the west one, forms a sort of porch decorated with an inner colonnade including applied Carystian pilasters. Spawforth and Walker 1985, 97–98, and plate II, fig. 3, noting both the great size of the excavated building's main hall and its unusual juxtaposition with the building's wider eastern end, suggest that the edifice was the meeting place of the Panhellenion, not a temple (see below, on the Temple of Hera and Zeus Panhellenios). See also Karivieri 1994, 91–92; Martini 1985 (identifying the Library of Hadrian as Pausanias's Sanctuary of all the gods); G. Dontas, *AAA* 1 (1968): 221–24 and *AAA* 2 (1969): 1–3; Travlos 1971, 439 and figs. 557–63, cf. 324 and 531;

Kokkou 1970, 159–61; Willers 1990, 25; Beaujeu 1955, 232–36; K. Ziegler, *RE* 18.3 (1949): 703, 707–26, s.v. Pantheion.

5. POSSIBLE CHANGES TO "*ROMAN AGORA*," PROBABLY AFTER 126/127

On the basis of archaeological data the renovations to the "Roman Agora," including the installation of the eastern gate and an internal colonnade around the central court (originally more than one hundred columns), have been dated to the early second century. The quadriporticus measures ca. 112 × 96 meters; the courtyard, 82 × 57 meters. The columns are of unfluted Hymettan marble, with Pentelic bases showing similar profiles at the eastern gateway and quadriporticus; the Ionic capitals and epistyle of quadriporticus are also Pentelic. Quadriporticus and courtyard were paved with white marble. Hadrian's decree regulating the sale of Athenian olive oil (Oliver, #92 = *IG* II² 1100 = *SEG* XV 108; see chapter 5, n. 35 and following), engraved on the northern jamb of the middle bay of the entrance to the "Roman Agora" (the Gate of Athena Archegetis) and with a terminus post quem of 126/127, may have been inscribed while the internal courtyard and quadriporticus were being renovated. Although the Roman Agora has long been thought to have served Athens's commercial activity, more recently its suitability for imperial cult has also been underlined. See Travlos 1971, 28–29; H. S. Robinson, "The Tower of the Winds and the Roman Market-Place," *AJA* 47 (1943): 302–5; I. T. Hill, *The Ancient City of Athens* (Chicago, 1953), 205–6; M. Hoff, "The Early History of the Roman Agora at Athens," in Walker and Cameron 1989, 1–8; Shear 1981, 359–60; A. S. Benjamin and A. E. Raubitschek, "Arae Augusti," *Hesperia* 28 (1959): 85.

6. *TEMPLE OF HERA AND ZEUS PANHELLENIOS*, ?131/132

Pausanias begins his list of buildings that Hadrian gave to the Athenians with a temple of Hera and Zeus Panhellenios and a temple or shrine "sacred to all gods" (*theois tois pasin hieron koinon,* Paus. 1.18.9; see above on the "Pantheon"). The passage is so unclear that some think three temples are meant, one each to Hera and Zeus Panhellenios and a separate "Pantheon" (cf. Travlos 1971, 429–31), some two distinct temples to Zeus and Hera (Beaujeu 1955, 178–79n. 2), and some only one temple (P. Godfrey and D. Hemsoll, "The Pantheon: Temple or Rotunda?" in *Pagan Gods and Shrines of the Roman Empire,* ed. M. Henig and A. King [Oxford, 1986], 207n. 33). Cassius Dio calls the Panhellenion a shrine (*sekon*), saying that Hadrian allowed the Greeks to build it in his honor (Cass. Dio 69.16.2). C. P. Jones (1996, 29–33) argues that Dio and Pausanias refer to two distinct structures, a temple of Zeus (and Hera?) Panhellenios that

Hadrian gave to the Athenians, and a smaller shrine to Hadrian himself that the emperor allowed the Greeks to build. I believe that Hadrian "Panhellenius" was identified with Zeus Panhellenios, and the temple of Hera and Zeus Panhellenios included a shrine (at least a statue) of Hadrian Panhellenius. The temple, perhaps designated the Panhellenion, was special to the Panhellenion League, and the conflation of Hadrian and Zeus is paralleled at Smyrna, Cyzicus, and Athens, at the Olympieion. Remains of a building, ca. one hundred meters south of the Olympieion and north of the Ilissos, have been tentatively associated with the shrine of the Panhellenion: their mortar foundations and exterior poros walls, and the prominent exedrae in their design, have parallels in other Hadrianic buildings. The rectangular peristyle measures 65.40 × 45.26 meters, with eastern entrance 6.96 meters wide; a central exedra, 10 meters diameter, projects from both north and south walls. At the back (west) part of the court are the foundations of a small building, 11.40 × 15.50 meters. Architectural fragments suggest the Corinthian order. See also Karivieri 1994, 91–93; Spawforth and Walker 1985, 97; contra, Willers 1990, 62–67.

CHAPTER 8

City Foundations, New and Renewed

THE ARRAY of benefactions Hadrian gave to various cities throughout the Roman world is epitomized in the cities he either founded ex novo or reconstructed extensively after previous devastation. Epigraphic, numismatic, or literary evidence place in this relatively small group Cyrene and Hadrianopolis in Cyrenaica, which Hadrian "refounded" or founded at the beginning of his reign; Stratonicea-Hadrianopolis and Hadrianoutherae, Hadrianoi, and Hadrianeia, founded in Mysia in 123 and 131/132; Antinoopolis in Egypt, founded 30 October 130; and Colonia Aelia Capitolina, established in Judaea in a lengthy and disastrous process from before 132.[1] (See endpapers and fig. 15.) These eight cities, which I term new foundations,[2] are attested by fairly abundant data. Colonia Aelia Mursa in Pannonia Inferior (?A.D. 133), presumable foundations of Hadrian such as Forum Hadriani in Lower Germany, and most cities called Hadrianopolis (such as modern Edirne in European Turkey), are not treated here because of the deficiency of evidence for them.[3] The majority of Hadrian's new foundations are in the Greek East, contrasting with his changes of city status, which are almost completely restricted to the Latin West (see chapter 3). Only Colonia Aelia Mursa and Colonia Aelia Capitolina are obviously Roman creations in which Hadrian settled veterans as new colonists.

Compared to the foundations of Trajan and earlier emperors, Hadrian's colonies and new cities are startlingly few in number; indeed, his two veteran colonies, Colonia Aelia Mursa and Colonia Aelia Capitolina, are the last such coloniae in the history of Rome.[4] Beginning with the reign of Augustus, the *pax Augusta* had gradually reduced the strategic benefits of colonies and municipia created ex novo. Even when establishing Aelia

---

[1] The name of the province was changed from Judaea to Syria Palaestina only after the Bar Kokhba War, but an exact date cannot be pinpointed: Mildenberg 1984, 98.

[2] As compared to Athens's "City of Hadrian" and Italica's "Nova Urbs," both discussed in chapter 7.

[3] For Aelia Mursa, for example, see the remarks of Mócsy 1974, 119, who cannot decide if the foundation was a *deductio* or not. M. Zahrnt, "Hadrians Wirken in Makedonien," in *Inscriptions of Macedonia* (Thessaloniki, 1996), 229–39, has now tentatively suggested that Hadrian founded three "Hadrianopoleis" in Macedonia.

[4] Zahrnt 1991 emphasizes the relative scarcity of Hadrian's colonies; see also Zahrnt 1988b, 229. A. Birley points out to me that a case can be made for a later example, Vaga in Africa. This city, to which Septimius Severus gave the status of colony before 193, later received veteran settlers from the same emperor: *CIL* VIII 14395, and Gascou 1982, 209–10.

Capitolina and Mursa, whose military contexts have recently been advanced, Hadrian's motivation is thought to have followed an imperial policy of equalizing the number of colonies in a province to the number of legions stationed there.[5] Hadrian encouraged urban self-administration in strategic locales in other ways, as we saw in chapter 3, by changes of city status that promoted the development of Roman administrative organization on the levels of individual cities and entire regions.[6] Further, the spectacular benefits Hadrian gave to certain cities, such as Athens, Smyrna, and Italica, made these represent Rome in the provinces, though colonies had previously played that role (cf. Gell. *NA* 16.13.9, and chapter 7). The Rome these Greco-Roman showcases symbolized was a Rome of Hadrian's making, open to distinct traditions and regional differences but strongly privileging Greco-Roman culture. Athens, Smyrna, Italica, and other choice cities were transfigured to include unmistakable references to the Roman emperor. Hadrian's new foundations embody the same ideology.

Though few in number, Hadrian's "new cities" are invaluable sources for understanding Hadrian's methods and goals in dealing with cities throughout the empire. They disclose both his promotion of a new understanding of the Roman empire, and the limitations of this vision. As sustained and conscious creations, they have revealing documentation, particularly Antinoopolis. In this chapter, therefore, I go into greater detail on individual cities than previously: the data confirm the inferences I have drawn in the preceding chapters. Strikingly, the earliest and latest cities in this group, Cyrene (with Cyrenaican Hadrianopolis) and Colonia Aelia Capitolina, are inextricably tied to Jewish revolts. Hadrian "refounded" or founded the Cyrenaican cities after the devasting Second Jewish Revolt, and his "foundation" of Colonia Aelia Capitolina is said by Cassius Dio to have triggered the Third Jewish Revolt, the Bar Kokhba War (see below). To the detriment of the empire, Hadrian's encouragement of cultural diversity and his attention to local differences did not extend to the Jews and other nonparticipants in the Graeco-Roman urban ideal.[7] But this will emerge from the following discussion, which is arranged in rough chronological order.

CYRENE AND OTHER CYRENAICAN CITIES

In A.D. 115 the "Second Jewish Revolt," a series of Jewish insurrections, broke out first in Cyrenaica and Alexandria, next in central Egypt, and ul-

---

[5] Mócsy 1974, 118–19; Isaac 1980–81, 49–50; Zahrnt 1991, 481–85.

[6] I intend to treat Hadrian's grants of municipal or colonial status to *canabae* in a future article.

[7] Cf. e.g., De Lange 1978. Goodman 1983, 154, and C. R. Whittaker, in *JRS* 68 (1978): 192, stress Rome's general lack of interest in villages and other nonurban communities.

timately in Judaea, Mesopotamia, and Cyprus.[8] The revolt was generally quelled before Hadrian's accession, but fighting continued in Alexandria and possibly elsewhere.[9] The insurrection had been especially violent in Cyrenaica. Cassius Dio reports the horrible deaths of 220,000 here (68.32.1–3), and Orosius speaks of fighting and desolation throughout the countryside, asserting that only Hadrian's "colonies" could repopulate the land (7.12.7b). The words of these historians are substantiated by the virtual disappearance of Jews from Cyrenaica and Egypt outside of Alexandria after this revolt.[10] The revolt was costly also in terms of property: Jewish enclaves were destroyed; in turn, the Jews apparently targeted pagan monuments and buildings closely associated with Roman rule and with Graeco-Roman religion and culture. Many of the restoration inscriptions from Cyrene specify that reconstruction came after "wrecking and burning" (the baths beside the Sanctuary of Apollo), "overthrowing and burning" (the Caesareum), "breaking up and destroying" (the road to Apollonia), "burning and plundering" (the Temple of Hecate), and "[being] thrown down" (the Temple of Zeus), all devastation said to have occurred in the Jewish tumult.[11] A menorah was carved into the road leading southwest from Cyrene to Balagrae and Ptolemais,[12] a striking symbol of Jewish exasperation and determination to overturn the status quo. The archaeological and epigraphic evidence for devastation is particularly clear at Cyrene, thanks to excavations and explorations undertaken by Italian and British teams since the 1920s. For the following description I am indebted to one of the more recent primary investigators, Dr. Susan Walker.[13]

---

[8] Pucci 1981; Fuks 1961; Reynolds 1958–59; Applebaum 1979, 242–344; Laronde 1988, 1045–49.

[9] For the suppression of the revolt in Cyrenaica by 117, see Smallwood, #313 (= *SEG* XVII 584 = *Türk Tarih Bell* 9 (1947): 101–4, #19, quoted in Fraser 1950, 84n. 37: an inscription from Attaleia); fighting in Alexandria and elsewhere in Egypt still in 117, Pucci 1981, 121–32.

[10] Egypt: Foraboschi 1988, 821–23; Cyrenaica (esp. Ptolemais-Barca): Reynolds 1990, 73, and Applebaum 1979, 342–43, 285–92. There has been little archaeological work at Berenice and Ptolemais-Barca. Hereafter I refer to Ptolemais-Barca as Ptolemais.

[11] Baths, Smallwood, #60 = *AE* 1928, 2; Caesareum, n. 37 below; road, Smallwood, #59 = *AE* 1951, 208; Temple of Hecate, *SEG* IX 168; Temple of Zeus, inscription published in *PBSR* 26 (1958): 31–33. Susan Walker has pointed out to me the contrast of such vivid vocabulary with the more generic formulae customary on restoration inscriptions. The intensity suggests the continuing alienation of the gentiles from the Jews. Applebaum 1979, 352, map 6, maps structures in Cyrene damaged by the revolt. Papyri document the devastation in Egypt, especially in the area of the Fayum: Foraboschi 1988, 822–23.

[12] Romanelli 1943, fig. 32 at p. 160.

[13] Dr. Walker has generously let me see an annotated draft of the paper she gave in January 1993 at the symposium on architectural sculpture at the National Gallery of Art, Washington, DC. I have also consulted her published work on Cyrene: Spawforth and Walker 1986, 96–101, and Walker 1985. Whatever mistakes there may be in the following are mine.

Trajan had initiated plans for reconstructing Cyrenaica, but Hadrian was predominantly responsible for Cyrene's rebirth. Before Trajan's death three thousand legionary veterans had been chosen to sail to Cyrene as colonists.[14] These Trajanic colonists have not left clear traces at Cyrene or elsewhere in Cyrenaica, however, and it is Hadrian who is termed "founder" and "savior" in Cyrene's inscriptions.[15] Even without the destructive catalyst of the Jewish insurrection, Cyrene seems appropriate for Hadrian's interest. Eight kilometers inland on a limestone coastal ridge (now Gebel el Akdar in eastern Libya), Cyrene was the first Greek settlement in this fertile but relatively narrow corridor of communications from Alexandria west.[16] (See fig. 12.) Cyrene had been founded by Greeks from Thera around 631 B.C., in accordance with an oracle from Delphi (Hdt. 4.150–58), and the new Greek colony was later strengthened by a second wave of Greek immigrants.[17] Along with its neighboring cities it was annexed by Ptolemy I, to remain more or less under Egyptian hegemony until Ptolemy Apion willed the kingdom of Cyrenaica to Rome in 96 B.C.[18] Then Cyrene and its neighboring cities were "free," as were most cities in other Greek territory bequeathed to Rome; only in 74 B.C. was the area made a quaestorian province. Cyrene functioned as the provincial capital of Cyrenaica during the turbulent last half-century of the Republic.[19] The accession of Octavian-Augustus brought prosperity to Cyrenaica, whose splendid cities also earned it the name Pentapolis ("Five-Citied"). The first Cyrenaican entered the Roman senate during the reign of Nero.[20] Cyrene's famous past involved Apollo and Greek colonization, Hellenistic

[14] See Smallwood, #313 (the inscription referred to in n. 9 above), commemorating the leader Trajan chose for the expedition.

[15] Oliverio et al. 1961–62, ##56 and 56bis (*soter kai euergetes*); *SEG* IX 136 (*soter kai ktistes;* A.D. 138); *SEG* XVII 809 with *SEG* XVIII 731 (*ktistes kai tropheus kai nomothetes;* A.D. 128/129; cf. *IG* VII 70–72, from Megara). This construct is echoed in Orosius's reference to Hadrian's "colonies" mentioned above. For a few possible traces of the colonists in Cyrenaica, see Reynolds 1958–59, 27, and Reynolds 1990, 73 (Ptolemais). Applebaum 1979, 287, mentions an epitaph of a veteran of the legio XV Apollinaris, found at Teucheira, referring to the large size of the city and its former sizable Jewish population. He contends that the Trajanic colonists settled here. A dubious sestertius, known from only one example in the Cabinet of France, calls Hadrian *restitutor Libyae: BMC, Emp.* III, p. 524, Toynbee 1934, 121. See below for Trajan's earlier building donations to Cyrene.

[16] Topography: Applebaum 1979, 1–7; Kraeling 1962, 1–3.

[17] The second group came from many parts of Greece: Broholm, *RE* XII (1924): 157–62, s.v. Kyrene (2); Applebaum 1979, 8–52.

[18] Laronde 1987.

[19] Laronde 1988, 1011–15, noting the problematic definition of the province of Crete and Cyrenaica.

[20] Ibid., 1015–28, noting also Augustus's Edicts of Cyrene and the mistrustful animosity between Hellenes and Romans in Cyrenaica. The five cities of the Pentapolis were Berenice, Teucheira, Ptolemais, Cyrene, and Apollonia: Romanelli 1943, 28.

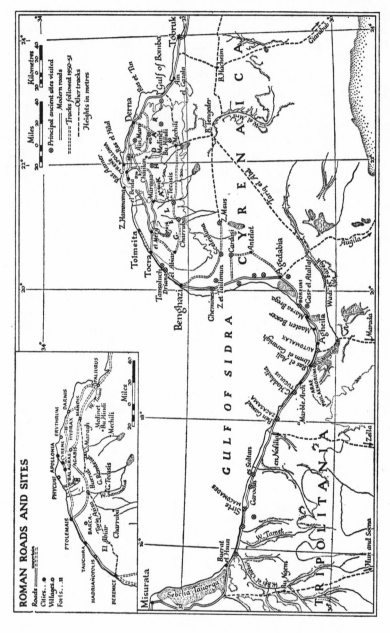

Fig. 12. Modern routes and ancient sites in Cyrenaica (Libya).

kings, and Augustus himself. The combination of an illustrious Greek heritage and the figure of Augustus must have attracted Hadrian to Cyrene, as it apparently did to Athens's Olympieion.[21]

Hadrian's letters to Cyrene, discussed below with other inscriptions from the city and its art and architecture, stress Cyrene's Greek roots. Hadrian evokes the city's legendary foundation and ancestral Greek ties, including Sparta's foundation of Thera, Cyrene's metropolis. Spawforth and Walker aptly place this emphasis within the wider context of the Panhellenion and the promotion of the Greek past and Greek culture.[22] Yet many of the structures Hadrian himself had restored also display imperial Roman characteristics,[23] thereby acknowledging Cyrene's present. (See fig. 13.) Spawforth and Walker note particularly Hadrian's collaboration with surviving members of Cyrene's elite: his letter of 134 urges its citizens "to come together and repopulate your city, and become not only residents but also founders of your fatherland."[24] The injunction expresses well the cooperative relationship of emperor and municipal elite Hadrian apparently strove for, even as it underlines the anachronism of much of Hadrian's thinking. The exhortation belies the reality, and the ideology, of imperial foundations. In the Roman world only an emperor could found new cities. His singular power can be exemplified on coins from Colonia Aelia Capitolina, which depict the emperor alone as founder and father of the new community (fig. 18).[25]

The earliest known restoration Hadrian undertook is the road connecting Cyrene to its port Apollonia, nineteen kilometers northeast. (See fig. 12.) This was achieved in 118 or 119 by a cohort of Roman soldiers of unknown identity (Smallwood, #59 = AE 1951, 208).[26] One milestone of the restored road was erected within Cyrene itself, not far from the northern gate and the sanctuary of Apollo west of it.[27] Since the milestone is located neither a mile from the next stone nor one from the head of the road,

[21] Hadrian may not even have visited the city: Halfmann 1986, 193. Birley 1997, 152, however, citing Oliver, #122 (who takes the document to be an address by Hadrian in person to the people of Cyrene because of its length and the frequent use of the second person plural), suggests that Hadrian visited Cyrene in 123.

[22] Spawforth and Walker 1986, 96–101.

[23] Reynolds 1978, 118, terms Hadrian's early restorations "official works."

[24] Ibid., 113, lines 25–30; Spawforth and Walker 1986, 96–97; Oliver, #122.

[25] Cf. Salmon 1970, 153, and Levick 1967, 36–37; for a numismatic representation of Octavian dressed as a priest behind a plow and apparently in front of a city wall, see H. A. Grueber, *Coins of the Roman Republic in the British Museum* (London, 1910), II:17, #4363, pl. 60.8 (issued 29–27 B.C.).

[26] The text is incorrectly printed in *SEG* IX 252: see *PBSR* 18 (1950): 83–91. A similar milestone is published in *AE* 1928, 1. Trajan had had the road paved in A.D. 100 by recruits from Cyrenaica: Smallwood, #424 = *SEG* IX 251, *SEG* XIII 619b.

[27] *JRS* 40 (1950): 89, D4, found in situ.

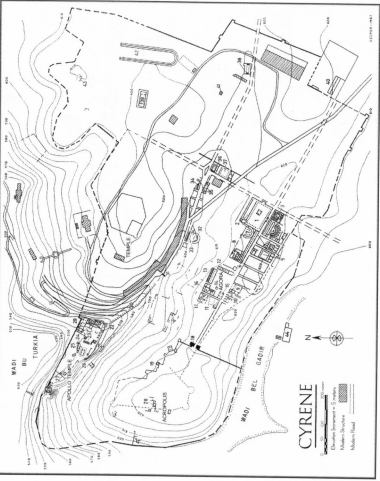

Fig. 13. Plan of Cyrene. The first milestone of the road to Apollonia, Cyrene's port, which Hadrian had rebuilt immediately upon accession, is found inside the gates of the city somewhat near the Trajanic Baths. Hadrian's restorations cluster in the sanctuary of Apollo at the northwest edge of the city (the upper left on this plan), the location of the Temple of Hecate as well as the Baths of Trajan, and in the southern-central region of the city, where are the Caesareum and its attached basilica.

its primary purpose seems symbolic.[28] It forcefully negates the appropriation of Cyrene's roads earlier signified by the insurgents' carved menorah.

In 119, according to a marble inscription in Latin (not found in situ), Hadrian had restored a set of baths with its porticoes, a ball court, and other unspecified adjacencies (Smallwood, #60 = *AE* 1928, 2).[29] These seem to be the baths Trajan had donated to the city at the beginning of his reign (cf. Smallwood, #399). At the northwest corner of the Sanctuary of Apollo, the large handsome baths (ca. 3,600 square meters overall) feature a long rectangular hall.[30] (See fig. 13.) Walker notes that this restoration would have reasserted the Roman imperial presence in the city. Furthermore, the baths' site, conveniently near the newly completed road and the Fountain of Apollo, made reconstruction relatively easy, as well as ensuring an impressive and accessible location.[31] The use of Latin alone, rather than the simultaneous use of Latin and Greek common in Cyrene's inscriptions of the imperial period,[32] may have emphasized the Roman character of the structure.

Another inscription proclaims in Latin and Greek that Hadrian restored the Temple of Hecate in 119 (*SEG* IX 168).[33] This small podium temple, facing south and located west of the baths and northeast of the temples of Apollo and of Artemis, had been constructed at the beginning of the second century A.D.[34] Although not one of the most important shrines of the sanctuary, the Temple of Hecate was the first decisively Roman temple in the sacred area.[35] Its immediate reconstruction by Hadrian may have encouraged others, for around this time the Temple of Isis was restored by a local priest of Apollo, who dedicated his work to Hadrian's health and long reign; the Temple of Artemis seems to have been restored by someone now unknown, also in honor of Hadrian (*SEG* IX 171); and the Temple of Apollo saw renewed cult activity.[36] Hadrian had succeeded in inspiring Cyrene's elite to cooperate with him in renewing the city's religious life.

[28] Walker (1993) notes also that the location, east of the baths, is "near double columns and a piazza, which marked the formal entrance to the reopened city at some distance within the defensive north gate."

[29] = *Africa Italiana* 1 (1927–28): 321–24.

[30] Yegül 1992, 397 and 400, and figs. 487, 488, 491c.

[31] Walker 1993, 3. The renovation of Cyrene's baths, if they are those originally donated by Trajan, may strengthen the credibility of Hadrian's alleged restoration of Trajan's baths at Antioch. See chapter 6, n. 113.

[32] See R. G. Goodchild 1971, 40, on Cyrene's bilingual official inscriptions.

[33] = *Africa Italiana* 2 (1928–29): 118–19n. 3, with fig. 8 = *AE* 1929, 9.

[34] R. Goodchild 1963, 64–65; Stucchi 1975, 199, fig. 189, pl. I, no. 19; Pressice 1990, 149.

[35] Pressice 1990, 149.

[36] Temple of Isis: Oliverio et al. 1961–62, 260, #72, with Ensoli Vittozzi 1992, 219 and pl. XII, 1; naos and portico, perhaps of the Temple of Artemis, *SEG* IX 171, with L. Pernier, "L'Artemision di Cirene," *Africa Italiana* 4 (1931): 216–20, 227–28, and Stucchi 1975, 243, figs. 34–35 (attribution doubted by Laronde 1988, 1051, and Applebaum 1979, 276).

In 118 Hadrian restored the Caesareum in the southeast sector of the excavated ancient city (fig. 13), according to a Latin and Greek inscription (*SEG* XVII 804),[37] but the extent of his work is unknown. A vast Doric quadriporticus (ca. 96 × 60 meters, with courtyard ca. 86 × 55 meters), the Caesareum was adapted sometime in the first century A.D. from an early-second-century B.C. gymnasium into a center for imperial cult, complete with freestanding temple.[38] Two gabled Doric (tetrastyle) propylaea cut through the high exterior walls, as entrances into the precinct from Cyrene's major north-south and east-west streets.[39]

According to a Latin inscription, in 119 or soon thereafter Hadrian restored the judicial basilica that had run lengthwise across the Caesareum's north side for at least a generation.[40] (See fig. 13.) The Roman proconsul used this hall for judicial proceedings during his visits to the city as assize center.[41] The long rectangular basilica, about 96 × 25 meters, was divided internally into a nave and two aisles. Its Hadrianic reconstruction gave it a western semicircular apse, which displayed statues of Nemesis, Tyche, and others now lost, as well as a dedication to Hadrian made in 118 (*AE* 1946, 177 = *SEG* XVII 808).[42] The reuse of architectural elements and the use of native limestone rather than imported marble suggest that the reconstruction was felt to be urgent.[43] The internal colonnades of the basilica were Doric, harmonizing with but not identical to the neighboring Caesareum.[44]

The famous statue of Hadrian in Greek dress (see fig. 14, and n. 56 below) was found within the cella of the Temple of Apollo. New propylaea were also erected for the sanctuary sometime in Hadrian's reign, though not by him: *SEG* IX 190, with Laronde 1988, 1051.

[37] *SEG* XVII 804 = L. Gasperini, "Le iscrizioni del Cesareo e della Basilica di Cirene," *QAL* 6 (1971): 10–12, ##C5–7, and cf. pp. 12–15, ##C8–14; Reynolds 1958–59, 161–62, #IVa; cf. *JRS* 40 (1950): 89–90, D3.

[38] The central temple in the courtyard has design comparanda in the Traianeum and Olympieion (chapter 7). For the Caesareum, see Ward-Perkins and Ballance 1958, and M. Luni, "Il Foro di Cirene tra secondo e terzo secolo," in *L'Africa romana—Atti V. Conv. di Studio: Sassari, 11–13 dic. 1987* (Sassari, 1988), 271–77.

[39] *SEG* XVII 804 was on the eastern propylaeum: M. Luni, *L'Africa romana IX*, ed. A. Mastino (Sassari, 1992), 143–45. The walls were embellished externally only with a Doric entablature and slight indentation at the bottom: Ward-Perkins and Ballance 1958, 140–49.

[40] Smallwood 1952, 37–38; Reynolds, in Ward-Perkins and Ballance 1958, 162, #IVb.

[41] Reynolds 1978, 114–15, 120–21; Luni 1990; Applebaum 1979, 282. By ca. A.D. 100 the basilica replaced rooms along the Caesareum's north side.

[42] Ward-Perkins and Ballance 1958, 149–55; R. G. Goodchild 1971, 72–73; Luni 1990, 106–12, also suggesting that the large niche in the center of the Hadrianic west apse held a marble group of Sabina, Trajan, and Hadrian, later moved to the "Temple of Commodus."

[43] Walker 1993.

[44] Spawforth and Walker 1986, 100–101: the later second-century use of Doric style in rebuilding the sanctuary of Apollo was a conscious archaism. Cf. Hadrian's reconstruction of the Ionic Temple of Dionysus at Teos.

At the end of his reign Hadrian again attended to Cyrene. A Greek dedication made in A.D. 138 to Hadrian, "savior and founder," and to Antoninus Pius mentions Hadrian's donation of statues to the city he had embellished (*SEG* IX 136).[45] Even if these did not depict Hadrian himself,[46] like many of those erected in Athens's Olympieion seven years earlier, they bore witness to Hadrian's concern for Cyrene's embellishment. From 134 comes a fragmentary letter in which Hadrian adjures the recipient "Greeks" to save their "mother Cyrene" and refers to gifts and grain. The truncated list of names that follows is headed by *theos Hadrianos;* if its interpretation as a list of donors is correct, it means that Hadrian gave grain or something else to Cyrene.[47] The identity of these "Greeks" is not clear. J. M. Reynolds suggests that Hadrian is addressing Greeks in Cyrenaica, not Greeks in general.[48] But "Greeks" here, as in Antinoopolis and in Cibyra of the Panhellenion League (see below, and chapter 7), may include those who embraced Greek culture but were not of pure Greek ancestry.[49]

A separate dossier of imperial letters presents new laws that Hadrian gave to Cyrene, apparently basing them on those of Cyrene's ancestral Sparta,[50] as well as his promise of a gymnasium for the ephebes of the city (Reynolds 1978, 113, lines 31–35, written 134/135).[51] Hadrian's laws are alluded to by a separate public inscription of 128/129, which honors him as *ktistes, tropheus,* and *nomothetes* (founder, nurturer, and lawgiver: *SEG* XVII 809 with *SEG* XVIII 731). In contrast, nothing yet corroborates the gymnasium Hadrian promised to Cyrene in 134/135 and in which, he says, the ephebes "would really appreciate imperial generosity."[52] The imperial letter recording these last two donations is the one in which Hadrian urges the Cyrenaeans to partake in their own refounding (cited at the beginning of this chapter). Hadrian enumerates his civic benefactions to Cyrene, apparently to inspire citizens to similar acts.

---

[45] *AE* 1919, 96, found at the Temple of Hadrian and Antoninus (formerly known as the Capitolium) on the southwest side of the Agora. Although the Greek is ambiguous, I follow Reynolds (1978, 118) in attributing the statues to Hadrian rather than to Antoninus Pius (as does Applebaum 1979, 280).

[46] Laronde 1988, 1051, and F. Chamoux, "Un Sculpteur de Cyrène: Zénion, fils de Zénion," *BCH* 70 (1946): 69–71, hold that the statues were of deities.

[47] Inscription published by Oliverio et al. 1961–62, 257, #68. Reynolds 1978, 118, proposes that the list is of donors. Laronde 1988, 1050, and Robert and Robert, *Bull.Ep.* 1964, #562, suggest that the list is of eponymous magistrates.

[48] Reynolds 1978, 118.

[49] Libyans had been gradually incorporated with Cyrene's Greeks after the fifth century B.C.: O. Masson, "Grecs et Libyens en Cyrénaïque, d'après les témoignages de l'épigraphie," *AntAfr* 10 (1976): 49–62.

[50] Reynolds 1978, 113, lines 36–44, and pp. 118–19; Spawforth and Walker 1986, 97; see Oliver, #123; note the parallel with Antinoopolis and Naucratis and Miletus.

[51] = Oliver, #123, citing previous discussions superseded by Reynolds.

[52] Reynolds 1978, 113, lines 34–35, and p. 118, presuming this to be the Hadrianic gymnasium of Hermes and Heracles. Walker is more cautious in her 1993 paper.

One final aspect of Hadrian's interest in and encouragement of Cyrene is suggested by the last letter in the dossier, which Antoninus Pius wrote in 153/154.[53] It documents Pius's unfavorable response to the citizens of Ptolemais, who had requested permission to hold contests in their own city rather than continue participating in the common sacrifice and *agon* at Cyrene. Rejecting the innovation, Antoninus Pius reaffirms Cyrene's primacy. The available evidence does not allow us to determine whether Antoninus Pius was following up some initiative of Hadrian concerning imperial cult games held at Cyrene. Such encouragement by Hadrian would not be surprising, given this emperor's attested interest in ephebic education at Cyrene and his frequent promotion of imperial games elsewhere (see chapter 5).

Cyrene was Cyrenaica's primary recipient of imperial generosity after the Second Jewish Revolt, and during Hadrian's reign and later the city was termed *metropolis*.[54] To our knowledge, Cyrene was one of only a few cities outside of Greece or Asia admitted to the Panhellenion, a decision involving Hadrian himself.[55] Hadrian's patronage established Cyrene as foremost in Cyrenaica, and on an equal footing with other members of the Panhellenion (except Athens). His interest in Cyrene's Greek heritage seems reflected in the remarkable standing portrait of Hadrian installed in the city within a generation of his death (fig. 14). Unique among all depictions of Roman emperors until Julian the Apostate, the statue represents Hadrian in Greek dress, wearing a chiton and himation (tunic and cloak).[56]

Cyrenaican Hadrianopolis, once known solely from the Antonine Itinerary and late geographers, was located in field work and excavations of the late 1960s near Driana, thirty-six kilometers east of Benghazi (the ancient Berenice) and thirty-three kilometers west of ancient Teucheira. (See fig. 12.) The city is witnessed by a seventeen-kilometer aqueduct, remains of an orthogonal plan, traces of houses over numerous buried cisterns, two ancient limestone quarries one kilometer southwest of the urban nucleus, and smaller finds and inscriptions.[57] Despite the implication of its name,

---

[53] Reynolds 1978, 114, lines 77–85; preferable to Oliver, #124.

[54] Reynolds 1978, 113, lines 19 and 21 (= Oliver, #121, lines 19 and 21), and pp. 117–18; *SEG* IX 170, of A.D. 161; and see the citations below for Hexapolis.

[55] Spawforth and Walker 1986, 96–97. Cyrene's admission occurred within three years of the Panhellenion's foundation. C. P. Jones 1996, 47–53, now contends that Ptolemais was also admitted to the Panhellenion by Hadrian (in 134/135), though with only one delegate (in contrast to Cyrene's two). Since this conclusion seems at least partly based on a controversial understanding of the last letter of the dossier, that from Antoninus Pius (C. P. Jones 1996, 49–50, follows Oliver in reading "Capitolia"), I am not fully convinced by his arguments.

[56] The statue may date to the late Antonine period. See Rosenbaum 1960, #34, pl. 26.1–2, 27.1; Niemeyer 1968, 90, #31, pl. IX.1; Walker 1991, back cover.

[57] Jones and Little 1971 compile and discuss the evidence; more briefly, B. Jones 1985, 27, 33–36. A fragmentary Proconnesian marble column was among the finds.

Fig. 14. In this portrait from Cyrene, Hadrian wears Greek dress: the *pallium,* or himation, over his tunic, laced sandals, and a pine crown on his head.

that Hadrianopolis was a city newly founded by Hadrian, ceramic evidence reveals that the second-century settlement incorporated or supplanted one from the mid first century A.D.[58] Occupation continued at least into the third century. Current scholarly thinking is that after the Second Jewish Revolt Hadrian fortified an existing city with Trajanic colonists and renamed it in his own honor.[59] Although its lack of a good natural port thwarted Hadrianopolis's prosperity, the settlement was symbolically important. Its "creation" by Hadrian transformed the epithet of Cyrenaica

[58] B. Jones 1985, 27, 33–36: perhaps Cauculi Vicus, attested by Scylax, *Periplus* 108.

[59] Reynolds 1958–59, 26–27; Walker 1993. Laronde 1988, 1050, suggests that Hadrian chose this location halfway between Berenice and Teucheira so that its veteran settlers could easily control the two cities, formerly with strong Jewish populations. R. G. Goodchild 1961, 87, infers from its central location that Hadrianopolis was intended to be a center of Hellenism. Jones and Little 1971, 59–60, infer the agrarian importance of the settlement from a massive rock-cut cistern in fields traversed by the aqueduct.

from "Pentapolis" to "Hexapolis" ("Six-Citied") during the late second century and possibly the third.[60]

Hadrian may have dealt personally with Apollonia and Ptolemais, two other cities of Cyrenaica.[61] Yet his association with Cyrene's port city is attested only by Apollonia's membership in the Panhellenion, and by the city's dedication to him as *oikistes* that was in the Olympieion at Athens (*IG* II² 3306).[62] Without further excavation we cannot authenticate Hadrian's (re)founding of this city: at the moment his only known liberality to the port is the rebuilt road from Cyrene, which benefited metropolis and port equally. At Ptolemais, about fifty kilometers west of Cyrene on the coast, Hadrian twice may have been the eponymous priest of Apollo, if Reynolds's reconstruction of a fragmentary text is correct.[63] Yet as shown in chapter 4, Hadrian's assumptions of municipal priesthoods and magistracies were fairly common; they rarely correlate with other activity at the honored city. Further finds are needed to document his interest in Ptolemais.[64] Apollonia and Ptolemais may simply have benefited indirectly from Hadrian's attention to Cyrene after the Second Jewish Revolt. The entire region quickly regained a prosperity that intensified into the third century.[65] Throughout this *floruit,* Cyrene was Cyrenaica's most splendid city, its metropolis, not least because of Hadrian's patronage.[66]

STRATONICEA-HADRIANOPOLIS AND OTHER MYSIAN CITIES

Hadrian's four "new" cities in Mysia (Asia), Stratonicea-Hadrianopolis, Hadrianoutherae, Hadrianoi, and Hadrianeia (see fig. 15), are often connected with his visit to the region in 123, a supposition buttressed in the case of Stratonicea-Hadrianopolis by references in his letter to it dated A.D.

---

[60] R. G. Goodchild 1961, on "the city of Cyrene, the metropolis of the Hexapolis" (= *SEG* XX 727 = *AE* 1963, 140; A.D. 185–92); for a text of Hexapolis of A.D. 165/166. See J. Reynolds, "Four Inscriptions from Roman Cyrene," *JRS* 49 (1959): 99.

[61] Hadrian has been associated with a basilica in Teucheira: referring to an unpublished inscription excavated here by Goodchild, Reynolds 1978, 120, says that Hadrian donated a basilica to the city. Walker 1993, similarly referring to an unpublished inscription (the same?) from Teucheira, says only, "at Teucheira a basilica was built in [Hadrian's] reign and there are a number of dedications to him."

[62] Laronde 1988, 1049, implausibly dates the dedication to 129. Without conclusive evidence, he also suggests that Hadrian had centuriated the region west of Apollonia. Apollonia was a member of the Panhellenion: chapter 7, n. 14.

[63] Reynolds 1990, 65n. 2; cf. S. Applebaum, in *JRS* 40 (1950): 90, #1, with note.

[64] Reynolds 1990, 65–66, remarks on the inadequacy of Ptolemais's evidence.

[65] Laronde 1988, 1052–60; Lloyd 1990, 41.

[66] Reynolds 1990: there still is insufficent evidence for why Diocletian chose Ptolemais, rather than Cyrene, as the capital of his new province of Libya Pentapolis.

CITIES in
ASIA MINOR

Map projection:
Lambert's Conformal Conic

Approximate scale:
1 : 6,888,000

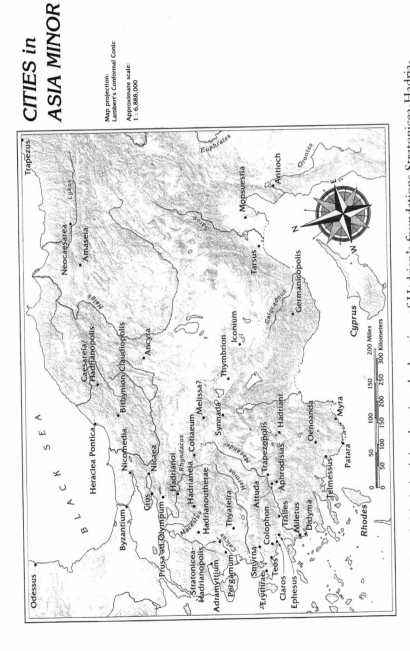

Fig. 15. Mysia in Asia, showing the location of Hadrian's foundations Stratonicea-Hadria-nopolis, Hadrianoutherae, Hadrianoi, and Hadrianeia.

127. Hadrian's motivation is unclear for establishing this group of cities in the upper plain of the Caïcus River and further north in central and eastern Mysia.[67] It is usually interpreted as due to a "conviction that civilization could best be promoted by urbanization" in this "scarcely Hellenized" region.[68] Since Mysia has received only spotty archaeological investigation, it is difficult to verify the last assumption.[69]

Stratonicea-Hadrianopolis is illuminated by a dossier of letters from Hadrian to this city, about fifty kilometers east of Pergamum in the environs of modern Kirkağaç (Oliver, ##79–81).[70] Hadrian reconstituted as a polis, renamed Stratonicea-Hadrianopolis, an earlier sympolity ("twin city") of two Hellenistic communities, Stratonicea and Indeipedion. Stratonicea-Hadrianopolis lies on the borders of Mysia and Lydia, in a rich agricultural region at the upper reaches of the Caïcus River.[71] It commands the road from the Macestus valley to the Caïcus valley where it intersects the inland route between Smyrna and Cyzicus.[72] Antiochus I of Syria had founded Stratonicea in the early third century B.C. in honor of his wife Stratonice, locating the new city over a previous settlement from which nothing now remains. Little is known of Stratonicea's history until its refounding by Hadrian. It issued coins in the early second century B.C., and individual ephebes are attested from the city in the second and first centuries B.C. From numismatic evidence L. Robert has argued that Stratonicea was subordinate to its partner in the sympolity, the polis of the Indeipediatai, until Hadrian's reconstitution of the political arrangement in 123 made the Indeipediatai obsolete as an independent political entity.[73] The letter from Hadrian to Stratonicea-Hadrianopolis dating to the beginning of 127 refers to the city as "newly founded."[74] Coins and other inscriptions establish Hadrian as the founder of this "new" city, an act he probably accomplished in 123.[75]

---

[67] For instance, the earthquake of A.D. 120 (see chapter 6, n. 46) seems not to have precipitated it. Dr. John L. Boatwright (U.S. Geologic Survey) kindly informs me that the fault lines under Cyzicus, Nicea, and Nicomedia do not run very close to Stratonicea-Hadrianopolis, Hadrianoi, or Hadrianeia, and that Stratonicea-Hadrianopolis is in a different fault zone.

[68] E.g., Magie 1950, 616–17; cf. V. Chapot, *La Province romaine proconsulaire d'Asie* (Paris, 1904), 98–103.

[69] See Robert 1962, 198–202.

[70] Robert and Robert, *Hellenica* 6 (1948): 80–84, also publish the complete dossier of three letters with continuously numbered lines. Many of the other publications, such as that of Smallwood (#453), present only one letter.

[71] Ruge 1940; Robert 1962, 43–74.

[72] Robert 1962, 46–50.

[73] Ibid., 66.

[74] Lines 8–9 of Oliver, #79 = *IGR* IV 1156a = *Syll.*³ 837 = Smallwood, #453. Cf. Robert and Robert, *Hellenica* 6 (1948): 80.

[75] Ruge 1940, 1245–46, and *Hellenica* 11–12 (1960): 56, #2, for the coins; inscriptions: *IGR* IV 1156, 1158–59, and above, n. 70. For the date of the foundation, see Halfmann 1986, 199–200.

Hadrian's letter, with two others from him to the city, is inscribed on a stele. The earliest missive records Hadrian's responses to the city about its finances and physical aspect. Hadrian grants taxes from the surrounding land to Stratonicea-Hadrianopolis rather than taking them for Rome;[76] and he orders the owner of a neglected house, Tiberius Claudius Socrates, either to restore it or to sell it to a neighbor so that it not fall down from decrepitude. The emperor calls these matters "only just and necessary to a recently established city." Similar imperial concern for cities' finances is evident in the Flavian municipal charter (chapter 3) and documented in chapter 5;[77] Hadrian's interest in the physical fabric of cities is mirrored in Pausanias (e.g., 10.4.1), in chapters on building and rebuilding in civic charters beginning in the last century of the Republic,[78] and in the later strictures in the *Digest* that curatores rei publicae or the *praeses provinciae* (governor of the province) oversee such matters.[79] In the dossier's second letter Hadrian acknowledges the city's thanks to T. Avidius Quietus, the former proconsul of Asia, for benefactions made during his office (in A.D. 125/126). In the third, Hadrian approves the city's honorary decree for its ambassador Ti. Claudius Candidus Iulianus, from whom he had learned of the previous two matters.

The letters disclose an interesting mix of Greek and Roman elements in the new political organization. The polis has magistrates, council, and assembly, here called *archones, boule,* and *demos,* in a tripartite system common to other poleis, and its adherence to Rome is marked by the Roman calendar date for the delivery of the three letters to the new city, the day before the Ides of March.[80] Stratonicea-Hadrianopolis apparently incorporated as new citizens all citizens of the sympolity, some of whom, like Candidus Iulianus, already had Roman citizenship.[81] There is no trace of

[76] Broughton 1934, 222–23, suggests that the revenues were from nearby patrimonial land given to the city to support its growth; equally plausibly, Burton 1993, 17–18, suggests that Hadrian granted the city "the right to levy new direct (or indirect) taxes on its territory." See also chapter 5.

[77] E.g., the Flavian municipal charter stipulates that the provincial governor approve cities' debts of more than fifty thousand HS. Such concern is also obvious in the correspondence of Pliny and Trajan.

[78] Lex Tarentina, lines 32–38; lex Col. Gen., chapter 75; Flavian municipal law, chapter 62; cf. *ILS* 6043. See further Lewis 1989; Spitzl 1984, 67, 80–82, 115; Garnsey 1976; and Murga 1976, 36–46. Specific references for the laws can be found in chapter 3, nn. 36–38.

[79] E.g., *Dig.* 1.18.7, 39.2.46; Y. Janvier, *La Législation du Bas-Empire romain sur les édifices publics* (Aix-en-Provence, 1969).

[80] Lines 5–6, 21–22, 27–28, 37, 43–44, 51–52, of text in Robert and Robert, *Hellenica* 6 (1948): 80–84.

[81] Other Roman citizens named in the documents are the archon [———] Lollius Rusticus, a C. Iulius Hippianus, and a C. Epile[———]; Apollonius, son of Philip and the town's ambassador to Hadrian for the third letter, evidently does not have Roman citizenship: lines 17, 21–22, 48, 50, 51, 53–54 of text in Robert and Robert, *Hellenica* 6 (1948): 80–84. For the growth of Roman citizenship among the upper classes in the Greek East, remarkable in the Trajanic-Hadrianic period, see Stahl 1978, 20–25.

new enfranchisements or settlements. Hadrian's letters reinforce pride in the new city. By identifying local notables,[82] they helped established the city's hierarchy. Moreover, the letters display the nexus of power connecting local elite, provincial governor, and emperor himself.

Literary and numismatic evidence is key for Hadrianoutherae, "Hadrian's Hunts," near modern Balikesir, Turkey. Sixty kilometers north of Stratonicea-Hadrianopolis and connected to it by a minor road, Hadrianoutherae is at the crossroads of the major route between Cyzicus and Pergamum and the road running west from coastal Adramyttium into the interior of Mysia (fig. 15).[83] Hadrian traversed this heavily wooded, fertile region in A.D. 123 and/or in 131/132.[84] According to Hadrian's biography (*HA, Hadr.* 20.13; cf. Cass. Dio 69.10.2, Malal. XI 280.20), Hadrian founded the city Hadrianoutherae where he had hunted and killed a she-bear.[85] We cannot date the foundation more closely than to give it a terminus post quem of A.D. 123. The origin of Hadrianoutherae's citizens is unknown. Little remains save coins struck by the city, and they accentuate Hadrian's habits. Some depict the emperor on horseback about to throw a spear at a fleeing bear; others, a bear's head.[86] Hadrian's "leisure" pursuits were thus publicly commemorated. The region's association with Hadrian and hunting was so strong that a statue erected in Stratonicea-Hadrianopolis to Hadrian, founder and settler (*ktistes* and *oikistes* are both used), honors him as Zeus "of the Chase" (*Kynegesios*). The dedicant was Ti. Claudius Candidus,[87] who thus publicly reciprocated his earlier prominence in Hadrian's letter to the city.

Hadrianeia, more than forty kilometers east of Hadrianoutherae in the mountainous area of Abrettene, and Hadrianoi, some sixty kilometers farther northeast near Mt. Olympus (fig. 15), have been elucidated by E. Schwertheim's publication of their inscriptions and coins.[88] Their names,

---

[82] The dossier from Stratonicea-Hadrianopolis itself, erected by the city, confirms that Candidus Iulianus's prestige rested at least in part on his effectiveness with the emperor. Candidus Iulianus may also have intervened successfully with Hadrian for the city's right to strike coinage: Robert, *Hellenica* 11–12 (1960): 56, 59–60.

[83] Robert 1962, 195, 389, 416.

[84] See Magie 1950, 1476n. 20; Halfmann 1986, 199–200.

[85] Gawantka and Zahrnt 1977, 310n. 15, contend that Hadrian's successful bear hunt prompted Hadrian's renaming an existing city (not founding a new one), but they adduce no corroboration. The biography places this information with other discussion of Hadrian's love for his horses and dogs. Hadrian's successful hunt of a she-bear is also depicted on one of the Hadrianic Tondi: see Boatwright 1987, 192–93.

[86] Imhoff-Blumer, *Nomisma* 6 (1911): 10–11; H. von Fritze, *Ant. Münzen Mysiens* (Berlin, 1913), I:194–95 (non vidi).

[87] Originally published by Gawantka and Zahrnt 1977; again, with a new interpretation of Hadrian's epithet, by Robert and Robert 1978.

[88] Schwertheim 1987, 133–48, replacing Magie 1950, 616–17, 1476–77.

like the inception of their coinage during Hadrian's reign, testify to these cities' foundation by Hadrian, as do their dating systems, beginning in 131/132, and an inscription from Hadrianoi honoring Hadrian as *soter kai ktistes* (savior and founder). Schwertheim convincingly dates the foundations to 131 or 132.[89] Hadrian probably hunted in this area, famous for thick forests and plentiful game.[90] Yet Schwertheim also suggests less idiosyncratic reasons for the two new cities: the exploitation of timber and the establishment of structures and road systems that would urbanize and unite Rome's imperium.[91] He notes that neither foundation occurred at known cult centers in the region, but some kilometers distant, at sites easier of access.

Hadrianoi, modern Orhaneli, lies south of Mt. Olympus at the crossing of the road leading south from Prusa and the east-west route along the Rhyndacus; Hadrianeia, modern Dursunbey, is between the Macestus and Rhyndacus rivers on an east-west road linking Hadrianoutherae and Cotiaeum (fig. 15).[92] Both new cities had the typically Greek polis organization, with the one unusual feature of strategoi (generals) as well as archons as magistrates.[93] Some of their citizens were citizens of other cities who owned estates in this area. To judge from the case of P. Aelius Aristides, who had citizenship at Smyrna and Hadrianoi, such individuals were liable to liturgies in their ancestral and new city alike.[94] Other citizens of the two Hadrianic foundations, presumably, were less wealthy natives of the region. The citizens epigraphically attested include those with the Roman franchise and individuals with good Greek names, indigenous names, or with epi-

[89] Schwertheim 1985; Schwertheim 1987, 156–57, correcting the speculative date of 123. Although the later date coincides with Hadrian's second visit to the region, his actual presence was not required for the foundations.

[90] Schwertheim 1987, 157–58, noting the coins' references to hunting; see also Robert and Robert 1978, 442–52. Also attractive may have been the famed Mysian Mt. Olympus and Sanctuary of Zeus Pandemos near Hadrianeia: Schwertheim 1985, 41.

[91] From the increased number of later cities in the region, Robert and Robert argue that Hadrian was successful in opening up Mysia to a higher culture (Greek) and to the imperial economy: Robert and Robert 1978, 449–50.

[92] Schwertheim 1987, 158–59. Older maps call Orhaneli "Beyce," and Dursunbey "Balat."

[93] Ibid., 159, attributes this to the area's past control by Pergamum: strategoi were usual in Pergamene political organization. Perhaps the strategoi oversaw the territories, and the archons the urban areas. The phylae in Hadrianoi were numbered, not named: *IHadrianoi* #17.

[94] P. Aelius Aristides was born in 118 on ancestral estates in Mysia (in the later territory of Hadrianoi), and educated in Smyrna, Pergamum, Athens, and other centers. His family was granted Roman citizenship by Hadrian in 123. Aristides successfully petitioned for immunity from liturgies in both Smyrna and Hadrianoi, including the post of Hadrianoi's eirenarch, to which he had been appointed in 154 by the governor of Asia. See Behr 1968, 1–19. Some would place Aristides's birthplace not at Hadrianoi, but at Hadrianoutherae (Swain 1991, 159, citing Robert, *Études anatoliennes* [Paris, 1937], 207n. 1).

thets indicating origins farther afield.[95] In both cities local gods and more customary ones of the Greco-Roman pantheon were honored, as was the imperial cult.[96] Evidence survives to show that Hadrianoi, at least, embraced culture: sometime in the second century the city honored the philosopher T. Avianius Bassus Polyaenus with a statue (*IHadrianoi* #52). Hadrianoi furnishes the best support for the interpretation of Hadrian's Mysian foundations as attempts to encourage Greco-Roman culture within the area.

ANTINOOPOLIS

Antinoopolis is perhaps the most famous of Hadrian's foundations, and certainly the one that best reveals the instability, or perhaps the irrelevance, of traditional concepts of Hellenization and Romanization when applied to Hadrian's era.[97] In antiquity the city's fame came from its association with Hadrian's beloved companion Antinoos.[98] This singularity still attracts modern scholars, as does the unparalleled wealth of documentary evidence, which helps offset the modern destruction of the site. While accompanying Hadrian and the imperial court up the Nile in October 130, Antinoos drowned near Hermopolis Magna, in what was variously declared an accident, suicide, or ritual offering as surrogate for Hadrian himself (Cass. Dio 69.11.2–4; *HA, Hadr.* 14.5–6; Aur. Vict. *Caes.* 14.7–9).[99] Antinoos was declared a hero-god.[100] Hadrian named and founded a city for him on the east bank of the Nile. Antinoopolis may indeed mark where the youth had drowned, as Cassius Dio claims (69.11.3), but its location had many advantages: an excellent harbor, a temple of Ramses II, and native

---

[95] *IHadrianoi* ##1, 3, 41, 58, and passim.

[96] E.g., *IHadrianoi* ##131, 132.

[97] The commonly used "Antinoe" is a modern abbreviation. For the various names of the site, see Calderini 1966, I.2:74–77; Meyer 1994, 92, with references. The first modern investigation of Antinoopolis was published by E. Kühn, *Antinoopolis* (Göttingen, 1913).

[98] Especially true among Christians: P. Guyot, "Antinous als Eunuch: zur christlichen Polemik gegen das Heidentum," *Historia* 30 (1981): 250–54; A. Hermann, "Antinous infelix. Zur Typologie des Heiligen-Unheiligen in der Spätantike," in *Mullus. Festschrift T. Klauser,* ed. A. Stuiber and A. Hermann (Munich, 1964), 159–64.

[99] See, e.g., Zahrnt 1988a, 671–72. J. Schwartz, *Chronique d'Égypte* 44 (1969): 164–68, corrects the date of 134 proposed by Follet 1968, 54–74. Antinoos, perhaps nineteen years old at the time of his death, is often regarded as fundamental to an understanding of Hadrian's principate: Birley 1994, 192–96. See also R. Lambert, *Beloved and God* (London, 1984).

[100] In accordance with the Egyptian practice of deifying those who drowned in the Nile, and without consultation of the Roman senate: see, e.g., Beaujeu 1955, 242–45. D. Kessler, in Meyer 1994, 117–29, discusses the Egyptian elements of Antinoos's cult.

inhabitation.[101] The new city Antinoopolis was granted local autonomy and other privileges, like the other three Greek poleis in Egypt (Naucratis and Alexandria to the north, and Ptolemais to the south).[102] Yet the Greek elements of Antinoopolis, though undeniable, should not be overemphasized.[103] Greek forms are showcased in its urban layout and political and social life, but Antinoopolis also evinces the architectural majesty, social and political mobility, and adherence to the imperial house characteristic of Rome's greatest cities of the era.

Antinoopolis was planned orthogonally (fig. 16). Featuring monumental structures that encouraged passage, such as its theater, tetrapyla, and colonnaded streets (all rare among Hadrian's building donations; see chapter 6), its design lent itself to a rational administrative system.[104] The city rose to either side of a wadi cutting west into the Nile. The major streets, a north-south one parallel to the Nile (1,800 meters long), and two east-west ones crossing it, were unusually wide, sixteen meters. Doric colonnades (five meters wide) bordered the north-south road and the southern cross street.[105] Tetrapyla rose at the two major intersections.[106] Overall, the principal roadways are reminiscent of those in the great cities of Roman

---

[101] Meyer 1994, 91–92, 97–109; Zahrnt 1988a, 675–77; the harbor is mentioned already in a papyrus of 140: Calderini 1966, I.2:91–92.

[102] Lewis 1983, 25–27.

[103] Its significance for our understanding of Hadrian's urban work is all the more unusual if we accept the distinction of Egypt from other Roman provinces, argued by Bowman 1986, 37–38, Lewis 1983, 14–17, and others. Through re-examination of the Obelisk of Antinoos and other evidence, Meyer 1994 (especially the contribution of D. Kessler, 91–149) highlights the Egyptian features of Antinoopolis.

[104] Most plans of Antinoopolis are based on the elegant but overly confident reconstruction E. Jomard made for the Napoleonic expedition of 1798 (1820–30, vol. 4, chap. 15). New investigations are underway: E. Mitchell 1982 (new plan); Baldassarre 1988; Donadoni 1974. The prominent city wall probably dates to the third century: E. Mitchell 1982, 172–73. For Antinoopolis, P. Pensabene, *Elementi architettonici di Alessandria e di altri siti egiziani* (Rome, 1993), 273–89, basically synthesizes Mitchell and Jomard. For the architectural concepts, see MacDonald 1986.

[105] E. Mitchell 1982, 174–75; Baldassarre 1988, 279–80, noting that nothing remains of the northern cross street. The larger streets may be the "public streets" recorded in a papyrus of 212 and by others: Calderini 1966, I.2:87–88. The city's orientation is not true north-south, but follows the northeast-southwest course of the Nile.

[106] Jomard noted tetrapyla at both crossings: one, with an inscription of A.D. 232 (*IGR* I 1143), probably dates to the third century; the other, perhaps the "tetrastylon of Antinoos" documented in A.D. 176 (Calderini and Daris 1988, 39), presumably dates to the original foundation. The only other instance of tetrapyla among Hadrian's donations are those in the reconstruction of Nicaea and Nicomedia, if Robert correctly interprets the unusual *tetraplateia* of the Chronicles as crossroads of large porticoed avenues, ornamented by tetrapyla: see chapter 6, n. 46.

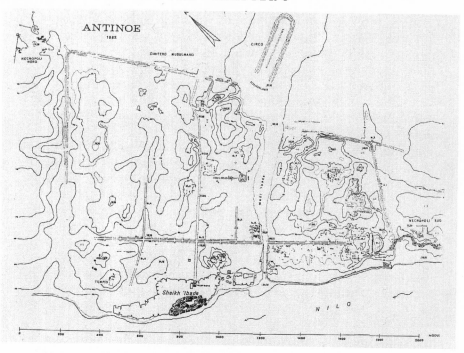

Fig. 16. Antinoopolis. On this plan are clearly visible the regular divisions of the city blocks, fronted with colonnades along the major north-south street. The outline of the theater can be discerned at the southern end of the major street, and to the east was Antinoopolis's hippodrome, used in the games for Antinoos.

Syria.[107] Smaller streets along the north-south street divided the city into regular blocks (32.50 meters wide), which were assigned letters and a subsidiary enumeration (perhaps for administrative purposes).[108] A forum or agora, and a *praetorium* (governor's residence), are documented by papyri.[109] Near the southern end of the north-south road rose the theater, documented as under construction in 138 and still visible in foundation trenches.[110] A stadium (or circus) lay to the east, aligned with the wadi.[111]

[107] Baldassarre 1988, 282–84.

[108] Ibid., 281; Calderini 1966, I.2:82–87. In Egypt only Alexandria had a similar system.

[109] Calderini 1966, I.2:88–93; Calderini and Daris 1988, 39.

[110] Calderini 1966, I.2:90 (papyri); physical remains of the theater, eighty-five meters long on scaenae frons and forty-three meters deep: E. Mitchell 1982, 176–77; Baldassarre 1988, 278–79, 281.

[111] Dimensions about 300 × 77 meters: Baldassarre 1988, 281.

These two structures, well placed for accessibility and visibility, were central to the famous games established here in Antinoos's honor, the Antinoeia,[112] and they have Egyptian comparanda only in Alexandria.

Some of the other documented public buildings of Antinoopolis also relate to the cult of Antinoos, which had strong Egyptian characteristics as well as elements of the imperial cult as practiced in the Greek East. The gymnasium and baths were surely used for the training and care of Antinoopolis's ephebes and competitors for the games; the temples, especially the sanctuary of Osiris-Antinoos, must have figured in processions.[113] The Obelisk of Antinoos, now on the Pincian Hill in Rome, once stood at Antinoopolis's temple in the new city. It depicts the new god Osiris-Antinoos praying for Hadrian and for Sabina.[114]

Careful thought was given to the new city's future. Flooding of the wadi was inhibited by two stone walls bordering it near the Nile.[115] The Via Nova Hadriana, equipped with cisterns, stations, and watchtowers, cut east through the desert to Myos Hormos on the northern Red Sea, to link with a coastal road south to Berenice. New survey work by S. E. Sidebotham is clarifying this road and its significance for the transport of Egypt's valuable stone and granite, and for Antinoopolis's role in Rome's overseas trade.[116] The new city's territorium, rare in Egypt where most land outside urban centers was imperially owned, lay on either side of the Nile. It included important alabaster quarries.[117] Equally unusually in Egypt, the city and its surrounding area did not constitute a *nomos* (a small administrative unit under supervision of a strategos), but a more autonomous nomarchy that reported directly to the Roman epistrategos (Roman equestrian official in charge of one of the three administrative divisions of Egypt) and the Roman prefect.[118] The Roman prefect of Egypt periodically came to An-

[112] Meyer 1994, 126–29; Decker 1973; *Bull.Ep.* 1952, #191–93. Competitions included wrestling, rowing races, horse races in the stadium, and musical contests.

[113] For references to these buildings, see Calderini 1966, I.2:88–93; Calderini and Daris 1988, 39. The sanctuary had an oracle room.

[114] Currently on its north side. The main text of the obelisk is translated by A. Grimm, in Meyer 1994, 28–88; the illustrations at the sides' tops are discussed by D. Kessler, ibid., 133–36.

[115] E. Mitchell 1982, 175; Baldassarre 1988, 281–82.

[116] *IGR* I 1142 = *OGIS* 701 = A. Bernand, *Pan du désert* (Leiden, 1977), 216–32, #80; Baldassarre 1988, 282–83; S. E. Sidebotham, *Dumbarton Oaks Papers* 48 (1994): 266–67; S. E. Sidebotham and R. E. Zitterkopf, "Survey of the Via Hadriana by the University of Delaware: The 1996 Season," forthcoming in the Newsletter of the American Research Center in Egypt.

[117] Meyer 1994, 92, 94; Montevecchi 1990, 190. Zahrnt 1988a, 689–90, notes the rarity of city territory for an Egyptian city, and the similarities this feature of Antinoopolis offers to the establishment of new Roman municipia and coloniae elsewhere. In later years troops protected the boundaries of Antinoopolis.

[118] Montevecchi 1990, 190.

tinoopolis to hear cases, and the epistrategos of Heptanomia seems to have resided there.[119] Like other provincial cities, however, Antinoopolis was self-governing and settled local judicial questions.

Citizens of Antinoopolis, "the new Hellenes,"[120] had unusual privileges, although these were embedded in a typically Greek political organization. Cassius Dio's description of the new city as a synoicism (69.11.3) is not entirely correct, since most of the new citizens seem to have been selected by lot from high-status individuals. Some Antinoites came from Ptolemais to the south, and others from the privileged class of "the 6,475 Hellenes in the Arsinoite nome" to the north.[121] Other new citizens with Roman names, including veterans, are attested in the reign of Antoninus Pius, but they had probably come to the new city earlier; these men, who served in the auxiliary forces and the fleet, also had high standing in the cities and villages of Egypt.[122] Although nothing reveals the fate of local Egyptians, recent work argues strongly for their continuing presence in the city.[123] The New Hellenes of Antinoopolis were divided into ten phylae (each with five demes), mimicking the organization of Athens. Most phyle names refer to Hadrian and members of the imperial house, including Antinoos, and most deme names refer to Athens.[124] The citizens had a boule (council), demos, and magistrates (probably *prytaneis*).[125] Their laws were modeled on those of Naucratis, the oldest Greek colony of Egypt,[126] in an anachronistic touch similar to many others we have seen. Yet the ostensible "Greek-

[119] Zahrnt 1988a, 698. On Roman administration and legal matters in Egypt, see Bowman 1986, 65–74.

[120] Zahrnt 1988a, 686, cites the documentation; Montevecchi 1990, 189, points to the rarity of this term in Roman Egypt.

[121] Montevecchi 1990, 188; Zahrnt 1988a, 686–88; Meyer 1994, 95–97; N. Lewis 1983, 40–41.

[122] Alston 1995, 62, 218n. 33; Braunert 1964, 213–19; Zahrnt 1988a, 686; Montevecchi 1990, 187–88. The right to enroll in the auxiliaries and fleet was restricted to those of "Greek" ancestry, and Montevecchi attributes these individuals' selection as Antinoites to their ancestry rather than to their service to Rome.

[123] Kessler in Meyer 1994, esp. 109–110; Zahrnt 1988a, 686–87.

[124] Kessler in Meyer 1994, 159–62; Calderini 1966, I.2:105–9; Weber 1907, 250. I list the phylai, followed by their known demoi in parentheses: Hadrianioi (Zenios, Olympios, Kapitolieus, Sosikosmios), Athenais (Artemisios, Eleusinios, Erichthonios, Marathonios, Salaminios), Ailieus (*sic*) (Apideus, Dionysieus, Polieus), Matidioi (Demetrieus, Thesmophorios, Kallieknios, Markianios, Plotinios), Neruanioi (Genearchios, Eirenieus, Hestieus, Propatorios), Oseirantinoeioi (Bithynieus, Hermaieus, Kleitorios, Parrhasios, Musegetikos), Paulinioi (Isidios, Megaleisios, Homognios, Philadelphios), Sabinioi (Harmonieus, Gamelieus, Heraieus, Trophonieus, Phytalieus), Sebastioi (Apollonieus, Asklepios, Dioskurios, Heraklios, Kaisarios), and Traianioi (Ktesios, Nikephorios, Stratios).

[125] Zahrnt 1988a, 688; Sherk 1992, 267.

[126] Zahrnt 1988a, 688–89. The months of Antinoopolis's calendar were named after the months of the calendar of Miletus, the metropolis of Naucratis.

ness" of the new foundation was inseparable from the Roman empire of Hadrian.[127]

Building on the fundamental work of H. Braunert, Zahrnt has listed the extraordinary privileges of Antinoopolis's new citizens, which he emphasizes as "Roman."[128] Although citizens of Antinoopolis retained family holdings from their ancestral homes elsewhere, they were exempt from liturgies (civic duties) in the cities of their possessions, as well as from *tutela minorum* (the care of minors) of non-Antinoites (compare the case of Aelius Aristides at Hadrianoi, at n. 94 above). Antinoites had no poll tax. They did not have to pay sales tax on any transaction made in Antinoopolis, and they paid no tolls for goods they imported for their own use. If they became involved in any judicial proceeding in Egypt, they had the right to return to Antinoopolis for trial. Antinoites could enroll in the Roman legions. At least some new citizens seem to have been allotted land.[129] Most uncommon of all, by a unique form of *epigamia* (the right of intermarriage) children of Antinoite and Egyptian spouses became citizens of Antinoopolis, regardless of which of their parents was a citizen of Antinoopolis.

Other privileges affected the city as a whole. The property of a defaulting debtor could be taken by the city, once claims by the imperial fiscus were satisfied. The Roman prefect of Egypt, rather than a member of the local elite, oversaw the Megala Antinoeia celebrated annually in Antinoopolis after 131. Although this cut off one important means for individuals to connect with the emperor (cf. the discussion of the Demostheneia in chapter 5), it may account for the longevity of these games compared to ones elsewhere for Antinoos.[130] Hadrian himself established an alimentary fund for Antinoite children, a manifestation of imperial favor unparalleled outside of Italy.[131]

Some of these privileges are unique to Antinoopolis; others have analogues in one or more of the other Greek poleis in Egypt.[132] No other city, however, had all the privileges of Hadrian's new foundation, and no Greek city anywhere possessed the right of *epigamia* as it existed in Antinoopolis. O. Montevecchi links this last privilege to the persistent underpopula-

---

[127] In my stress on the Roman elements of Antinoopolis, I depart from H. I. Bell, "Antinoopolis: A Hadrianic Foundation in Egypt," *JRS* 30 (1940): 133–47, and others.

[128] Zahrnt 1988a, 690–701; Braunert 1962. Less well known is the excellent article by Hoogendijk and van Minnen 1987, noting the Antinoites' privileges on 71–74.

[129] Zahrnt 1988a, 697: perhaps the "Greek soldiers" in the Fayum.

[130] Antinoopolis's games are attested into the third century, and occasioned civic emulation in Oxyrhynchus in 200: Calderini 1966, I.2:102; N. Lewis 1983, 39.

[131] Montevecchi 1990, 191; H. I. Bell, "Diplomata Antinoitica," *JEA* 33 (1933): 514–28; Wilcken, *Arch. f. Pap.* 11 (1935): 300, for parallels with Italy. See chapter 5, n. 41.

[132] N. Lewis 1983, 25–28.

tion of the Greeks in Egypt, and Zahrnt notes it as a way to stimulate the Hellenized Egyptian elite to immigrate to Antinoopolis from elsewhere.[133] Zahrnt further compares Antinoopolis's *epigamia* to the increased opportunities for Roman citizenship offered in the West by the institution of *Latium maius*, by which not only magistrates but councillors of Latin municipia qualified for Roman citizenship.[134] In both cases Rome encouraged active participation in Roman civic life on the part of individuals formerly without Roman citizenship.

The privileges accorded to the "New Hellenes" of Antinoopolis underscore that Hadrian's urbanization should not be evaluated by material benefactions alone. The vitality of cities, and of Rome itself, depended on the willingness of individuals to assume municipal duties. Hadrian's liberality to cities throughout the empire rewarded individuals for such service, while simultaneously inducing others to serve. His travels and his wide knowledge, even his notorious curiosity and one-upmanship, enabled him both to appreciate the diversity of the Roman empire and, as with Antinoopolis in middle Egypt, to shape his largesse to local needs and traditions.

COLONIA AELIA CAPITOLINA

Yet the limitations of Hadrian's empire are clear in the last foundation I discuss in detail, Colonia Aelia Capitolina. Hadrian's empire was based on cities, and the Jews' distinct religious practices had always made their integration into Greco-Roman urban life awkward.[135] The fragile accommodation was destroyed by Hadrian's Colonia Aelia Capitolia. In supplanting Jerusalem in Judaea, Hadrian brazenly suppressed local mores and expressly prohibited the native population from this symbolic spot. The extreme measures precluded any possibility of continued compliance on the part of the Jews, and they, and in turn the Romans, resorted to violence.

Hadrian's establishment of a veteran colony here is entangled with the history of the Third Jewish Revolt of 132–35, the Bar Kokhba War. According

---

[133] Montevecchi 1990, 183–95; Zahrnt 1988a, 699–701. Kessler, in Meyer 1994, 110, points to this right as part of the evidence that the Egyptians of the area were not completely ignored in the new foundation.

[134] Zahrnt 1988a, 701–6. See discussion of *Latium maius* in chapter 3, n. 7 and chapter 1, n. 58.

[135] For instance, there were few cities but many villages in Palestine; the practice of Jewish ritual was disturbing to polytheistic city-dwellers; Jews were generally not educated in Greek rhetoric, the sine qua non of political and cultural discourse; and Jews did not serve in the army, since service would entail breaking the Sabbath. See Rajak 1984; Rajak 1985; Goodman 1983, esp. 141–54.

to some ancient and modern writers, the revolt was the consequence of Hadrian's decisions to found the colony and to build a temple to Jupiter Optimus Maximus over the site of the Jewish Temple at Jerusalem (Cass. Dio 69.12.1). Another catalyst is said to have been Hadrian's universal prohibition of circumcision (*HA, Hadr.* 14.2).[136] Other sources consider the revolt to be the cause, not the consequence, of Hadrian's activity (Euseb. *Hist. Eccl.* 4.6.1–4). This casts Hadrian's decisions as punitive, for the military colony would then be imposed chiefly to maintain order.[137] Since coins of the new colony have been found in hoards alongside coins struck by the Jewish rebels, Aelia Capitolina must have been founded before the revolt broke out, although we cannot determine the effect of the foundation on the insurrection's outbreak.[138] We should assume that the colony was begun before 132, but completed only after the war.[139] The process may have been started when Hadrian passed through the region in 129–30 (Epiph. *Mens.* 14 = *PG* 43, 260f; cf. Cass. Dio 69.12.2).[140] For my purposes, however, the most important aspects of Colonia Aelia Capitolina are its closed nature and its message to the provincial population. Henceforth Jews were forbidden entry to their holiest city,[141] and many scholars call Hadrian's ban on circumcision a deliberate attempt to destroy Jewish ethnic character.[142] In stark contrast to Antinoopolis, Colonia Aelia Capitolina stifled the needs and desires of its region's inhabitants.

[136] The assertion that the war was caused by Hadrian's prohibition of the Jews "to mutilate their genitalia" (*HA, Hadr.* 14.2) is supported by Smallwood 1959 and 1960; cf. Schürer 1973, I:534f.

[137] Schäfer 1981 discusses this and the other two reasons primarily advanced in Jewish and Roman sources for the revolt, the hypothesis that Hadrian, soon after coming to power, allowed the Jews to rebuild the temple but later withdrew his permission, and Hadrian's intention to rebuild Jerusalem as Colonia Aelia Capitolina. Mildenberg 1984, 73–109, surveys the sources. Smallwood 1976, 433–38 (refuted by Zahrnt 1991, 477–80), advances four reasons for the colony's foundation: (1) to further Hadrian's general policy of Romanization; (2) to gratify the Jews by restoring their devastated city; (3) to suppress the resurgent Jewish nationalism by substituting a secular city for Jerusalem; and (4) to counteract Jewish restlessness through a military foundation. See at n. 4 of this chapter.

[138] Zahrnt 1991, 475–77; Mildenberg 1984, 100–101, with other numismatic evidence.

[139] As do most, e.g., Smallwood 1976, 433. The war did not end until late 135, or perhaps later.

[140] Halfmann 1986, 193, 207, correcting Epiphanius's untenable date of 117. Hadrian's visit of 130 is also linked to the activities of the legio VI Ferrata in 130 on the aqueduct at Caesarea and the Caparcotna road, the positive attitude toward Hadrian of the Jewish Fifth Sibylline oracle, and the magnificent bronze cuirassed statue of Hadrian found near Bet Shean in 1975: Bowersock 1980, 134. For the statue, see G. Foerster, "A Cuirassed Bronze Statue of Hadrian," *Atiqot* 17 (1985): 139–60, and R. A. Gergel, "The Tel Shalem Hadrian Reconsidered," *AJA* 95 (1991): 231–51.

[141] Harris 1926.

[142] See Mildenberg 1984, 102–9, with many other references. This ban, however, also affected Nabateans, Samaritans, and Egyptians. Perhaps, as G. W. Bowersock puts it (*JRS* 65 [1975]: 185), "Hadrian simply considered the practice abhorrent."

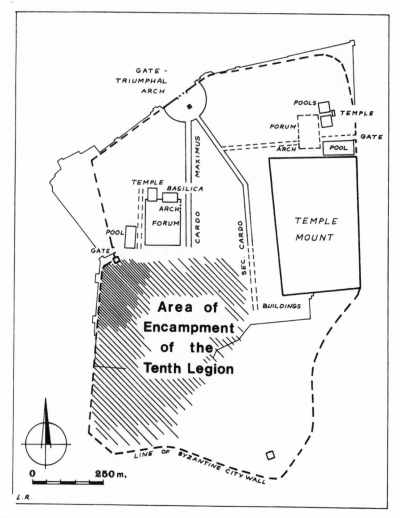

Fig. 17. Plan of Colonia Aelia Capitolina, showing known monuments of the Hadrianic foundation and the camp of the Tenth "Fretensis" legion.

Colonia Aelia Capitolina (fig. 17) was a military colony, a traditional and official settlement of veterans. It did not involve the local population in any constructive way.[143] As Jews, the few locals who had resettled at or around Jerusalem after A.D. 70 could not enter the new colony.[144] Colonia Aelia Capitolina was to be self-sufficient, and much of the material used in new

[143] Zahrnt 1991, 470–71, also noting the lack of evidence about the local population at Hadrian's only other military colony, Colonia Aelia Mursa in Pannonia.
[144] Lifshitz 1977, 487; Harris 1926.

construction came from a brick and tile factory operated by the Tenth Fretensis Legion, encamped at Jerusalem since A.D. 70.[145] The colonists, called "Greeks" in some of the ancient sources, probably were veterans of the legio X Fretensis and other Roman troops in and near the province.[146] Exempt from taxation (though without the *ius Italicum*), the colonists received allotments of land around the city.[147] The colony was just north of the camp and presumable outbuildings of the Tenth Fretensis.[148] Water was brought in by the "high-level" aqueduct, built or reconstructed by the legion.[149]

The colony was distinctly Roman, a point worth stressing against the general assumption that the new colony is due to a "hellenizing" policy on Hadrian's part, as assumed by some.[150] Some of the coins of the new colony (fig. 18) depict on their reverse Hadrian as founder, ploughing with bull and cow the *sulcus primigenius* (aboriginal furrow) that established the colony's *pomerium* (sacred boundary); in the background is a *vexillum* (military standard), and the legend is COL[ONIA] AEL[IA] KAPIT[OLINA] COND[ITA].[151] Reverses of other coins show Jupiter Capitolinus seated between Minerva and Juno within a distyle temple, with the legend COL[OLNIA] AEL[IA] KAP[ITOLINA] or CAPI[ITOLINA].[152] The name of the

[145] Barag 1967; Geva 1984, 243–45, 253; B. Arubas and H. Goldfus, "The Kilnworks of the Tenth Legion Fretensis," in *The Roman and Byzantine Near East: Some Recent Archaeological Research,* JRA Supp. Series 14 (Ann Arbor, 1995), 95–107.

[146] The term *Greeks* seems to be used to distinguish the colonists from the Jews: Malal. XI 279.11–12; Zonar. 11.23; Cedr. 249 B–C; cf. Zahrnt 1991, 275–76, 282; Isaac 1980–81, 46–47, 51; Millar 1990, 29. A second legion, apparently the legio VI Ferrata, was stationed at Caparcotna in northern Judaea probably in the early 120s. Together with the Legio X Fretensis, which had been in Jerusalem since the First Jewish Revolt, its presence marked the transformation of Judaea into a consular province. About the same time a garrison was established in Caesarea: Mildenberg 1984, 81; H. G. Pflaum, *IEJ* 19 (1965): 232. Bowersock 1980, 133, explains the military reorganization of Judaea as a response to the Second Jewish Revolt of 115–17.

[147] *Dig.* 50.15.1.6; Zahrnt 1991, 482; Avi-Yonah 1966, 114, 155–56.

[148] Geva 1984, esp. 246–50: after A.D. 70 only a small detachment of the Tenth Legion remained in Jerusalem, with other squadrons encamped nearby and in Caesarea.

[149] A. Mazar, "The Aqueducts of Jerusalem," in *Jerusalem Revealed,* ed. Y. Yadin (Jerusalem, 1975), 79–84; Geva 1984, 252.

[150] See Zahrnt 1991, 478–80, for a clear refutation of such a policy; for the concept, see Schäfer 1981, 92. Millar 1990, 29–30, however, notes the difficulty of assessing the colony's "Latin" character later.

[151] G. F. Hill, *British Museum Catalogue of the Greek Coins of Palestine* (London, 1914), p. 82, #2; Kadman 1956, p. 80, #1, cf. ##2–9 and p. 154, #1; Rosenberger 1972, pl. #1.

[152] Hill (see n. 151 above), p. 82, #1; Kadman 1956, p. 80, #3, and Rosenberger 1972, pl. #2. Similar to these are bronzes with a reverse type showing Tyche, left, within a hexastyle temple with COL[ONIA] AEL[IA] KAPIT[OLINA] COND[ITA]: Kadman, p. 80, #2, cf. #4. A second group of Aelia coins consists of small bronzes with the signs of the legio X Fretensis; a third, with busts of Hadrian, Sabina, Aelius, or Antoninus Pius: Mildenberg 1984, 99– 100, Hill, pp. 82–83, ##3–5.

Fig. 18. Reverse of coin from Colonia Aelia Capitolina, depicting Hadrian as founder of the colony. He ploughs the *sulcus primigenius* (aboriginal furrow) that established the colony's *pomerium* (sacred boundary). The *vexillum*, or military standard, in the background represents the veteran status of the colony's new inhabitants. The legend, COL[ONIA] AEL[IA] KAPIT[OLINA] COND[ITA], translates "The founding of Colonia Aelia Capitolina."

colony identifies it with Hadrian and the cult of Jupiter Optimus Maximus on the Capitoline at Rome,[153] permanently asserting the message of the coins. The political organization of the colony was Roman: duumviri, aediles, and decurions are documented.[154]

The layout and buildings of Hadrian's colony (fig. 17) have been obscured by the continuous inhabitation and reconstruction of the city, now sacred to three religions, and by the decidedly "anti-pagan" nature of most literary sources. The city's plan was determined by the location of the Fretensis camp in Jerusalem's southern sector, by the site's contours, by a pre-existing rough grid established by Herod Agrippa, and by the political orientation of the province, whose capital was north at Caesarea.[155] The main city entrance was a monumental three-bayed arch, now known as the Damascus Gate, which opened onto a paved court with a freestanding column within the city. This ensemble, originally constructed by Herod Agrippa, was rebuilt and rededicated by the colony's new decurions.[156] On

[153] The name Capitolinus may have evoked both the Capitoline cult of Rome and Hadrian's epithet Olympios: Zahrnt 1991, 479n. 43.

[154] Lifshitz 1977, 484. Municipal assemblies are rarely recorded after the first century A.D.: see chapter 3, n. 58 and following.

[155] See Geva 1984, 248–52, and Wilkinson 1975, 135. The area of the new colony was about 950 × 600 square meters.

[156] J. B. Hennessy, "Preliminary Report of Excavations at the Damascus Gate, Jerusalem,

the basis of Jerusalem's depiction on the mid-sixth-century Madaba map, it is usually assumed that from the oval court ran two wide and colonnaded streets, one running south to the camp and the other southwest to a small plaza near the northwest corner of the Temple Mount.[157]

Just to the west of the main north-south street and separated from it by a monumental wall (1.5 meters wide) pierced by a triple arch, was the main forum of Aelia Capitolina. Today the environs of the Church of the Holy Sepulcher and the Muristan compound,[158] this probably housed the new colony's Capitoline temple.[159] Although Cassius Dio reports that the war was ignited by Hadrian's temple to Jupiter on the site of Jerusalem's Temple (69.12.1–2), Eusebius and Epiphanius discredit the location, and archaeology confirms that the Temple Mount was desolate until the sixth century.[160] Statues of Jupiter and of Hadrian (the latter perhaps an equestrian one) were featured at or in the Capitolium, and/or at the Temple Mount.[161] Imperial statuary often embellished Capitolia,[162] and Hadrian's Olympieion in Athens and Temple of Zeus at Cyzicus vaunted his image.

Other temples of the new colony must have been highlighted in the city plan,[163] and the list of Hadrian's buildings in the *Chronicon Paschale* includes two public baths, a theater, a nymphaeum of four porticoes, a mon-

---

1964–66," *Levant* 2 (1970): 22–27; Wilkinson 1975, 135. The colony's walls have a terminus post quem of the third quarter of the second century and may be much later than that: Geva 1984, 251, 254.

[157] But recent excavations of the "Cardo Maximus" (the main north-south of these two streets) reveals its date to be Byzantine rather than second century: D. Chen, "Dating the Cardo Maximus in Jerusalem," *PEQ* 114 (1982): 43–45. For the Madaba map: G. Ortolani, "Cartografia e architettura nella 'Carta di Madaba,'" *Palladio* n.s. 7.14 (1994): 55–68; M. Piccirillo, *The Mosaics of Jordan* (Amman, 1993); H. Donner and H. Cüppers, *Die Mosaikkarte von Madeba,* vol. I (Wiesbaden, 1977); M. Avi-Yonah, *The Madaba Mosaic Map* (Jerusalem, 1954).

[158] Vincent and Abel 1914–26, II:1–217, 875–902.

[159] Comparanda in Todd 1985, and I. M. Barton, "Capitoline Temples in Italy and the Provinces (Especially Africa)," *ANRW* II.12.1 (1982): 259–342. I identify Cassius Dio's temple with the "three-chambered one" of the *Chronicon Paschale* (1.474).

[160] Euseb. *Hist. Eccl.* 8; Epiph. *Mens.* 14; Wilkinson 1978, 178–79; Grelle 1972, 227–28.

[161] Hieron. *In Jes.* 2.19 = *PL* 24.49, *Comm. in Matt.* 24.15, locating the statue on the Temple Mount; cf. the Pilgrim of Bordeaux (two statues of Hadrian there: *Palestinae descriptiones,* ed. Tobler, p. 4) and Cedrenus, ed. Bekker, 1.438; Nicephorus Callistus, *Eccl. Hist.* 3.24, Chrysostom, *Orat. adv. Judaeos* 5.11, and Origen, in *GCS* Orig. 12, pp. 193–94. See also Jeffreys et al. 1986, 148.

[162] As at Brescia, Gabii, and Ferentium: Todd 1985, 62.

[163] Other deities worshiped in the colony include Tyche, Serapis, Victoria, Dea Roma, and Syrian gods: Lifshitz 1977, 486–87, Vincent and Abel 1914–26, II:887–89. Pausanias follows his report of the Bar Kokhba War with a comment on Hadrian's ubiquitous sanctuaries to the gods: 1.5.5.

umental gate of twelve entrances, and a quadrangular esplanade. None of these buildings has been securely located. Nor have the smaller forum, temple, and triumphal arch discovered north of the Temple Mount wall been identified.[164] The only other "Hadrianic" edifice is a triple arch dedicated to Hadrian and perhaps to Antoninus Pius as well, situated about 350 meters north of the Damascus Gate.[165]

Overall, what remains of Colonia Aelia Capitolina avows its Romanness, its adherence to the emperor and the imperial house, and its exclusion of the Jews. This could not be announced more dramatically than on the city's gates. Some gates glorified the imperial house in their inscriptions; though conventional, these proclamations of Roman might symbolically challenged the Jews, excluded from the city. Moreover, Eusebius specifies that one city gate carried the statue of a boar (Euseb. *Chron.* 47, Helm). Although the boar was one of the traditional emblems of the Tenth Fretensis Legion, the swine signified uncleanliness to the Jews, the point of Eusebius's passage.[166] Hadrian's prohibition of Jews from the new colony is the legal expression of the same insult. Colonia Aelia Capitolina reaffirmed Rome's military might and humiliated the provincials who had dared to oppose it.

Despite the implication of the new colony's epithet, Aelia, Hadrian's family name, this is the one municipal activity of Hadrian's that least reflects him, unless we deny all the positive qualities credited to this self-contradictory man.[167] On a less personal and more institutional level, Colonia Aelia Capitolina manifests the ruthless single-mindedness that had won Rome's domain during the Republic. To maintain its provinces, imperial Rome had had to modify this stance, to compromise, and to admit the conquered to higher status; Rome had to give as well as take. Most of Hadrian's interactions with cities exemplify the varied means by which the Roman empire governed to the mutual benefit of capital and provinces. Colonia Aelia Capitolina laid bare the military oppression and totalitarian measures Rome could employ to preserve supremacy and empire. Al-

[164] See *Chron. Pasch.* 1.474, also maintaining that Hadrian divided the city into seven regions for administrative purposes. For the area near the Temple Mount, see P. Benoit, "Découvertes archéologiques autour de la Piscine Bethesda," in *Jerusalem through the Ages* (Jerusalem, 1968), 48–57; Vincent and Abel 1914–26, II:669–742.

[165] Vincent and Abel 1914–26, II:35–39, fig. 14.

[166] Eusebius focuses on this latter meaning, Vincent and Abel 1914–26, II:35, on the former. Eusebius's passage may be tendentious, although the brick stamps used by the legion do depict a boar: Barag 1967, 245–46.

[167] Cf., e.g., Zahrnt 1991, 278–79. The turn against the Jews seems to have been precipitous: see Grelle 1972, 226, citing (among other references) legends of Hadrian's friendly disputes with rabbis and the coins struck at his arrival in the province that proclaim ADVENTUI AUG. IUDAEAE and RESTITUTORI IUDAEAE: Strack 1933, 138–48. See also n. 140 above. Schäfer 1981 concludes that Hadrian was less solely culpable for the war than often assumed.

though the war reaffirmed Rome's determination to maintain sovereignty at all costs, Hadrian himself realized that this was a sacrifice, according to a verbatim account in Cassius Dio (69.14.1–3).[168] The historian details the devastation of the Bar Kokhba War: fifty Jewish outposts and 985 villages were razed, 580,000 insurgents were slain, many more civilians perished by famine and fire, and numerous Romans fell. He then notes that Hadrian's report to the senate strikingly omitted the customary opening phrase of such missives: "If you and your children are in health, it is well; I and the legions are in health."

A good emperor should avoid thus weakening Rome; he should work to create and maintain consensus, rather than spark or encourage rebellion. Ill and increasingly estranged himself, Hadrian died within three years of the Bar Kokhba War. In Judaea, renamed Syria Palaestina after the revolt, neither Hadrian nor any subsequent emperor played the beneficent role Hadrian had assumed in Cyrenaica after the Second Jewish Revolt. The area was never fully integrated into the Roman empire. Although the Roman empire depended on its cities for its peaceful administration, the emperor's personal encouragement of these cities and their elites was crucial for the compliant performance of their tasks.

[168] For the veracity of the quotation, see Baldwin 1985, 197. Hadrian may have visited Judaea during the war: Syme 1988, 167; T. D. Barnes, *JRA* 2 (1989): 254.

CHAPTER 9

Hadrian's Civic Benefactions
and the Roman Empire

HADRIAN is writ large in my text, just as he is in the ancient sources that tend to accord him sole agency in the events of his reign. His shadow should not obscure the innumerable others essential for both the municipal achievements of his period and the ultimate success of the principate itself. It would be fallacious to focus on Hadrian alone, interpreting, for example, his benefactions to Athens, Achaea, and Asia simply as the manifestation of his philhellene predilections. Although Hadrian's archaism, intellectual curiosity, one-up-manship, and other personal traits did prompt some benefactions he made as emperor, Roman imperial ideology and economy, the growth of the imperial cult, the fierce competition between cities, and the era's stress on image, the past, and finesse were just as influential. Moreover, other individuals were crucial to every phase of the changes described in this book. This cooperation seems to me to be the most significant aspect of Hadrian's municipal activity.

Most fundamentally, the empire's citizens and subjects furnished the resources for "Hadrian's" projects and changes. The taxes, duties, dues, and contributions exacted from those within Roman control are the indispensable, but largely anonymous, basis of Hadrian's work. They supplied stipends for the soldiers working on Hadrian's aqueducts in Caesarea and Sarmizegetusa; more generally, they met the costs of Hadrian's gifts of grain to Athens and other grants. How conscious Romans could be of this exchange is exemplified by Hadrian's exorbitant aqueduct at Alexandria Troas, which was bitterly resented and denounced because its costs allegedly absorbed the tribute of Asia's "500 cities." Funding for Hadrian's civic benefactions also came more directly from individuals, through liturgies or more spontaneous contributions, in keeping with the euergetism characteristic of imperial Rome. The road repairs around Aeclanum were paid for by the area's landowners as well as by Hadrian, and other donors are catalogued together with Hadrian in the list from Smyrna discussed in chapter 7. Hadrian exhorted Cyrene's citizens to come forward as "founders," joining him in reconstructing the city after the Second Jewish Revolt. Even where direct evidence is lacking, as with Italica, we should assume that most large building projects financially involved the local elite.

Individuals of many different types were responsible for attracting Hadrian's attention to a town. State officials could alert him to local needs, as when the "corrector of the free cities" Herodes Atticus detailed for Hadrian the lamentable water supply of Alexandria Troas. Ti. Claudius Candidus Iulianus, of Stratonicea-Hadrianopolis, and other ambassadors incessantly relayed petitions about their cities' needs and wants. At other times a man's accomplishments and personal standing brought him into Hadrian's circle, with ensuing benefits for his town. For example, Polemo's brilliance so captivated Hadrian that the emperor lavished gifts upon Polemo's adopted Smyrna, switching his favor from nearby Ephesus to the Ephesians' chagrin. Demosthenes's phenomenal wealth and detailed plans for Oenoanda's games apparently triggered Hadrian's public sanction of that city's Demostheneia. Less famous intermediaries can be identified for cities such as Tralles, where A. Fabricius Priscianus Charmosynus gained Hadrian's permission and contributed money himself to boost the city's grain supply.

Many were required to implement Hadrian's changes in cities. Officials such as L. Aemilius Iuncus, the "corrector of the free cities of Achaea," and T. Avidius Quietus, proconsul of Asia, were authorized by Hadrian to settle intra- and inter-city squabbles hindering his decisions for Coronea and Aezani. Arrian's modification of Trapezus's sanctuary of Hermes, which he initiated as governor of Cappadocia, suggests that officials could also take immediate action anticipating Hadrian's ratification. Perhaps viewed as less intrusive were C. Ennius Firmus, Patrocles, and others of Hadrian's curatores whom Hadrian appointed to cities such as Beneventum and Nicaea, since he tended to select local men in this capacity, and for limited tasks. Even the less privileged in cities surely contributed to construction: as we saw in chapter 3, a town's citizens and its incolae had to provide five days of free labor and a yoke of oxen for public building projects.[1] Coronea is our clearest example of locals' participation as laborers and/or foremen. In the aggregate, Hadrian's interactions with cities could involve all strata of Roman population, cutting vertically through the steep hierarchies of the empire.

It is vitally important, however, that such cooperation was voluntary, not coerced. Hadrian achieved this, for the most part, by his personal involvement with cities and by his public appreciation of those who cooperated with him. Apparent links with Hadrian were forged each time someone served as magistrate or priest in a town the year Hadrian assumed its eponymous magistracy. Every time a man took a political position in a "new" Hadrianic colony or municipality, worshipped at a civic temple or tomb Hadrian had restored or built, or participated in a city's "Hadrianeia" games (or others with his name, even ones not sponsored by Hadrian himself), another personal tie was created. The authority and glory of the all-powerful emperor reflected on those associated with him. Similarly, the frequency with which Hadrian's praise of individuals is recorded indicates its

---

[1] Chapter 3 at n. 68; see Liebenam 1900, 401–2, 417–30, for other references.

significance in the competitive Roman empire.[2] The emperor's favor conveyed power, and those below him strove to get his attention. The higher they stood in local hierarchies, the easier their access to the emperor. They raised their status in their cities by assuming liturgies, giving benefactions, or attaining prominence through their brilliance, as Polemo did in Smyrna. This nexus of power relations, from the emperor down, was a much less costly way to achieve the empire's cohesion and cooperation throughout Italy and the provinces than the display and use of state violence.

The array of Hadrian's interventions—more than 210, distributed in more than 130 cities—brings into relief the size and complexity of the Roman empire. The two most obvious bonds of this far-flung and diverse domain are the Roman emperor and the importance of cities and their elites. The variety of Hadrian's interactions with cities reveals both the multiplicity of means by which he maintained a beneficent presence in Rome's cities and the wide range of duties city magistrates undertook for local and central governments. The Hadrianic material underscores the direct correlation of these two phenomena. But other patterns and conclusions can also be discerned from my investigation.

Hadrian dealt with cities and their representatives regularly throughout his twenty-one years on the throne. At his accession he reportedly remitted, or lowered, the crown tax due from Italian and provincial cities; at the end of his life he willed money to Signia and left unfinished projects in Puteoli, Athens, and elsewhere. Some of his benefactions date to when he was traveling outside Rome: Halfmann, for example, has used Hadrian's benefactions to help date his trips. Yet this correlation is not universally true. It does not apply, for instance, to his largesse to many cities near Rome and the imperial villas, such as Castrimoenium, Nomentum, Lanuvium, and Caiatia. Moreover, his tax remissions and exemptions generally date to his accession and are not associated with his presence. And the profusion of civic games and festivals he supported, as well as the ninety or so known structures he patronized and emblazoned with his name, date from throughout his reign.

Hadrian's travels surely helped locate his activity, but they are not exclusively determinant. Hadrian's hunting trip in Mysia in A.D. 123 can be mapped by plotting his foundations there, and his itinerary in Achaea in A.D. 124/125 is presumed from his donations to the province's celebrated sanctuaries and cities. Yet Hadrian's presence did not automatically entail a benefaction. Although he scarcely would have missed Olympia while in the Peloponnesus, nothing yet attests a benefaction by him there or to Elis. So far there is no record of donations or any other marks of his favor to

---

[2] This perceived power is obvious in Hadrian's letter to Ephesus promoting the sea captains L. Erastus and Philokyrios for election to the city council (Oliver, ##82 A–B).

Tibur and Baiae, his favorite residences. Conversely, Hadrian certainly did not see every city he benefited. Cassius Dio expressly tells us that Hadrian never visited his home town, Italica, as emperor, although he showered it with honor and gifts, and Cyrene may never have seen the emperor in person. One reason for this divergence is the ubiquity of municipal embassies, which approached Hadrian whether he was at home or abroad. For instance, in A.D. 129 Astypalaea's ambassadors met Hadrian in Laodicea on Lycus while he was traveling to Caria, whereas Gigthis's ambassador gained in Rome the greater Latin right for the city, be it from Hadrian or Antoninus Pius. The emperor's physical presence in cities was not necessary for his benefactions, although it could occasion them.

A look at the endpapers, which situate in the Roman empire most of the cities Hadrian benefited, reveals more significant geographical patterns. Most of these cities are located in Italy (and central Italy at that), in Africa and Mauretania Caesariensis, and in the Greek East, especially in Achaea, Asia, Bithynia-Pontus, Syria, and Cyrenaica. A smattering of cities along the Danube benefited from him. But Hadrian is known to have interacted personally with not one city in Britannia, Mauretania Tingitana, or Arabia, and three or fewer each in the Gallic and German provinces, in Hispania and Lusitania, in Egypt, and in Corsica, Sardinia, and Sicilia. One could argue that there simply were not as many cities for him to attend to in the far north and west, or in Egypt and Arabia, as there were in Italy, North Africa, and the Greek East. If this is true, however, Hadrian's apparent lack of interest in these regions argues against concluding that he had any conscious program of "urbanization" or "Romanization" (in the older model of directly transmitting Roman norms to the provinces). No evidence points to a conscious policy on Hadrian's part to materially improve whole cities or provinces. On the other hand, while cities in other areas formerly under Roman control were later progressively abandoned, the regions with the greatest number of Hadrian's civic benefactions—Asia, central Italy, and North Africa—maintained dynamic cities into the seventh century.[3] Hadrian's attention and material support may have contributed to the longevity of urban traditions and structures in the three favored regions.

Less apparent on the endpapers is the typological distribution of Hadrian's benefactions. Changes of city status (see below) are his only type of intervention known for the Danubian regions (except his aqueduct at Sarmizegetusa), and this type accounts also for almost all the marks of Hadrian's favor in Mauretania and Africa. Hadrian's curatores tend to be appointed to cities in Italy. His support for cities' games and festivals, his

[3] For cities in the later Roman empire, see, e.g., A. Cameron, *The Mediterranean World in Late Antiquity, AD 395–600* (London, 1993), 152–75; S. J. B. Barnish, "The Transformation of Classical Cities and the Pirenne Debate," *JRA* 2 (1989): 385–400.

alterations of honorific titles, and his renovations of cities' tombs are basically limited to the Greek East. Yet other types of Hadrian's municipal interaction cannot be mapped so easily. Hadrian's two changes to citizen rolls and councils are on opposite sides of the Mediterranean, in Tarraconensis and Asia. The cities in which Hadrian assumed eponymous magistracies and priesthoods are scattered from Baetica to Thracia and Asia, although they all seem to be of venerable heritage. Hadrian's engineering and building donations, approaching one hundred, are found in a wide swath across the northern area of the Mediterranean, from Baetica to Syria; if one includes buildings in his new and renewed foundations, the distribution goes from Pannonia to Middle Egypt. A clear distribution pattern of building types within these regions, however, cannot be determined.

The frequency of Hadrian's building donations helps explain the later tradition that he traveled with an attendant corps of builders and architectural designers (*Epit. de Caes.* 14.4–5). Although the army and local populations must have been the usual construction laborers and foremen (as in Caesarea and Coronea), the design similarities of Italica's Traianeum and Athens's Library of Hadrian suggest that Hadrian may indeed have traveled with plans and architects.[4] Some standardization was inevitable, at any rate, in these and other buildings to which Hadrian donated marble columns and other materials from the imperial fiscus, for such products came in standard sizes (see chapter 7).[5] Their appearance throughout the empire helped create a "Roman" visual vocabulary. But the record of Hadrian's municipal activity also includes instances in which he made use of native resources, as when his restoration in Caiatia used marble from the nearby quarries of Cubulteria. Overall, Hadrian's building activities in cities manifest the same commingling of local and imperial that I find characteristic of his municipal interaction, and they were beneficial for provinces and Rome alike.

A broad division can be distinguished between benefactions affecting new or newer cities, and those affecting older ones. On the one hand are Hadrian's new city foundations and grants of municipal or colonial status to towns in Africa, Mauretania, and along the Danube: at least some of these affected locales not highly urbanized (such as Thambes and other African towns yet to be located). On the other hand, the great majority of Hadrian's marks of favor, and particularly those of an engineering or architectural nature, went to cities boasting a distinguished past. Many are in the most respected Greek cities (whose ancestry was also honored in the League of the Panhellenion, which Hadrian founded), or in cities in

[4] Cf. L. Haselberger, "Architectural Likenesses: Models and Plans of Architecture," *JRA* 10 (1997): 77–94.

[5] Here we might also think of Hadrian's increased control of timber, indicated in the imperial cedar forests in Lebanon: see chapter 5, n. 3.

Latium Vetus, the ancient heartland of Rome. Yet Hadrian's reconstruction of a temple or donation of an aqueduct could not guarantee revitalization of any particular town, as we saw with the continued decrepitude of Megara and Gabii. A Roman city was much more than a collection of buildings or even the numerous inhabitants dwelling in them. The community had to share rituals and norms, responsibility for self-administration, and duties to Rome.

The evidence in this book points to the use of religion and the incorporation of the past as distinguishing Hadrian's municipal activity and fundamental to his encouragement of civic life and the *pax Augusta*. They are seen most clearly in the civic festivals with which Hadrian is associated, the numerous religious structures he restored and built, and his assumption of eponymous priesthoods. Hadrian's emphasis on religion and revival of traditions combined to ensure that the figure of the emperor was integral to the religious life of numerous cities. Games and religious sites he patronized simultaneously evoked local traditions and the central power of Rome, embodied in the emperor and his family. In the outstanding case of Athens's Olympieion, "the great achievement of Time" (Philostr. *VS* 533), Hadrian completed an archaic temple to have it comprise statues of Hadrian himself, presided personally at its dedication ceremonies, which featured the great sophist Polemo, and linked the sanctuary with the Panhellenion and the Panhellenia games. Hadrian's benefaction thus brought the past into the present, celebrated its relevance, and established means for its continued applicability and conferral of advantages to the favored city.

Although Hadrian's municipal activity furthered the cohesion of the empire, buildings, political practices, and culture were no more uniformly "Roman" in the Mediterranean world after Hadrian's reign than before it.[6] Hadrian could not legislate such uniformity, nor force it upon all populations: this is most clear in the devastating Third Jewish Revolt, which is inextricably associated with Hadrian's prohibition of circumcision and his imposition of a Roman veteran colony on the Jews' holy city Jerusalem. But Hadrian typically avoided such egregious mistakes during his reign. His municipal interactions encouraged the spread of Roman norms and values more peacefully. Hadrian's benefactions created personal ties between emperor and city elites, and they added the Roman imperial presence to games, cults, titles, and the urban space of cities themselves. Just as significantly, his largesse materially strengthened cities. Hadrian thus demonstrated that the value of urban life was intrinsic to the Roman empire itself.

---

6 The increasing abandonment of Augustan classicism in the arts, the growing strength of the Second Sophistic, and the development of Christianity are all examples of lesser rather than greater uniformity.

BIBLIOGRAPHY

This bibliography contains items fundamental to my topic. Individual works on points appearing only once are cited in full in the footnotes. In referring to periodicals I generally follow the conventions of the *American Journal of Archaeology*.

Abbott, F. F., and A. C. Johnson. 1926. *Municipal Administration in the Roman Empire*. Princeton, NJ.

Abmeier, A. 1990. "Zur Geschichte von Apollonia am Rhyndakos." In *Mysische Studien*. Asia Minor Studien 1. Bonn, 1–16.

Adams, A. 1989. "The Arch of Hadrian at Athens." In Walker and Cameron 1989, 10–16.

Akurgal, E. 1983. *Ancient Civilizations and Ruins of Turkey*. 5th ed. Ankara.

Alcock, S. E. 1993. *Graecia Capta: The Landscapes of Roman Greece*. Cambridge, Eng.

Alexander, P. J. 1938. "Letters and Speeches of the Emperor Hadrian." *HSCP* 49:141–77.

Alföldy, G. 1991. "Epigraphische Notizen aus Kleinasien I. Ein Beneficium des Augustus in Ephesos." *ZPE* 87:157–62.

Almagro-Gorbea, M. 1982. *El santuario de Juno en Gabii*. Rome.

Alston, R. 1995. *Soldier and Society in Roman Egypt: A Social History*. London.

Anderson, G. 1993. *The Second Sophistic: A Cultural Phenomenon in the Roman World*. London.

André, J.-M. 1993. "Hadrien, littérateur et protecteur des lettres." *ANRW* II.34.1:583–611.

Andrei, O. 1984. *A. Claudius Charax di Pergamo. Interessi antiquari e antichità cittadine nell'età degli Antonini*. Bologna.

Applebaum, S. 1979. *Jews and Greeks in Ancient Cyrene*. Leiden.

Arafat, K. W. 1996. *Pausanias' Greece: Ancient Artists and Roman Rulers*. Cambridge, Eng.

Aupert, P. 1989. "L'Aqueduc nord d'Argos." *BCH* 113:722–31.

———. 1994. "L'Eau curative à Argos." In *L'Eau, la santé, et la maladie dans le monde grec*. BCH supp. 28. Paris, 193–99.

Avi-Yonah, M. 1966. *The Holy Land from the Persian to the Arab Conquests (536 B.C. to A.D. 640): A Historical Geography*. Grand Rapids, MI.

Baldassarre, I. 1988. "Alcune riflessioni sull'urbanistica di Antinoe (Egitto)." *Annali. Sezione di Archeologia e Storia Antica*. Naples, 275–84.

Baldwin, B. 1985. "Dio Cassius on the Period A.D. 96–180: Some Problematic Passages." *Athenaeum* 63:195–97.

Barag, D. 1967. "Brick Stamp-Impressions of the Legio X Fretensis." *BJb* 167: 244–67.

Bardon, H. 1968. *Les Empereurs et les lettres latines d'Auguste à Hadrien*. 2nd ed. Paris.

Barnes, T. D. 1984. "The Composition of Cassius Dio's *Roman History*." *Phoenix* 38:240–55.

Bauman, R. A. 1980. "The *Leges iudicorum publicorum* and Their Interpretation in the Republic, Principate and Later Empire." *ANRW* II.13:103–233.

Bean, G. E. 1978. *Lycian Turkey: An Archaeological Guide*. London.

Beard, M. 1985. "Writing and Ritual: A Study of Diversity and Expansion in the Arval Acta." *PBSR* 53:114–62.

Beard, M., and J. North, eds. 1990. *Pagan Priests: Religion and Power in the Ancient World*. Ithaca, NY.

Beaujeu, J. 1955. *La Religion romaine à l'apogée de l'empire*. Paris.

Behr, C. A. 1968. *Aelius Aristides and the Sacred Tales*. Amsterdam.

Bell, H. I. 1940. "Antinoopolis: A Hadrianic Foundation in Egypt." *JRS* 30:133–47.

Benario, H. W. 1980. *A Commentary on the "Vita Hadriani" in the "Historia Augusta."* American Classical Studies 7. Chico, CA.

Bendala Galán, M., ed. 1993. *The Hispano-Roman Town*. Barcelona.

Benjamin, A. S. 1963. "The Altars of Hadrian in Athens and Hadrian's Panhellenic Program." *Hesperia* 32:57–86.

Berger, A. 1953. *Encyclopedic Dictionary of Roman Law*. Philadelphia.

Bernhardt, R. 1971. *Imperium und Eleutheria. Die römische Politik gegenüber den freien Städten des griechischen Ostens*. Hamburg.

———. 1980. "Die Immunitas der Freistädte." *Historia* 29:190–207.

Beschaouch, A. 1979. "Éléments celtiques dans la population du pays de Carthage." *CRAI*, 403–4.

Birks, P. 1988. "New Light on the Roman Legal System: The Appointment of Judges." *Cambridge Law Journal* 47:36–60.

Birley, A. R. 1981. "The Economic Effects of Roman Frontier Policy." In *The Roman West in the Third Century*, ed. A. King and M. Henig. Oxford, 1981, 39–53.

———. 1994. "Hadrian's Farewell to Life." *Laverna* 5:176–205.

———. 1997. *Hadrian: The Restless Emperor*. London.

Blake, M. E., D. T. Bishop, and J. D. Bishop. 1973. *Roman Construction in Italy from Nerva through the Antonines*. Philadelphia.

Blanco Freijeiro, A. 1982. "La Itálica de Trajano y Adriano." In *Itálica. Actas de las Primeras Jornadas sobre Excavaciones Arqueológicas en Itálica. Sevilla, Septiembre 1980*. Madrid, 291–98.

Blázquez, J. M. 1980–81. "Urbanismo y Religión en Itálica (Bética, Hispania)." *AttiCAntCl* 11:233–63.

Bleicken, J. 1974. "*In provinciali solo dominium populi Romani est vel Caesaris*. Zur Kolonisationspolitik der ausgehenden Republik und frühen Kaiserzeit." *Chiron* 4:359–414.

Blume, F., K. Lachmann, and A. Rudorff. 1848–52. *Die Schriften der römischen Feldmesser*. Berlin. Reprinted Hildesheim, 1967.

Boatwright, M. T. 1987. *Hadrian and the City of Rome*. Princeton, NJ.

———. 1989. "Hadrian and Italian Cities." *Chiron* 19:235–71.

———. 1997a. "Italica and Hadrian's Urban Benefactions." In Caballos and León 1997, 116–35.

————. 1997b. "The Traianeum in Italica (Spain) and the Library of Hadrian in Athens." In *The Interpretation of Architectural Sculpture in Greece and Rome,* ed. D. Buitron-Oliver. Studies in the History of Art 49. Washington, DC, 193–217.

Bolin, S. 1958. *State and Currency in the Roman Empire to 300 A.D.* Stockholm.

Borchhardt, J., et al. 1975. *Myra. Eine lykische Metropole in antiker und byzantinischer Zeit.* Istanbuler Forschungen 30. Berlin.

Bosch, E. 1967. *Quellen zur Geschichte der Stadt Ankara im Altertum.* Ankara.

Bowersock, G. W. 1969. *Greek Sophists in the Roman Empire.* Oxford.

————. 1980. "A Roman Perspective on the Bar Kochba War." *Approaches to Ancient Judaism* 2:131–41.

————. 1985. "Hadrian and Metropolis." *Bonner HAC 1982/83.* Bonn, 79–86.

Bowie, E. L. 1982. "The Importance of Sophists." *YCS* 27:29–59.

Bowman, A. K. 1986. *Egypt after the Pharaohs, 332 BC–AD 642: From Alexander to the Arab Conquest.* Berkeley and Los Angeles.

Bowman, A. K., and G. Woolf, eds. 1994. *Literacy and Power in the Ancient World.* Cambridge, Eng.

Bradford, A. S. 1986. "The Date Hadrian Was Eponymous *Patronomos* of Sparta." *Horos* 4:71–74.

Braunert, H. 1962. "Griechische und römische Komponenten im Stadtrecht von Antinoopolis." *JJP* 14:73–88.

————. 1964. *Die Binnenwanderung: Studien zur Sozialgeschichte Ägyptens in der Ptolemäer-und Kaiserzeit.* Bonn.

————. 1966. "*Ius Latii* in den Stadtrechten von Salpensa und Malaca." In *Corolla memoriae Erich Swoboda dedicata.* Graz, 68–83. Reprinted in *Politik, Recht und Gesellschaft in der griechisch-römischen Antike. Gesammelte Aufsätze und Reden,* ed. K. Telschow and M. Zahrnt. Stuttgart, 1980, 305–21.

Bremen, R. van. 1983. "Women and Wealth." In *Images of Women in Antiquity,* ed. A. Cameron and A. Kuhrt. London, 223–42.

Breton, J.-F. 1980. *Inscriptions grecques et latines de la Syrie.* Vol. VIII.3. Paris.

Broughton, T. R. S. 1929. *The Romanization of Africa Proconsularis.* Baltimore.

————. 1934. "Roman Landholding in Asia Minor." *TAPA* 65:207–39.

————. 1938. "Roman Asia." Vol. IV.4 of *An Economic Survey of Ancient Rome,* ed. T. Frank. Baltimore.

Brunt, P. A. 1974a. "C. Fabricius Tuscus and an Augustan dilectus." *ZPE* 13:161–85.

————. 1974b. "Conscription and Volunteering in the Roman Imperial Army." *Scripta Classica Israelica* 1:90–115. Reprinted in *Roman Imperial Themes,* by P. A. Brunt. Oxford, 1990, 188–214.

————. 1976. "The Romanisation of the Local Ruling Classes in the Roman Empire." In *Assimilation et résistance à la culture gréco-romaine dans le monde ancien,* ed. D. M. Pippidi. Bucharest, 161–73. Reprinted in *Roman Imperial Themes,* by P. A. Brunt. Oxford, 1990, 266–81.

————. 1980. "Free Labour and Public Works at Rome." *JRS* 70:81–100.

————. 1981. "The Revenues of Rome." *JRS* 71:161–72. Reprinted in *Roman Imperial Themes,* by P. A. Brunt. Oxford, 1990, 330–46.

Brunt, P. A. 1990. "Publicans in the Principate." In *Roman Imperial Themes*, by P. A. Brunt. Oxford, 354–432.

Bürchner, 1927. *RE* III.A.1, 2nd series: 730–64, s.v. Smyrna.

Burnett, A., M. Amandry, and P. P. Ripollès. 1992. *Roman Provincial Coinage*. Vol. I, *From the Death of Caesar to the Death of Vitellius (44 BC–AD 69)*. London.

Burrell, B. 1981. *HSCP* 85:301–3.

Burton, G. P. 1979. "The Curator Rei Publicae: Towards a Reappraisal." *Chiron* 9:465–87.

———. 1993. "Provincial Procurators and the Public Provinces." *Chiron* 23:13–28.

Caballos, A., and P. León, eds. 1997. *Italica MMCC*. Seville.

Caballos Rufino, A. 1994. *Itálica y los Italicenses*. Seville.

Cadoux, C. J. 1938. *Ancient Smyrna: A History of the City from the Earliest Times to 324 A.D.* Oxford.

Calandra, E. 1996. *Oltre la Grecia. Alle origini del filellenismo di Adriano*. Naples.

Callu, J.-P., et al. 1992. "Introduction générale, Vies d'Hadrien, Aelius, Antonin." Vol. I.1 of *Histoire Auguste*. Paris.

Calderini, A. 1966. *Dizionario dei nomi geografici dell'Egitto greco-romano*, vol. I.2. Madrid.

Calderini, A., and S. Daris. 1988. *Dizionario dei nomi geografici dell'Egitto greco-romano*, supp. 1. Milan.

Camodeca, G. 1980. "Ricerche sui curatores rei publicae." *ANRW* II.13:453–534.

Canto, A. M. 1979. "El acueducto romano de Itálica." *MDAI (M)* 20:282–338.

Carrié, J.-M. 1992. "La 'Munificence' du prince. Les Modes tardifs de designation des actes impériaux et leurs antécédents." In *Institutions, société et vie publique dans l'empire romain au IVe siècle ap. J.-C.*, ed. M. Christol et al. CollEFR 159. Paris, 411–30.

Cartledge, P., and A. Spawforth. 1989. *Hellenistic and Roman Sparta, A Tale of Two Cities*. London.

Castrén, P. 1983. *Ordo populusque Pompeianus: Polity and Society in Roman Pompeii*. Rome.

Champlin, E. 1976. "Hadrian's Heir." *ZPE* 21:79–89.

———. 1980. *Fronto and Antonine Rome*. Cambridge, MA.

Chastagnol, A. 1977. "Le problème du domicile légal des sénateurs romains à l'époque impériale." In *Mélanges offerts à Léopold Sedar Senghor*. Dakar, Senegal, 43–54.

Chouquer, G., M. Clavel-Lévêque, F. Favory, and J.-P. Vallat. 1987. *Structures agraires en Italie centro-méridionale. Cadastres et paysages ruraux*. CollEFR 100. Paris.

Clavel-Lévêque, M. 1986. "L'espace des jeux dans le monde romain: Hégémonie, symbolique et pratique sociale." *ANRW* II.16.3:2405–2563.

Cook, J. M. 1973. *The Troad: An Archaeological and Topographical Study*. Oxford.

Corbier, M. 1974. *L'aerarium Saturni et l'aerarium militare. Administration et prosopographie sénatoriale*. Rome.

———. 1977. "Le Discours du prince d'après une inscription de Banasa." *Ktema* 2:211–32.

————. 1987. "L'Écriture dans l'espace romain." In *L'Urbs: Espace urbain et histoire*. CollEFR 98. Rome, 27–60.

————. 1991. "City, Territory and Taxation." In *City and Country in the Ancient World*, ed. J. Rich and A. Wallace-Hadrill. London, 211–39.

Cotton, H. 1984. "The Concept of *Indulgentia* under Trajan." *Chiron* 14:245–66.

Cox, C. W. M., A. Cameron, and J. Cullen. 1988. *Monuments from the Aezanitis*. Ed. B. Levick, S. Mitchell, J. Potter, M. Waelkens, and D. Nash. *MAMA* IX. London.

Crawford, M. 1970. "Money and Exchange in the Roman World." *JRS* 60:40–48.

————. 1986. "The Monetary System of the Roman Empire." In *L'Impero romano e le strutture economiche e sociali delle province*, ed. M. H. Crawford. Como, 61–69.

————. 1988. "The Laws of the Romans: Knowledge and Diffusion." In González and Arce 1988, 127–40.

Crawford, M. H., ed. 1996. *Roman Statutes*. BICS supp. 64. London.

Curty, O. 1995. *Les parentés légendaires entre cités grecques*. Geneva.

Daniels, C. 1983. "Town Defences in Roman Africa: A Tentative Historical Survey." In Maloney and Hobley 1983, 5–19.

Davies, R. W. 1968. "Fronto, Hadrian and the Roman Army." *Latomus* 27:75–95.

Day, J. 1942. *An Economic History of Athens under Roman Domination*. New York.

De Caro, S., and A. Greco. 1981. *Campania*. Bari.

Decker, W. 1973. "Bemerkungen zum Agon für Antinoos in Antinoupolis (Antinoeia)." *Kölner Beiträge zur Sportswissenschaft* 2:38–56, 213–14.

de Lange, N. R. M. 1978. "Jewish Attitudes to the Roman Empire." In *Imperialism in the Ancient World*, ed. P. D. A. Garnsey and C. R. Whittaker. Cambridge, Eng., 255–81.

Delorme, J. 1960. *Gymnasion*. Paris.

Desanges, J. 1972. "Le Statut des municipes d'après les données africaines." *RHD* 50:353–73.

Diaz Martos, A. 1985. *Capiteles Corintios romanos de Hispania. Estudio-Catalogo*. Madrid.

Dodge, H. 1991. "Ancient Marble Studies: Recent Research." *JRA* 4:28–50.

Donadoni, S. 1974. *Antinoe (1965–68)*. Rome.

D'Orgeval, B. 1950. *L'Empereur Hadrien, oeuvre législative et administrative*. Paris.

Downey, G. 1961. *A History of Antioch in Syria from Seleucus to the Arab Conquest*. Princeton, NJ.

Drew-Bear, T., and F. Richard. 1994. "Hadrien et Erastos, nauclère d'Ephèse." In *L'Afrique, la Gaule, la religion à l'époque romaine. Mélanges à la mémoire de M. Le Glay*. CollLat 226. Brussels, 742–51.

Duncan-Jones, R. 1982. *The Economy of the Roman Empire: Quantitative Studies*. 2nd ed. Cambridge, Eng.

————. 1990. *Structure and Scale in the Roman Economy*. Cambridge, Eng.

Dupuis, X. 1992. "Nouvelles promotions municipales de Trajan et d'Hadrien: Àpropos de deux inscriptions récemment publiées." *ZPE* 93:123–31.

Duthoy, R. 1974. "La Function sociale de l'augustalité." *Epigraphica* 36:134–54.

Duthoy, R. 1976. "Recherches sur la répartition géographique et chronologique des termes *sevir Augustalis, Augustalis* et *sevir* dans l'empire romain." *EpigStud* 11:143–214.

———. 1978. "Les *Augustales." *ANRW* II.16.2:1254–1309.

———. 1979. "Curatores rei publicae en Occident durant le Principat." *Ancient Society* 10:171–238.

Eck, W. 1979. *Die staatliche Organisation Italiens in der hohen Kaiserzeit.* Munich.

———. 1980. "Die Präsenz senatorischer Familien in der Städten des Imperium Romanum bis zum späten 3. Jahrhundert." In *Studien zur antiken Sozialgeschichte: Festschrift F. Vittinghoff,* ed. W. Eck, H. Galsterer, and H. Wolff. Cologne/Vienna, 283–322.

———. 1987. "Die Wasserversorgung im römischen Reich: Sozio-politische Bedingungen, Recht und Administration." In *Die Wasserversorgung antiker Städte.* Geschichte der Wasserversorgung 2. Mainz am Rhein, 49–101.

———. 1996. "I *legati Augusti pro praetore* italici sotto Adriano e Antonino Pio." In *Tra epigraphia, prosopografia e archeologia,* by W. Eck. Rome, 155–63.

Edwards, D. R. 1996. *Religion and Power: Pagans, Jews, and Christians in the Greek East.* Oxford.

Engesser, F. 1955. *Der Stadtpatronat in Italien und den Westprovinzen des römischen Reiches bis Diocletian.* Freiburg.

Ensoli Vittozzi, S. 1992. "Indagini sul culto di Iside a Cirene." In *L'Africa romana: Atti del IX Convegno di Studio Nuovo, 13–15 dic. 1991,* ed. A. Mastino. Sassari, 167–250.

Ensslin, W. 1954. *RE* 22.2:1257–1347, s.v. "praefectus."

Fant, J. C. 1992. "The Roman Imperial Marble Yard at Portus." In *Ancient Stones: Quarrying, Trade and Provenance,* ed. M. Waelkens, N. Herz, and L. Moens. Leuven, 115–20.

———. 1993. "Ideology, Gift, and Trade: A Distribution Model of the Roman Imperial Marbles." In *The Inscribed Economy,* ed. W. V. Harris. Ann Arbor, MI, 145–70.

Fein, S. 1994. *Die Beziehungen der Kaiser Trajan und Hadrian zu den "litterati."* Stuttgart.

Fernández Gómez, F. 1991. "Nuevos fragmentos de leyes municipales y otros bronces epigráficos de la Bética en el Museo Arqueólogico de Sevilla." *ZPE* 86:121–36.

Février, P.-A. 1983. "Armée et aqueducs." In *Journées d'études sur les aqueducs romains—Tagung über römische Wasserversorgungsanlagen, Lyon (26–28 mai 1977).* Paris, 133–40.

Fishwick, D. 1987–92. *The Imperial Cult in the Latin West.* 2 vols., each in 2 parts. Leiden.

Flacelière, R. 1971. "Hadrien et Delphes." *CRAI,* 168–85.

Follet, S. 1968. "Hadrien en Égypte et en Judée." *RPh* 42:54–77.

———. 1976. *Athènes au IIe et au IIIe siècle: Études chronologiques et prosopographiques.* Paris.

———. 1992. "Hadrien *ktistès kai oikistès:* Lexicographie et realia." In *La Langue et les textes en grec ancien: Actes du colloque P. Chantraine,* ed. F. Létoublon. Amsterdam, 241–54.

Foraboschi, D. 1988. "Movimenti e tensioni sociali nell'Egitto romano." *ANRW* II.10.1:807–40.

Forbes, C. A. 1955. "Ancient Athletic Guilds." *CP* 50:238–52.

Forni, G. 1953. *Il reclutamento delle legioni da Augusto a Diocleziano*. Milan.

Foss, C. 1975. "Aleipterion." *GRBS* 16.2:217–26.

Fossey, J. M. 1986. *The Ancient Topography of Eastern Phokis*. Amsterdam.

———. 1991. "The City Archive at Koroneia." In *Studies in Boiotian Inscriptions*, by J. M. Fossey. Epigraphica Boeotica 1. Amsterdam, 5–26.

Fougères, G. 1898. *Mantinée et l'Arcadie orientale*. Paris.

Fraser, P. M. 1950. "Hadrian and Cyrene." *JRS* 40:77–90.

Frederiksen, M. W. 1959. "Republican Capua: A Social and Economic Study." *PBSR* 27:80–130.

Freeman, P. W. M. 1993. "'Romanisation' and Roman Material Culture." *JRA* 6:438–45.

Frere, S. S. 1984. "British Urban Defences in Earthwork." *Britannia* 15:63–74.

Freyberger, K. S. 1990. *Stadtrömische Kapitelle aus der Zeit von Domitian bis Alexander Severus: Zur Arbeitsweise und Organisation stadtrömischer Werkstätten der Kaiserzeit*. Mainz am Rhein.

Friesen, S. 1995. "The Cult of the Roman Emperors in Ephesos: Temple Wardens, City Titles, and the Interpretation of the Revelation of John." In *Ephesos, Metropolis of Asia*, ed. H. Koester. Valley Forge, PA, 229–50.

Frisch, P. 1983. *Die Inschriften von Parion*. IK 25. Bonn.

Fuchs, M. 1987. *Untersuchungen zur Ausstattung römischer Theater in Italien und den Westprovinzen des Imperium Romanum*. Mainz am Rhein.

Fuks, A. 1961. "Aspects of the Jewish Revolt in A.D. 115–117." *JRS* 51:98–104.

Gabba, E. 1988. "Riflessioni sulla lex Coloniae Genetivae Iuliae." In González and Arce 1988, 169–84.

Galsterer, H. 1988a. "Municipium Flavium Irnitanum: A Latin Town in Spain." *JRS* 78:78–90.

———. 1988b. "The Tabula Siarensis and Augustan Municipalization in Baetica." In González and Arce 1988, 61–74.

Galsterer-Kröll, B. 1972. "Untersuchungen zu den Beinamen der Städte des Imperium Romanum." *EpigStud* 9:44–145.

García Iglesias, L. 1975. "La hipotética inscripción del Teatro de Mérida, reconstruida por Hübner." *Revista de Estudios Extreménos* 31:591–602.

García y Bellido, A. 1960. *Colonia Aelia Augusta Italica*. Madrid.

———. 1965. "La Italica de Hadriano." In *Les Empereurs romains d'Espagne*, ed. A. Piganiol. Paris, 7–26.

———. 1985. *Andalucía monumental. Itálica*. Seville.

Garnsey, P. 1970. *Social Status and Legal Privilege in the Roman Empire*. Oxford.

———. 1974. "Aspects of the Decline of the Urban Aristocracy in the Empire." *ANRW* 2.1:229–52.

———. 1976. "Urban Property Investment." In *Studies in Roman Property*, ed. M. Finley. Cambridge, Eng., 123–36.

———. 1988. *Famine and Food Supply in the Graeco-Roman World: Responses to Risk and Crisis*. Cambridge, Eng.

Garnsey, P., and R. Saller. 1987. *The Roman Empire: Economy, Society and Culture.* Berkeley and Los Angeles.

Garzetti, A. 1974. *From Tiberius to the Antonines.* London.

Gascou, J. 1972. *La Politique municipale de l'Empire romain en Afrique proconsulaire de Trajan à Septime-Sévère.* CollEFR 8. Rome.

———. 1979. "L'Emploi du terme *respublica* dans l'épigraphie latine d'Afrique." *MEFR* 91:383–98.

———. 1982. "La Politique municipale de Rome en Afrique du Nord, I et II." *ANRW* II.10.2:136–229, 230–320.

Gauthier, P. 1985. *Les Cités grecques et leurs bienfaiteurs.* Athens.

Gawantka, W., and M. Zahrnt. 1977. "Eine neue Inschrift der Stadt Stratonikeia-Hadrianopolis in Lydien." *Chiron* 7:305–14.

Geagan, D. J. 1972. "Hadrian and the Athenian Dionysiac Technitai." *TAPA* 103:133–60.

———. 1973. "A Decree of the Council of the Areopagus." *Hesperia* 42:352–57.

Geva, H. 1984. "The Camp of the Tenth Legion in Jerusalem: An Archaeological Reconsideration." *IEJ* 34:239–54.

Giménez-Caudela, T. 1981. "Una contribución al estudio de la ley Irnitana. La manumisión de esclavos municipales." *Iura* 32:37–56.

Ginouvès, R. 1969. *Laodicée du Lycos. Le Nymphée.* Quebec.

Glaser, F. 1987. "Brunnen und Nymphäen." In *Die Wasserversorgung antiker Städte.* Geschichte der Wasserversorgung 2. Mainz am Rhein, 118–31.

Gleason, M. W. 1995. *Making Men: Sophists and Self-Presentation in Ancient Rome.* Princeton, NJ.

Glucker, C. A. M. 1987. *The City of Gaza in the Roman and Byzantine Periods.* BAR Int. Ser. 325. Oxford.

Golvin, J.-C., and C. Landes. 1990. *Amphithéâtres et gladiateurs.* Paris.

González, J. 1986. "The Lex Irnitana: A New Copy of the Flavian Municipal Law." *JRS* 76:147–243.

González, J., and J. Arce, eds. 1988. *Estudios sobre la Tabula Siarensis.* Madrid.

Goodchild, R. 1963. *Cyrene and Apollonia: An Historical Guide.* 2nd ed. London.

Goodchild, R. G. 1961. "The Decline of Cyrene and Rise of Ptolemais: Two New Inscriptions." *QAL* 4:83–95.

———. 1971. *Kyrene und Apollonia.* Zurich.

Goodman, M. 1983. *State and Society in Roman Galilee, A.D. 132–212.* Totowa, NJ.

Gordon, R. 1990a. "From Republic to Principate: Priesthood, Religion and Theology." In Beard and North 1990, 177–98.

———. 1990b. "Religion in the Roman Empire: The Civic Compromise and Its Limits." In Beard and North 1990, 233–55.

———. 1990c. "The Veil of Power: Emperors, Sacrificers and Benefactors." In Beard and North 1990, 199–231.

Graindor, P. 1930. *Un Milliardaire antique. Hérode Atticus et sa famille.* Cairo.

———. 1934. *Athènes sous Hadrien.* Cairo.

Greco, E., and M. Torelli. 1983. *Storia dell'urbanistica. Il mondo greco.* Rome.

Greenidge, A. H. J. 1894. *Infamia: Its Place in Roman Public and Private Law.* Oxford.

Grelle, F. 1972. *L'autonomia cittadina fra Traiano e Adriano. Teoria e prassi dell'organizzazione municipale.* Naples.

Gros, P. 1984. "L'*Augusteum* de Nîmes." *RAN* 17:123–34.

Gros, P., and M. Torelli. 1992. *Storia dell'urbanistica. Il mondo romano.* 2nd ed. Rome.

Gsell, S. 1901. *Les Monuments antiques de l'Algérie.* Vol. I. Paris.

———. 1911. *Atlas archéologique de l'Algérie.* Paris.

Guarducci, M. 1941. "Adriano e i culti misterici della Grecia." *Bollettino. Museo dell'Impero Romano* 12:145–58.

Habicht, C. 1969. *Die Inschriften des Asklepieions.* Altertümer von Pergamon, vol. VIII.3. Berlin.

———. 1985. *Pausanias' Guide to Ancient Greece.* Berkeley and Los Angeles.

Hahland, W. 1950. "Der Fries des Dionysostempels in Teos." *JÖAI* 38:66–109.

Halfmann, H. 1979. *Die Senatoren aus dem östlichen Teil des Imperium romanum bis zum Ende des 2. Jahrhunderts n. Chr.* Göttingen.

———. 1986. *Itinera principum.* Stuttgart.

Hanard, G. 1987. "Note à propos des *leges Salpensana* et *Irnitana:* Faut-il corriger l'enseignment de Gaius?" *RIDA* 34:173–79.

Hanell, K. 1935. *RE* 16.2:2422–28, s.v. "neokoroi."

Hannestad, N. 1986. *Roman Art and Imperial Policy.* Aarhus.

Hardy, E. G. 1912. *Three Spanish Charters and Other Documents.* Oxford.

Harl, K. W. 1987. *Civic Coins and Civic Politics in the Roman East, A.D. 180–275.* Berkeley and Los Angeles.

———. 1996. *Coinage in the Roman Economy, 300 B.C. to A.D. 700.* Baltimore.

Harmand, L. 1957. *Le Patronat sur les collectivités publiques.* Paris.

Harris, R. 1926. "Hadrian's Decree of Expulsion of the Jews from Jerusalem." *HThR* 19:199–206.

Hauschild, T. 1972/1974. "Römische Konstruktionen auf der oberen Stadtterrasse des antiken Tarraco." *ArchEspArq* 45/47:3–44.

Heilmeyer, W.-D. 1970. *Korinthische Normalkapitelle.* Heidelberg.

Heiss, A. 1870. *Description générale des monnaies antiques de l'Espagne.* Paris.

Holford-Strevens, L. 1988. *Aulus Gellius.* London.

Honoré, T. 1987. "Scriptor Historiae Augustae." *JRS* 77:156–76.

Hoogendijk, F. J. A., and P. van Minnen. 1987. "Drei Kaiserbriefe Gordians III. an die Bürger von Antinoopolis. P. Vindob. G 25945." *Tyche* 2:47–74.

Hopkins, K. 1978. "Economic Growth and Towns in Classical Antiquity." In *Towns in Societies,* ed. P. Abrams and E. A. Wrigley. Cambridge, Eng., 35–77.

———. 1980. "Taxes and Trade in the Roman Economy." *JRS* 70:101–25.

Howgego, C. 1994. "Coin Circulation and the Integration of the Roman Economy." *JRA* 7:5–21.

Imhoof-Blumer, F. 1883. *Monnaies grecques.* Paris.

Isaac, B. 1980–81. "Roman Colonies in Judaea: The Foundation of Aelia Capitolina." *Talanta* 12/13:31–54.

———. 1992. *The Limits of Empire: The Roman Army in the East.* 2nd ed. Oxford.

Jacques, F. 1983. *Les Curateurs de cités dans l'Occident romain de Trajan à Gallien.* Paris.

Jacques, F. 1984. *Le Privilège de liberté. Politique impériale et autonomie munici-pale dans les cités de l'Occident romain (161–244)*. Rome.

Jarrett, M. G. 1971. "Decurions and Priests." *AJP* 92:513–38.

Jeffreys, E., B. Croke, and R. Scott, eds. 1990. *Studies in John Malalas*. Sydney.

Jeffreys, E., M. Jeffreys, R. Scott, et al. 1986. *The Chronicle of John Malalas: A Translation*. Melbourne.

Johnston, D. 1985. "Munificence and Municipia: Bequests to Towns in Classical Roman Law." *JRS* 75:105–25.

———. 1987. "Three Thoughts on Roman Private Law and the Lex Irnitana." *JRS* 77:62–77.

Jomard, E. 1820–30. "Description d'Antinoé." In *Description de l'Egypte*, ed. C. L. F. Panckoucke. 2nd ed. Paris, 10:413–28. The illustrations are in vol. 4.

Jones, A. H. M. 1940. *The Greek City from Alexander to Justinian*. Oxford.

Jones, B. 1985. "Beginnings and Endings in Cyrenaican Cities." In *Cyrenaica in Antiquity,* ed. G. Barker, J. Lloyd, and J. Reynolds. BAR Int. Ser. 236. Oxford, 27–41.

Jones, C. P. 1996. "The Panhellenion." *Chiron* 26:29–56.

Jones, G. D. B., and J. H. Little. 1971. "Hadrianopolis." *Libya Antiqua* 8:53–67.

Jouffroy, H. 1986. *La Construction publique en Italie et dans l'Afrique romaine*. Strasbourg.

Kadman, L. 1956. *The Coins of Aelia Capitolina*. Jerusalem.

Kalcyk, H., and B. Heinrich. 1989. "The Munich Kopäis Project." *Boeotia Anti-qua* I:55–71.

Karivieri, A. 1994. "The So-Called Library of Hadrian and the Tetraconch Church in Athens." In *Post-Herulian Athens,* ed. P. Castrén. Helsinki, 89–113.

Kaser, M. 1956. "*Infamia* und *ignominia* in den römischen Rechtsquellen." *ZRG* 73:220–78.

Keay, S. J. 1992. "The 'Romanisation' of Turdetania." *Oxford Journal of Archae-ology* 11:275–315.

Kenny, E. J. A. 1935. "The Ancient Drainage of the Copais." *Liverpool Annual of Archaeology and Anthropology* 22:189–206.

Keppie, L. 1983. *Colonisation and Veteran Settlement in Italy, 47–14 B.C.* London.

———. 1984. "Colonisation and Veteran Settlement in Italy, 47–14 B.C." *PBSR* 52:77–114.

———. 1991. *Understanding Roman Inscriptions*. Baltimore.

Kienast, D. 1959–60. "Hadrian, Augustus und die eleusinischen Mysterien." *JNG* 10:61–69.

———. 1990. *Römische Kaisertabelle*. Darmstadt.

———. 1993. "Antonius, Augustus, die Kaiser und Athen." In *Klassisches Alter-tum. Spätantike und frühes Christentum. Adolf Lippold zum 65. Geburtstag gewidmet*. Würzburg, 191–222.

Kloft, H. 1970. *Liberalitas principis. Herkunft und Bedeutung. Studien zur Prinzi-patsideologie*. Cologne.

Kokkou, A. 1970. "[Hadriáneia érga eis tas Athénas]." *ArchDelt* 25A:150–73.

Kornemann, E. 1900. *RE* 4.1:511–88, s.v. "coloniae."

———. 1933. *RE* 16.1:570–638, s.v. "municipium."

Kraeling, C. H. 1962. *Ptolemais: City of the Libyan Pentapolis*. Chicago.

Kubitschek, J. W. 1889. *Imperium Romanum tributim discriptum*. Vienna. Reprinted Rome, 1972.

Laffi, U. 1966. *Adtributio e contributio: Problemi del sistema politico-amministrativo dello stato romano*. Pisa.

———. 1971. "I terreni del tempio di Zeus ad Aezanoi." *Athenaeum* n.s. 49:3–53.

La Genière, J. de. 1990. "Le Sanctuaire d'Apollon à Claros. Nouvelles découvertes." *REG* 103:95–110.

Lämmer, M. 1967. *Olympien und Hadrianeen im antiken Ephesos*. Cologne.

Lane Fox, R. 1987. *Pagans and Christians*. New York.

Langhammer, W. 1973. *Die rechtliche und soziale Stellung der "Magistratus municipales" und der "Decuriones" in der Übergangsphase der Städte von sich selbstverwaltenden Gemeinden zu Vollzugsorganen des spätantiken Zwangsstaates (2.– 4. Jahrhundert der römischen Kaiserzeit)*. Wiesbaden.

Laronde, A. 1987. *Cyrène et la Libye hellénistique. Libykai Historiai*. Paris.

———. 1988. "La Cyrénaïque romaine (96 av. J.-C.–235 ap. J.-C.)." *ANRW* II.10.1:1006–64.

Larsen, J. A. O. 1938. "Roman Greece." Vol. IV.3 of *An Economic Survey of Ancient Rome*, ed. T. Frank. Baltimore.

Lavagne, H. 1986. "Rome et les associations Dionysiaques en Gaule (Vienne et Nîmes)." In *L'Association Dionysiaque dans les sociétés anciennes*. CollEFR 89. Paris, 129–48.

Le Bas, P., and W. H. Waddington. 1870. *Inscriptions grecques et latines recueillies en Asie Mineure*. Paris. Reprinted Meisenheim/Glan, 1972.

Lebek, W. D. 1993. "La *Lex Lati* di Domiziano (Lex Irnitana): Le Strutture giuridiche dei capitoli 84 e 86." *ZPE* 97:159–78.

Le Bohec, Y. 1989. "Inscriptions inédites ou corrigées concernant l'armée romaine d'Afrique." *AntAfr* 25:191–221.

Le Glay, M. 1976. "Hadrien et l'Asklépieion de Pergame." *BCH* 100:347–72.

Lehmann-Hartleben, K. 1923. *Die antiken Hafenanlagen des Mittelmeeres*. Leipzig.

León, P. 1988. *Traianeum de Italica*. Seville.

———. 1989. "La Afrodita de Itálica." In *Festschrift für Nikolaus Himmelmann. Beiträge zur Ikonographie und Hermeneutik*, ed. H.-U. Cain, H. Gabelmann, and D. Salzmann. Beihefte der Bonner Jahrbücher 47. Mainz am Rhein, 405–10.

———. 1992. "Zur Neustadt von Italica." In *Die römische Stadt im 2. Jahrhundert n. Chr. Der Funktionswandel des öffentlichen Raumes*, ed. H.-J. Schalles, H. von Hesberg, and P. Zanker. Xantener Berichte 2. Cologne, 87–97.

León Alonso, P. 1982. "La zona monumental de la Nova Urbs." In *Itálica. Actas de las Primeras Jornadas sobre Excavaciones Arqueológicas en Itálica. Sevilla, Septiembre 1980*. Madrid, 97–132.

Leopold, J. W. 1986. "*Consolando per Edicta*: Cassiodorus, *Variae*, 4, 50 and Imperial Consolations for Natural Catastrophes." *Latomus* 45:816–36.

Le Roux, P. 1986. "Municipe et droit Latin en Hispania sous l'Empire." *RHD* 64:325–50.

Leveau, P. 1993. "Mentalité économique et grands travaux: Le Drainage du lac Fucin. Aux origines d'un modèle." *AnnESC* 48:3–16.

Levick, B. 1967. *Roman Colonies in Southern Asia Minor.* Oxford.

————. 1985. *The Government of the Roman Empire: A Sourcebook.* Totowa, NJ.

Levin, S. 1989. "The Greek Oracles in Decline." *ANRW* II.18.2:1599–1649.

Lewin, A. 1995. *Assemblee popolari e lotta politica nelle città dell'impero romano.* Florence.

Lewis, A. D. E. 1989. "Ne quis in oppido aedificium detegito." In *Estudios sobre Urso: Colonia Iulia Genetiva,* ed. J. González. Seville, 41–56.

Lewis, N. 1983. *Life in Egypt under Roman Rule.* Oxford.

Lewis, N., and M. Reinhold. 1990. *Roman Civilization.* 3rd ed. New York.

Liebenam, W. 1900. *Städteverwaltung im römischen Kaiserreich.* Leipzig.

Lifshitz, B. 1977. "Jérusalem sous la domination romaine. Histoire de la ville depuis la conquête de Pompée jusqu'à Constantine (63 a.C.–325 p.C.)." *ANRW* II.8:471–744.

Liou, B. 1969. *Praetores Etruriae XV populorum (Étude d'épigraphie).* Brussels.

Lloyd, J. A. 1990. "The Cities of Cyrenaica in the Third Century AD." In *Giomata lincea sulla archeologia cirenaica.* Rome, 41–53.

Lo Cascio, E. 1981. "State and Coinage in the Late Republic and Early Empire." *JRS* 71:76–86.

Lolos, Y. A. 1997. "The Hadrianic Aqueduct of Corinth (With an Appendix on the Roman Aqueducts in Greece)." *Hesperia* 66:271–314.

Lomas, K. 1995. "Urban Elites and Cultural Definition: Romanization in Southern Italy." In *Urban Society in Roman Italy,* ed. T. J. Cornell and K. Lomas. London, 107–20.

Luni, M. 1990. "Il Ginnasio-'Caesareum' di Cirene nel contesto del rinnovamento urbanistico della media età ellenistica e della prima età imperiale." In *Giomata lincea sulla archeologia cirenaica.* Rome, 101–12.

Luzón Nogué, J. M. 1989. *La Itálica de Adriano.* 4th ed. Seville.

MacDonald, W. L. 1986. *The Architecture of the Roman Empire.* Vol. II. New Haven.

Mackie, N. 1983. *Local Administration in Roman Spain, A.D. 14–212.* BAR Int. Ser. 172. Oxford.

MacMullen, R. 1959. "Roman Imperial Building in the Provinces." *HSCP* 64:207–35.

————. 1982. "The Epigraphic Habit in the Roman Empire." *AJP* 103:233–46.

————. 1984. "Notes on Romanization." *BASP* 21:161–77. Reprinted in *Changes in the Roman Empire: Essays in the Ordinary,* by R. MacMullen. Princeton, NJ, 1990, 56–66.

Macready, S., and F. H. Thompson, eds. 1987. *Roman Architecture in the Greek World.* London.

Macro, A. D. 1976. "Imperial Provisions for Pergamum: *OGIS* 484." *GRBS* 17:169–79.

Magie, D. 1950. *Roman Rule in Asia Minor to the End of the Third Century after Christ.* 2 vols. Princeton, NJ.

Maloney, J., and B. Hobley, eds. 1983. *Roman Urban Defences in the West.* CBA Research Report 51. London.

Mann, J. C. 1983. *Legionary Recruitment and Veteran Settlement during the Principate.* London.

Martín, F. 1982. *La documentación griega de la cancillería del emperador Adriano.* Pamplona.

Martini, W. 1985. "Zur Benennung der sog. Hadriansbibliothek in Athen." In *Lebendige Altertumswissenschaft. Festgabe zur Vollendung des 70. Lebensjahres von Hermann Vetters.* Vienna, 188–91.

Matthews, J. F. 1984. "The Tax Law of Palmyra: Evidence for Economic History in a City of the Roman East." *JRS* 74:157–80.

Mattingly, D. J., ed. 1997. *Dialogues in Roman Imperialism: Power, Discourse and Discrepant Experience in the Roman Empire.* JRA supp. ser. 23. Portsmouth, RI.

Meiggs, R. 1973. *Roman Ostia.* 2nd ed. Oxford.

Merkelbach, R. 1978. "Der Rangstreit der Städte Asiens und die Rede des Aelius Aristides über die Eintracht." *ZPE* 32:287–96.

———. 1987. *Nikaia in der römischen Kaiserzeit.* Opladen.

Metcalf, W. E. 1974. "Hadrian, *Iovis Olympius.*" *Mnemosyne* 27:59–66.

Meyer, H., ed. 1994. *Der Obelisk des Antinoos. Eine kommentierte Edition.* Munich.

Mildenberg, L. 1984. *The Coinage of the Bar Kochba War.* Frankfurt/Salzburg.

Millar, F. 1964. *A Study of Cassius Dio.* Oxford.

———. 1968. "Local Cultures in the Roman Empire: Libyan, Punic and Latin in Roman Africa." *JRS* 58:126–34.

———. 1977. *The Emperor in the Roman World, 31 BC–AD 337.* Ithaca, NY. Reprinted with a postscript, Ithaca, NY, 1992.

———. 1983. "Empire and City. Augustus to Julian: Obligations, Excuses and Status." *JRS* 73:76–96.

———. 1990. "The Roman *Coloniae* of the Near East: A Study of Cultural Relations." In *Roman Eastern Policy and Other Studies in Roman History,* ed. H. Solin and M. Kajava. Helsinki, 7–58.

———. 1993. *The Roman Near East, 31 BC–AD 337.* Cambridge, MA.

Miller, S. G. 1972. "A Roman Monument in the Athenian Agora," and "Addendum to 'A Roman Monument in the Athenian Agora.'" *Hesperia* 41:50–95, 475–76.

———. 1990. *Nemea.* Berkeley and Los Angeles.

Millett, M. 1990. "Romanization: Historical Issues and Archaeological Interpretation." In *The Early Roman Empire in the West,* ed. T. Blagg and M. Millett. Oxford, 35–41.

———. 1991. "Roman Towns and Their Territories: An Archaeological Perspective." In *City and Country in the Ancient World,* ed. J. Rich and A. Wallace-Hadrill. London, 169–89.

Mitchell, E. 1982. "Osservazioni topografiche preliminari sull'impianto urbanistico di Antinoe." *Vicino Oriente* 5:171–79.

Mitchell, S. 1979. "Iconium and Ninica: Two Double Communities in Roman Asia Minor." *Historia* 28:409–38.

———. 1984. "The Greek City in the Roman World: The Case of Pontus and Bithynia." In *Praktika* [Proceedings of the Eighth International Congress of Greek and Latin Epigraphy, Athens, 1982]. Athens, 120–33.

———. 1987. "Imperial Building in the Eastern Roman Provinces." *HSCP* 91:333–65.

———. 1990. "Festivals, Games and Civic Life in Roman Asia Minor." *JRS* 80:183–93.

Mitchell, S. 1993. *Anatolia: Land, Men, and Gods in Asia Minor.* Vols. I and II. Oxford.

Mitford, T. B. 1974. "Some Inscriptions from the Cappadocian *Limes.*" *JRS* 64:160–75.

———. 1980. "Cappadocia and Armenia Minor: Historical Setting of the *Limes.*" *ANRW* II.7.2:1169–1228.

Mócsy, A. 1962a. *RE Supp.* 9:517–776, s.v. Pannonia.

———. 1962b. "Ubique Res Publica." *Acta Antiqua Hung* 10:367–84.

———. 1968. *RE Supp.* 11:1003–4, s.v. Municipium.

———. 1974. *Pannonia and Upper Moesia: A History of the Middle Danube Provinces of the Roman Empire.* Trans. S. Frere. London.

Moffatt, A. 1990. "A Record of Public Buildings and Monuments." In *Studies in John Malalas,* ed. E. Jeffreys, B. Croke, and R. Scott. Sydney, 87–109.

Mommsen, T. 1887. *Das römische Staatsrecht.* 3rd ed. Vol. II.2. Leipzig.

Montevecchi, O. 1990. "Adriano e la fondazione di Antinoopolis." In *Neronia IV. Alejandro Magno, modello de los emperadores romanos,* ed. J. M. Croisille. Coll-Lat 209. Brussels, 183–95.

Moretti, L. 1953. *Iscrizioni agonistiche greche.* Rome.

Morley, N. 1996. *Metropolis and Hinterland: The City of Rome and the Italian Economy, 200 B.C.–A.D. 200.* Cambridge, Eng.

Morris, I. 1992. *Death-Ritual and Social Structure in Classical Antiquity.* Cambridge, Eng.

Mourgues, J.-L. 1987. "The So-Called Letter of Domitian at the End of the Lex Irnitana." *JRS* 77:78–87.

Mühlenbrock, S. 1994. "Hadrian in Alexandria Troas? Eine neue Inschrift." In *Neue Forschungen zu Neandria und Alexandria Troas.* Asia Minor Studien 11. Bonn, 193–95.

Münsterberg, R. 1973. *Die Beamtennamen auf den griechischen Münzen.* New York.

Murga, J. L. 1976. *Protección a la estética en la legislación urbanística del Alto Imperio.* Seville.

———. 1985. "Las acciones populares en el municipio de Irni." *BIDR* 88:209–50.

Neesen, L. 1980. *Untersuchungen zu den direkten Staatsabgaben der römischen Kaiserzeit (27 v. Chr.–284 n. Chr.).* Bonn.

Negev, A. 1964. "The High Level Aqueduct at Caesarea." *IEJ* 14:237–49.

———. 1972. "A New Inscription from the High Level Aqueduct at Caesarea." *IEJ* 22:52–53.

Nicols, J. 1979. "Zur Verleihung öffentlicher Ehrungen in der römischen Welt." *Chiron* 9:243–60.

———. 1988. "On the Standard Size of the Ordo Decurionum." *ZRG* 105:712–19.

———. 1990. "Patrons of Greek Cities in the Early Principate." *ZPE* 80:81–100.

Niemeyer, H. G. 1968. *Studien zu den statuarischen Darstellungen der römischen Kaiser.* Berlin.

Nierhaus, R. 1965. "Zum wirtschaftlichen Aufschwung der Baetica zur Zeit Trajans und Hadrians." In *Les Empereurs romains d'Espagne,* ed. A. Piganiol. Paris, 181–94.

———. 1966. "Hadrians Verhältnis zu Italica." In *Corolla memoriae Erich Swoboda dedicata*. Graz, 151–68.

Nir, Y. 1985. "The Destruction of the Roman High Level Aqueduct and the Herodian Harbour at Caesarea." In *Harbour Archaeology*, ed. A. Raban. BAR Int. Ser. 257. Oxford, 185–94.

Nock, A. D. 1930. "[Sunnaos Theos]." *HSCP* 41:1–62.

Nörr, D. 1965. *RE Suppl.* 10:433–73, s.v. "origo."

———. 1966. *Imperium und Polis in der hohen Prinzipatszeit*. 2nd ed. Munich.

North, J. 1992. "The Development of Religious Pluralism." In *The Jews among Pagans and Christians in the Roman Empire*, ed. J. Lieu, J. North, and T. Rajak. London, 174–93.

Nutton, V. 1978. "The Beneficial Ideology." In *Imperialism in the Ancient World*, ed. P. D. A. Garnsey and C. R. Whittaker. Cambridge, Eng., 209–21.

Oliver, J. H. 1953. *The Ruling Power: A Study of the Roman Empire in the Second Century after Christ through the Roman Oration of Aelius Aristides*. Transactions of the American Philosophical Society 43.4. Philadelphia.

———. 1970a. "Hadrian's Reform of the Appeal Procedure in Greece." *Hesperia* 39:332–36.

———. 1970b. *Marcus Aurelius: Aspects of Civil and Cultural Policy in the East*. Hesperia supp. 13. Princeton, NJ.

———. 1989. *Greek Constitutions of the Early Roman Emperors from Inscriptions and Papyri*. Memoirs of the American Philosophical Society 178. Philadelphia.

Oliverio, G., G. Pugliese Carratelli, and D. Morelli. 1961–62. "Supplemento Epigraphico Cirenaico." *ASAA* 39–40 (n.s. 23–24): 221–375.

Parker, H. M. D. 1971. *The Roman Legions*. Cambridge, Eng.

Patterson, J. R. 1987. "Crisis. What Crisis? Rural Change and Urban Development in Imperial Appennine Italy." *PBSR* 55:115–46.

Peacock, D. P. S., and V. A. Maxfield. 1997. *Mons Claudianus: Survey and Excavation, 1987–1993*. Vol. I. Cairo.

Pensabene, P. 1973. *Scavi di Ostia*. Vol. VII, *I Capitelli*. Rome.

Pesce, G. 1941. *I rilievi dell' anfiteatro campano*. Rome.

Petzl, G. 1987. *Inschriften von Smyrna*. Vol. II.1. IK 24.1. Bonn.

Pickard-Cambridge, A. W. 1968. *The Dramatic Festivals of Athens*. 2nd ed. Revised by J. Gould and D. M. Lewis. Oxford.

Piganiol, A. 1962. *Les Documents cadastraux de la colonie romaine d'Orange. Gallia* supp. 16. Paris.

Piso, I. 1993. *Fasti Provinciae Daciae*. Vol. I. Bonn.

Plácido, D. 1992. "La ley olearia de Adriano." *Gerión* 10:171–79.

Pleket, H. W. 1973. "Some Aspects of the Athletic Guilds." *ZPE* 10:197–227.

———. 1975. "Games, Prizes, Athletes and Ideology: Some Aspects of the History of Sport in the Graeco-Roman World." *Stadion* 1:49–89.

———. 1984. "City Elites and Economic Activities in the Greek Part of the Roman Empire: Some Preliminary Remarks." *Praktika* [Proceedings of the Eighth International Congress of Greek and Latin Epigraphy, Athens, 1982]. Athens, 131–44.

Poliakoff, M. B. 1989. "Guilds of Performers and Athletes: Bureaucracy, Rewards and Privileges." *JRA* 2:295–98.

Posner, E. 1972. *Archives in the Ancient World.* Cambridge, MA.

Pressice, C. P. 1990. "Nuovi altari nel santuario di Apollo a Cirene. Indagini preparatorie per la ricostruzione grafica delle fasi architettoniche dell'area sacra." In *Giornata lincea sulla archeologia cirenaica.* Rome, 121–55.

Price, S. R. F. 1984a. "Gods and Emperors: The Greek Language of the Roman Imperial Cult." *JHS* 104:79–95.

———. 1984b. *Rituals and Power.* Cambridge, Eng.

Pucci, M. 1981. *La rivolta ebraica al tempo di Traiano.* Pisa.

Pülz, S. 1989. *Untersuchungen zur kaiserzeitlichen Bauornamentik von Didyma.* IstMitt, Beiheft 35. Tübingen.

Rajak, T. 1984. "Was There a Roman Charter for the Jews?" *JRS* 74:107–23.

———. 1985. "Jewish Rights in the Greek Cities under Roman Rule: A New Approach." *Approaches to Ancient Judaism* 5:19–35.

Rebuffat, R. 1986. "Les Fortifications urbaines du monde romain." In *La Fortification dans l'histoire du monde grec.* Paris, 345–61.

Reynolds, J. M. 1958–59. "The Jewish Revolt of A.D. 115 in Cyrenaica." *PCPS* 185:24–28.

———. 1978. "Hadrian, Antoninus Pius and the Cyrenaican Cities." *JRS* 68:111–21.

———. 1982. *Aphrodisias and Rome.* London.

———. 1988. "Cities." In *The Administration of the Roman Empire (241 B.C.–A.D. 193),* ed. D. C. Braund. Exeter, 15–51.

———. 1990. "Some Inscriptions of Roman Ptolemais." In *Giornata lincea sulla archeologia cirenaica.* Rome, 65–74.

Rickman, G. 1971. *Roman Granaries and Store Buildings.* Cambridge, Eng.

———. 1985. "Towards a Study of Roman Ports." In *Harbour Archaeology,* ed. A. Raban. BAR Int. Ser. 257. Oxford, 105–14.

Rigsby, K. J. 1987. "Megara and Tripodiscus." *GRBS* 28:93–102.

Ringel, J. 1975. *Césarée de Palestine. Étude historique et archéologique.* Paris.

Robert, J., and L. Robert. 1978. "Hadrien Zeus Kynégésios." *BCH* 102:437–52.

Robert, L. 1938. *Études épigraphiques et philologiques.* Paris.

———. 1954. *Les Fouilles de Claros.* Ankara.

———. 1962. *Villes d'Asie Mineure.* 2nd ed. Paris.

———. 1963. *Noms indigènes dans l'Asie Mineure greco-romaine.* Paris.

———. 1969. "L'Oracle de Claros." In *La Civilisation grecque de l'antiquité à nos jours,* ed. C. Delvoye and G. Roux. Brussels, 305–12.

———. 1977. "La Titulature de Nicée et de Nicomédie: La Gloire et la haine." *HSCP* 81:1–39.

———. 1978. "Stèle funéraire de Nicomédie et séismes dans les inscriptions." *BCH* 102:395–408.

———. 1980. *À travers l'Asie Mineure.* Paris.

———. 1984. "Discours d'ouverture." *Praktika* [Proceedings of the Eighth International Congress of Greek and Latin Epigraphy, Athens, 1982]. Athens, 35–45.

Rodá, I. 1997. "Los mármoles de Itálica. Su comercio y origen." In Caballos and León 1997, 166–76.

Rodger, A. 1990. "The Jurisdiction of Local Magistrates: Chapter 84 of the Lex Irnitana." *ZPE* 84:147–61.

Rogers, G. M. 1991. *The Sacred Identity of Ephesos.* London.

———. 1992. "The Assembly of Imperial Ephesos." *ZPE* 94:224–28.

Roldán Gómez, L. 1987. "Técnica edilicia en Itálica. Los edificios públicos." *ArchEspArq* 60:114–22.

Romanelli, P. 1943. *La Cirenaica romana.* Verbania.

———. 1959. *Storia delle province romane dell'Africa.* Rome.

Rosenbaum, E. 1960. *A Catalogue of Cyrenaican Portrait Sculpture.* London.

Rosenberger, M. 1972. *The Rosenberger Israel Collection.* Vol. I. Jerusalem.

Rossner, M. 1974. "Asiarchen und Archiereis Asias." *Studi Clasice* 16:101–42.

Ruge, W. 1940. *RE Suppl.* 7:1244–50, s.v. Stratonikeia-Hadrianopolis.

Şahin, S. 1978. *Bithynische Studien.* IK 7. Bonn.

———. 1979. *Katalog der antiken Inschriften des Museums von Iznik (Nikaia).* Vol. I, *Nr. 1–633.* IK 9. Bonn.

Saller, R. P. 1982. *Personal Patronage under the Early Empire.* Cambridge, Eng.

Salmon, E. T. 1970. *Roman Colonization under the Republic.* London.

Sartori, M. 1989. "Osservazioni sul ruolo del *curator rei publicae.*" *Athenaeum* 67:5–20.

Schäfer, P. 1981. "The Causes of the Bar Kokhba Revolt." In *Studies in Aggadah, Targum and Jewish Liturgy in Memory of J. Heinemann,* ed. J. T. Petuchowski and E. Fleischer. Jerusalem, 74–94.

Scheer, T. 1993. "Mythische Vorväter. Zur Bedeutung griechischer Heroenmythen im Selbstverständnis Kleinasiatischer Städte." Diss., University of Munich.

Schlumberger, J. 1974. *Die Epitome de Caesaribus. Untersuchungen zur heidnischen Geschichtsschreibung des 4. Jahrhunderts n.Chr.* Vestigia 18. Munich.

Schneider, A. M., and W. Karnapp. 1938. *Die Stadtmauer von Iznik (Nicaea).* Berlin.

Schulz, A., and E. Winter. 1990. "Historisch-archäologische Untersuchungen zum Hadrianstempel von Kyzikos." In *Mysische Studien.* Asia Minor Studien 1. Bonn, 33–82.

Schürer, E. 1973. *History of the Jewish People in the Age of Jesus Christ.* Vol. I. Ed. G. Vermes and F. Millar. Edinburgh.

Schwertheim, E. 1983. *Die Inschriften von Kyzikos und Umgebung.* Vol. II. IK 26. Bonn.

———. 1985. "Zu Hadrians Reisen und Stadtgründungen in Kleinasien. Eine neue Gründungsära." *EpigAnat* 6:37–42.

———. 1987. *Die Inschriften von Hadrianoi und Hadrianeia.* IK 33. Bonn.

Seston, W. 1962. "Le Décret de Digne et la fin de l'autonomie municipale en Occident." *REA* 64:314–25.

Shear, T. Leslie, Jr. 1981. "Athens: From City-State to Provincial Town." *Hesperia* 50:356–77.

Sherk, R. K. 1969. *Roman Documents from the Greek East.* Baltimore.

———. 1970. *The Municipal Decrees of the Roman West.* Buffalo, NY.

———. 1990a. "The Eponymous Officials of Greek Cities, Part I." *ZPE* 83:249–88.

———. 1990b. "The Eponymous Officials of Greek Cities, Part II." *ZPE* 84:231–95.

———. 1991. "The Eponymous Officials of Greek Cities, Part III." *ZPE* 88:225–60.

Sherk, R. K. 1992. "The Eponymous Officials of Greek Cities, Part IV." *ZPE* 93:223–72.

———. 1993. "The Eponymous Officials of Greek Cities, Part V." *ZPE* 96:267–95.

Sherwin-White, A. N. 1966. *The Letters of Pliny: A Historical and Social Commentary.* Oxford.

———. 1973. *The Roman Citizenship.* 2nd ed. Oxford.

Sillières, P. 1990. *Les voies de communication de l'Hispanie méridionale.* Paris.

Simhäuser, W. 1989. "La jurisdiction municipale à la lumière de la lex Irnitana." *RHD* 67:619–50.

Sisson, M. A. 1929. "The Stoa of Hadrian at Athens." *PBSR* 11:50–72.

Smallwood, E. M. 1952. "The Hadrianic Inscription from the Caesareum at Cyrene." *JRS* 42:37–38.

———. 1959. "The Legislation of Hadrian and Antoninus Pius against Circumcision." *Latomus* 18:334–47.

———. 1960. "Addendum." *Latomus* 20:93–96.

———. 1976. *The Jews under Roman Rule.* Leiden.

Spawforth, A. J. S. 1989. "Agonistic Festivals in Roman Greece." In Walker and Cameron 1989, 193–97.

Spawforth, A. J., and S. Walker. 1985. "The World of the Panhellenion, I. Athens and Eleusis." *JRS* 75:78–104.

———. 1986. "The World of the Panhellenion, II. Three Dorian Cities." *JRS* 76:88–105.

Spitzl, T. 1984. *Lex Municipii Malacitani.* Vestigia 36. Munich.

Stadter, P. 1980. *Arrian of Nicomedia.* Chapel Hill, NC.

Stahl, M. 1978. *Imperiale Herrschaft und provinziale Stadt.* Göttingen.

Strack, P. L. 1933. *Untersuchungen zur römischen Reichsprägung des zweiten Jahrhunderts.* Vol. II, *Die Reichsprägung zur Zeit des Hadrian.* Stuttgart.

Strocka, V. M. 1981. "Römische Bibliotheken." *Gymnasium* 88:298–329.

Strong, D. E. 1953. "Late Hadrianic Architectural Ornament in Rome." *PBSR* 21:118–51.

Stucchi, S. 1975. *Architettura cirenaica.* Rome.

Swain, S. 1991. "The Reliability of Philostratus's *Lives of the Sophists.*" *ClassAnt* 10:148–63.

———. 1996. *Hellenism and Empire: Language, Classicism, and Power in the Greek World, A.D. 50–250.* Oxford.

Syme, R. 1958. *Tacitus.* 2 vols. Oxford.

———. 1964. "Hadrian and Italica." *JRS* 54:142–49.

———. 1965. "Hadrian the Intellectual." In *Les Empereurs romains d'Espagne,* ed. A. Piganiol. Paris, 243–53.

———. 1968. *Ammianus and the Historia Augusta.* Oxford.

———. 1971. *Emperors and Biography.* Oxford.

———. 1983. "Hadrian and Antioch." In *Bonner HAC 1979/1981.* Bonn, 321–31.

———. 1988. "Journeys of Hadrian." *ZPE* 73:159–70.

Talbert, R. J. A. 1984. *The Senate of Imperial Rome.* Princeton, NJ.

———. 1989. "The Decurions of Colonia Genetiva Iulia in Session." In *Estudios sobre Urso: Colonia Iulia Genetiva,* ed. J. González. Seville, 57–67.

Teja, R. 1980. "Die römische Provinz Kappadokien in der Prinzipatszeit." *ANRW* II.7.2:1083–1124.

Thomas, E., and C. Witschel. 1992. "Constructing Reconstruction: Claim and Reality of Roman Rebuilding Inscriptions from the Latin West." *PBSR* 60:135–77.

Thulin, C. 1923. *Opuscula agrimensorum veterum.* Leipzig.

Tobin, J. 1997. *Herodes Attikos and the City of Athens: Patronage and Conflict under the Antonines.* Amsterdam.

Todd, M. 1985. "Forum and Capitolium in the Early Empire." In *Roman Urban Topography in Britain and the Western Empire,* ed. F. Grew and B. Hobley. London, 56–66.

Toneatto, L. 1983. "Tradition manuscrite et éditions modernes du *Corpus Agrimensorum Romanorum.*" In *Cadastres et espace rural: Approches et réalités antiques. Table ronde de Besançon, mai 1980.* Paris, 21–50.

Toynbee, J. M. C. 1934. *The Hadrianic School.* Cambridge, Eng.

Travlos, J. 1971. *Pictorial Dictionary of Ancient Athens.* New York.

Treggiari, S. 1969. *Roman Freedmen during the Late Republic.* Oxford.

Trillmich, W., and P. Zanker, eds. 1990. *Stadtbild und Ideologie. Die Monumentalisierung hispanischer Städte zwischen Republik und Kaiserzeit.* Munich.

Veyne, P. 1990. *Bread and Circuses.* Trans. B. Pearce. London. Originally published as *Le Pain et le cirque. Sociologie historique d'un pluralisme politique.* Paris, 1976.

Vincent, H., and F. M. Abel. 1914–26. *Jérusalem Nouvelle.* Vol. II. Paris.

Wacher, J., ed. 1987. *The Roman World.* 2 vols. London.

Waelkens, M. 1989. "Hellenistic and Roman Influence in the Imperial Architecture of Asia Minor." In Walker and Cameron 1989, 77–88.

Walker, S. 1979. "Corinthian Capitals with Ringed Voids: The Work of Athenian Craftsmen in the Second Century A.D." *AA,* 103–29.

————. 1985. "The Architecture of Cyrene and the Panhellenion." In *Cyrenaica in Antiquity,* ed. G. Barker, J. Lloyd, and J. Reynolds. London, 97–104.

————. 1991. *Roman Art.* London.

————. 1993. "Hadrian and the Renewal of Cyrene." Paper presented at a symposium on Architectural Sculpture at the National Gallery of Art, Washington, DC, January 1993. Used by courtesy of the author.

Walker, S., and A. Cameron, eds. 1989. *The Greek Renaissance in the Roman Empire.* London.

Wallace-Hadrill, A. 1982. "Civilis Princeps: Between Citizen and King." *JRS* 72:32–48.

————. 1983. *Suetonius: The Scholar and His Caesars.* New Haven.

————. 1986. "Image and Authority in the Coinage of Augustus." *JRS* 76:66–87.

————. 1988. "Greek Knowledge, Roman Power." *CP* 83:224–33.

————. 1990. "Roman Arches and Greek Honours: The Language of Power at Rome." *PCPS* n.s. 36:143–81.

————, ed. 1989. *Patronage in Ancient Society.* London.

Walter, O. 1922–24. "Antikenbericht aus Smyrna." *JÖAI* 21–22:224–60.

Wankel, H. 1979. *Die Inschriften von Ephesos.* Vol. Ia. IK 11.1. Bonn.

Ward-Perkins, B. 1984. *From Classical Antiquity to the Middle Ages.* Oxford.

Ward Perkins, J. B., and M. H. Ballance. 1958. "The Caesareum at Cyrene and the Basilica at Cremna (With a Note on the Inscriptions of the Caesareum by J. M. Reynolds)." *PBSR* 26:136–94.

Watkins, T. H. 1983. "*Coloniae* and *Ius Italicum* in the Early Empire." *CJ* 78:319–36.

Weber, W. 1907. *Untersuchungen zur Geschichte der Kaisers Hadrianus.* Leipzig.

Weiss, P. 1982. "Textkritisches zur Athleten-Relatio des Plinius (*Ep.* 10.118)." *ZPE* 48:125–32.

———. 1995. "Hadrian in Lydien." *Chiron* 25:213–24.

Whittaker, C. R. 1990. "The Consumer City Revisited: The *Vicus* and the City." *JRA* 3:110–18.

———. 1997. "Imperialism and Culture: The Roman Initiative." In Mattingly 1997, 143–63.

Wilber, D. N. 1938. "The Plateau of Daphne: The Springs and the Water System Leading to Antioch." In *Antioch-on-the-Orontes, 2: The Excavations, 1933–36,* ed. R. Stillwell. Princeton, NJ, 49–56.

Wilkinson, J. 1975. "The Streets of Jerusalem." *Levant* 7:118–36.

———. 1978. *Jerusalem as Jesus Knew It: Archaeology as Evidence.* London.

Willers, D. 1990. *Hadrians panhellenisches Programm. Archäologische Beiträge zur Neugestaltung Athens durch Hadrian.* Basel.

Williams, W. 1967. "Antoninus Pius and the Control of Provincial Embassies." *Historia* 16:470–83.

———. 1976. "Individuality in the Imperial Constitutions: Hadrian and the Antonines." *JRS* 66:67–83.

———. 1979. "Caracalla and the Authorship of Imperial Edicts and Epistles." *Latomus* 38:67–89.

Williamson, C. 1987. "Monuments of Bronze: Roman Legal Documents on Bronze Tablets." *ClassAnt* 6.1:160–83.

Wilmanns, G. 1873. *Exempla inscriptionum latinarum in usum praecipue academicum.* Vol. II. Berlin.

Wiseman, J. 1978. *The Land of the Ancient Corinthians.* Göteborg.

Woolf, G. 1990. "Food, Poverty and Patronage: The Significance of the Epigraphy of the Roman Alimentary Schemes in Early Imperial Italy." *PBSR* 58:197–228.

Wörrle, M. 1971. "Ägyptisches Getreide für Ephesos." *Chiron* 1:325–40.

———. 1988. *Stadt und Fest in kaiserzeitlichen Kleinasien. Studien zu einer agonistischen Stiftung aus Oenoanda.* Vestigia 39. Munich.

Wycherley, R. E. 1959. "Pausanias in the Agora of Athens." *GRBS* 2:21–44.

———. 1963. "Pausanias at Athens, II." *GRBS* 4:157–75.

Yegül, F. 1992. *Baths and Bathing in Classical Antiquity.* Cambridge, MA.

Yorke, V. W. 1896. "Excavations at Abae and Hyampolis in Phocis." *JHS* 16:291–312.

Zabehlicky, H. 1995. "Preliminary Views of the Ephesian Harbor." In *Ephesos: Metropolis of Asia,* ed. H. Koester. Harvard Theological Studies 41. Valley Forge, PA, 201–13.

Zahrnt, M. 1979. "Die 'Hadriansstadt' von Athen." *Chiron* 9:393–98.

———. 1986. "Zum Fiskalgesetz von Palmyra und zur Geschichte der Stadt in hadrianischer Zeit." *ZPE* 62:279–93.

——— 1988a. "Antinoopolis in Ägypten: Die hadrianische Gründung und ihre Privilegien in der neueren Forschung." *ANRW* II.10.1:669–706.

———. 1988b. "Vermeintliche Kolonien des Kaisers Hadrian." *ZPE* 71:229–49.

———. 1988c. "Zum römischen Namen von Augburg." *ZPE* 72:179–80.

———. 1989a. "Ein hadrianisches Municipium in der Hispania Tarraconensis?" *ZPE* 79:173–76.

———. 1989b. "Latium maius und Munizipalstatus in Gigthis und Thisiduo in der Africa Proconsularis." *ZPE* 79:177–80.

———. 1991. "Zahl, Verteilung und Charakter der hadrianischen Kolonien (unter besonderer Berücksichtigung von *Aelia Capitolina*)." *Stuttgarter Kolloquium zur Geographie des Altertums* 2:463–86.

Ziegler, R. 1985. *Städtisches Prestige und kaiserliche Politik*. Düsseldorf.

———. 1993. *Kaiser, Heer und Städtisches Geld: Untersuchungen zur Münzprägung von Anazarbos und anderer ostkilikischer Städte*. Vienna.

———. 1995. "Zur Einrichtung des Kilikischen Koinon. Ein Datierungsversuch." *Asia Minor Studien* 16:183–86.

Index

References to ancient sources as documentation, and references to places and people as a guide to location or chronology, are not included in this index. Cities in this index are ones with which Hadrian has been closely associated. Most buildings are indexed under the city in which they are found, including ones at Rome.

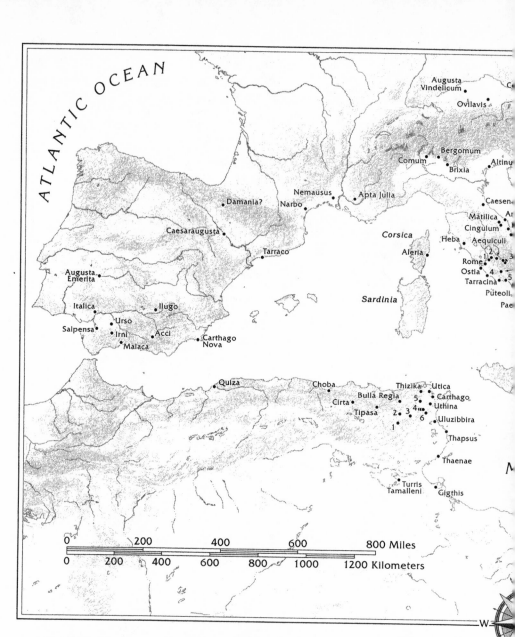

CITIES in HADRIAN'S EMPIRE

Africa Proconsularis

1. Althiburos
2. Lares
3. Zama Regia
4. West to east: Bisica Lucana, Avitta Bibba, Thuburbo Maius
5. Thisiduo
6. Abthugni

Italy

1. Nomentum
2. Trebula Mutuesca
3. West to east: Alba Fucens, Lucus Angitiae, Marsi Marruvium
4. Antium
5. Formiae
6. Capua
7. Calatia
8. Neapolis

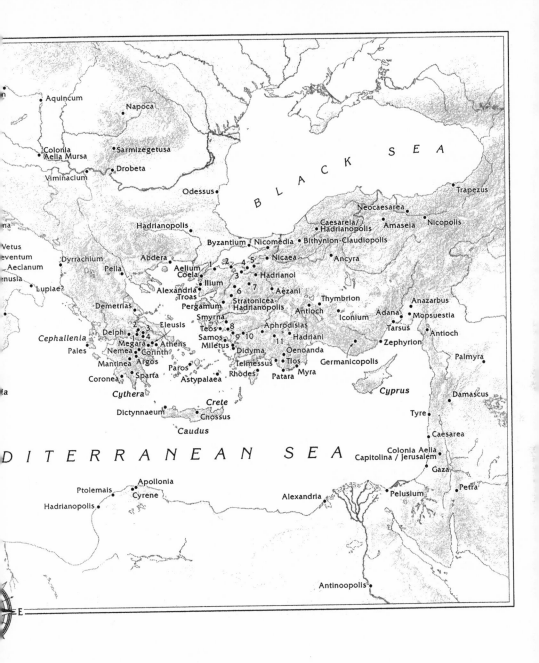

Boeotia

1. Coronea
2. South to north: Abae, Hyampolis
3. Thespiae
4. Thisbe

Approximate scale: 1 : 15,318,000

Map projection: Lambert's Conformal Conic

Asia Minor

1. Parium
2. Cyzicus
3. Miletupolis
4. Apollonia on the Rhyndacus
5. Prusa ad Olympum
6. Hadrianoutherae
7. Hadrianeia
8. Colophon
9. Ephesus
10. Tralles
11. Diocaesaria